1. VIEW OF NATAL BAY, FROM THE BEREA.

A La. Barners, Litho. 92 Paternoster Row .

HISTORY

OF

THE COLONY OF NATAL,

SOUTH AFRICA.

TO WHICH IS ADDED,

AN APPENDIX,

CONTAINING

A BRIEF HISTORY OF THE ORANGE-RIVER SOVEREIGNTY AND OF THE
VARIOUS RACES INHABITING IT, THE GREAT LAKE N'GAMI,
COMMANDOES OF THE DUTCH BOERS, &c., &c.

BY

THE REV. WILLIAM C. HOLDEN,

UPWARDS OF FIFTEEN YEARS A RESIDENT IN THE COLONY.

WITH THREE MAPS,
AND NINETEEN ILLUSTRATIONS ON WOOD AND STONE.

LONDON:
ALEXANDER HEYLIN, 28, PATERNOSTER-ROW.
GRAHAM'S-TOWN :—GODLONTON, WHITE, AND CO.
CAPE-TOWN :—A. S. ROBERTSON.
NATAL:—J. CULLINGWORTH, D'URBAN; J. ARCHBELL, PIETERMARITZBURG.
MDCCCLV.

LONDON:
PRINTED BY WILLIAM NICHOLS,
32, LONDON WALL.

PREFACE BY THE EDITOR.

At the conclusion of this "History," (pp. 332–334,) the reader will find the substance of Mr. Holden's Preface; and will admire it for the modesty, frankness, and sincerity which breathes in every sentence. In the commencement of the first chapter, also, he has briefly given his reasons why a first undertaking of this kind, imperfect as it is, ought to be received with favourable indulgence. As he thought that "some one should engage in the attempt" without delay, "and leave to future topographers to communicate the results of their researches in a more comprehensive History;" he has, at considerable risk, labour, and expense, embarked in the enterprise himself, and commits its merits and its failings, alike, to the kindness of his friends, and the lenity of his censors. Being the first description of the Colony of Natal on an extended plan, it will be deemed worthy of much commendation for its suggestions and aspirations, though, in common with all new undertakings, it does not pretend to be faultless in its execution.

But Mr. Holden might, on another account, prefer still stronger claims to the forbearance of critics. This "History" was finished at the close of 1852, and transmitted for publication to one of his friends in London, who communicated with him on the subject; and, after a lapse of some months, I was induced, in the summer of 1853, to superintend the volume while passing through the press, and to incorporate all the additional information which the author might subsequently transmit. The composition had advanced beyond the tenth sheet, and a good part of it was printed off, when, at the end of 1853, I received advice that Mr. Holden had hastily composed a small work on the Orange-River Sovereignty, the abandonment of which by the British Government was then in contemplation. In it he had adduced the strongest arguments of those who were opposed to the abandonment of British control over that important territory; and it was his wish that it should form an Appendix to the "History," and should also be published as a separate pamphlet, if it arrived in sufficient time to aid the appeal of the able Deputation from the Colony, that was sent to avert what was then generally viewed as an impending calamity.   The manuscript was unfortunately detained several months at Algoa Bay, and did not reach London till late in the Spring of 1854, when its publication as a pamphlet could have been of no service to those who had arrived to oppose the intended withdrawal of British rule and occupancy. The debate on the subject was commenced and concluded, May 29th, 1854; and the Orange-River Sovereignty was again left to care for itself.   I then proceeded, according to instructions, to arrange all the materials available for the Appendix; but I was prevented from fulfilling my purpose by a severe attack of illness, from which I have but lately recovered.   Having applied myself again to the task, I find such an accumulation of events, between 1853 and the commencement of 1855, as have seldom been recorded in the annals of a rising community.   The principal of these I have enumerated in my "Concluding Observations;" (p. 456;) and many of them were so important as to demand a considerable modification and abridgment of the materials which I had previously received and prepared.

These mortifying, yet unavoidable, hindrances have prevented the earlier appearance of the book, though they have probably contributed to the greater completeness of certain portions, and have afforded me an opportunity of glancing at some of the most recent occurrences in those distant regions; the communication with which seems still to be very slow and unsatisfactory, when compared with some of our older and more populous colonies. Among other matters which have, on this account, received a larger share of elucidation, is that of the Dutch Boers.   Many of them had shown a violent antipathy against all British rule and interference; for which, it cannot be denied, they had strong ground in our fitful conduct towards them, when endeavouring to find a resting-place for the soles of their feet; and, having, after long wanderings, migrated beyond the Vaal River, they formed a new and extensive settlement under the name of the Trans-Vaal Republic.   Mr. Holden has evinced much candour and fairness in describing their principles, habits, and actions, in pp. 77, 78, and in various parts of the Appendix, especially pp. 380–391.   But several of their own dispatches and official documents having lately appeared in the colonial journals, and been transferred, with strong tokens of approbation, to the columns of some most influential newspapers in this country, I have, as became an Englishman and a Christian, expressed, in language which cannot be mistaken, my extreme detestation of their cruel and dastardly conduct towards the natives, and have warned them of the disastrous consequences to themselves which such reprehensible proceedings invariably produce. The reader will find those remarks at the close of the Appendix. For them the author is not responsible; but their publication seemed needful, when such important changes in the whole administration of British authority in the South-African provinces are in a state of hopeful progress.

The numerous engravings and maps which accompany the letter-press descriptions, are explanatory of the subjects which they severally represent. The two engravings on wood, on pages 67 and 71, will enable the reader to form a faint idea of the manner in which Kafir wars were formerly conducted, and of those nimble and undaunted skirmishers with whom our brave and well-appointed army, under the lamented Sir George Cathcart, had more recently to contend. These half-civilized men have, of late years, been rendered far more formidable, from the immense quantities of rifles with which they have furnished themselves, and in the use of which they have become very expert.

The author had prepared for publication another work, highly illustrative of some of the topics discussed in this " History," which ought to have been its companion. But he considers it more prudent to defer its appearance, till he has ascertained the degree of encouragement which this earlier production will obtain. That book will give a complete account of the Natal and Zulu Kafirs; their origin, history, language, customs, &c. Its title and contents will be found on the last leaf of the present volume.

THE EDITOR.

May 14*th*, 1855.

CONTENTS.

APPENDIX.

MAPS.

- ILLUSTRATIONS ON WOOD AND STONE.

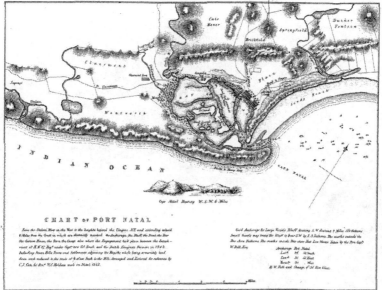

Cape Natal Bearing W.S.W 6 Miles

CHART of PORT NATAL.

From the Umlass River in the West to the heights behind the Congos NE and extending inland
6 Miles from the Coast in which are distantly marked. Rondebergs, the Bluff the Point, the Bar,
the Custom House, the Town the Camp also where the Engagement took place between the detachment of H.M.S. Reg.t under Capt. now Col. Smith, and the Dutch Emigrant Farmers in 1842.
including Rivers Hills Towns and Settlements defining the Bay,the whole being accurately laid
down and reduced to the Scale of ⅜ of an Inch to the Mile. Arranged and Entered for reference by
C.J. Cato for Revd W.C.Holdens work on Natal 1852.

Good Anchorage for Large Vessels Bluff bearing S.W.bearing 7 Miles 6½ fathoms
Small Vessels may bring the Bluff to bear S.W by S 3 fathoms The marks outside the
Bar Shew Fathoms The marks inside, Bar shew Feet Low Water Taken by the Port Capt.t
W. Bell. Esq.

Anchorage Port Natal
Lat.t   29   54 South
Lon.t   30   51 East
Variation   30   West
H. W. Full and Change 4h 30 Bar tides.

Miles

A. E. Evans. Litho. 52. Paternoster Row

HISTORY OF NATAL.

CHAPTER I.

THE description of Natal, which promises to become one of
the most important of the colonial possessions of Great Britain in
South Africa, must necessarily be brief and imperfect, in consequence of its having been only very recently recognised as a
British dependency, the scattered state of its population, the few
and incomplete surveys of some parts of the coast and of the interior, and, generally, in consequence of the paucity of appropriate
and available materials. Some one, however, it is thought, should
engage in the attempt; leaving future topographers, when they
obtain more ample information, to communicate the results of their
researches in a more correct description and a more comprehensive history. With this apology for undertaking to write on the
"cradling" of a nation, now in its infancy, and in consideration of the favourable opportunities which I have enjoyed of
obtaining information, I may venture to adopt the words of
Cicero, with a slight alteration in the name of the subject: "*Non
alienum fuit* [*mihi*] *de* NATALIS *quasi incunabulis dicere.*"

To any intelligent man who casts his eye over a map of the
world, the great advantages of situation which Natal possesses
will be at once apparent. Inhabiting a region remarkably tem-
perate, the settlers will soon be induced to direct their energies
to pursuits more congenial to some of them than the cultivation
of the soil, and the skilful exploration of its riches. Do any of
these enterprising men wish to enter into profitable commercial
relations with the East Indies? they have a fine prospect before

them; for, on passing over the northern part of the Indian Ocean, they enjoy the privilege of trading with Madagascar, Sumatra, Borneo, and other large and fruitful islands, and of ultimately taking a part in the lucrative and increasing traffic connected with India and China. Do they wish to proceed to those rich and fruitful Colonies of Australasia, to offer their more useful and necessary produce in exchange for gold and other metals which are now obtained there in lavish abundance? they have only to sail over the southern portion of the same great ocean, with scarcely an intervening island to divert them from a direct course; and they find themselves in a friendly Colony, peopled by their own countrymen, a great portion of which lies nearly within the same degrees of latitude as Natal, and in which commercial skill and energy are sure to obtain their reward.

When an end shall be put, on the part of the mother country, to that vacillating and theoretic system of colonial legislation, which has hitherto been the bane of this and of others of the British dependencies; and when Natal shall be not only suffered, but likewise encouraged, to develope her varied and valuable resources; then we may expect her to take a high position among the most productive and commercial communities. This bright era is now dawning; and will soon communicate that security to the possessors of the soil, and that confidence to the mercantile interest, from the want of which both of them have lately been in a languishing condition.

From this general and more formal introduction, we descend to the humble task of delineating Natal, its numerous appliances and advantages, and its fair and legitimate prospects. In the present Chapter and in that which succeeds it, the reader will find as ample an account of this new Colony, as under existing circumstances can be expected.

AFTER the voyager to Natal has traversed the mighty ocean for three weary months, he feels a sudden thrill go through his frame on hearing the joyful exclamation, *"Land O!"* A thousand exciting thoughts and feelings rush through his soul whilst he hastens with his fellows on deck, to hear the mate ask the man aloft, *"Where?"* when no sooner is the answer given, than all simultaneously rush to the point of observation; and a motley, anxious company are seen stretching the organs of vision, until in the far distant horizon appears an object like a dim dark line, if they are coming from the southward, extending into the Indian Ocean, or like a small island, if coming from the north-eastward. That dim line enlarges, and becomes better defined, the nearer you approach: it is *the Bluff of Natal!*

Such a description of the Natal Bay, and of the adjacent country, as will convey a correct idea to the distant stranger and to the newly-arrived emigrant, has never yet been given. In order to supply this *desideratum,* I have procured drawings and charts from the best artists on the spot; and gentlemen of experience and ability have kindly communicated to me the results of their knowledge and skill, (among whom the harbour-master must be specially mentioned,) that nothing may be lacking to render the volume as complete as possible; and I trust that these specimens of artistic ability, with the brief observations made upon them, will supply all the information which the reader may desire.

The drawings and charts, embracing the latest observations and discoveries, having been prepared expressly for this work with the greatest care and labour, they may be consulted with perfect confidence, and relied upon as correct. The writer owes a debt of gratitude to the accomplished gentlemen who have so promptly responded to his call, and who have furnished him with materials on various subjects which, from the nature of the case, it was beyond the range of his ability to supply; and he takes the present opportunity of thanking them for their generous services.

D'Urban, the port town of Natal, is situated on the north side of the Bay; and behind it, at about a distance of two miles and a half, is a range of hills known as the Berea, formerly occupied by Captain Gardiner, from the site of whose intended house our view of the Bay is taken.

The engraving placed as a frontispiece to this volume, shows at once one part of the town, the lower part of the Bay, with one of the islands partially exhibited, and the tongue of land stretching down to the Point, covered with ever-green trees. It likewise delineates the crescent towards the sea, and marks the inland bank on the border of the Bay.

The greater part of the town and the upper part of the Bay are excluded from view by the hills and trees on the right, to give which would have involved the necessity of confusion in the rest, and would have prevented a just idea of the parts described.

The Bluff in bold grandeur rises in front to an altitude of two hundred and fifty feet, covered with trees and under-wood in perpetual green, to the water's edge; and, striking out to the eastward, is commissioned to say to the Indian Ocean, "Hitherto shalt thou come, but no further."

On the point of this headland a light-house is built, and a flag-staff erected. By the light of the one, the care-worn and anxious mariner may be warned of proximate danger, and, in the darkest night, conducted to a safe anchorage: by the other he may converse with those who are in charge, in the alphabet of colours, and obtain information essential to the right direction of his vessel, upon the observance of which depends his own safety and that of others. The lamps for the beacon have not yet arrived from England. They will be placed in such a position that a vessel, when steering for the anchorage, must *anchor immediately she shuts-in the sight.*

On the extreme left of the drawing is depicted a ship lying at anchor in the roadstead, the depth of water and distance from land being accurately laid down in the Chart, page 1. Inside the Bay, the vessels are seen lying safely at anchor; and it is gratifying to observe with what perfect composure they seem to treat the raging of the most violent storms, defying their fury, and gently bending, as if in dutiful compliment to the terrible artillery of Heaven. Here they can be brought to within a few yards of the landing-place, making the discharge of cargoes a comparatively small item of labour and expense. With but little outlay, a jetty might be constructed, so as to render the use of boats needless; and doubtless, as it is the interest of the landing-agents to have such an accommodation, they will shortly procure its erection.

In the Bay a few sailing-boats are shown. Sometimes ten or twenty of these small craft are seen at once, spreading their tiny sails to the wind, and moving as if by magic upon the water's surface. Some of the gentlemen (not of the turf) take greater pleasure in sailing lifeless boats than in riding fiery steeds; and they occasionally try the relative merits of their small craft by what is laconically called "racing," when the winner comes off with considerable *éclat*.

The Bluff and the Island are the resort of pleasure-parties on festal and bridal occasions, when the members of a newly-formed band of interesting young men try their musical skill, inviting the echo of the water, or the bank of the Bluff, to give effect to their instrumental performances. It rarely happens that an accident occurs, except when the hat of a careless fellow or a conceited wag is blown off; or when, by the capsizing of his boat, he gets a good ducking, by which his courage is cooled, and he is reduced a few inches lower in self-esteem,—a result of no small benefit.

This general good fortune, however, has made some parties presumptuous, and recently led to a catastrophe of a distressing nature. The queen's birthday this year (1852) was very stormy, in which a strange coincidence was perceptible between it and the same day ten years ago, when the elements of war were raging; showing us that, without the strife of man, human beings may be hurried into eternity when they least expect it. A storm arose, a strong wind blowing from the westward; notwithstanding which, several parties crossed in boats to the Bluff in the morning; and, in the evening, when returning, one of the boats had no sooner come from under the shelter of the high land than, receiving the full force of the gale, she capsized, and plunged the passengers into the water. By great exertions they got upon the boat again, as it lay keel upwards; but, from the power of the wind above and the force of the current below, she again turned over, when all of them were a second time plunged into deep water. Three of them sank to rise no more alive: these were two interesting females, and a coloured man who had exerted himself to save them. The husband of one of the females was rescued with the greatest difficulty, through the care of a gracious Providence, being almost spent when taken up by those sent to his rescue. Some other parties were also in imminent jeopardy of being carried out to sea, never to return home. This painful event spread an air of sadness over our small community, and will probably read a lesson of caution to all for the future, and thus be productive of beneficial results.

The Bay, as shown in the engraving, is at high-water-mark; being then five miles long, and three broad. The tide rises five and a half feet at spring tides, which occur at the full and the dead of the moon; so that when the tide fills the Bay, it is a magnificent sheet of water, being in reality an inland lake, skirted with mangrove and other trees to the water's edge, which afford a rich and varied aspect. As these trees are never divested of their foliage, they exhibit in winter, as well as in summer, the same unvarying freshness and verdure. At high water the small boats emerge from their hiding-places, and are seen sailing in all directions, giving animation to the beautiful and placid expanse. At low water a large part of the Bay is laid bare, as seen in the Chart; thus allowing waggons to pass along the sands without difficulty, excepting in those parts where the channels are marked.

It will be evident to every observer, that the body of water flowing into the Bay at high tide, and on the turn issuing out of it, must be enormous; the channel for which is very narrow, close under the Bluff, and consequently causes the immense fluid mass to rush in and out with great violence. Under the skilful management of an experienced engineer, this rapid transit of the tidal waters, in conjunction with the fresh water to be brought into it from the neighbouring streams, might be advantageously employed to remove the accumulation of sand which constitutes the Bar, and eventually to effect its disappearance.

The reader will find, at the commencement of this Chapter, an accurate Chart of the Bay and of the country immediately adjacent; in which the depth of water is given in different places, and the particulars embraced are reduced to measurement, on a scale of five-eighths of an inch to the mile.

Having given a general outline, I may now detail some of the particulars connected with the interesting objects which it embraces.

In this Chart the anchorage in the roadstead outside is distinctly and accurately laid down, with the exact position in which vessels should lie: the variations of the needle are also marked, which at this point are probably as great as in any part of the world. The anchorage in the roadstead is perfectly safe whilst the wind is from the south-west; vessels may bring up in ten and a half fathoms' water, the Bluff bearing south-west two miles.

Large vessels making Natal with the wind strong from the eastward, should keep under sail until communication is obtained by signal from the flag-staff on the Bluff: Marryatt's signals are to be used. The Cape Natal Bluff can be seen for more than sixteen miles from seaward; and vessels are recommended to signalize immediately when they come in sight, and *to keep well to the eastward*, as there is at all times a strong westerly current, by which vessels often get to leeward of the port, and are drifted down as far as St. John's, while not paying proper attention to the course of the current. An instance of this has just occurred in the case of the "Gitana," which made the anchorage, but was afterwards drifted down, and for a fortnight was not seen or heard of, and fears were entertained that she was lost. But, nearly a month after she had first spoken the port, she made an entrance.

It is the opinion of experienced nautical men, that if proper care is taken, there never need be a wreck at Natal; except that sometimes an accident will occur which no human prudence can foresee, and no care prevent. In all other cases, the sea-room is so ample, and the anchorage so good, that vessels may easily get out. But if the wind is strong from the eastward or north-east, it is better either to get under weigh, or to slip the anchor, not attempting to ride out the storm, (unless the tackling be very good and plenty of cable be given,) as the anchor will either drag or the cable break, by which time the vessel is probably too far toward the shore to escape. This was the case with the " Minerva." She had dragged her anchor some distance before it was detected, it being in the night, and she being too near in-shore; and when the crew tried to get her out, she was driven on the ledge of rocks at the Bluff Point. But it is thought by some who are well qualified to form a judgment, that the " Minerva" did not drag her anchor, but parted, and let go another, and, before it would hold, she was too close in-shore.

If these precautions be observed, the roadstead of Natal will be found to be incomparably safer than either Table Bay, or Algoa Bay, or the Mouth of the Buffalo.

It may not be out of place here to state, that the harbour-master, Captain Bell, is a thoroughly efficient officer, whose judgment may always be followed with safety. The pilots, like-

wise, are sober, honest, skilful men, who may be trusted either
to bring vessels in, or to take them out.

On referring to the Chart, the letter A is placed on the summit
of the Bluff: it shows the position of the light-house and flag-
staff, which are well displayed in the drawing of the vessel crossing the Bar. (Wood-cut, No. III., page 10.)

The Bluff is a bold promontory, two hundred and thirty feet
high, stretching some distance into the Indian Ocean, as though
on purpose to make a channel, under its lee bank, for the passage
of ships and commerce with the natives. On the western bank
the breakers roll with tremendous fury. After a strong gale has
continued some days, the sea comes up from the vast Indian Ocean
wrought up to tempest, and, leviathan-like, breaks upon the rocks,
foaming and roaring, as if in hollow groans. It was here that
the ill-fated vessel, the "Minerva," was wrecked; and the writer
of these pages looked on with intense and painful interest,
whilst the passengers were landed, who were nearly three hundred
in number.

THE BAR, in No. III., is a sand-bank thrown up by the sea
breaking on one side, and sent back again by the tide ebbing on
the other. This also is distinctly marked in the Chart with the
name written across it. This is, and has been, in truth, a great
barrier to the prosperity of Natal. It is there shown to be nine
feet at low water; but instances have occurred since the place was
occupied by the English, when, for weeks together, it was not as
deep at high water, and vessels inside have been effectually locked
in, and others outside have been completely excluded. Long and
bitter complaints have been raised against government for not
having attempted to improve this dangerous entrance. Some
wattle-work has been lately constructed, and is still in progress;
but the general impression is, that it is either entirely useless or
inadequate to meet the difficulty.

In order that something more effectual may be done, an
ordinance is now proposed to be passed for the formation of a
committee or corporation, to devise and adopt the best plans for the
removal of this inconvenience. Whilst, on the one hand, suitable
works are required to confine the water to one channel, so as to
sweep away the sand by the force of the outward current, it is, on
the other hand, extremely desirable to bring the Umgeni river

from the north-east, and the Umlazi river from the south-west, into the Bay. This might be done, without any enormous outlay, by bringing these tributary streams, in well-constructed channels, along the marshes which are shown in the Chart, and over which they have probably flowed at some former period. It is especially desirable that the Umgeni should be thus brought out with as little delay as possible, as there is a strong stream of water flowing down that river at all times. The large body of water thus brought into the Bay, when forced out at ebb tide

through a confined channel, would drive away the mass of sand which might have accumulated on the Bar outside.

Some persons, however, have indulged in the conjecture, that, instead of proving beneficial, these rivers would bring down more sand, which would tend to render the Bay more shallow, and not remove the Bar. But strong demonstrative proof has already been given of the fallacy of this opinion; for, in the great flood of 1848, the Umgeni overflowed its banks, and became one grand extended sheet of water, reaching from the bed of the river to the Bay, in some parts nearly a mile broad, and pouring an immense body of water into the Bay; the other two small

rivers, Umbilo and Umhlatusan, also overflowed, and discharged
their streams into the head of the Bay. By this rapid flow of
water, the Bar was quite removed, and sixteen feet of water were
found there for a long time afterwards. Besides, a conduit from
these streams would be extremely beneficial to the town of
D'Urban, and contribute greatly to the health and comfort of the
inhabitants, by supplying it with good water, and carrying off
all noxious animal or vegetable deposits, which, as population
increases, would be in danger of accumulating.

III.—THE BACK BEACH.   THE MAYFLOWER CROSSING THE BAR.

This gives a very correct representation of a vessel crossing
the Bar. When I and my family were at the same spot, the
"Mazeppa" struck for about a quarter of an hour; and each
heavy roll of the surf, as it broke over her, tore away part of
her bulwarks. It was then found necessary to lighten her; and,
amongst the other things thrown overboard, were two four-
pounders, one of which was buried in deep water, and the other
was the very gun that is shown in the wood-cut, (Chap. VI.,)
of *the "Mazeppa" leaving the Bay*, and was employed by the
Boers at that time in firing into her, when sailing off to the
Cape, to acquaint the governor with Captain Smith's critical

position, and to solicit instant succour. The detention of our little vessel on the Bar seemed to have been brief after the captain sang out, "All is right! she is in deep water again!" Within a few minutes we were under the lee of the Bluff, and, "lo! there was a great calm."

But, from this description, it is not by any means to be inferred that the Bar is always rough and dangerous. I have stood on the Back Beach, and seen five vessels come in, one after another, in the most gallant style, not one of which touched the Bar, or was washed by a single spray. The coasting vessels generally appear as if either they knew the winds and the waves, or the winds and the waves knew them.

Let the Bar be removed, the steamers brought into active operation, and Natal's resources be developed, and the Colony will stand second to none in interest and value to the British crown and the English public.

The next object of consequence is the point marked B on the Chart. This is a sand-spit, which extends down to within about two hundred yards of the Bluff, where the bed of the deep channel runs, along which all vessels entering and leaving the Bay must pass. On the sand-spit the Custom-House and Cato's large store are marked. On a hill just behind, a large block-house is erected, which contains military ammunition and stores, and is guarded by soldiers; from which they could rake any vessel lying in the offing, and shatter those who attempted to cross the Bar in a hostile manner. The house of Captain Bell, the harbour-master, also stands on a hill close by, and a number of undefinable small buildings are found near, in which soldiers, sailors, and boatmen are domiciled.

As you take your stand near the Custom-House, life in all its varied colonial colours and forms is presented to view. The ships are lying at anchor one hundred yards from shore, and the sailors are busily engaged in discharging their cargoes; the boats are plying to and from the vessels; the jolly tar is singing his song in his own way, whilst he is winding up his goods from the hatchway, or lowering them into the boats; and the master or the mate is ever and anon acting high life upon deck when all is not done to his satisfaction, or when an unfortunate bag of sugar or rice happens to be damaged, or when some cases enumerated in the bill of lading cannot readily be found, and are not forth-coming. On the beach may be seen one or two Englishmen and eight or ten naked Kafirs, whose duty it is to discharge the cargo of the boat. When something rather heavy has to be handed on shore, these natives, not having been accustomed to hard work in the form of combined exertions, often let it fall into the water. The owner of the package, if at a distance, is unconscious of the damage he is sustaining through these black gentlemen; or, if standing near, he utters horrid curses or deep complaints. At a few yards' distance stands the Collector of Customs, looking as gravely as if the affairs of a great nation depended on the present moment. The other Custom-House officers are found in their places, and performing their several duties. I believe these gen-tlemen are not remiss; but, whilst they are faithful to their sove-reign, are not oppressive in their exactions upon her subjects.

Near them is to be seen a primitive English, Dutch, or Hot-tentot waggon-driver, impatient of delay, storming and fuming, because, forsooth, he cannot be loaded up at once; as though those about him had no other business than to attend to his wishes. Sometimes not less than four or six waggons are waiting at the same time to be loaded. As soon as he gets his comple-ment of goods, he sets to work to "load up," as it is called, with half-a-dozen Kafirs to help him; the only concern of each appa-rently being—for each man to throw all the weight on another, and to take none himself. This being cleverly done, the bale or bag is deposited again on the sand, instead of being lodged in the waggon. When, after much labour, the waggon is at length loaded, and the wheels are sunk deeply in the sand, the driver takes his long whip, and, at the top of his stentorian voice, shouts or shrieks to his dull team of twelve oxen. But he now finds that one of them has got out of his yoke, the neck-strap of ano-ther is broken, or that a yoke-skea has divided asunder, or, worse than all, that his worthless leader has taken his departure to take snuff with his friend, or to look out for a "*klein stuck flesch*," ("a little bit of meat,") until the poor man's temper is tried, and he is either in a perfect rage, or is ready to cry through vexa-tion; whilst all around him are as unconcerned and unmoved as the bags of sugar and rice with which his waggon is laden.

Let not the reader suppose this description to be fictitious: it is true to the life. It does not, however, always happen that things are equally annoying. The patience of other parties, besides waggon-drivers, is sometimes severely tested. But these remarks are common to all new sea-ports, till they become more frequented, and till all the appliances of science are brought into action to lessen the amount of human labour, and to teach the most illiterate of men the benefits of strenuous and combined exertions. As these fresh ports are improved, and visited by larger ships, the captains of which are men of intelligence, the labourers at the wharves, and the "in-shore" men, are taught to be more active and energetic, and soon become equal to their compeers in other parts of the world.

The next letter, C, shows Cato's flag-staff. This was erected when the writer and his family were in the "Mazeppa," lying outside, and had anchored too near the Bar, where a dreadful sea struck her, carried away her bulwarks, and buried her for the time being, whilst those on shore and those on board doubted whether she would ever "right" again. The site of this flag-staff is called "the Back Beach;" and there is a road from the town to it, through the bush, without being obliged to go round the Point.

D shows the town of D'Urban, of which I shall say more in another place; only observing here, that, a few yards from the the water's edge, the ground rises several feet; and that, when the buildings in the town are further advanced, they will show a line of villas, almost in the form of a crescent, with gardens reaching down to the verge of the water, presenting a pretty appearance in a charming situation.

The "British Camp" is seen near Congella, it being well-nigh encircled by the marsh, and the Zulu road passing close by it on the left hand.*

E shows the exact spot where Captain (now Colonel) Smith engaged in deadly strife with the Dutch Boers, who, from behind the trees there shown, directed the artillery of death against our veteran troops, at midnight's solemn hour, until the calm moon-

---

* The reader will find two wood-engravings in Chapter VI. The first represents the camp as it was hastily formed when first attacked by the Dutch Boers; and the second, in a different site, shows what it was when the suitable erections were completed by the military.

light disappeared amidst the sheet of fire which was lighted up by the instruments of slaughter, and the peaceful night was invaded by the noise of battle,—cannons, muskets, shouts, groans, and death,—all uniting to record the event, and perpetuate its memory. On the part of the British, thirty-four were killed, sixty-three wounded, and six missing; besides two Hottentot waggon-drivers who were killed, and one English waggon-driver wounded. This must have been sharp service, when more than two-thirds were either killed, wounded, or missing. A full account of this engagement is given in the Chapter on the taking of Natal by the English.

F marks the place where the boats were lying with the howitzers under Lieutenant Wyatt, who was sent to assist the troops on this momentous occasion, whilst Congella, situated just in front of it, unmistakeably shows where the Boers' camp lay,—to take which was Captain Smith's object. Only one house now remains of those which formed part of the Dutch town and camp at that time; but allotments of land have recently been sold, and some English families are settling.

On leaving Congella, and proceeding on the Umlazi road close toward the Umbilo river, you pass through a beautifully wooded tract of country; and on the hills to the right a number of allotments are marked off, containing about twenty acres each, nearly all of which are now purchased, and a number of houses erected. The situation is beautiful; and when from it you look over the Bay or down into the river, nature appears dressed in its richest colours and most varied forms.

Proceeding onwards after crossing the Umbilo river, the old Maritzburg road is shown, striking off to the right, and passing over a hill marked "Sea View." This was the residence of the late Mr. Dunn and family. It was here that Captain Smith first halted when coming from the Umgazi to take Natal from the Boers, and where he thought of fixing his camp. On this spot Mr. Dunn gave the British troops a cordial welcome, and the best assistance which his circumstances allowed; at the same time expressing his surprise, that so small a force was sent, and stating his apprehensions that they were inadequate to the task. On his inquiring if another force was not dispatched by sea to support them, Captain Smith replied, that *he was not afraid to meet all*

the Boers, and as many more.   Mr. Dunn smiled to think of his
small force attempting an encounter with fifteen hundred of the
best-armed men in the Colony, each of them furnished with a
sword, a pistol, and a double-barrelled gun.   The brave captain,
however, found that he had more than enough to do with these,
when afterwards half of his force was either cut off or disabled at
Congella, and he was besieged a month in his camp, and reduced
to eating horse-flesh and forage-corn.

The residence of Mr. Dunn was rightly called "Sea View,"
as the prospect from it is extremely fine, exhibiting a perfect
panorama.   In front, numerous mangrove trees, with their dark
shining foliage and beautiful forms, line the fine Bay stretched
along; before the Custom-House the ships are seen lying at
anchor; and, beyond the Point, the wide ocean extends, until
lost in the far distant horizon.   To the right, the bold Bluff
rears its noble head, crowned with a cap of trees and brushwood,
always green, and striking out into the ocean "in form majestic."
On the left, beautifully wooded scenery presents its soft and
varied face in contrast to the almost stern appearance of the
Bluff.   Beyond all, lies the town of D'Urban: land and water,
hills and valleys, grass and trees, houses and gardens, are interspersed,—all conspiring to constitute this one of the most complete pictures of pleasant natural scenery which the eye ever
beheld.   The Umlazi road then leads on towards Kafirland,
crossing the Umhlatusan, beyond which Claremont Town is
marked; but it is the site for a *town intended,* two or three
houses being all that are at present erected.   The Umlazi river
is next crossed, the road leading on to the Isipingo; both of
which unite at the mouth, and empty themselves into the Indian
Ocean.   In the neighbourhood of these rivers, many hundreds
of acres of low swampy land are found, covered with tall reeds
or long flags: if drained and put into cultivation, they would
produce very large crops of rice or sugar-cane.

G shows the site of the Agricultural and Horticultural Gardens, lying in a convenient spot under the Berea Hill.   Operations have been carried on here for a little more than a year;
and in the Chapter on the productions of the Colony, will be
found an account of what is doing there.

H denotes the spot on which a windmill has just been erected

on the top of the Berea, to the right of the Pietermaritzburg
road: it is a very prominent object, strongly built of sandstone
from the neighbourhood, being, I think, the first in the Colony of
Natal. A little further to the right is a black square spot, where
I believe Captain Gardiner's house stood, and where Sidney Peel,
Esq., has now built, and commenced cultivation. The Berea
Hills, as shown on the Chart, extend from the Umbilo river to
the Umgeni, the road to Pietermaritzburg going nearly through
the middle. They are covered with dense bush, much of which
has not been penetrated; and in which elephants, panthers, monkeys, and other wild animals, find a safe retreat. The elephant-
hunters would rather go a hundred miles another way than
attempt to follow these huge creatures into their bushy haunts.
The reason is, the bush is so impervious, on account of thick
underwood, that if the elephant is wounded, but not mortally,
the hunter has a bad prospect of escape, if pursued. When
writing a critique on the pamphlet of Mr. Methley,—where, speaking of elephants, he describes them as having all fled into the
interior along with the Dutch Boers,—the editor of an English
journal humorously says, " I doubt not but it would have put
this good gentleman's courage to the test, had he attempted to go
through the Berea on the Maritzburg road after dusk in the evening; for, often in the day-time, men of tolerably stout hearts
have scampered away, when they have met these unwieldy and
unwelcome guests." Not long since a German was killed, a few
miles from the Bay, by a panther, the skin of which lies harmlessly
on the floor of our parlour, being now an object of ornament as
well as of usefulness, rather than of terror. Johannes Meyer, a
respectable Dutchman, was killed by one of these ferocious beasts,
a short time ago, beyond the Umhloti. Happily, fatal effects are
not frequent in their occurrence. Elephants and tigers, or panthers, are occasionally killed; and the methods of trepanning and
exterminating them, adopted in different parts of the Colony,
display great ingenuity, and prove efficacious.

In the north part of the Chart is the Umgeni. This is a large
river, which flows a considerable distance; and, even in the
driest seasons, pours a large volume of water into the ocean.
Many hundred acres near its banks are low and flat; which
being sometimes overflowed by it, a rich alluvial soil is deposited;

and very fine reeds grow in great abundance. At some seasons of the year alligators are found here. A Kafir boy was seized by one of these monsters some months ago, and not heard of again ; and a stout, athletic Kafir man, whom I saw shortly afterwards, had a piece of flesh taken out of his thigh as large as my hand, in consequence of which he would probably be maimed for life. Since the traffic in the Bay has increased, these monsters are rare in their appearance. I have seen only one of them; and it quickly swam to the opposite bank, and was lost in the reeds.

In the upper part of the Chart is shown "Sea-Cow Lake," so called from the number of hippopotami that still inhabit it. I have seen the heads of some half-dozen of these large amphibious animals, while basking themselves on a sunny day; and I could relate some ludicrous stories concerning those who went to shoot them when they left their watery retreat at night, and whose courage failed them at the intended time of attack : but I forbear. This lake, with the scenery around, is very beautiful, especially in a land where such objects rarely occur. It is fed by the Little Umhlanga river, which flows along the bottom of the farm Duiker Fontein.

The plots of land marked on the north of the Umgeni are adapted for cotton plantations and other tropical products.

I have now given what may be deemed a tolerably compendious account of Port Natal, as shown in the Chart, and in other Plates; that will convey, to the minds of those at a distance, information in reference to the points brought under observation, on which they may rely. The drawing of the entrance at the bottom of the Chart shows the appearance of Natal as seen from the sea, bearing west-south-west, six miles distant.

I close this Chapter by appending a Table, showing the depth of water on the Bar for six months; and another, enumerating the winds and weather for one month, June; which is one of the dry winter months, at which time the easterly winds chiefly prevail. These Tables have been kindly supplied by the harbour-master.

DEPTH OF WATER ON THE BAR AT HIGH WATER.

		Ft. In.				Ft. In.
1852. January	3rd	9 . 6	1852. April	1st		9 . 9
,,	5th	11 . 0	,,	3rd		11 . 3
,,	6th	11 . 3	,,	5th		11 . 6
,,	8th	11 . 9	,,	8th		12 . 0
,,	9th	10 . 9	,,	9th		12 . 0
,,	11th	10 . 8	,,	10th		11 . 9
,,	12th	10 . 6	,,	11th		10 . 9
,,	17th	9 . 9	,,	12th		10 . 9
,,	19th	8 . 6	,,	15th		10 . 6
,,	20th	9 . 0	,,	16th		11 . 3
,,	21st	9 . 6	,,	17th		11 . 6
,,	22nd	10 . 0	,,	24th		10 . 6
,,	23rd	10 . 3	,,	25th		10 . 6
,,	30th	8 . 0	,,	26th		10 . 0
,,	31st	8 . 0	,,	27th		10 . 4
February	5th	10 . 0	,,	29th		10 . 3
,,	8th	9 . 6	,,	30th		10 . 6
,,	12th	8 . 0	May	1st		11 . 0
,,	15th	8 . 4	,,	2nd		12 . 0
,,	20th	9 . 8	,,	4th		13 . 0
,,	21st	9 . 6	,,	5th		13 . 0
,,	22nd	9 . 6	,,	7th		12 . 0
,,	23rd	9 . 6	,,	15th		9 . 0
,,	24th	9 . 9	,,	16th		10 . 0
,,	26th	10 . 0	,,	17th		10 . 0
,,	29th	8 . 0	,,	18th		10 . 6
March	2nd	9 . 3	,,	19th		11 . 0
,,	3rd	9 . 3	,,	20th		11 . 0
,,	4th	9 . 6	,,	21st		11 . 0
,,	5th	10 . 0	,,	23rd		9 . 9
,,	6th	11 . 0	June	2nd		10 . 3
,,	10th	9 . 6	,,	3rd		11 . 6
,,	11th	11 . 9	,,	4th		11 . 6
,,	12th	11 . 6	,,	11th		8 . 0
,,	13th	11 . 0	,,	12th		8 . 6
,,	14th	10 . 6	,,	14th		9 . 0
,,	15th	10 . 9	,,	15th		9 . 0
,,	19th	11 . 3	,,	16th		9 . 9
,,	22nd	13 . 0	,,	21st		11 . 0
,,	26th	11 . 6	,,	23rd		10 . 0
,,	28th	10 . 0	,,	28th		9 . 4
,,	29th	9 . 9	,,	29th		10 . 0
,,	30th	9 . 3	,,	30th		10 . 0

WIND AND WEATHER.

JUNE 1st. The whole of this day, light airs from the Eastward, and fine weather.

2nd. Light airs from the N.E., and fine clear weather.

3rd. First part of this day, light airs from the N.E.: latter part, light airs from the East.

4th. The whole of this day, light airs from the Eastward, and fine weather.

5th. The whole of this day, light airs from the Eastward, and fine weather.

6th. Morning and noon, calm and fine weather: at 4 P.M. light airs from the Eastward.

7th. First part of this day, fresh winds from the S.W.: at 5. 30. P.M. winds with rain: at 8 P.M. moderate weather.

8th. The whole of this day, light airs from the Eastward, and fine weather.

9th. This day, light airs from the Eastward, and fine clear weather.

10th. Morning, light airs from the N.E. and fine weather: at 3 P.M. light airs from S.W. and cloudy weather.

11th. Morning, light airs from the S.W. and fine clear weather: at 4 P.M. light airs from the Eastward: at 8 P.M. light winds from S.W.

12th. The whole of this day, light airs from the Southward, and fine weather.

13th. This day, light winds from the Southward, and fine clear weather.

14th. This day, light airs from the Southward, and fine clear weather.

15th. The whole of this day, light winds from S.S.W., and fine clear weather.

16th. Morning, light airs from the N.W.: noon, light airs from the Eastward: at 8 P.M. fine clear weather.

17th. Morning, light airs and variable: noon, wind steady at N.E.: 8 P.M. fine weather.

18th. First part of this day, light airs from the S.W.: noon, the wind increased to a heavy gale: at 8 P.M. fine weather.

19th. The whole of this day, fresh gales from the S.W., and clear weather.

20th. First part of this day, light airs from the N.W.: at 4 P.M. light airs from S.S.E.

21st. Morning, light airs from the N.W., and fine weather: at 8 P.M. light breeze from N.E.

22nd. The whole of this day, light winds from the N.E., and fine weather.

23rd. Morning, light winds and variable: at 4 P.M. fresh breeze from N.E.

24th. Morning, light airs and variable: at 10 A.M. moderate breeze from N.E. which continued throughout the day.

25th. The whole of this day, light winds and variable.

26th. This day, light airs from the Southward, and fine clear weather.

27th. This day, light winds from the Southward, and fine weather.

28th. Morning, light airs from the S.S.W., and cloudy weather: noon, veered to S.S.E.: at 4 P.M. moderate at N.E.

29th. Morning, light airs and variable: at 11 A.M. the wind came from the N.E., and blew steadily throughout the day.

CHAPTER II.

GEOGRAPHICAL POSITION AND NATURAL HISTORY OF NATAL.

THE Colony of Natal is bounded, on the north-east, by the Tugela and Umzinyati rivers; on the north-west, by the Umzimkulu;* on the south-east, by the Indian Ocean; and on the north-west, by the Quahlamba Mountains. It stretches along the coast of the Indian Ocean about 150 miles; but if the extension named below be added, it will give about 80 miles more of coast range, running parallel with the Umzimkulu, inland, to the Quahlamba. It mostly lies between 29° and 32° south latitude, and 29° and 32° east longitude.

In the maps which have hitherto appeared, the latitude and longitude have been incorrectly laid down; even in the last, by Dr. Stanger, in the Blue Book. After the strictest inquiry and numerous observations, taken from on board vessels and on shore, it appears, that in the longitude of Natal there is an error of twelve or fifteen miles, and in the latitude one of several miles. The latitude and longitude given in the Map at the end of this volume is the result of strict and continued observation by the most competent persons, and will be found as nearly correct as possible. There are also several rivers laid down in this Map, which have never appeared in any other. It will be seen from it, that the country is well watered.

There are no harbours from Kafirland to Delagoa Bay, except Port Natal and St. Lucia. Of the latter but little is yet known, nor is any traffic carried on there: of the former a full account is given in the preceding Chapter. A reef of rocks runs out near the mouth of the Umkomas river to the north-east, on which vessels that are lying in near the coast are in danger of striking.

---

* This was the old boundary, till the limits were extended to the Umtafuna by the local government some time ago; but there appears to be uncertainty as to the confirmation of the arrangement by the home government.

It does not fall within the design of the writer, or the province of this work, to attempt giving an extensive or scientific account of the natural history of Natal. This would require a volume, not a chapter, and would open a wide field of investigation to the philosopher. Of the zoological, botanical, and mineralogical productions, little is known. What has been written in reference to other countries on these subjects, will either not apply to this at all, or only partially. The whole will require to be reduced to a new system of analysis, and experiments must be made which may lead to satisfactory conclusions. All that I shall, therefore, attempt in the present instance will be, to give a general outline of the natural history of the country, leaving it to be filled up as opportunities may occur.

A personal friend, of considerable scientific ability, has kindly placed at my disposal the result of his thoughts and investigations on the subject; the substance of which I now lay before the reader. It should be added, that the remarks apply particularly to the coast-land :—

" The surface of the land for five or ten miles from the shore rises with a gentle angle, and is every where strongly undulated. From one extremity to the other, there is an almost painful succession of similar hills and vales, rising and falling in endless monotony. The traveller fords a stream, ascends a hill, descends, crosses a brook; and this is the whole variety of an ordinary day's journey along the coast division. If he sees ahead of him (as he does in the vicinity of Natal Bay) a level plain, three or four miles across, he hails with joy this interruption in the fatiguing monotony of grass-covered hills and ravines. However interesting, at first, the sight might be, who would not tire of beholding, day after day, the *congealed motionless* waves of the ocean ?

" This coast-land is almost destitute of trees, except along the courses of the numerous streams, and close upon the shore. For most of the distance, a dense jungle extends from the beach inland, varying in width from two rods to as many miles. Scarcely any timber valuable for building purposes is found near the coast, except the red mangrove, which abounds at the mouths of some of the larger rivers. Through almost every part of this coast division, waggons can find their way, without their owners being required to

bestow labour in making the roads. Numerous little streams of
pure water rise and flow along the ravines, whose hidden waters
are marked by the ranker vegetation which skirts their course.

"The shore is generally low and sandy, though often bold
cliffs advance into the waves, and rocky pinnacles shoot up from
the midst of the water. Every where, at low water, rocky *strata*
appear below the sandy beach, rendering the approach of vessels
impossible. There is an ocean current flowing parallel with the
coast towards the south-west.

"The land gradually rises, as it recedes from the coast, till,
at varying distances of from five to fifteen miles, the elevation
suddenly terminates in rocky precipices crowning a valley, and
forming a natural boundary to the coast division. At short
intervals, this wall has been cleft asunder for the passage of the
rivers, sometimes leaving perpendicular walls on either side,
matched to each other, from five hundred to two thousand feet
high. Into the valleys succeeding upon the coast range, there
are but few places of access for waggons. The hollows are
nearly filled with innumerable round, grass-covered hills, rising
from one hundred to two thousand feet high. The appearance of
these valleys, as viewed from the surrounding heights, has been
compared to the ocean stirred from its depths, and then suddenly
congealed; but such a comparison utterly fails to convey an
adequate idea of the magnificence of the view, and of the mighty
forces which burst open the earth's crust, and protruded from its
fiery depths, in such infinite confusion, the lofty hills and frag-
mentary mountains, which fill the deep gulf between the first and
second range of table-lands.

"It is to be observed that most of the rocks in these valleys
are of the primary formation. Near Isidumbi, the station of the
Rev. J. Tyler, is a granite boulder, 30 feet thick, 140 long, and
95 broad, extreme measure. One end is elevated 34 feet from
the ground, and the other end about 10 feet, resting on three
rocks, not more than 4 to 8 feet in diameter. The rocks on
which it rests are split into shivers, as if the boulder had fallen
from above upon them, and partially crushed them.

"In the midst of these valleys rise lofty mountains, of the
same geological character as the distant table-lands, but entirely
detached and isolated. Some present at the summit a horizontal

surface, several acres in extent, always covered with a carpet of luxuriant grass. Others rise in sharp or rounded peaks. Others are carved into a thousand fantastic shapes. It requires but little imagination to behold the towers and battlements, the domes and spires, of some Titanic empire; all weaker remains of which have long since sunk into the earth, or been washed away by floods. *There* lies prostrate a Cyclopean form, beside his crumbling tower;—*here* is a large sphinx, looking from high battlements;—and *yonder* a gigantic lion crouches, as if about to spring upon his prey.

"Beyond this valley series, the ground gradually rises, and stretches out in broad table-land, almost wholly destitute of trees, often cut deep by ravines and rivers, and sometimes interrupted by ranges of mountains, the sides of which are covered with dense forests. As we penetrate inland about fifty miles, the peaks of the Quahlamba Mountains, four or five thousand feet above the level of the sea, are visible in the distance.

"Natal abounds in streams of pure water. There are upwards of a hundred rivers, (taking both great and small,) whose embouchures are into the Indian Ocean; besides branches and branchlets innumerable, with which the country is every where intersected. Seldom does one travel an hour along the coast country, without crossing rivulets of transparent water. These vary in size, from the merest brook, three miles in length, to the Utukela (Tugela) and Umzimkulu, which are 150 yards wide, and 200 miles long. Of these, only the Utukela, the Umkomazi, and the Umzimkulu have their sources as far inland as the Quahlamba Mountains.

"On each series of table-lands distinct classes of rivers rise and flow to the ocean. The general direction of the rivers is south-east, at right angles to the coast. Those rivers which have their sources from fifty to one hundred miles inland, are very numerous, and afford abundant water-power. Their passages through the first and second ranges of table-lands are often picturesque and grand. Usually the high lands are apparently split asunder, and on either side stand perpendicular walls of sandstone, of granite, or of basalt, rising many hundred feet above the sullen waters that chafe and roar through their deep foundations. Cascades and falls are frequent. The Falls of the Umgeni, near Pietermaritzburg, are 276 feet in perpendicular height.

The traveller riding on the table-lands beholds before him nothing but grassy plains, or blue mountains in the far distance; when suddenly the earth opens,—he hears the roar, and sees the sparkling waters, of a river far, far below; to pass which he must lead his stumbling horse down precipices, through deep, dank ravines, and over plains of rocky fragments hurled down from the overhanging heights, as if to retard the march of the victorious current to its ocean home.

"None of the rivers in Natal are navigable for ships; and most of them, for the greater part of the year, are closed up by sand-banks at the mouth. Nearly all the streams are perennial; for the rainy season happens during summer: but they flow in channels so deep below the level of the adjacent country as to render them unavailable for facility of irrigation. There are but a few localities in the whole district to which water can be conducted from neighbouring streams, without the aid of machinery to elevate it. The water of the rivers is soft and clear, and, running over beds of granite and trap rocks, is but slightly impregnated with minerals. It is said, however, that the waters of several rivers (as the Umgeni and Umhloti) are slightly alkaline.

"The soil varies in character and fertility in different sections. Near the coast, there is a preponderance of sandy soils; but, at a few miles from the sea, loams prevail, varying in colour from yellow and dark brown to a deep red. Shining scales of mica are abundantly distributed, and have more than once been mistaken by the ignorant for 'Afric's golden sands.' In large sections the soil is strongly impregnated with iron, the ore of which frequently protrudes, and is found in abundance towards the Quahlamba Mountains. In the last-mentioned region strongly magnetic iron ore has been discovered.

"The soil is not generally rich, though by proper cultivation it is rendered moderately productive. The natives never manure the land; and every year they burn all the vegetation, which, if left to decay, would form a rich mould. They change their gardens often; for under their treatment the land soon wears out. The two chief articles of consumption and cultivation by the natives are, Indian corn, and a grain called *amabele*, which, in its kernel and growth, somewhat resembles broom corn. Pumpkins, squashes, melons, and calabashes flourish well, and are extensively

IV.—SKETCH OF THE UMGENI WATER-FALL, ABOVE PIETERMARITZBURG.

cultivated. Besides these, the natives raise sweet potatoes, an edible root resembling the *arum*, and called *idumbi*, the common potato, beans, and a sort of millet of which they make beer. Along the sea-coast a valuable fruit called the *itungula*, resembling in form and size a large plum, is abundant, and is much used by Europeans for preserves and jellies. Most of the wild fruits are valueless. The banana, pine-apple, oranges, lemons, limes, papaw, and most tropical fruits, flourish under cultivation near the coast. A little inland, peaches and apples, pomegranates and quinces, grow well. In the vicinity of Port Natal, two, and even three, crops of Indian corn may be raised in one year on the same ground. Wheat, so far as limited experiments show, does not flourish along the coast division; but towards the Quahlamba Mountains it does.

"In the extensive grassy plains, many cattle, goats, and sheep are pastured. Nearly the whole surface of the country is burnt over once or twice a year; not all at once, but in sections, so that at all seasons the flocks and herds may have abundance of fresh grass. The flames, once kindled in the dry grass, run rapidly before the wind, rousing from their retreats the birds of night, wolves and hyænas, that flee howling and screaming away; and startling from mid-day sleep the roebuck and antelope, whose graceful bounds and winged speed soon place them beyond the reach of the devouring fire. A winter evening in Africa presents no more charming sight than those long lines of fire sweeping over the plains, descending into some deep valley, where their raging thirst shall be quenched in a crystal brook, or gathering round some lofty hill, whose precipitous sides they climb, dance a moment on its summit, and then expire. In two or three days after the fire has blackened the earth, countless numbers of a little leafless flower (one of the *amaryllaceæ*) shoot up, whose bowed heads seem to supplicate Heaven's mercy for the scorched earth, and whose glorious beauty is enough to entice the treasures of the clouds to their feet. In two weeks, the under-grass puts forth its leaves, and the earth is spread with a flowery carpet of richest green.

"The climate of Natal is delightful. Free alike from extremes of heat and of cold, it realizes, as nearly as any land, the idea of eternal spring. From May till September but little rain falls;

for four months there is almost uninterrupted sunshine, with a
clear bracing atmosphere. During this season the thermometer
ranges from 50° to 80° at Port Natal. The average of the thermometer for five years, in the winter, was 70°; and in the
summer, 82°. During the years 1845 to 1850, the temperature
ranged between 53° and 90° in the shade. The temperature near
the ground, on a low spot along the coast, during a winter's
night, often falls below the freezing point. The summer nights,
except in a moist low situation, seldom show a temperature many
degrees below 70°. At a spot about five miles from the sea, on
a hill about 300 feet high, with an angle of elevation of about
30° facing the east, the thermometer during summer generally
rose to the *maximum* of the day about eight o'clock A.M., and
began to fall before two P.M. The hot winds along the coast
are unfrequent, and do not exhibit such high degrees of heat as
are spoken of in Australia, seldom exceeding 90° or 95°. In an
airy situation the summer heat does not usually exceed 80° along
the coast, as a strong breeze from the E.N.E. or S.W. ordinarily
prevails at that season. During winter the winds are generally
calmer.

"Of course in a country so mountainous as this, the temperature varies in different localities, with nearly similar latitudes.
At Ifumi, about five miles from the sea, and perhaps 600 feet
high, the thermometer has risen at mid-day in the shade to 110°,
and sunk at night to 43°. In some places not far from the
coast, in latitude 30° 30', hoar frosts are frequent during the
winter months; and, as we go inland to the more elevated regions,
the range of the temperature is greater. At the Quahlamba
Mountains snow always falls in winter, often in large quantities.

"Neither foreigners nor natives seem to be subject to any
disease peculiar to the climate, and many have come here from
Europe with decided gain to their health. The only malignant
disease to which Europeans seem exposed is dysentery, which,
if not speedily checked, assumes a fatal character. Several
gentlemen who were afflicted with *bronchitis* in England, have
been greatly benefited by a residence in this Colony. Among
the natives pulmonary diseases are common and fatal; but these
are induced by their excessive imprudence, and not by the
character of the climate.

"In the warm season violent thunder-storms are frequent. Immense quantities of electricity are discharged; and rain falls so copiously that the large rivers are rendered unfordable for many weeks. From September to March, scarcely a week passes without the fall of more or less rain. The magnificence and awfulness of thunder-storms in Natal surpass description. Sometimes, during a storm, so rapid are the discharges of electricity, that the whole firmament constantly glows with flame. Clouds rise from opposite directions; and while they approach each other, the lightning assumes a thousand different forms and motions. Fiery serpents grapple and rush athwart the sky: arrows and javelins fly and meet in mid heaven: meteors, of various hues, are shot down from the zenith. Now pours down to earth a cataract of crimson blood; a stream of molten iron is shot on high; then a sulphurous column,—blue, yellow, and red,—spreading into innumerable branches as it rises, and crowning the clouds with wreaths of fire. Overhead a vast chasm is rent in the glowing heavens, through whose walls appear tenfold fiercer flames. Now the whole brasen firmament seems cracked into millions of falling fragments. Above all, louder and still louder, roars and crashes the awful thunder.

"The geology of Natal has been but little studied; yet some features are manifest to the most cursory observer. The perpendicular sides of the table-lands and mountains, in the coast division, generally present *strata* of red sandstone; and what, perhaps, strikes a foreigner most, is the perfect horizontalism of these *strata*. In several places, the mountains seem to have been worn by water up to the very top of the rocks. One can hardly resist the impression, that the widest valleys have been washed out, or, at least, have once been filled with water. Many of the rounded hills in these valleys are *moraines*. Nearly all the streams flow over beds of gneiss, granite, or trap rock; and in their channels abound large boulders of those rocks. All the varieties of quartz are found in the beds of the streams, and on the lower hills. As we pass along the beach, we may travel a few miles on *strata* of sandstone; then intervenes a couple of miles of basalt or pudding-stone, gneiss or granite. All of these are found in distinct sections along the coast, each occupying in succession from fifty rods to five miles. From the Ilovo river to the Umpambinyoni,—a distance in latitude of perhaps eighteen miles,—at an elevation of 300 or 400 feet above the sea, is a continuous mass of greenstone conglomerate, surmounted, towards the northern part, by Ifumi Hill,—a mass of sandstone, some three miles in circumference, and 200 or 300 feet high above the surrounding country. Imbedded in this greenstone are fragments, both angular and worn, of quartz, granite, porphyry, jasper, sienite, varying from the size of a pea to that of a bushel measure. Adjoining this formation on the north, and also in other places in the district, is found slate-stone. But little lime, and none of pure quality, has been discovered near the coast, except in the form of shells and corals. There are seen large banks of shells in several places, many feet above the present level of the sea. Coal has been discovered near the junction of the Utukela and Umzinyati rivers, but not of good quality; as have also copper and lead, but in limited quantities. On the Umtwalumi river is found a black oxide of iron, resembling lava, in which are cemented particles of coarse siliceous sand, and pebbles of quartz. No fossils, except a few ammonites, have as yet been found.

" The animals most abundant in Natal are such as are common to other parts of Africa. Elephants, lions, buffaloes, leopards, wolves, hyænas, hippopotami, and alligators abound. Several species of bucks, antelopes, monkeys, and baboons, are every where found. There are also wild hogs, ant-eaters, wild cats, wild dogs, and many species of smaller animals. Serpents are abundant and poisonous. There are several species whose bite is fatal. The puff-adder, the cobra, and the python are the largest. Not unfrequently are reptiles found in our houses, or hanging from trees, and concealed in narrow paths.

" Of insects there is an endless and amazing variety. The scorpion and scolopendra are here, with many varieties of flies, and several thousand kinds of beetles. But the most troublesome of the insect tribes to man and beast are those commonly called ' bush-ticks.' During the warm season, these abound every where in the coast division. On every spire of grass, they await the passing of some living creature, to which they tenaciously cling, bury their heads in the flesh, and, while they suck the blood, infuse a subtle poison, which excessively irritates the skin, and causes painful and obstinate sores. Though at first so small as to be scarcely visible, if not removed, they increase in a few days to the size of the end of the finger ; then drop off from the festering flesh, and breed millions more. Neglected cattle are sometimes destroyed by them.

"Africa has been described as a land of ' rivers without water, flowers without fragrance, and birds without song ;' but such a description does not apply to Natal. Birds are here in endless variety, adorned with surpassingly beautiful plumage, and uttering notes as sweet as those which sing beneath European skies. The ' Whip-poor-Will,' which all night long makes the woods ring with music ; the turtle-dove, whose soft call will cause lions to start ; the *amassingisi,* whose concert-notes are like the distant sound of instruments floating over some tranquil lake ;—these alone are sufficient to redeem Natal from the slander, so far as regards the feathered tribes.

"Of birds of prey, the eagle, the vulture, and several species of hawks and kites, are found here. The crane, the ibis,—Egypt's sacred bird, both black and white,—the bustard, a species of turkey, the swallow, the pheasant, the partridge, the honey-bird, the humming-bird, the parrot, and multitudes of others, are here to be met with. Happy is he in Africa who lives near a wood, and wakes betimes to hear the morning hymn of praise poured forth by thousands of merry birds.

"The botany of Natal is but little familiar to the public. We know of only one man who has attempted to arrange and describe South-African plants ; and his description embraces only the region around the Cape of Good Hope. In analysing plants, all European and American works are deficient ; for, while by their aid most specimens can be traced to known *genera,* the specific and family differences are not pointed out. Very many South-African trees, shrubs, and plants have the same generic characters as are known in America and Europe ; but we have not seen one indigenous vegetable which does not in some feature differ from their foreign kindred. To a person newly arrived from the higher latitudes of New England, the entire novelty of the general features of all vegetation in Natal makes him feel as if landed in a new planet. There is a great variety of trees ; but, along the coast, all are stunted, gnarled, and crooked, very few being fit for timber. The tree which most strongly attracts the attention of the stranger is the *euphorbia,* which resembles, more than any thing else, a species of cactus grown to the height of thirty or forty feet. The castor-oil tree abounds; also the trees yielding gum-arabic. These last are often so scattered in the open country as to bear great resemblance to extensive orchards. A singular tree, called by the natives *umtombi,*—from the quantity of milky juice which exudes from its bark when pierced,—fastens itself, when young, upon another tree, and, after a few years, completely envelopes and kills it in its embrace."

CLIMATE OF NATAL.

Meteorological Table, from Observations taken by Mr. John Ecroyd, of Briercliffe, near D'Urban, Port Natal. (late of Rochdale.)

Year.	Month.	AT SUNRISE.			AT NOON.			AT EIGHT P.M.			Monthly Average of Mean Temperature.	Number of Days on which Rain fell.	Rain in inches.
		Max.	Min.	Mean.	Max.	Min.	Mean.	Max.	Min.	Mean.			
		Deg.	Deg.	Deg.	Deg.	Deg.	Deg.	Deg.	Deg.	Deg.	Deg.		
1850	November	71	50	64	85	63	75	77	57	69	69	7	2·08
	December.	71	64	69	89	71	77	78	65	71	72	16	4·61
1851	January ..	75	61	71	87	70	80	81	69	75	75	15	11·23
	February .	74	60	70	85	70	79	81	66	74	74	14	3·17
	March ...	72	58	65	86	72	79	78	62	71	71	10	1·15
	April......	71	58	62	84	69	77	75	63	70	69	2	1·07
	May	67	50	57	81	57	73	73	49	65	65	5	4·96
	June	63	45	55	78	60	71	70	51	62	63	6	1·53
	July	64	37	48	86	61	70	63	50	56	58	2	1·08
	August ...	67	40	51	78	51	72	69	51	59	61	4	0·90
	September	71	45	59	80	59	72	70	53	64	65	8	3·04
	October...	72	48	62	88	66	75	78	57	66	67	7	2·24
	November	72	62	67	86	69	78	77	66	71	72	15	5·32
	December.	75	59	69	86	69	78	77	62	71	73	22	6·57
1852	January...	77	63	70	92	74	84	80	65	73	76	12	4·66
	February .	78	65	71	91	68	79	80	67	74	75	17	13·66
	March ...	74	60	66	83	69	76	77	66	71	71	14	3·51
	April......	70	48	62	82	68	74	74	55	68	68	11	4·15
	May	72	42	53	79	65	70	64	52	57	60	4	1·05
	June	56	40	48	76	66	71	64	45	55	58	1	3·36

CLIMATE OF ENGLAND.

METEOROLOGICAL NOTES PUBLISHED IN "THE FRIEND."

	COMBE DOWN, near Bath.		DUBLIN.		ACKWORTH.		FALMOUTH.		KENDAL.		STAMFORD HILL.	
	Rain in inches.	Number of Rainy Days.	Rain in inches.	Number of Rainy Days.	Rain in inches.	Number of Rainy Days.	Rain in inches.	Number of Rainy Days.	Rain in inches.	Number of Rainy Days.	Rain in inches.	Number of Rainy Days.
1851. January ...	4·05	28	4·15	19	...	...	7·31	28	10·0	21	3·34	17
February ..	1·31	13	0·31	7	...	...	0·78	7	3·73	12	0·88	10
March ...	5·00	21	2·05	14	2·32	21	6·67	25	3·33	19	4·58	21
April	1·12	14	1·35	11	2·25	19	1·80	14	1·94	12	1·78	14
May	1·01	13	1·36	9	1·29	15	1·02	9	1·15	12	1·07	8
June	...	...	1·81	12	2·92	14	1·67	10	5·09	16	...	...
July	2·46	19	2·53	14	2·26	16	4·41	20	4·87	14	...	...
August ...	3·00	12	1·57	18	2·36	15	2·61	15	4·59	19	2·14	10
September.	0·59	7	1·17	4	...	...	1·21	5	2·12	6	0·35	6
October ...	3·43	17	3·04	11	...	...	3·77	18	6·22	23	1·94	16
November.	0·89	11	1·12	10	0·54	9	3·65	24	1·76	8	0·70	12
December.	1·99	15	0·77	8	1·16	9	2·29	9	2·64	11	0·80	9
1852. January ...	6·32	23	2·27	15	...	...	7·19	23	9·88	24	3·85	19
February ..	1·63	15	2·12	11	1·08	12	1·51	14	7·90	13	1·22	10

CHAPTER III.

EARLY HISTORY OF NATAL, FROM ITS DISCOVERY BY VASCO DE
GAMA IN 1497, TO THE ARRIVAL OF LIEUTENANT FARE-
WELL IN 1823.

AT the close of a century which had given birth to the
printing-press, and during which the nations of Europe had
been from time to time excited by reports of maritime feats and
discoveries, each one more daring and more successful than the
former, Vasco de Gama set forth from Lisbon, on July 9th, 1497,
to make another attempt to accomplish the long-cherished object
of reaching the Indies by sea; and thus to secure to his king and
nation a share in that commerce, which had for so many years
enriched the republic of Venice.

As early as 1412, the Portuguese made the first addition to
the knowledge of the African coast, beyond what had been the
southern limit of the intercourse of European nations with Africa,
by doubling the formidable Cape Nun, and proceeding as far as
Cape Bojador. From that time till Vasco de Gama, in the
voyage above referred to, succeeded in the great object of his
ambition, the Portuguese were honourably distinguished among
the nations of Europe by the interest taken by them in maritime
discovery, and by the zeal and pertinacity with which they applied
themselves to the exploration of the coasts of Africa. In select-
ing this field of investigation, they were, no doubt, impelled
at once by the traditions handed down by classical writers
respecting the circumnavigation of Africa by the Phœnicians,
(though the accounts of that enterprise, as interpreted by the
limited knowledge of geography which obtained in the fifteenth
century, were so vague and indefinite as to detract little from the
claim to independent merit and originality which the Portuguese
may justly prefer in this field of distinction,) and by the circumstance that the north-west of Africa was almost the only known

line of coast, open to the investigations of the mariners of the age, which yet remained unexplored. Limited as was the intercourse of the central and southern nations of Europe with Russia and other northern states, and imperfect as was their knowledge of the Scandinavian seas, the means of communication between them sufficed for all the exigencies of commerce; and the descriptions of the coast obtained from the inhabitants of the shores of those northern seas, would, notwithstanding their vagueness, dispel any thing like mystery and romance that might be associated with naval expeditions in that quarter, and reduce the attractiveness of such an undertaking to a matter of bare utility. But such was not the case with Africa: that land of golden sands shone from afar with all the tempting lustre of rare riches and adventure.

The eyes of King John of Portugal, and of his distinguished son, Prince Henry, were therefore directed to the shores of Africa; and they nobly commenced a series of voyages which, after the rough sea had kindly forced their captains to be bold, and compelled them to leave the shore which they were hugging too closely for success, led first to the discovery of the Madeira Isles, (where a colony was settled, and the vine and sugar-cane were introduced,) and were followed by results every way commensurate with the means employed. At the death of Prince Henry, however, in 1463, the discoveries of the Portuguese on the coast of Africa had not reached the Equator. It is interesting to us, as Britons, to remember, that it was a nephew of our great King Henry IV. who, a younger son of a royal race, employed his talents and influence in improving the art of navigation, and extending the limits of geographical knowledge; and who, while his cousin, Henry V. of England, was gaining the barren honours of military renown on the fields of France, was opening new fields for commerce, and turning his discoveries to practical account by the establishment of the first modern colony on African soil.

The zeal for African exploration did not die with him with whom it originated. It was pursued by the Portuguese with various success, until, in 1492, Bartholomew Diaz reached the Cape of Good Hope. The destitute and shattered state of his fleet prevented him from personally ascertaining, by further examination, that he had reached the most southerly point on the African Continent : but the results of his voyage, and reports from other quarters, left no doubt on the mind of the Portuguese king, that these long-continued efforts were now about to be crowned with success. A small squadron was forthwith fitted out, for the purpose of continuing the discoveries of Diaz, and was placed under the command of Vasco de Gama. It was he who, after doubling the Cape of Good Hope, and coasting along the shores of what is now the Cape Colony, arrived at length, on Christmas-day, 1497, at the Bay of NATAL, and, in giving it a name, associated it with the auspicious day on which it was discovered.

The coast and Bay of Natal were, at various times, visited by the Dutch, English, and Portuguese,—occasionally by parties wishing to explore the country to ascertain its capabilities for the purposes of trade; but mostly by the crews of vessels unhappily wrecked on its inhospitable shores.

The first time that Natal was visited by the English appears to have been in 1683, when, an English ship having been wrecked near Delagoa Bay, the crew, about eighty in number, made their way overland to Cape Town, and received the assistance of the unsophisticated natives of the tribes through whose territory they travelled. The account given by them of the land on the eastern coast agrees pretty well with the present characteristics of the district, though civilization has driven some of the animals therein named to seek their habitation in the more retired spots of the interior. They state that "the natural fertility of the countries travelled through made the inhabitants lazy, indolent, docile, and simple. Their rivers are abundantly stored with good fish and water-fowl, besides manatees, or sea-cows, and crocodiles; their woods, with large trees, wild cattle and deer, elephants, rhinoceroses, lions, tigers, wolves, foxes for game; also many sort of fowls and birds, with ostriches."

In a MS. preserved in the Public Library at Cape Town, the Port of Natal is thus described: "The river of Natal falls into the Indian Ocean in 30° S. latitude. Its mouth is wide and deep enough for small craft; but there is there a sand-bank, which at the highest flood has not more than ten or twelve feet water. Within this bank the water is deep. This river is the principal one on the coast of Natal, and has been frequently visited by merchant vessels."

This statement is of importance in connexion with the question of the former course of the rivers near the Bay of Natal. The Bay is large, and may be described as of a circular shape, with two small rivers, and some lesser streams, running into it. At low tide the greater part of it is left uncovered; and any one riding round the Bay has ocular demonstration that the quantity of fresh water falling into it is comparatively trifling. On each side of the Bay, stretching along in the direction of the coast, is a flat, not much raised above high water-mark, and separated from the sea, on the southern coast, by a range of sandstone hills; on the northern, by low hillocks of loose sand. Along this latter flat, the Umgeni, one of the largest of the Natal rivers, has twice within the last ten years, on the occurrence of heavy floods, made its way into the Bay. Was this its ordinary course two hundred years ago, when the above description was written?

On the one hand, the mouth of the Umgeni is now often choked by the sand of the sea-shore; and the position of the land between the Bay and the Umgeni is such that the supposition is almost involuntarily forced upon even ordinary observers, that the river, at some prior period, had its course through the Bay. Moreover, we can hardly suppose that such experienced seamen as Holland then sent forth could mistake the Bay as it now exists for a large river. On the other hand, it must be admitted that the inquiries which the colonists made among the natives at the time of these floods, supplied no evidence of the river having had another course than its present one.

In the year 1686, a Dutch ship, the "Stavenisse," was wrecked at the entrance of the Bay of Natal. After one or two ineffectual attempts to escape in the boats and by land, they set to work to build a small craft out of the timbers of the wreck. In a twelve-month this vessel was completed, and sailed for the Cape, without compass or chart, leaving some of the crew behind, (and amongst them four Englishmen and a Frenchman,) who did not care to expose themselves to the dangers of such a voyage. The little vessel, however, arrived in safety at Table Bay.

In the course of the next year, the Dutch Company at the
Cape, excited by the accounts of the amazing fertility and strange
productions of Natal, dispatched another vessel, to make further
discoveries at Natal, and along the coast as far as Delagoa Bay.
After completing the survey of that place, they sailed for Natal
Bay, and there rescued two of the seamen left behind by the
"Stavenisse;" and, when coasting along in latitude 33°, and
off the territory of the Magoses, (now called the Amakosas,)
another seaman of the "Stavenisse" swam off to them. These
persons gave much information respecting Natal and the inhabitants, which, at this time of day, it is not a little amusing to
peruse. They state, among other marvels, "One may travel
two or three hundred *mylen* through the country, without any
cause of fear from men, provided you go naked, and without any
iron or copper; for these things give inducement to the murder
of those who have them. Neither need one be in any apprehension about meat and drink, as they have in every village, or
kraal, a house of entertainment for travellers, where these are
not only lodged, but fed also. Care must only be taken, towards
nightfall, when one cannot get any further, to put up there, and
not to go on before morning. In an extent of one hundred and
fifty *mylen*, travelled by your servants along the coast, to the
depth of about thirty *mylen* inland, and through five kingdoms,—
namely, the *Magoses, Makriggas*, the *Matimbas, Mapontes*, and
Emboas,—they found no standing waters, but many rivers with
plenty of fish and full of sea-cows. There are many dense forests,
with short-stemmed trees: but at the Bay of Natal are two
forests, each fully a *myl* square, with tall, straight, and thick
trees, fit for house or ship timber; in which is abundance of
honey and wax: but no wax is to be had from the natives, as
they eat the wax as well as the honey.

"In all the time of their stay in that country, or of travelling
through it, they found but one European,—an old Portuguese,
in the country of the Mapontes. He had been shipwrecked
there about forty years before, while returning from India. The
wreck, built of teak, is still to be seen on shore; and, as the
Africans state, several brass and iron cannon are still to be found
there. This Portuguese had been circumcised, and had a wife,
children, cattle, and land. He spoke only the African language,

having forgotten every thing,—his God included. They cultivate three sorts of corn, as also calabashes, pumpkins, water-
melons, and beans. They sow annually a sort of earth-nut, and
a kind of underground bean, both very nourishing, and bearing a
small leaf. Tobacco grows there wild, and, if they knew how to
manage it, would, in all probability, be equal to the Virginian.

"The true European fig grows wild, also a kind of grapes,
which are a little sour, though well-tasted : they are best boiled.
They have also a kind of tree-fruit, not unlike the father-land
medlar, and not unpleasant to eat. Wild prunes grow abundantly on the shore, and are well-tasted. There are also wild
cherries, with long stalks, and very sour. Finally, they have
a kind of apple, not unpleasant eating, but which are not ripe
until they fall from the tree : before they fall, they are nauseous,
and cause flatulency. The country swarms with cows, calves,
oxen, steers, and goats. There are few sheep, but no want of
elephants, rhinoceroses, lions, tigers, leopards, elands, and harts,
as well of the Cape kind as the father-land, with branched horns;
rheboks of various kinds, wild hogs, dogs, buffaloes, sea-cows,
crocodiles, and horses. The latter they do not catch or tame,
although they approach within ten or twelve paces : they are
finely formed and quite black, with long manes and tails, incredibly swift, and of great strength. Some have the tail black,
and others white." They also say, that they "saw two animals
feeding together in the wilderness, in size and colour like the
elephant; having a head like the horse, a short tail, but long
neck, very tame, and totally unknown in Europe. (Giraffe?)

"There are many kinds of snakes, scorpions, large and small,
also centipedes, toads and frogs, ostriches, geese, ducks, pigeons,
red and brown partridges, abundance of pheasants and *Pauws*,
with a shining top-knot and tail. (Balearic crane?) In the
rivers are eels and congers, and in the Bay of Natal king's-fish
and sun-fish, known in India and here, as may be further seen
from the annexed account taken down from the mouths of our
men."*

The officers in command of the expedition, also, while at Port
Natal, entered into a treaty with the chief of the district for the

* CHASE's "Reprint of Natal Papers," &c., vol. i., pp. 8, 9.

purchase of the Bay and some surrounding land, the medium of
exchange being beads, copper, iron-work, &c.; and they were
specially directed to affirm, in the purchase-deed, that the goods
so given were of the value stated in their instructions.   The land
was bought and assigned accordingly.   But the purchase did not
secure to the Dutch any benefit equivalent to the value of the
goods given, trifling as that was: for, on visiting the place a few
years after, to take possession, they found that the chief with
whom the contract was made was dead; and his son, on being
reminded of the treaty, replied, "My father is dead: his skins"
(that is, clothes) "are buried with him in his house, which has
been burnt over him; and the place is fenced in, over which
none now must pass: and as to what he agreed to, it was for
himself; I have nothing to say to it."

About the commencement of the eighteenth century, Port
Natal was visited by the English for the purpose of securing victims for the nefarious slave-trade, in which they appear to have
been successful.

In 1721, the Dutch established a factory at Port Natal, but
soon abandoned it; and, till the arrival of Farewell and his party
in 1823, as detailed in the next Chapter, the intercourse of the
white man with the inhabitants of Natal was principally the
result of shipwrecks along the rock-bound coasts.

CHAPTER IV.

HISTORY OF THE FIRST ENGLISH SETTLERS, FROM THE ARRIVAL OF LIEUTENANT FAREWELL IN 1823, TO THE TAKING OF NATAL FROM THE DUTCH IN 1842.

A FEW pages have sufficed to give the leading particulars of interest connected with Natal, from its discovery by Vasco de Gama, on Christmas-day, 1497, to the year 1823; but as, after this date, it becomes the stage on which civilized man is to act his part, events thicken around us, and call for a more detailed account. It was only about three years before this time, (in 1820,) that Tshaka, (or Chaka,) like a desolating scourge, over-ran Natal with his armies, making his name a terror to all who heard it, until no nation dared to stand before his wrath, but all fled, like frighted birds or deer, to their safe retreats in the dense bush. Directly after Natal had thus been swept, Fynn, Farewell, and others arrived.

The designation of this Chapter might be "The Knight-Errantry of Natal," the chivalrous and romantic having a large place in this period of its history, which bears some likeness to Scott's "Tales of a Grandfather," and the works of some of our early English historians.

The knights and squires,—*alias*, Kafir chiefs,—who figured in the adventures of these times, had their thousands of vassals, whom they could summon to fight against their enemies, or against each other, as occasion might require. They had not, certainly, their fortified castles, surrounded by moats, defended by ramparts, and mounted with guns; but they had—what served their purpose equally well—the dense bush, into which they could flee with their people, and remain until the enemy had wasted his energies, and taken his departure. Accordingly, when the sound of alarm was heard from Tshaka or Dingaan, a council of safety was called, at the end of which the sage warriors would say, with the greatest composure, " We hope the report is not true; but if it is, we can go into the bush, supposing it is not desirable to fight." This course they accordingly took, as necessity arose; and on their return generally found their houses of straw burnt down, and their palaces of clay destroyed, whilst sundry small articles had disappeared.

These pugnacious gentlemen had not, to be sure, the sturdy peasantry of England or Scotland under their command; but they had soldiers who, under the circumstances, served their purpose much better. The Natal Kafirs had so far collected and increased under their English lords, that in the early part of 1838 it was computed that they could bring 3,000 or 4,000 fighting-men into the field, who, with their wives and children, would probably make up 10,000 people. These warriors, being armed with muskets and trained for battle, constituted no mean force when an enemy had to be confronted.

When they went forth to battle, they carried their own commissariat with them, not requiring ships and waggons to convey their stores, neither wives nor children encumbering their progress. Their provisions consisted chiefly of what fell in their way, or what they could take from the foe. Their powers of endurance were also very great; they could fast long, and travel far, without exhaustion; could take their enemies by surprise, or, when surprised by others, flee into the bush, thus living secure in the midst of alarms.

The difficulty of obtaining correct information on the subjects embraced in this Chapter has been extreme. The most exciting parts, however, of the narration are those on which I can best rely, having obtained them from living persons of undoubted veracity, who either took part in what they relate, or lived in Natal at the time. There is no existing author who has given any continued and correct account of these times. Captain Gardiner says but little upon the subject, nor was much to be expected from him, considering the peculiar position which he occupied; and Mr. Isaacs is an author on whom I cannot rely, even during the period which his two volumes embrace, terminating in the beginning of 1831, and leaving a chasm of eleven years, of which only some short notices have been given by Mr. Chase. Indeed, the most respectable living witnesses of the earlier times of the settlement affirm, that there was not one amongst their number who was in circumstances to give a fair and impartial account of what took place. Their mutual quarrels were so serious, and carried on with so much fire and bitterness, that they were incapacitated to write a history of the times and transactions.

Not only was this the case in reference to the relations of the settlers to each other, but there was also much in the personal history of each individual, which it would not be convenient to publish to the world. Nor shall I seek to drag from oblivion more than is needful for a just view of what transpired, or to correct many errors which have been made current, confining myself to a refutation of one which runs through Mr. Isaacs's work, and which appears to have a bearing upon all matters connected with those times.

Being myself utterly unable to understand Mr. Isaacs's account, I sought from various respectable individuals in Natal, who lived in the times referred to, the information required; and having consulted those to whom I have had access, I have compared notes, and sought to arrive at the truth, and give an honest account of the whole. If any thing related is thought to be derogatory to any person, either living or dead, I can only say that I have sought to avoid giving any thing of a disagreeable nature, which was not called for by historical faithfulness. I have no party predilections in the matter, and no personal ends or wishes to gratify. Nor am I aware that these transactions would ever have seen the light, had I not searched them out, and placed them before the public. Some may think it was needless to take the pains; but others will thank me for my trouble. The last of the living actors are now passing away; and although the busy emigrant may not have leisure to attend to these matters now, yet in process of time he will be glad to read the record of what occurred, in years gone by, on the spot where his house is built, or his cattle are grazing. Could poor Farewell rise from his grave, and see what is now passing near the place where his fort of clay was erected,—the site on which the extensive premises are built in the market-place, as shown in Plate No. XII.,—how confounded would he be to behold the emporium of trade, where his straw house before stood,—the Post-Office, from which the news of the day and the literature of the world are distributed,—

and, in the upper story, the magistrate sitting with all the *insignia* of office, and the lawyers disputing in flowing gowns!

Mr. Isaacs is much displeased with a former writer, for saying that the settlers had Kafir wives, or concubines, &c. He certainly had better have not adverted to the matter; for the fact is, whatever he and others may say to the contrary, that, with scarcely an exception, they all had Kafir wives and concubines, and as many of them as suited their wishes or convenience, varying from one or two to ten. Let any man attempt to deny it, and we will give him demonstrative proof to the contrary, by pointing to a mixed colour of skin, and a peculiar physical conformation in the rising progeny, which speak for themselves. A certain black lady, whom I could name, is the widow of one of these young men: she is the great "*inkosi kasi*," that is, the chief wife or widow of this young gentleman; and sometimes honours her guests with a sight of the arm-chair in which her late spouse used to sit. It is said that she has about one hundred kraals under her, containing a thousand people, over whom she is queen. Other proofs might be given, if requisite; but this is needless. Some of these men were *Kafir chiefs*, in the proper sense of the word, except that the skin was not quite black.

Then in reference to laying aside the clothes and wearing blankets, Mr. Isaacs might as well have been silent. I have good grounds for believing that sometimes it was not convenient to get them; but that frequently they cared nothing at all about them, and dressed like Kafirs without reluctance. It is much more easy for man to descend in the scale of being from the civilized to the savage, than to rise from the savage to the civilized; and in strange lands, surrounded by barbarous life, great care is required in the settler to prevent such a degrading lapse. To attempt to deny facts like these, is useless; and it is better to admit them, and say it was so, but that it was to a great extent the result of the circumstances in which the parties were placed. Every man did what was right in his own eyes: and woe to the man who dared to interfere with or oppose his fellow! Lynch-law was the order of the day.

Never was there a more heterogeneous company on the face of the earth, than those who figured away at Natal at this time,—

English, Kafirs, Zulus,—officers, hunters, and sailors,—deserters and traders. Of parsons there was not one, or all the blame of their misdeeds might have fallen on his unfortunate head.

Amongst the natives there were the remnants of the tribes scattered by Tshaka, collected and collecting under their white chiefs; gathering around whom, they said, "Let us be called by your name, fight your battles, and enjoy your protection;" whilst Tshaka, and afterwards Dingaan, treacherous and bold, walked upon their heights, like the lion watching for his prey, and waiting the most convenient opportunity for scattering and destroying the affrighted tribes.

Amongst the first personages who performed their part on this novel stage, were H. Fynn, Lieutenant Farewell, and, a year later, Lieutenant King. Isaacs also came with King, and figured here. But in their feeble state it was most unfortunate that they quarrelled so seriously as to be unable to act together, thus rendering it needful for each to take care of himself as best he could. The probability is, that each wanted to be the *inkosi inkulu*, "great chief," with his Zulu majesty, and the others were not willing to allow it; so that each in his turn went to the "great place" to pay his respects to Tshaka or Dingaan, and deliver presents, seeking to ingratiate himself into the favour of his savage lord, and possibly doing this at the expense of others; whilst Tshaka reaped the benefit, playing a double game, and deriving profit from the weakness and folly of these misguided men.

It was in 1823 that Lieutenant Farewell, of the Royal Marines, joined with Mr. Alexander Thompson in an exploring expedition to the Eastern Coast of Africa. In trying to commence operations at St. Lucia, their boats were capsized, and some of their men were lost, but Farewell and Thompson escaped; upon which they ran their vessel (the "Saltbury") into Natal, and tried to open a communication with Tshaka, but failed. On the return of Lieutenant Farewell to the Cape, he was of opinion that favourable openings for commerce presented themselves at Natal; and induced about twenty persons to join him in his favourite scheme of founding a new Colony. Amongst this number was Lieutenant King, who, instead of coming with the first party, proceeded to England to lay their plans before the Admiralty, and, if possible, excite interest and obtain assistance there.

Lieutenant Farewell also applied to Lord Charles Somerset, the governor of the Cape, to have his proposed Colony fully recognised by the English government, as a regular dependency of the British empire. A copy of the correspondence may be seen in Chase. But in this attempt Farewell did not succeed, and therefore had no alternative but either to abandon the enterprise, or to undertake it without that encouragement and support which appeared essential to success. Nothing daunted, however, these intrepid adventurers pursued their course; and in March, 1824, the sloop "Julia" arrived with Messrs. Farewell, Peterson, Hoffman, and others. Mr. H. Fynn was also of this first party, but came overland, and arrived a few weeks earlier than his companions in the "Julia." On his arrival, in company with a few others, in the early part of 1824, having set the people to erect some temporary buildings on what is now the market-square of D'Urban, he proceeded towards Tshaka's country, and opened a communication with him by messengers; upon which Tshaka, wishing Mr. Fynn to defer his personal visit, sent him a present of forty oxen and some ivory, desiring him to wait until a suitable reception could be prepared. On Mr. Fynn's return, he met Messrs. Farewell, Peterson, and Hoffman, with the remainder of the adventurers who had arrived.

The following year Lieutenant King returned from England to the Cape, and, in company with Mr. Isaacs, proceeded to Natal in the "Mary," which was wrecked on entering the Bay, but without any loss of life occurring. It was out of this wreck, with the addition of Natal wood, that the "Tshaka" was built, which was afterwards seized in Algoa Bay, as coming from a foreign port. This was on her second visit to that place, and appears to have been an act of severity, if not of injustice.

The first three leading characters on the stage of Natal had now made their appearance,—Fynn, Farewell, and King; to whom Isaacs might be added: but there was a fifth individual of some note, named Jacob, a Kafir.

Jacob, it would appear, was a shrewd, wily Kafir, from the frontier of the old Colony, where he was detected in cattle-stealing, for which he was sent to Cape Town to be tried, when, being found guilty, he was dispatched to Robin Island at the time the notorious Lynx was there; but Captain Owen, of the

" Leven,"* needing some one to go with him to Delagoa Bay, an arrangement was made for Jacob to accompany him in the capacity of servant and interpreter; upon which he was handed over to the care of Mr. Fannin, one of whose boats being capsized at St. Lucia, Jacob escaped, and was named *"Thlambamanzi,"* having saved himself from being destroyed by the water. He was then taken by the natives to Tshaka, who prided himself on favouring foreigners of all nations, and by whom he was treated with great caution for a while. But, as this great chief found that Jacob knew much about the English, having been to Graham's Town and the Cape, and as a few English from Natal were frequently visiting him, he made use of Jacob as interpreter and go-between,—a dignity which, in the reign of Dingaan, Tshaka's successor, cost him his life. He was now raised to considerable power and influence by the Zulu chief, being made a captain of some note: he was much at the "great place;" but his usual abode was near the Umtongaart river.

Jacob must have been a very shrewd fellow. Amongst other things, he told the Zulu monarch that he was a prophet, and would tell him and his captains what would come to pass in the last days; namely, "that an *umfundis*" ("teacher" or "missionary") "would come and ask to sit among his people, and build his house, and teach them the Great Word; afterwards another and another would come, until the place was full. Then they would make war upon his people, and conquer them, taking their land, and destroying their nation." So said Jacob about the year 1825.† Accordingly, when Captain Gardiner made application to Dingaan to allow a missionary to reside with him, this was the answer he received, (as related by that gentleman in his work,) without knowing who was the author of it; and; after his utmost efforts, Captain Gardiner could not obtain permission. Subsequently, whilst Captain Gardiner was absent in England, the Rev. Aldin Grout, of the American mission, applied to Din-

---

* To this gentleman we are indebted for most of what is known of the Natal coast. He commanded the "Leven" sloop-of-war and a small squadron, with which he surveyed the coast.

† Some say that it was an aged Hottentot, and not Jacob, who made this statement; or it may be that one made it at one time to one chief, and the other at another time to another chief.

gaan for the same purpose, and received the same reply. However, he afterwards gave permission; and Mr. Grout was about to proceed to his location, when Captain Gardiner returned from England, bringing with him the Rev. Mr. Owen, of the Church Missionary Society, who went to Dingaan instead of Mr. Grout, and was at his kraal when Retief and his party were so brutally murdered.

Jacob was thus the connecting link between the Zulu despot and the settlers,—a position which, in the end, cost him his life. Whilst Tshaka lived, all went well with him; but, when that chief was murdered by Dingaan in 1828, Jacob did not stand so high with his successor as he had done with Tshaka, it being the policy of Dingaan to cut off all who had favour or power under Tshaka, lest they should give him trouble, or plot his ruin. Mr. Isaacs lays the English language under contribution to find epithets sufficiently strong to describe the villany of this so-called "arch-fiend," who, though certainly a dangerous man, was probably not so bad as represented, as will be seen when the progress of events is recorded. I should not have said so much about this man, if he had not acted so prominent a part in connexion with the English settlers, and formed part and parcel of the occurrences that took place.

Having thus distinctly set before the reader the leading characters in this drama, we shall proceed to note what transpired.

The first object of the English settlers was to secure the friendship of Tshaka; and, had they had the good sense to allow one of their number to be the acknowledged organ of communication betwixt themselves and that great Kafir chief, they would have secured his favourable consideration. Tshaka, being a perfect despot, and not knowing how there could be equals in chieftainship, or how to treat with each separately, could form no conception of republican principles. So, when the settlers could not agree to have a representative, each one did his best, by presents, and in other ways, to ingratiate himself with his Zulu majesty; which afforded him an opportunity of playing a double, and often profitable, game; giving or withholding his friendship and protection, as suited his passion or caprice; making and unmaking them chiefs by turns; and bestowing or withdrawing the country at his pleasure. In this course of conduct he continued to the end of his career.*

In order fully to understand the state of things in those times, it must not be forgotten that the Natal territory, which had a short time before been swarming with human beings, was comparatively depopulated and laid waste. There were still many people in it; but these lay, like hunted deer, hid in dense bush or deep ravine, and only crawled out stealthily to see and hear what was going on around, speedily disappearing if danger threatened. In these hidden haunts they lived on roots, or small patches of cultivated corn, hid by the trees or rocks; and persons passing through the country would have supposed that no human being dwelt in it. Along some parts of the coast, they subsisted on fish and roots; and one tribe resorted to the horrid practice of cannibalism.

Thus "scattered and peeled," these feeble and frightened creatures were glad to range themselves under the banner of any parties who were likely to afford them protection. The few English settlers, therefore, were placed in a position to collect the remnants around them; a circumstance which increased their importance, and gave them facilities of defence, if attacked by enemies, opening, at the same time, a source from which they might obtain supplies of food, &c.

In this manner the early settlers became Kafir chiefs by the force of circumstances, and formed a nucleus around which the people might collect.

According to the best information which I have obtained, Mr. H. Fynn was the first to collect about forty of these desolate wanderers around him; by which act he exposed himself to the displeasure of Tshaka, for preserving those who had been his foes, and against whom he had fought: for, according to Zulu law, not one enemy was allowed to live; not even the dog of a hostile party might be preserved alive. What a fearful picture of fallen, depraved humanity! Let those who talk of the dignity of human nature without the Gospel, ponder it well, as they have it here in unadulterated perfection.

To these refugees others were added from time to time, until

---

* Lieutenant Farewell's interpreters were "Fire" and "Frederick." I presume both were Hottentots.

E

the number has swelled into what, eight years ago, was estimated at 100,000.   Although Fynn took the lead in this particular, Farewell, King, and others, collected many people around them who lived near the Bay, and gradually extended themselves, as they found their number and strength increase.

These three leaders, being divided, had each his own separate establishment.   Farewell fixed on the site of the present Market-square, near to which the large store of Middleton, Wirsing, and Co. now stands; King chose the Bluff, at the bottom of which, opposite the Island, the schooner "Tshaka" was built; whilst Fynn located on the Umbilo river, about five miles from the Bay.

The erection of the "Tshaka" (schooner) was no small task for this little band of enterprising men to accomplish.   It appears that the crew of the "Mary," under the able management of Lieutenant King, got out a considerable portion of the wreck of that vessel by great labour and perseverance; with which, and with timber cut out of the bush on the Bluff, they built the "Tshaka," so named after the Zulu chief, but afterwards called the "Elizabeth and Susan."   They were three years in constructing this little vessel, which certainly ought to have been christened "Natal."   Mr. Hatton was one of the chief agents in her building; but the quarrels between him and Mr. King were so serious, as to make it doubtful whether she would ever get to sea.   King and Hatton, the first two ship-builders at Natal, both died here, as if to take possession of the country for shipping purposes.

The schooner being completed, notwithstanding the many reverses which arose, she was launched on the 10th of March, 1828, having been three years in building.   The difficulties which had been surmounted were of no ordinary kind, and her completion in the face of them was a trophy of the labour and perseverance displayed in her erection.   On the 30th of April, Messrs. King, Farewell, and Isaacs embarked, taking with them Sotobe and Bosomboser, two of Tshaka's principal chiefs, who were sent on a mission of friendship to the old Colony, in order to obtain information, and, if desirable, to proceed onward to England; Jacob acting as the interpreter.

On May 4th, the "Tshaka" cast anchor in Algoa Bay, and was boarded by Mr. Francis, the port-captain, and Mr. Ware,

the surgeon.   She was detained here three months, during which
time many communications passed betwixt the government authorities, Messrs. Farewell and King, and the Zulu chiefs; but
these were of such a nature as rather to fill the minds of the
barbarians with disgust and contempt, than excite within their
breasts feelings of admiration and esteem.   At length the
"Helicon" was sent, and took the chiefs on board to convey
them to Natal.   It sailed on the 9th of August, in company
with the "Tshaka," and they made the Cape of Natal on the
17th.   The entire particulars of the voyage, with subsequent
events, are recorded by Mr. Isaacs.

The "Tshaka" afterwards took another voyage to Algoa Bay,
when she was seized by the authorities, as coming from a foreign
port; and, if the account given by Mr. Isaacs is correct, its
seizure was certainly a very pitiable and contemptible, if not
illegal, affair.

These pioneers of a new Colony—which is now rising to so
much importance in the Christian and commercial world, to the
shores of which thousands of emigrants have come, and probably
thousands more will shortly follow them—had enough to do
to obtain food and raiment, often enduring considerable hardship
and privation, buying a little corn as they could, shooting bucks,
and, when hard pressed, going to Tshaka for cattle, being beggars
at the door of the great king; where they sometimes met with
cold reception and rough treatment, but generally obtained part
or all of that for which they came.

The time had now arrived when death was to make a serious
inroad upon the settlers, and two of those who had been the chief
instruments in bringing Natal into notice, were to be numbered
with the silent dead.   King and Farewell, as they had begun to
excite interest about Natal and take active measures together,
were not long divided in death; the former meeting his end
quietly on the Bluff, the latter being cut off by the hand of the
murderer in whose protection he had confided.

On the return of the "Tshaka" from her first voyage, Lieutenant King was taken seriously ill about August 18th.   This
illness was greatly aggravated by many circumstances of disappointment and chagrin which had arisen out of their visit to
Algoa Bay, and by the perplexities and difficulties which arose in

connexion with the return to Tshaka of the two chiefs whom they had taken with them. These particulars it is not needful to detail; but they doubtless preyed upon his spirit, and had much to do with hastening his end.

He was attended, I believe, by his mother and sister, and Isaacs and Fynn, during his last illness; and he sent a request to Farewell to come and visit him on this deeply painful occasion, so that they might be reconciled to each other, and he might die in peace; but so deep was the feeling of resentment in Farewell's breast, that he declined the interview,—a melancholy instance of the extent to which bad feeling may triumph over the dictates of reason and the voice of humanity. But whilst I regard the act as utterly inexcusable, I can by no means unite with Mr. Isaacs and some others in those unrestrained and wholesale epithets of abuse which his work contains. So violent had been Mr. King's rage against Mr. Farewell, that, on one occasion at least, he is reported to have come over in a boat from the Bluff, with his people, to destroy him utterly by force; but, upon more full and careful inquiry, I am induced to think that it was to challenge him to fight a duel. This was shortly after the arrival of Mr. King, and is only one instance given to show the height to which their quarrels were carried.

The last hours of Lieutenant King were made as easy as they could be by the presence and attentions of his friends. He expressed deep concern for his mother and sister, of whom he often spoke. His character among his friends stood well; and he was followed to his early grave by the respect and regrets of most who knew him. He was buried on what was called "Mount Prospect," on the Bluff side of the Bay, which it overlooks, with the Islands, and the town of D'Urban, on the opposite side. Mr. Henry Fynn has now built here, and resides on the spot where this early adventurer is buried, and is enclosing the grave, on which a tablet will be placed.

No sooner had the grave closed upon Lieutenant King, than the first great mover in Natal colonization was destined to meet his fate by the treacherous assagai stab, in a manner from which the heart recoils with chilling horror.

Lieutenant Farewell left Natal for Graham's Town, for purposes of trade, shortly after the death of Lieutenant King;

whence he started on his return in the month of July, 1831, in company with Messrs. Walker and Thackwray, and about thirty Hottentots, who proceeded safely on their journey until they arrived on the borders of Amamponda-land, adjoining the present Colony of Natal ; when they were murdered under the following circumstances : " From Amadolo, this company proceeded to the residence of Fakoo, (Faku,) on the 26th of August, intending afterwards to visit the encampment of Quetoo, (Quecha,) whom Mr. Farewell knew while at Port Natal. Respecting this part of their design the Umpondo chief warmly remonstrated with them, and represented it as an extremely perilous measure, that might not only endanger the lives of the party, but likewise involve them in great trouble. Not being disposed, however, duly to consider Fakoo's (Faku's) argument, or recent events, and having received a message, informing them that the Amaquabi had numbers of elephants' tusks which they wished to dispose of, they resolved on carrying their plans into effect at all hazards. Hence, after travelling with their waggons until within twenty or thirty miles of the place, Messrs. Farewell, Walker, and Thackwray, attended by interpreters, &c., went forward on horseback. Quetoo (Quecha) received them with apparent kindness, ordered a beeve to be slaughtered for their use, and gave them various other tokens of friendship. Scarcely, however, had night-shade fallen, before his mien greatly altered, as did that of his attendants also ; for both their words and actions then assumed an air of hostility. This was sufficiently manifest to our travellers themselves, but more especially to the interpreters, who repeatedly hinted that the aspect of things was indicative of evil. The chief seems to have signified a wish to prevent their procedure to Natal, being, probably, fearful that they might render Dingaan assistance against him. After informing them of the wound he had received from the gun of a white man, Lochenburg's horses were brought, and exhibited in triumph ; and, in their rage, the savage throng cruelly goaded and most barbarously treated the poor animals, as if to annoy their visitors, or induce them to say something on which a quarrel might be grounded. Messrs. Thackwray and Walker now became very uneasy ; but Mr. Farewell was still unwilling to believe that their host would venture to do them any personal injury.

"Their fears being somewhat quieted, and the natives having retired, they laid themselves down to sleep, and all remained tranquil until near the dawn of the following day. Their tent was then suddenly surrounded, and all three were horribly massacred, together with five of their native servants, who slept in a hut hard by. Three only escaped to tell the dreadful tale; and one of these was obliged desperately to fight his way through, in doing which he shot three of the barbarians, and received one or two slight wounds himself. The ruffians then set off to plunder the waggons, which they knew to be not far distant. On seeing them advance, the people in charge, both English and Hottentots, immediately fled into the woods, so that there was no further obstacle in the way. The draught-oxen, thirty or forty in number, constituted the first object; and, having secured these, they next ransacked the waggons completely. Here they found several thousand pounds of beads, which to them were, of course, more precious than gold; and likewise quantities of clothing, wherewith they dressed themselves as well as they were able. Ten or twelve horses also fell into their hands, together with several guns belonging to the party. Thus laden, they returned without doing any injury whatever to the waggons, or so much as attempting to pursue the survivors. These, after remaining in the forests until their way out became quite clear, hastened back again to Morley, whence the intelligence of their misfortunes was first received in the Colony."

Thus fell the enterprising Farewell,—after years of toil, privation, and suffering, in the prosecution of his favourite scheme, the colonization of Natal,—just at the point when he fondly hoped his wishes were about to be realized, and his plans consummated in complete success. Let the colonist of the present day, placed in more favourable circumstances, drop his tear over these pioneers of civilization in Natal, and raise his tribute of praise to that Being who has highly favoured him above those who went before.

The scenes which immediately followed were of a most exciting nature. Henry Ogle and John Cane had been in the employ of Farewell, and now took his people and cattle, which they divided between them, and fully entered upon their career of Kafir chieftainship.

When the "Tshaka" returned, before Lieutenant King died,

the box of presents from the English authorities was opened by him; and as the presents did not appear of sufficient value, King added a large looking-glass to them.* But when the whole was forwarded, the chief was dissatisfied, and resolved on sending John Cane to Graham's Town and the Cape on the business, with Jacob for interpreter. During the absence of Cane, Tshaka met his tragical end, in a manner which was a fit consummation of his career of blood and death, and which proves that "there is a God that judgeth upon the earth," and ruleth alike amongst civilized and savage; and who shall stay His hand, when He stretches it forth in wrath to chastise?

The death of Tshaka was an event of great importance both to the Zulu nation and to the Natal settlers. To give a full account of this monster chief does not fall within the range of my present design, but is reserved for the volume on the natives, in which the scene is accompanied by a plate, in elucidation of the manner in which that tragedy was perpetrated. To leave his death without notice, would, however, be improper and inexcusable, as it is an integral part of passing transactions.

This chief has been called "the Modern Attila." In many things he differed from that "Scourge of God;" but in others, unhappily, they bore too close a resemblance. Another of his designations has been, "the Hyæna Man," as being descriptive of the revolting scowl and dark treachery of that ferocious beast; and he was also styled "the Great Elephant," as one who, with the weight of his ponderous body, could at once crush his victim beneath his feet. Before Tshaka's day, the Zulu tribe from which he sprang was not remarkably great or strong, being a nation of pedlars, the great tobacco-sellers of the country. His father's name was Usenzengakona; his mother's name, Unandi, from the Ilangeni tribe.

Tshaka early displayed extraordinary powers of both body and mind. His physical form was tall and well-proportioned; his appearance, commanding and, when excited, terrific; and his exploits were such as to compel wonder and fear. His mental

* Among the presents sent by the Cape government to Tshaka, were one or two cases containing sheets of very thick copper, which were too heavy to be conveyed to Tshaka on men's backs, the only mode of carriage at that time: the boxes were therefore opened, for the purpose of dividing the contents into convenient packages.

powers were not at all inferior, as his deeds declare : but here
the baser passions at once assumed the reins, and the intellectual
powers became the servants of suspicion, jealousy, hatred,
revenge, lust, and ambition, producing relentless cruelty and
unbounded ferocity. The circumstances in which he was placed
afforded full opportunity for the developement of all these evil
passions combined, which were followed by effects of a most
appalling character.

By treachery and violence he got his father and brother cut
off, and then took possession of the throne thus vacated, in a
short time destroying his early friend and guardian, and seizing
his people and country as a lawful prize.* He then fought tribe
after tribe in his own country, cutting many of them off, root
and branch, and laying the remainder in abject wretchedness at
his feet. He introduced the short stabbing assagai in the place
of the long spear or assagai, in order that, instead of a hazardous
throw, his men might give the mortal thrust, the deadly stab.
He would not allow his warriors to marry, lest they should be
touched with the softer passions of the human breast, and be
rendered less reckless of life. With armies thus prepared, his
name became a terror through the land, but few being found
who could stand before them. With these he swept the countries as with the besom of destruction, and wasted them until
they were without inhabitant. He chased the other tribes as the
frighted deer to the mountain, or laid them dead in heaps on the
plain. Desolation and destruction stalked in his fiery course, his
path being tracked by blood and death.

Over the fertile country of Natal this tempest of destruction
swept, about the year 1820. Tshaka, having before conquered

* This has been the common report, and has passed current from one to another,
down to the present time. But his uncle, who was a boy of twelve or fourteen
when Tshaka was born of Unandi, his sister, declares that such was not the case;
but that Tshaka was born on a little river, called the Isiziba, near the Umhlatoos,
and, when a youth, went to the Umtetwas, of whom Udingiswao was chief; that,
whilst he was there, his father, Usenzengakona, died in peace; that Umakadama,
chief of the Ilangeni, the tribe from which Tshaka's mother came, then tried to get
the Zulu throne, when Tshaka obtained assistance from Udingiswao, chief of the
Umtetwas, with whom he had been staying, and, thus strengthened, returned, and
took the chieftainship, but without fighting; and that afterwards the Umtetwas
became subject to him, but Udingiswao was not killed by him.

all beyond the Umhlatoos, his nation's boundary, broke forth, like an irresistible flood, covering the land with a deluge of blood. According to every account, the country was swarming with human beings, who are represented as standing thick as the blades of grass; but the whole were not able to oppose the force of his arms, or arrest the progress of his victories. One or two severe battles were fought; but the shades of gathering night dispersed the combatants, and the light of the following morning found those who had stood opposed to the Zulus far distant, having availed themselves of the protection of darkness to flee and escape, whilst the Zulus looked around for the foe, but found him fled.

This mighty executioner of the human race not only spread terror abroad by the success of his arms, but was feared and dreaded at home, on account of the number who fell victims to his suspicion, or revenge, or caprice. Captains, men, women, children, all fell before the motion of his head, or the flourish of his hand: life was cheap, and blood was spilled like water. Terror reigned; pity was unknown; and savage human nature walked in state amidst suspicion, horror, murder, death. How dark is fallen humanity! how depraved and cruel the heart of man! and how melancholy are its workings, when left to its own natural developement!

At length this savage monster fell by the hand of his own brother Dingaan. It is affirmed by Tshaka's uncle, (before alluded to,) that Dingaan was the proper and lawful heir to the throne; and that Tshaka obtained it, instead of him, in the manner above stated, Dingaan not attempting to prevent it. But one day, at noon, or about four P.M., Dingaan came secretly upon Tshaka, whilst he was sitting in conversation with his counsellors, (of whom Adam Abantwana was one, whose figure will be given in my other volume,) and, assisted by others, allowed him no opportunity for defence or escape. Finding his dread fate at hand, this great destroyer implored life in the capacity of a servant; but, as he had shown no pity towards others, none was now exercised towards him. He died, in 1828, near the Umvoti river. "The stout-hearted are spoiled; they have slept their sleep; and none of the men of might have found their hands." "Who may stand in Thy sight, when once Thou art angry?"

Dingaan, his brother, immediately mounted the throne of the Zulus without opposition, and became the rightful king over the Natal settlers. His first great work was to cut off all the captains and people who had been favourable to Tshaka, so as to remove those at once who might in any way endanger the safety and perpetuity of his reign. This proceeding, as we shall see, placed the Natal settlers in circumstances of delicacy and difficulty.

It was thought for a while that Dingaan was much milder in disposition, and more disposed to cultivate the arts of peace, and to indulge in friendly intercourse with the whites, than Tshaka, his predecessor, had been. This kindliness is set forth by Mr. Isaacs as the result of Dingaan's intercourse with Europeans; but the sequel proves that he was not greatly in advance of him whom he had cut off.

It appears that Mr. John Cane was employed by him to go on a mission to Graham's Town, and Jacob was required to act as interpreter, which he did very reluctantly; and, on their return, instead of Cane going to the "great place," and laying before Dingaan the result of his mission, he sent the presents forward by natives, remaining himself with the settlers at Natal. This conduct irritated Dingaan exceedingly. He then sent for Cane and Fynn to the "great place," who refused to go; and this refusal formed the pretext for Dingaan sending down his army to cut off Cane.

According to Mr. Isaacs's account, Jacob had, on his return from Graham's Town, represented to Dingaan that the English were about to send a force against him, and reduce his people to submission, if not destroy them altogether; and he also did his utmost to induce Dingaan to cut off the English settlers. But Mr. Fynn gives another version of the affair, stating that, on the death of Tshaka, Dingaan sent for the European settlers and their people, professedly to assist him in war, but in reality to cut them all off by stratagem, it being the custom of new chiefs to cut off the friends and supporters of the old ones. Not feeling themselves safe, therefore, in going to Dingaan, he and others refused, which brought down the *impee*, "army," upon them, professedly only to destroy Cane's kraal, but, in reality, to cut off the whole; so that when the army arrived at Cane's place, (near the present Horticultural Gardens,) they found only a few of his effects, which they utterly destroyed, burning the huts, driving off his cattle, and leaving not a vestige behind. Cane had fled into the bush : they thought to take him by surprise, but he had received information of Dingaan's movements in time to make his escape.

Fynn, also, having been made acquainted with Dingaan's intentions, fled westward beyond the Umzimkulu. To cover his intentions, and prevent Fynn from being suspicious, Dingaan sent Umtobella to ask for beads ; but the army was at hand. Fynn fled ; but two regiments, about 3,000 Zulus, followed and overtook him in the night ; and about three o'clock A.M., whilst it was yet dark, his cattle were taken, and thirteen or fourteen Natal Kafirs were killed, before they knew that the army was upon them, or could collect themselves for defence. At the dawn of the following day, the Zulus, with the cattle, were fled. Cane then joined Fynn beyond the Umzimkulu, and the other English settlers fled. The former had about 3,000 Kafirs with them. Mr. Isaacs had either left just before, or gives no account of the affair concerning Fynn. " Umbulas Wætaga " was the Kafir name of Mr. Fynn. He was first made chief by Tshaka in 1825, and afterwards was declared " great chief " of the Natal Kafirs by Dingaan in 1831.

Shortly afterwards the English settlers were induced to return, by the assurances of Dingaan that he had no evil design against them. They demanded that their cattle should be given up, but in vain. Dingaan required them to give up seven native chiefs, who had been engaged in war against him ; but on their refusal he detained the cattle.

A little after this, Messrs. Collis and Cawood came overland to trade at Natal, and were very successful in their enterprise, making much money by their undertaking. The former was accidently killed by the explosion of a cask of gunpowder ; and the latter has, for some time past, been a respectable merchant in Somerset, in the old Colony.

Dingaan, ever restless and never satisfied, sent some of his people to spy out the land, and see if they could proceed against Ncipi, a chief who had escaped from a part of the Natal country, and also against Quecha, who had revolted from Tshaka. Their

report was favourable, and on two different occasions the armies
went down, taking the upper range of country as they went, and
the coast as they returned; but they obtained no cattle either
time, and occasionally they were reduced almost to starvation.
On their return from one of these forays they helped themselves
to food from the Natal Kafirs, which led to some fighting, and
many fears on the part of the peaceable; but the attack was
made rather to obtain food than with any hostile intentions; and
the affair was afterwards arranged with Dingaan, without leading
to consequences more serious. But Dingaan had the eyes of
some of the spies taken out, because they had told lies and
deceived him. An Englishman interceded for one of these, but
in vain; the stern command of the chief must be obeyed.

Mr. H. Fynn left Natal in 1834, and received a government
appointment on the frontier of the old Colony. One of his brothers, Frank Fynn, died, and his chief wife, *"inkosi kasi,"*
remains a widow, being "the great queen," having about one
hundred kraals under her, and a thousand people. She resides
near the Umzimkulu river, on the Natal side. Many of the
people still look up to Mr. H. Fynn as their chief, and are called
by his name.

The inhabitants of Cape Town, in June, 1834, forwarded to
England a memorial to the king in council, praying that measures
might be immediately taken for occupying Port Natal, and the
neighbouring country. Appended to this memorial was a statement, in support of its petition, written by Dr. Andrew Smith,
staff assistant-surgeon, who had recently explored the region
about Natal. The prayer of the memorial—though it requested
but trifling aid, in the shape of a magistrate, and a few policemen
or soldiers, to keep up some semblance of law and order—was
refused, on the insufficient ground that the Cape Colony could
not sustain any further pressure upon its finances; whereas competent resources would have been furnished by the sale of land to
settlers. The credit, or discredit, of the refusal must lie at the
door of Lord Monteagle, then Mr. Spring Rice, and Colonial
Secretary.

In 1835, Natal was brought into more prominent notice by
the arrival of Captain Allen Gardiner, of the Royal Navy, who
was a near relative of Lord Bexley, and appears to have been a

truly devoted Christian gentleman, but who, like many others
newly arrived from England, had formed very erroneous notions
of the mode of proceeding with the natives.   He published his
own Travels; so that, if the reader desires, he may consult them,
and obtain a full account of his doings and sayings from his own
hand.   He was very anxious to establish a mission among the
Zulus; and endured much fatigue, loss, and annoyance, in order
to accomplish his object, but did not at that time succeed.   Dingaan, however, gave him full permission to commence operations
near Port Natal, where the natives were already numerous.   He
then entered into the following treaty with the Zulu despot, which
was attended with unhappy results, and involved him in much
painful litigation with the settlers, as well as much suffering and
chagrin caused by the Zulu monarch :—

"A TREATY CONCLUDED BETWEEN DINGAAN, KING OF THE ZULUS,
AND THE BRITISH RESIDENTS AT PORT NATAL.

"DINGAAN, from this period, consents to waive all claim to
the persons and property of every individual now residing at Port
Natal, in consequence of their having deserted from him, and
accords them his full pardon.   He still, however, regards them as
his subjects, liable to be sent for whenever he may think proper.

"The British residents at Port Natal, on their part, engage
for the future never to receive or harbour any deserter from the
Zulu country or any of its dependencies, and to use every endeavour to secure, and return to the king, every such individual
endeavouring to find an asylum among them.

"Should a case arise, in which this is found to be impracticable, immediate intelligence, stating the particulars of the
circumstance, is to be forwarded to Dingaan.

"Any infringement of this treaty, on either part, invalidates
the whole.

"Done at Congella, this 6th day of May, 1835, in presence of
"UMTOBELLA,⎫ chief indunas and head counsellors of
ZAMBOOZA, ⎭   the Zulu nation.
"G. CYRUS, Interpreter.
"Signed on behalf of the British residents at Port Natal,
"ALLEN F. GARDINER."*

* CHASE's "Reprint of Natal Papers, Notices," &c., vol. i., p. 40.

This treaty, and the subsequent events, involved Captain Gardiner in great difficulties; and the journey to Zulu-land undertaken by this gentleman, as recorded in his work,—in which he took back some Zulu refugees, who were put to a slow and cruel death, —is harrowing to the feelings of every humane person.

In the year 1835, the American Board for Foreign Missions established a mission here; and the Revs. G. Champion, Aldin Grout, and Dr. Adams arrived, as the agents of the mission, which was then commenced, and has been continued to the present time, with varied success as well as discouragement.

About this time the town of D'Urban was also formed, and named after the honoured governor of the Cape, Sir B. D'Urban.

In the year 1837, Captain Gardiner, having taken a voyage to England, returned to Natal, and brought with him the Rev. Mr. Owen, of the Church Missionary Society; who was afterwards allowed to build a temporary residence near Dingaan's capital, and also assisted that chief in preparing the document for letting the Natal territory to the Dutch farmers, and was there when Retief and his party were cut off.

Captain Gardiner, on his return, was invested with magisterial authority, which he sought to exercise over the Natal settlers and natives, but to which they absolutely refused to submit; and, as the Boers were already on their march towards Natal, the English seriously contemplated uniting with them in forming an independent government,—a scheme which was of short-lived duration.

Thus stood matters when the eventful year 1838 commenced; the events of which, so far as the Dutch are concerned, are recorded in the Chapter on their emigration to Natal. This year broke in upon Natal and Zulu-land with storms, and blood, and death: savagism and civilization were brought into close contact and deadly strife. Without attempting to discuss the merits of the various questions which arise out of this deeply interesting subject for the consideration of the philosopher and Christian, I shall detail events as they transpired.

The Honourable H. Cloete, in his " Lectures on the Emigration of the Dutch Farmers to Natal," as quoted in the following Chapter, in narrating the order of events, has fallen into a slight error, and omitted some things which were done by the settlers; to give

a particular account of which, probably, did not fall within the
range of his design.   After full investigation into the events
which transpired about this time, I believe they occurred in the
following order.

In the early part of February, Retief, with seventy picked farmers
and thirty Hottentots, went to Dingaan's "great place," Umgungunhlovi, Umkongloof, or Congella, to negotiate the cession of
Natal to the Boers, in which he was assisted by the Rev. Mr.
Owen, of the Church Missionary Society.   But, when the treaty
had been drawn up and regularly signed, that treacherous despot
had the whole party cut off, as detailed in the next Chapter.
Immediately after this, the Zulus came into the Colony, and
butchered about six hundred Boers, including women and children, in the division of the Bushman's River.   Upon this, Piet
Uys and his clans, with as many farmers as they could muster,
went into Zulu-land to revenge the death of their friends and
families, who had been so wantonly and cruelly cut off at Dingaan's Kraal, and in the Bushman's-River territory.   Uys there
met with a tragical end; and his devoted son fell at his side, by
the Zulu assagai.   It was whilst Uys and his people were on this
"commando" that the Natal settlers, with their natives, went to
Utunjanbile, where Nombanga and Sotobe's Kraals were, and
took away 2,000 or 3,000 head of cattle, besides women and
children, meeting with no resistance, because the men were away
on commando against Uys and his party.   The defeat of the
Natal settlers to which Mr. Cloete refers occurred some weeks
after the death of Uys and his clan, the details of which I shall
now give, after furnishing an account of the first commando of
the Natal settlers, to which allusion has just been made.

It has been computed, by some of the residents then living,
that the English settlers could bring from 3,000 to 4,000 fighting men into the field, 400 of whom had guns, and some of
whom were very expert in the use of fire-arms,—these, with the
women and children, making some 10,000 natives.   Some of the
great leaders were Ogle, Cane, Biggar, and Stubbs, besides others
who occupied a less prominent place.   These either made an
arrangement with the Boers to go into Zulu-land at the time of
Uys's commando, or they thought that to be a favourable time for
them to make a descent, when Dingaan had his hands full with

the Farmers.   Accordingly, they settled their plans, and set off
on their march, but, unhappily, fell out by the way.   The dispute arose out of the right of precedence,—whether Cane and his
people were to go first, and take the post of honour, or Ogle and
his people; the former maintaining that it was their right, and
the latter being unwilling to yield it.   When they could not
otherwise settle the dispute, to fighting they went, and, with
their "kerries," made very sensible impressions on each other's
heads, arms, and legs.   About fifty returned home disabled,
passing by Dr. Adams's old mission-station on the Umlazi, where
some of their wounds were bound up.   It is said that Cane's
people gave Ogle's a sound thrashing at this time, and that the
latter vowed to be revenged when a suitable opportunity should
occur: this subsequently presented itself, when the affront was
bitterly repaid.

Having thus settled their quarrel, the victors advanced.   Leaving
Pietermaritzburg on the left, and passing by the present site of
York, in the upper Umvoti division, they came upon Nombanga
and Sotobe's Kraals, at Utunjanbile, which signifies "a rock,"
or "the two holes or gates of a rock."   These were two of Dingaan's great captains, who lived on the colonial side of the
Umtugela river.

Upon their arrival, all the men were absent on the commando against Uys and his party.   The women, children, and
cattle, being left unprotected, fell an easy prey into the hands of
the settlers, not more than about two Zulus being killed, and
none on the side of the settlers.   It is said that about 3,000
cattle were taken, and a considerable number of women and children, the women and girls being more costly than cattle.   These
appear large numbers; but, at that time, kraals were not
small and dispersed, as now, but large and close together:
besides, these were the settlements of captains of some
importance.

On the return of the settlers, the booty was divided amongst
them according to the proportion of people they had, each chief
settling with his own people.   When returning, John Cane
detected one of his great men secreting or stealing cattle, and
shot him at once without judge or jury.   They came through
Jarandal, probably by Inanda, the present station of the Rev.

D. Lindley, American missionary, and the residence of Mr. Mesham, the Kafir magistrate.

The excitement of this successful foray had not subsided, when Mr. Robert Biggar, who had been absent on a visit to the old Colony, returned; and, being dissatisfied with the share of the booty awarded him and his people on the last expedition, wished to proceed at once, and make another descent upon Dingaan, resolving to go alone if the others would not assist him. Upon this a council was called, at which a difference of opinion was displayed,—some wishing to proceed at once, and others being desirous that the commando should be a while delayed. It was at length determined that they should proceed at once: but Mr. Ogle would not consent to go; nor did he go, although his people went. There was, however, division, not only in the council, but amongst the people also, some of whom felt very unwilling to go, fearing that the consequences might not be favourable. But this hesitation was settled in a very summary manner: the alternative being either to go or be shot, it was quite enough to overcome their scruples; so go they did! But, whilst many were thus unwilling, others were equally enthusiastic, especially some of the Kafirs. The last commando had been so successful, and the cattle taken so numerous, that they were wrought up to the highest pitch of excitement; and old men who could only just walk were so inflamed with expectation and desire, as to go, assisted by their sticks, although expostulated with by those who saw their danger; but it was in vain to dissuade them.

This army consisted of about 18 English settlers, 30 Hottentots, and 3,000 Kafirs; 400 being armed, and all ranged under their respective leaders, the numbers of whose companies were apportioned to their rank. Many of these leaders were men of dauntless courage and desperate character.

This warlike party was designated "the grand army of Natal," and great demonstrations of joy and triumph were made; whilst all were equipped in the best manner which their circumstances allowed,—some with assagais, kerries, and shields, and others with guns, pistols, swords, and cutlasses, with the appendages of powder-horns, shot-flasks, bullet-bags, &c. Their nondescript hats were adorned with ostrich-feathers; and most of the leaders were mounted on horseback.

F

Thus equipped, full of expectation and hope, they started on their hazardous enterprise. On the evening of the third day, they came to the Umzinyati, above the Umtugela, and halted, sending forward Fumayo (a small chief under Cane) and his people to reconnoitre. These crossed the Umtugela, and found a detachment of Zulu spies at Kude's Kraal, and fired upon them. They then returned to the body of their army, and reported what had transpired; when a council of war was held, in which great division of sentiment existed. Biggar, and those who thought with him, wished to proceed at once and attack the enemy in his country, taking the aggressive; whilst Cane and his partisans argued, that it would be better for them to remain where they were, on the defensive, as the Zulus would be sure to make the attack, and they could then choose their own positions. But, after much discussion, all embraced the former proposition; and, having come to this resolution, they pushed forward at once, in order to take the enemy by surprise, before resistance could be organized. They quickly crossed the Umtugela, and, ascending the hill on the opposite side, came up to the Kraal of *Eudonda-kusuka*, that is, "tardy in starting," (marked 3 on the wood-engraving,) and surrounded it before daylight. A detachment of Dingaan's army was lying here, upon whom they opened fire with their guns; when the inmates of the huts, finding the firing directed low towards the ground on which they were lying, took hold on the tops of the houses, holding by the sticks which form the wattle-work. This plan was, however, quickly detected, on account of the huts sinking with the pressure, when the settlers directed their fire higher up, and the people fell wounded or dead. The whole kraal was destroyed, the people being killed, and the huts burnt.

As the morning of this awful day dawned, many of those who were attacked lying dead, and others being in the pangs of death, one man said, "You may do with me as you please, and kill me; but you will soon see and feel *the great elephant*," meaning Dingaan's army. This "elephant" soon appeared, and crushed them to death under his ponderous feet.

The wood-engraving No. V. presents a very correct view of this terrible battle. The land was very hilly, the hills stretching out something like the fingers of a man's hand when extended,

V.—THE BATTLE BETWEEN THE NATAL KAFIRS, UNDER JOHN CANE, AND THE ZULUS,
ON THE TUGELA RIVER.

rising to ridges in the centre, and descending to deep ravines on each side; the kraal being near the top of one of these ridges, and reaching down the slopes on each side. It was at a short distance from this kraal that "the great elephant" presented himself, and uttered his piercing cry and terrific scream, which, coming from thousands of infuriated savages wrought to the highest pitch of frenzy, must have had a terrible effect, being enough to make the stoutest heart quail.*

Dingaan did not appear in person in this notable battle, nor were the old warriors allowed to fight, the young men being destined to win the highest honours, and take the weapons of their foes as trophies, to perpetuate the memory of their conquest.

The Zulu captains commanding were Umahlebe, Zulu, and Nougalazi. These, with the old warriors, took their stand on the hill, from which they could see all that passed, and issue their commands accordingly (marked 10 in the Plate). Seven Zulu regiments, making about 10,000 men, (each regiment containing about 1,500,) were brought into the field of action. These were flushed with three successive victories:—1. The cutting off of Retief and his party at "the great place;" 2. The slaughter of the Boers in the Bushman-River district; and, 3. The defeat of Uys, and the dispersion of his people. Besides, they were full of rage at the loss of their cattle, women, and children at Utunjanbile, and the destruction of the kraal before their eyes, for which they were burning to be revenged. These circumstances led them to fight with a fury which could only be quenched in death. When they were shot down, if they could crawl, they would take an assagai, and try to inflict a fatal stab on one of their bitter foes, rendering it needful to fire upon them again until dead.

The Natal army had therefore to fight with the vigour of men whose lives were in a fearful balance, and who were made desperate by the greatness of the impending danger. They were drawn up near the kraal in question, the English and Hottentots

---

* In this wood-engraving, Nos. 1, 2, 5, 6, 8, and 9, represent the advance of the Zulus to the attack, from several points. No. 4 displays the Europeans, and those Hottentots who had fire-arms, commencing their retreat. No. 10 marks the position of the Zulu chiefs who were in command, and directed the operations.

with muskets in front, and the Kafirs with assagais in the rear.
The first division of the Zulu army came on with a fearful rush,
but were met by the steady fire and deadly shots of their foes,
which cut them down like grass.   They were checked, broken,
driven back, and defeated, many lying dead and dying at the
feet of the settlers.   Robert Joyce, or, as he was called, "Bob
Joyce," a deserter from the Seventy-second Regiment, had ten
men under him with guns, besides Kafirs; and such fearful execution did they do, that they cut a pathway through the Zulu
regiment, as they approached, until the Zulu commanders ordered
a change in the mode of attack.   This man I saw and attended
in his last sickness; he was one of the few who escaped.   He
died a penitent, greatly distressed for his sins.

This first division, however, only retreated to make way for
the Zulu forces to come from different points favoured by the
formation of the hills.   Cane sent Ogle's Kafirs to attack the
Zulus on the south-west, whilst he, with the main body of the
Natal army, took the north-east.   When Ogle's Kafirs had dispersed these, they were to come round and take the Zulus in flank :
instead of which,—the hour of revenge being come for the affront
which they received at Cane's hands,—when they had dispersed the
Zulus, they fled to the drift, upon which the Zulu chiefs exclaimed,
" O ! anti bagabalekana !" that is, " They can run or flee, can
they ?" (This cannot be shown in the engraving.)   The sight of
them running inspired fresh courage into the Zulus, who now
closed in from all quarters upon the diminished Natal army, coming
down as an overwhelming flood, the mighty masses of which it was
impossible to resist.   The strife was deadly in the extreme.   The
Zulus lost thousands of their people; they were cut down until
they formed banks over which those who were advancing had to
climb, as well as over the wounded, crawling and stabbing, tena-
cious of life, and selling it dearly.

Cane fought hard, and died of his wounds.   A fine old Kafir
man, who was present, gave me a description of his death the
other day.   He was questioned about other matters; but as soon
as he came to this, his eyes appeared to flash with excitement,
and his hands moved in all forms to express the firing of the guns
and the stabbing with the assagais.   He took a stick, and
held one point to his breast, to show where the assagai entered

VI.—DEATH OF JOHN CANE AND ROBERT BIGGAR, AT THE BATTLE ON THE TUGELA.

Cane's chest. He then gave his companion another stick, to show how a second assagai was buried between Cane's shoulders, whose gun was lying on his left arm, his pipe in his mouth, his head nodding, until he fell from his horse, and died. His horse was killed close by. (See No. VI.)* The last deed of this man was tragical. One of his own people, who had now thrown away his badge, was coming to snatch the assagai from his back, when Cane, supposing him to be a Zulu, shot him at once over his shoulder. Stubbs was stabbed by a boy, and, when he felt it was his death-wound, exclaimed, "Am I to be killed by a boy like you?" Biggar fell close by. The Natal army being surrounded and cut up, heaps of slain lay dead upon the field, to be devoured by beasts of prey, their bones being left to bleach under many summer suns. It is only now, after sixteen years, that the ground is beginning to be cleared of bones.

The work of destruction, however, was not yet complete. No sooner had the leaders fallen, than the Natal Kafirs threw away their badges and shields, and seized the shields of the Zulus, in order to favour their escape, whilst the swiftness with which they could run was their best defence. But, in making their escape, the Zulus knew their ground, and that the river must be crossed; and they therefore so surrounded them as to compel them to take one only course. No. 1, on the extreme left of the wood-engraving, (V.,) shows how the Zulus were mustered in force there to prevent escape, whilst the position of the various divisions on the right shows the impossibility of escape there. In flight, then, these wretched beings had no alternative but to take the path shown, at the bottom of which there is a descent of one hundred feet perpendicular to the river, leaving a hole at the bottom; and so numerous were the bodies heaped upon each other in this great grave, that at length, instead of leaping as represented, they walked over the bodies of those who filled the chasm. One of those who made the leap was Upepo, who was stabbed, as he went under the water, by a Zulu, who cursed him and said, "I have finished you:" but the death-wound was not given; for the man escaped.

---

* This wood-engraving represents the close of the battle, and the death of Cane and Biggar, the leaders of the Natal Kafirs. The remains of the burnt kraal, which was the first point of attack by the Natal party, is seen on the centre of the hill.

In order to complete the dire destruction of this day of blood and death, a division of Zulus was sent round to cut off those who might escape by the river. In the engraving these men are seen up to the arm-pits in the stream, stabbing any who might be in danger of escaping; and very few gained the opposite bank and lived. It was here that Blankenberg was killed. Of the few who escaped, some swam, some dived, and some floated along, feigning to be dead. One, Goba, crossed the river four times, and was saved at last. Petrus Roetzie (or "Piet Elias," as better known by many) entered the river lower than most of the others, and got into the long reeds of the opposite bank, where the Zulus searched for him, but in vain.

In this terrible battle fell John Cane, Robert Biggar, John Stubbs, Thomas Carden, John Russel, — Blankenberg, Richard Wood, William Wood, Henry Batt, John Campbell, — Lovedale, Thomas Campbell, with two or three other white men, leaving not half-a-dozen to return and tell their tale of woe. Of the Hottentots three or four returned; and of the Kafirs, very few, except Ogle's. The few who escaped arrived at home singly, many of them having been pursued nearly to the Bay, and owing their deliverance to the shelter of the bush and the darkness of night. Most of the particulars herein recorded I can vouch for as being correct, having conversed with several who were engaged in the transaction, and others who were residing at Natal at the time: but slight errors in some of the details may possibly be discovered, which, however, will not materially affect any of these statements.

I might make some observations on the conduct of some of the parties concerned, but think it better to allow the facts to speak for themselves, and the reader to draw his own conclusions; only dropping my tear over this sad waste of human life, without discussing the causes of it, or the manner in which the battle was lost by the settlers.

The honour of this victory was claimed by Umpanda, the present Zulu chief, who was at that time Dingaan's chief "*induna*," and on whom it devolved to call the army, and direct the various preparations, including the incantations of the doctors, by which the warriors were made strong for battle, and success obtained.

This defeat was quickly followed by Dingaan's army coming

down to the Bay,—an event which happened a few weeks after-wards,—when the English residents took refuge on the Island in the middle of the Bay, where they remained by day, and at night went on board the "Comet," which was lying at anchor there at the time.   Amongst those thus circumstanced, was the Rev. D. Lindley, of the American Mission, and the Rev. Mr. Owen, of the Church Missionary Society, who had just returned from Din-gaan's Kraal, after the slaughter of Retief and his party.   These, and many more, had, for two weeks and upwards, to live exposed to danger and death, and to look on whilst an army of furious savages were destroying their property.   The Zulus left not a vestige of any thing remaining, except perhaps the walls of some of the houses.   Furniture, clothes, dogs, cats, poultry, and every thing they could seize, were utterly destroyed.   They advanced as far as the Umlazi river, and threw a firebrand upon the roof of Dr. Adams's house; but it did not ignite, and no damage ensued.

No events of great interest transpired after what has now been related.   The occupancy of Natal brought an additional number of English traders; and things began to assume more of the settled character of civilized society.   But the English and the Dutch did not amalgamate.   The Boers were jealous of the English; and it is stated that they shot Biggar at the Bushman's River, whilst the lives of others were in great danger from the same cause.   It was therefore the occasion of great pleasure to the English settlers when they heard that the home-government were about to take possession of Natal, and that Captain Smith was ordered to move forward from the Umgazi post for this purpose.

We close this Chapter with the lively and humorous account of Joseph Brown the Bugler, whose letter is quoted elsewhere: "The next day's march, we came within twenty-five miles of Natal; and that evening there came four Englishmen out to meet us, all armed with swords, pistols, and doubled-barrelled guns. You may depend, it alarmed us very, very much to see them so well armed; but you would not believe how much they were overjoyed to see us.   They stated to the Captain that they were obliged to fly for refuge.   The Boers threatened to hang them and a good many more that stopped in the town.   The next day's march, we met the whole of the Englishmen coming out to meet us, all armed in the same manner as the first four. When they came up to us, they all shouted unanimously together, 'Welcome, welcome, boys! You are the brightest sight we saw this many a day. Our lives are in danger this month past, since they heard of the troops coming up, and we were all obliged to make our escape from the band of ruffians, who said they would hang us all if we would not go in arms against the troops that were coming up; but we never would consent, and we had to fly, leaving our property and houses behind us, to get some protection from you: and thanks be to the Almighty, you are at hand!' Now they told us many yarns about the Dutch barbarians, the ill-treatment they gave them, and how they made them pay heavy revenue and duties upon all kinds of goods which they purchased out of different vessels."

CHAPTER V.

THE EMIGRATION OF THE DUTCH FARMERS TO NATAL, WITH
THE SLAUGHTER OF RETIEF AND HIS PARTY AT DINGAAN'S
CAPITAL.

THE Dutch *Boers,* or "Farmers," now form a very large portion of the white population of South Africa, and are spread over
an extensive tract of country, including the Cape and Natal
Colonies, and what is now called "the Sovereignty," and the
Vaal Riveire (*Faal* or "Yellow River") Republic.

Their character and manners are very simple, approaching
sometimes to the rude. They are very hospitable, especially
among their own class, and also to those whom they know among
the English population. The families are often large, including
many children and grandchildren; but, so long as the father
lives, he is the head of the establishment, and is generally looked
up to with considerable veneration, and treated with great respect,
by the younger members of the family. The children usually
marry young, the girls at the age of fifteen years, and the boys
about eighteen or twenty. After marriage, they often remain
under the roof and care of the parents of one of them for a long
time, and move off only when they are in circumstances to
provide comfortably for themselves. Their habits are mostly
inactive. The old lady of the house takes her seat beside a table,
upon or near to which the coffee-kettle or tea-pot is usually
found; and, when a friend has sat down, in a few minutes he is
accosted with, "*Will Mynheer een kop coffee drink?*" "Will
the gentleman drink a cup of coffee?" which is no unwelcome
question, if the visitor has been travelling far in dust and heat;
and the coffee is found to be a refreshing beverage. A little girl
or boy, or a Hottentot, follows with some warm water and a
towel, which greatly relieves the skin of the hands and the face,
if they were before burning with heat. The two principal meals

are taken about eleven o'clock in the morning, and seven in the evening; and if you go three hours or three minutes before they sit down to table, it is all the same; for, as in America, the hours fixed for the meals are strictly adhered to, and you eat no sooner for being half an hour before time. The males are generally stout, when the season of youth is passed; but the females are, in the fullest sense of the word, *fat*. It not unfrequently happens, in the sleeping arrangements, that four or five beds are found in one room, and two or three married couples occupy them. This appears passing strange to a respectable pair of English strangers, on their first visit to these domiciles; but the Dutch usually do not undress, or only partially so, on going to bed.

The men frequently do but little beyond taking the oversight of the cattle, &c., night and morning. A good waggon and a fine span of twelve oxen are regarded as an indispensable appendage to the establishment; and with these the farmer finds his home in any part of the wilds of South Africa. But the Boers cannot endure to be annoyed with wild animals or troublesome natives. Their large flocks of sheep with heavy tails of fat, their extensive herds of cattle with long horns, and their fine troops of horses with sleek skins, must all dwell in peace and safety, or very soon the exclamation from the *"groot heer"* ("great master") is significantly heard, *"Myne vrouw, wy moet trek,"* "My wife, we must move."

Their religious sentiments are generally strong. They possess great respect and reverence for their ministers, to whom they look not. only for spiritual guidance, but often for direction in temporal matters; and if the minister is a good and consistent man, he will obtain great influence over them. They attach great importance to baptism, the Lord's supper, and confirmation, which, after the manner of the old country whence their ancestors came, are administered only at particular seasons of the year, generally at one of the great festivals of the church. They will sometimes travel a whole week, with an ox-waggon, to be present on these solemn occasions; and whilst many Englishmen will not leave their establishments for two hours to worship God on the Sabbath-day, these denizens of the wilderness will travel hundreds of miles, and be absent two weeks, for that good purpose.

I shall not in this place attempt to detail the causes which induced so many of the Boers to leave the Cape Colony from 1836 to 1843.   These are fully set forth by the Honourable H. Cloete, LL.D., in his "Lectures," recently delivered at Pieter-maritzburg, "on the Emigration of the Dutch Farmers," &c.; but I may observe in general, that their dissatisfaction arose chiefly from the manner in which the English behaved towards the natives: 1. In connexion with the Hottentots leaving the employ of their masters, and going upon mission-stations.   2. In the liberation of the slaves on the 1st of December, 1838; which occurring just in the midst of harvest, and all the slaves leaving on the very day of their liberation, the Farmers were left in a very destitute condition, and their agricultural operations were brought to a stand for the time being.   3. With regard to the unsatis-factory manner in which the Kafir question was settled after the war of 1834, when Sir Andries Stockenstrom became lieutenant-governor of the Eastern Province, and the Glenelg Treaties were brought into operation, which worked so unfavourably, and have been succeeded by two other most calamitous wars.

Having at that time heard something of the Natal country, they sent out a party to explore it.   "During the same period, the capabilities of this district of Natal had become obscurely known, from the visits of Lieutenant Farewell and Captain King; and the accounts of several of their companions being brought to the Cape, a society was soon formed for the exploration of Southern Africa; and Dr. Smith, with a respectable party of travellers, was fully equipped to examine and report upon its condition and advantages.   He succeeded in exploring the Bay of Natal, and visiting Dingaan in his chief town of Umkongloof; and the accounts which he brought back first attracted the atten-tion of the Dutch Farmers to this district, with a view to occupy-ing the same.   They quietly collected fourteen waggons; and a party headed by Piet Uys, Cobus Uys, Hans de Lange, Stephanus Maritz, and Gert Rudolph, started from Uitenhage in the begin-ning of the year 1834, taking the lower route along the eastern slopes of the Quahlamba or Drakenberg Range, following nearly the same track by which Dr. Smith and his party had explored this district.   Their arrival agreeably surprised the small party of English who had settled themselves down at the Bay, where

Messrs. Ogle, Toohey, and King, (who are now amongst us, and the only survivors of those settlers,) gave them a hearty reception; from whose accounts, and from their own explorations of the country, they soon came to the conclusion, that this would be a country in every way suited to them and their countrymen. They loitered here some time, shooting, and examining the country; and would have pursued their explorations still farther, if they had not been startled by the astounding intelligence that the Kafirs had made a sudden general irruption into the Eastern Province, and thus provoked a third Kafir war."*

At the close of the Kafir war of 1835, the Dutch were so dissatisfied with the arrangements made by the government with the Kafirs, that a large number of them resolved on leaving without delay, and seeking, in the interior and at Natal, freedom from the yoke of the British government, which they would no longer bear, being determined to pursue that unrestrained course which their interests or passions dictated. Accordingly, in the early part of 1836, about two hundred persons, headed by Hendrick Potgieter, crossed the Orange river, and, being quickly followed by many others from the divisions of Albany, Uitenhage, and Graaf-Reinet, spread themselves in different parts of what is now called " the Sovereignty," locating chiefly along the Modder, the Vet, and the Sand rivers.

I will here quote the graphic and able account of the Honourable H. Cloete, in the Lectures already quoted, which will at once give an accurate, clear, and touching description of the whole transaction : " Their numbers were about that time also increased by another large clan, headed by the venerable patriarch, Jacobus Uys, then about seventy years of age, and his eldest son, Pieter Uys, who, having visited this district before, cherished the idea of settling down here, in preference to going further into the interior of Africa. This party issued a manifesto, declaratory of their intention to shape their course towards Natal, and to secede from all those parties who seemed more intent to occupy the banks of the Vaal river, or what is now called 'the Sovereignty,' and even to proceed eastward to Delagoa Bay. This determination of the clans of Uys, Moolman, and Potgieter,

---

* See "Lectures on the Emigration of the Dutch Farmers, &c. By the HON. H. CLOETE." Page 31.

seems to have induced Retief also to follow their track; and he sent exploring parties from the Sand river, who at length succeeded in finding two or three paths across the Quahlamba, or Draaksberg, which might be made passable for waggons; for, up to that time, every attempt to cross that mountain range by waggons from the Zuurberg to the west, up to the Oliviers Pass, at the north-east extremity of our district, had failed.

"Retief succeeded, with his party, in crossing at one spot, and reached Port Natal in safety, where he met with a hearty reception from the British emigrants, who (strange to say) had also formed themselves into a little independent community; for, upon Captain Gardiner, of the navy, arriving among them, and asserting a magisterial authority over them, under the provisions of an extraordinary law, passed by the British legislature, and entitled, 'The Cape-of-Good-Hope Punishment Bill,' which he promulgated among them, they at once repudiated his interference, and maintained their independence from all authority, except from such as should emanate from themselves; in consequence of the then secretary for the colonies, Lord Glenelg, having expressly 'disclaimed, in the most distinct terms, any intention on the part of his majesty's government to assert any authority over any part of this territory.' This mutual feeling of independence seemed to serve as a bond of union between them; and there can be no doubt, that if a person like Retief had continued to be the acknowledged head of the Dutch emigrants, a more firm and lasting tie would have bound them together.

"Pieter Retief, however, in the conscientious view which he had always taken of these matters, felt that as both Tshaka and Dingaan had nominally given away this territory to various other persons before his arrival, the occupation of this country by him and his followers might thereafter subject them to disputes, either with the Zulu chiefs, or with such English emigrants as had received these ill-defined grants from the Zulu sovereigns. He therefore determined to proceed in person to Dingaan's capital, to negotiate with him a treaty of peace, and obtain a formal cession of such extent of territory as the latter might feel inclined to cede to him and the Emigrant Farmers.

"Upon reaching the Zulu chief's capital, Umkongloof, he accidentally found there a missionary of the Church of England,

(the Rev. F. Owen,) who materially assisted in apparently dis-
posing the chief to give him a kind reception; and upon
being made acquainted with the special object of Retief's mission, he at once promised him a formal cession of this territory,
upon his first recovering for him a quantity of cattle which
Sikonyella, a Mantatee chief, residing on the sources of the
Caledon river, had recently taken from him.   Retief accepted
these terms, and, returning to this district, at once called together several of the parties who were preparing to settle down in
this territory. They determined on an attack on Sikonyella; but,
before doing so, sent messengers to him, demanding restitution,
with a significant notice that it would be enforced : and this
communication had the desired effect; for Sikonyella immediately gave up seven hundred head of cattle, together with
sixty horses, and some guns, which he and his tribe had at
various times captured from small parties of Emigrating Farmers.

   " During these proceedings, which took place during the last
months of the year 1837, nearly a thousand waggons had already
descended, and passed down the slopes of the Draaksberg into
this district; and the Emigrant Farmers finding the country
already denuded of all population, (with the single exception of
one small party under the chief Matuan, who now still occupies
nearly the same ground,) they spread themselves over the whole
of the Klip river division, down to the Bushman's River, where
the remains of thousands of stone kraals clearly indicated that a
very dense population must have once been settled down; thus
also giving a promise of the great fertility of the soil, as it could
not otherwise have maintained so large a population.

   " Upon Retief's return to that part of this district, on his way
to Dingaan, with the cattle surrendered by Sikonyella, to be
delivered to the former, a sad presentiment seems to have come
over many of the heads of the parties, who, however, then still
acknowledged Retief as their leader.   Gert Maritz proposed that
he should proceed to Dingaan, with the cattle recovered, taking
only three or four men with him, arguing very justly that the
insignificance of such a force would be its best safeguard.   But
Retief appears to have desired to show Dingaan something like
a respectable force, and insisted on taking some forty or fifty of
his best horsemen with him, leaving it, however, optional to any

person to accompany him or to remain behind. This only induced an additional number of spirited young men to join; and during the last week of January, 1838, Pieter Retief, accompanied by seventy of the most respectable and picked men from among the Emigrants, with about thirty young Hottentots and servants riding or leading their spare horses, formed an imposing cavalcade, with which he crossed the Umzinyati, (or Buffalo river,) and, on the 2nd of February, arrived at Umkongloof, (Dingaan's capital,) and delivered over the cattle recovered from Sikonyella, with the receipt of which Dingaan expressed himself highly satisfied; and, having collected several of his regiments from the neighbouring kraals, he entertained them for two days with their favourite sham-fights, which give a fearful representation of their mode of warfare.

"On February 4th Dingaan had fixed for signing a formal cession of the whole of this district to Pieter Retief, for himself and the Emigrant Farmers for ever; and the Rev. Mr. Owen, then still residing with Dingaan, was requested to draw out and witness the instrument, which he accordingly did in English; and to this document Dingaan and some of his principal counsellors affixed their marks, after the tenor thereof had been fully interpreted to them by the Rev. Mr. Owen.

"Retief's business being thus satisfactorily ended, he made his arrangements to depart the next morning, when Dingaan desired him to enter his kraal once more to take leave of him, requesting, however, that his party should not enter armed, as this was contrary to their usage; and to this Retief unguardedly consented, leaving all their arms piled up outside of the kraal, while they sent their '*achter ryders*' to fetch and saddle their horses. Upon approaching Dingaan in his kraal, they found him surrounded (as usual) by two or three of his favourite regiments, when, after conversing with Retief, and some of his leading men, in the most friendly manner, he pressed them to sit down a little longer, offering them their 'stirrup-cup,' in some *chualla*, or maize beer, which the Kafirs enjoy as a favourite beverage. This was handed round to the whole party, who partook freely thereof; and while a number of them were thus sitting down, with the bowls in their hands,* Dingaan suddenly exclaimed,

---

* See this account corrected, pp. 84, 87.

'*Bulala amatagati*,' or, 'Kill the wizards;' and in an instant
three or four thousand Zulus assailed them with their knob-
kerries; and, although many of the Farmers, instantly drawing
their clasp-knives, (which they usually carry by them, and use in
cutting up the game they kill, or the viands they eat,) made a
determined resistance, and took the lives of several of their assailants, yet they soon fell, one after the other, under the overwhelming pressure of the thousands by whom they were charged
and beaten down ; and, after a desperate struggle, of half-an-
hour's duration, their expiring and mangled corpses were
dragged out of the kraal to an adjoining hillock, marked and
infamous as the Aceldama, or rather the Golgotha, where the
bones of all victims to the fury of this despot were hoarded up,
and became a prey to the wolves and vultures."

This tragic scene is strikingly set forth in woodcut No. VII.,
as here given. The proper Kafir name of Dingaan's capital, or
"great place," was Umgungunhlovi, meaning, in English, "the
rumbling noise of the elephant;" and it is estimated to have
contained two thousand large huts or houses, with ten head of
cattle belonging to each. Figure 1 shows the Dutchman
Retief and his party in the middle of the kraal : 2 represents
the Zulu warriors, not with "knob-kerries," as stated in the
Lecture, but with sticks three feet long. It was a capital crime
for a Zulu to take an assagai, or knob-kerry, to the king's
kraal, or "great place;" so that Dingaan, in requesting the
Boers to leave their guns outside, only asked them to observe
the law of his country. I mention this regulation, not to pal-
liate this awful butchery, but to explain Zulu law and usage.
Figure 11, at the bottom of the engraving, and outside of the
great enclosure, denotes the muskets of the Boers; and 2 exhibits
the furious onslaught, when, with savage ferocity, the Zulus rushed
to the dreadful work of death, exclaiming, "*Bambani abatagati*,"
that is, "Seize the witches." The person indicated by figure
3 is Dingaan retiring towards his labyrinth, his disappearing
behind the high fence being the signal for destruction. The king's
person must be guarded, must be safe. He retired, saying, "*Salani
guhle*," that is, "Sit," or, "Abide, comfortably;" or, "*Hamba
guhle*," that is, "Travel well." This was a fit finish to his consum-
mate treachery. 4 is the sentry house, leading into the labyrinth,

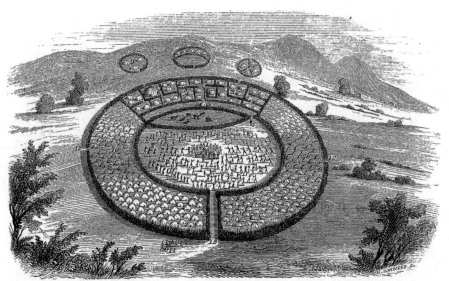

VII.—VIEW OF THE KRAAL, OR CAPITAL, OF THE KAFIR CHIEF DINGAAN.

which is constantly guarded by sentinels, so that no person may enter, except the king and those whom "the king delighteth to honour." 5 shows the labyrinth, where the entrance into these *kraals within kraals* is very small, and the fences are very high, so that, if a stranger gets into them, he is quite lost, and cannot find his way out. This is called *Tsiklohlo*. 6 shows the *intunkulu*, "chief house or palace," the high abode of the great Zulu king and despot. The rods of this house, instead of being horizontal, like common ones, must be perpendicular, and as straight as a dart, being covered with mats instead of thatch. It is twenty feet wide, and eight feet high. The crown on the top is called *tsikongo*, "pinnacle of the house or temple." This crown is curiously constructed from a very long piece of matting, which is folded or rolled into the particular form required. The adjoining houses are of similar construction, but are not equal to "the great house." The king's wives and servants occupy the other houses in the labyrinth. Figure 7, being the middlemost of the three small enclosures at the top of the engraving, presents to view the *emposeni*, "seraglio," where the king's chief wives dwell; and to enter which is death to any man, except the sacred person of the king. 8 is the *wamabele*, "provision kraal," where the stores of flesh or corn are kept. 9 represents the *tlabamkomo*, "slaughter-house," or kraal, where all the beasts are killed which supply the royal table, and feed the thousands of retainers about the chief. The figures 10, 10, are *tzinhla zenutu*, "multitudes of houses," forming the outer rim of the large enclosure; and surely they must baffle all description,—eight or ten thousand human beings being crowded together in so small a space. The figures 12, 12, exhibit *intuba* and *isango*, the "entrance" into the kraal, and the "huts of the people." To have a few thousand warriors at hand to murder Retief and his party, was no great matter, when the means where so ample.

This description of "Umgungunhlovi" may be relied upon as being in the main correct. I know of only one person who could give such an accurate and particular account of the wonderful specimen of barbarian art and contrivance which Dingaan's capital displayed; and it has been my good fortune to derive my information from him. I now resume my quotation from the Honourable Mr. Cloete's narrative:—

"Dingaan, following the precept of Cæsar, who deemed nothing done so long as any thing remained undone, ordered instantly ten of his regiments to march into the Natal territory, to attack all the Emigrant Farmers, (who, in perfect security, were spread over all the district, awaiting the return of their friends,) and exterminate them root and branch. It certainly is remarkable, that the doubts which the majority had entertained as to the good faith of Dingaan vanished so soon after the departure of Retief and his party. The young men were enjoying the pleasure of the chase, and supplying their friends with the game that abounded; and the women, seemingly also unsuspicious, were only waiting the return of their husbands, sons, and relatives; when the Zulu army, having divided itself into several small detachments, fell, at break of day, on the foremost parties of emigrants, near the Blue Krans river, and close to the present township of Weenen, which has obtained its name (meaning 'wailing or weeping') from the sad events of that day. Men, women, and children were at once surrounded and barbarously murdered, with horrors which I should be sorry to dwell upon and detail. Other detachments of Zulus surprised, in other places, similar small parties, who were likewise scattered over all the Klip-river division, and who all fell under the Zulu assagai. But from one or two waggons a solitary young man escaped, who, hastening to the parties whom he knew to be in the rear, at length succeeded in spreading the alarm among them; so that, as the Zulus advanced further into the district, two or three parties of Farmers had been able hastily to collect a few waggons, and arrange them into a *laager* or 'encampment,' where they made their preparations to secure their families just in time, before they were also attacked; and they thus succeeded in repelling the most daring attacks made upon them, not one of these *laagers* having been forced or penetrated by the Zulus. The latter, however, advanced farther southward, until they met a still stronger party of Emigrants, on the farm now called *Vecht Laager*, (at present the property of Mr. Ogle,) on the Bushman's River, where they sustained a very serious engagement, which lasted throughout the whole day, but where, when the Farmers' ammunition was nearly exhausted, luckily their last shot from a three-pounder, which had been rigged to the back of one of their waggons, struck down some of the leading Zulu chiefs, and forced them to a precipitate retreat.

" The moment these attacks were thus repulsed, the Emigrant Farmers sallied out from their *laagers*, to rescue, if possible, any of their friends who had been in advance, and to ascertain the havoc which had been caused among them ; when, upon reaching the stations which the latter had occupied, a scene of horror and misery was unfolded which no pen can describe. All the waggons had been demolished, the iron parts wrenched from them, and by their ruins lay the mangled corpses of men, women, and children, thrown in heaps, and abandoned to the beasts of prey. Amongst those heaps, at the Blue Krans river, they found, literally amongst the dead corpses, the bodies of two young females, about ten or twelve years of age, which still appeared to show some signs of vitality. The one was found pierced with nineteen, and the other with twenty-one, stabs of the assagai, leaving every part of their little frames completely perforated, and every muscle and fibre lacerated. The one was named Johanna van der Merwe, and the other Catharina Margaretha Prinslo. They were taken up and tended with the utmost care, and, strange to say, live to this day, the sole survivors of the immediate branches of those families ; but they are, and will ever remain, perfect cripples, although one of them (still more strange to say) has married, and is the mother of one or two children. But, with these solitary exceptions, all those small parties which had not been able to combine and concentrate themselves in *laagers*, were utterly destroyed ; and, in one week after the murder of Retief and his party, six hundred more victims were thus immolated by the fury and treachery of Dingaan and his army.

" The survivors of this fearful catastrophe, after recovering from the panic into which they had been thrown, resolved to avenge themselves for their dreadful loss.

" The whole clan of Uys, which, from some little feeling of jealousy of Retief, had lagged behind on the Draaksberg, and had thus escaped this onslaught, on hearing of this destruction, came down into the Klip river, with many other small parties of Farmers who were advancing towards this district ; and their precarious situation was soon made known to the English party resident at the Bay,* when the latter determined upon a movement on Dingaan, to support the cause of the Emigrant Farmers. But they, being few in numbers, took with them a body of 700 Zulus, 400 of whom were armed with guns, having learned to use them in their hunts of the elephant and buffalo. This party, which placed itself under the command of Mr. R. Biggar, crossed the Tugela at its mouth, and advanced a few miles across that river, when they attacked and destroyed the town of Tatabasooke, while the Zulu forces hid themselves in the Matikoola and Imsimdoosa rivers: but, advancing a little further, they were suddenly surrounded, and attacked at break of day, by three divisions of the Zulu army. After a desperate and murderous engagement, almost every European or man of colour belonging to the party here lost his life. A fearful number of the Zulus were also killed; but, of the English population of the Bay, R. Biggar, Blankenberg, Cane, Stubbs, Richard Wood, William Wood, Henry Batt, John Campbell, Thomas Campbell, and Thomas Carden, successively fell; and only one or two Europeans succeeded in fighting their way through these masses, to convey to the small party who had remained at the Bay the sad result of this engagement.† That portion of Dingaan's army followed up, as usual, their success, and advanced as far as the Bay; but the few English who survived took refuge on board of the 'Comet,' Captain Hadden, then luckily lying at anchor in the Bay; when, after sweeping away all the cattle, this detachment of Dingaan's army retired again into the Zulu country.

"Dingaan himself, with his principal forces, was, however, at this time still watching the Dutch Emigrant Farmers, who, having now collected about 400 fighting men in the Klip-river division, placed themselves under the command of Piet Uys and of Hendrick Potgieter, and advanced, about the same time, (in April, 1838,) towards Umkongloof, Dingaan's capital, intent upon destroying it, and expelling Dingaan from the country.

"This wily chieftain allowed the Emigrant Farmers to advance to within a few miles of his capital, where the approach to the town is closed in between two hills: and there the Zulu forces

---

* See corrected account in the preceding Chapter, p. 63.

† There is some error and discrepancy in this account of the English settlers from the Bay, which is fully explained in Chapter IV., pp. 64–74.

first showed themselves, but, gradually retiring, drew the Emigrant Farmers still farther into this hollow way; when, another division of the Zulu forces emerging from behind one of these hills, and cutting off all retreat, a desperate hand-to-hand fight ensued, the Farmers being so hemmed-in that they could not fire, then fall back rapidly on horseback, and again load and charge, as was their usual and efficient mode of warfare. They accordingly, as by one consent, directed all their fire on one mass of the Zulus, when, their fatal aim having cleared a path by bringing down hundreds in this volley, they rushed through, and thus escaped. But their chief and unquestionably most gallant commander, Piet Uys, having taken a somewhat different course, in a country but little known to them, found himself surrounded, with a small party of about twenty faithful followers and his favourite son, a young lad of twelve years of age, before a ravine, which their horses could not get over or clear.

" Finding himself wounded, he called to his followers to fight their way out, as he could not follow. All obeyed his command, except his loving son, who remained by his father, till both fell pierced with wounds. The remainder of their party, and the great majority of the Emigrant Farmers, having ultimately succeeded in thus fighting their way out of this trap, which had so ably been laid for them, effected a retreat out of the country without any further great loss of life; leaving, however, the *prestige* of victory with the Zulu chieftain, to whom the loss of several hundreds of his best warriors was always considered but of little moment, imparting only an exciting interest to his fiendish propensities and habits.

" The Emigrant Farmers were, however, so disheartened by the result of their attack, and that of the English settlers from the Bay, upon Dingaan's forces, that they gave up all hope of resuming hostilities for the present. They had been taught a lesson of prudence by the talent and daring displayed by the Zulu armies; and they accordingly kept a watchful eye upon their northern frontier, and sent messengers out in various directions, imploring farther accessions to their numbers, both from the Cape and the present ' Sovereignty.' Many parties, on hearing of their distressed state, came to join them; but this, at the moment, only increased their misery and wants, as, their cattle

and herds having been swept away, (these being still in the hands
of the Zulus,) and they having been prevented from cultivating
any lands, they were not only exposed to the greatest want, but
were actually in a state of famine; when some liberal-minded
countrymen of theirs at the Cape, hearing of their distressed condition, sent them supplies of food, medicine, and other necessaries
of life, which helped them through the miseries of the winter of
1838, during which season want, disease, and famine stalked
over the land, making fearful ravages among them.

"Dingaan, ever watchful when to attack his foe with advantage, being fully informed of their wretched condition, made another attack upon them in August, 1838: but, on this occasion,
the Emigrant Farmers (having their scouts always out, to give
them timely intimation of his advance) were every where prepared
to give him a warm reception; and, at every *laager*, the Zulu
forces were driven back and defeated with great loss, only two or
three lives having been lost among the Emigrants during several
successive engagements. But, although Dingaan was thus
defeated, the Emigrant Farmers were still contending, up to the
close of that year, with the greatest difficulties. Small parties
were pouring in to join them, but bringing little effectual support, until the beginning of December, when, the season appearing propitious, and a number of young men having come in
by the Sovereignty, 460 fighting and mounted men put themselves under the command of ANDRIES PRETORIUS, who had also
recently joined the Emigrants, among whom (having formerly
been a field-cornet in the Graaf-Reinet district) he had made
himself extremely popular.

"They were powerfully aided by the brave and sterling CARL
LANDMAN, who joined them with all those Emigrants who had
already commenced settling themselves down near the Bay; and
these combined forces, profiting from the experience of the past,
advanced with great caution, securing their position every evening;
so that, when they had nearly reached the Umslatoos river, they
were fully prepared, as, at the earliest dawn of day, on Sunday,
December 16th, 1838, the whole of Dingaan's forces, about
10,000 or 12,000 strong, attacked their position with a fury
far exceeding all their former attacks. For three hours they
continued rushing upon them, endeavouring to tear open all their

defences, and force the Emigrant camp, until Pretorius, finding
the Zulu forces concentrating all their efforts upon one side of
the camp, and their own ammunition nearly failing, ordered 200
mounted men to sally forth out of one of the gates at the rear
of the line which the Zulus were attacking; and these mounted
warriors, charging both flanks, and pouring their deadly volleys
upon the immense masses which were gathered together within a
small space, at length beat them off with fearful loss.   The
Emigrants assert that nearly 3,000 Zulus licked the dust before
they retreated; and their defeat must have been complete, since
Dingaan fled quite panic-stricken, set fire to the whole of his
town of Umkongloof, and hid himself, with the remnant of his
force, for a considerable time in the woods skirting the Umvaloos
river.

"The Emigrants having had only three or four men killed,
and as many wounded, in this decisive engagement, (among the
latter of whom was Pretorius himself,) advanced upon the town
of Umkongloof,* which they found still partially burning; and
on the awful hillock, outside of the town, they beheld, in one
vast pile, the bones and remains of Retief and their one hundred
companions in arms, who, ten months before, had fallen victims to
Dingaan's treachery, but whose deaths they were then in fact
avenging.   Many of the straps or *riems* by which they had been
dragged to this place of slaughter, were found still adhering to
the bones of the legs and arms by which they had been drawn
thither.   The skulls were frightfully broken, exhibiting marks of
the knob-kerries and stones with which they had been fractured;
and, singular to relate, the skeleton of their ill-fated leader, Retief,
was recognised by a leathern pouch or bandolier, which he had
suspended from his shoulders, and in which he had deposited
the deed or writing formally ceding this territory to the Emigrant
Farmers, as written out by the Rev. Mr. Owen, on the day previous to his massacre, and signed with the mark of Dingaan, by
which he agreed 'to resign to Retief and his countrymen the place
called Port Natal, together with all the land annexed; that is
to say,—from the Tugela to the Umzimvubu river, and from
the sea to the north, as far as the land may be useful and in my
possession.'

* The town shown in the wood-engraving VII., and described in p. 87.

"These are the very words of the original document, which was found still perfectly legible, and was delivered over to me by the Volkstraad in the year 1843, and is now (or ought to be) among the archives of the Colonial Office here.*

"After decently interring the remains of their unfortunate countrymen, the Emigrant Farmers found that their horses and ammunition were ill calculated to continue a harassing warfare upon Dingaan in his fastnesses; and they therefore resolved gradually to fall back, which they did with little loss, taking with them some 5,000 head of cattle, which they distributed among themselves, as the lawful and hard-earned trophies of this campaign.

"On their return from this successful inroad, they were not a little surprised to find that Sir George Napier (who had succeeded Sir Benjamin D'Urban in the government of the Cape Colony) had sent a small detachment of Highlanders, under the command of Major Charteris, to take possession of the Bay of Natal. This measure had been evidently taken, and in fact was acknowledged, in a Proclamation of the 14th of November, 1838, to have emanated from a desire to 'put an end to the unwarranted occupation of parts of the territories belonging to the natives, by certain Emigrants from the Cape Colony, being subjects of his majesty;' and that Proclamation gave the officer commanding these forces the further power to 'search for, seize, and retain in military possession, all arms and munitions of war which, at the time of the seizure of Port Natal, shall be found in the possession of any of the inhabitants.'

"Major Charteris returned immediately to the Cape, when the command of the detachment devolved on Captain Jervis of the Seventy-second Regiment; and from the vague and ill-defined nature of his instructions, some serious difference, if not conflict, might have arisen between him and the Emigrant Farmers, in regard to the authority and orders he had received to seize upon their gunpowder and ammunition: but the good sense and good feeling of that officer soon smoothed away every difficulty between them; and he delivered them up their gunpowder, which he had

---

* But this document cannot affect the English, who have distinctly denied the authority of the Dutch Boers to act in their behalf.

provisionally seized, upon their engaging not to use it in aggressive hostilities against the natives. The necessity of keeping and maintaining the detachment led to some regular demand for supplies, which kept up a mutual interchange of wants; and the most friendly intercourse was ever afterwards maintained between them. In the mean while, the Emigrant Farmers laid out this township of Pietermaritzburg, and what is now called 'the town of D'Urban.' *Landdrosts* were appointed to both townships: they established a more regular system of government; and, with the able assistance of Mr. Boshoff, (the present registrar of the court,) who about this time arrived in this district with his entire clan, various laws and regulations were framed, which gradually redeemed them from the state of anarchy into which they were fast falling.

"While the winter of 1839 was thus taken up by these duties and labours, Dingaan, somewhat recovering from the effects of his late defeat, commenced sending in some special messengers, first delivering up 316 horses which he at various times had captured, and thereafter professing every disposition to enter into amicable arrangements with the Emigrants. Their answer was plain and manly,—that they would not enter into any treaty of peace with him, unless ample restitution had been made of all their cattle and sheep, and until the value of their property, taken or destroyed by him and the Zulus, had been paid for. This led to frequent embassies, promises of restitution, and fixing places where some at least of the cattle, and some guns, were promised to be delivered; but the Farmers soon discovered that these messages and promises were mere pretexts to keep up a constant and regular espionage upon them; as one of these pretended messengers, or spies, being caught, admitted that he had been sent to report to Dingaan, whether the Farmers were gradually returning to their farms, or whether they still kept near to their *laagers,* thus clearly showing that he only waited the opportunity to attempt another *razzia* upon them. This naturally paralysed all their agricultural enterprises, and prevented them from spreading themselves about to carry on their farming pursuits, being thus kept constantly on the alert; when, in the inscrutable decrees of Providence, one of those events was brought about for which they were quite unprepared, in which they were not even the chief agents, but which led to their undisputed possession of the whole territory of Natal.

"There were at that time remaining alive only two brothers of Tshaka and Dingaan ; the elder, Panda, or Umpanda, (as he is called by his subjects,) and a young lad, Clu Clu. Umpanda had just reached manhood; but, brought up in the midst of debauchery and sensuality, he was known only for his unwarlike habits, and became the object of derision with the warriors, and of contempt with Dingaan, and he seemed for a time to give full scope to the indulgence of his passions, as most conducive to his own personal safety; while Dingaan's appetite for war was so insatiable that, notwithstanding his signal defeat by the Emigrant Farmers in the previous December, he had again mustered a strong army, with which he attacked Sapusa, but was defeated with fearful loss.

"It was therefore not unnatural that, even among the Zulus, a party was forming, deprecating these murderous wars, and apparently inclined to support Panda, with a view to bring about peace with the Emigrants and the surrounding nations. From that moment Dingaan determined to watch the opportunity of murdering his brother; but it appears that a hint of his intentions to this effect had transpired. Panda at once fled, with a number of followers; and, crossing the Tugela near its mouth, took possession of some lands near the Umvoti, and sent messengers, requesting the support and protection of the Emigrants. Some suspicion was at first entertained that this was a deep-laid plot between him and Dingaan, to inveigle them into the Zulu country; but, after repeated conferences, which were managed with great tact and ability by the *Landdrost* Roos of D'Urban, with G. Kemp, Moolman, Morewood, Breda, and several others, a formal treaty of alliance, offensive and defensive, was concluded with him; by the terms of which the Emigrant Farmers pledged themselves to support and defend Panda, while he, on the other hand, promised to support *them* in any attack upon Dingaan.

"The beginning of the year 1840 being considered the best season for commencing offensive operations, the Emigrant Farmers again mustered a force of 400 mounted warriors, who, under the chief command of Andries Pretorius, joined Panda's army, which was about 4,000 strong; and this combined force, in January, again entered the Zulu country, by the Sunday's River and Big-gar's Mountains; but, with proper caution, the Emigrants kept themselves at some distance from Panda's army, which, under the able guidance of Nonklaas, (at present still Panda's chief coun-sellor and captain,) seemed quite intent upon coming into action.

"While this commando was preparing and mustering their forces in this town, one of Dingaan's principal messengers, Tam-boosa, arrived here with one of those specious messages and offers of peace. He was, however, seized, with his attendant, Combi-zana; and, upon being rigidly questioned, frankly admitted that he had also been sent with a view of reporting to Dingaan the state of the combined army of Emigrants and Zulus under Panda. The latter, evidently embittered against this person, (one of Din-gaan's principal counsellors,) charged him with having been the chief cause of the murder of Retief and his party; that he had plotted and advised his (Panda's) death; and, in short, brought such a series of charges against him, that, contrary to every usage of civilized life, he was taken along with the army as a prisoner, until they reached the banks of the Buffalo or Umzinyati river, where a court-martial was formed, which, under the excited feel-ings of the occasion, soon passed sentence of death upon the unfortunate prisoners, which was carried into execution within a few hours after. Tamboosa not only nobly upbraided his execu-tioners with the violation of all usage towards messengers even amongst savages, but expressed his perfect readiness to die: he only implored—but in vain—mercy on behalf of his young attendant, who was only a camp-follower, and had thus been but doing his duty in following his master.*

"This may be said to have been the only blot which seriously reflected on the conduct of the Emigrant Farmers in their several engagements with the Zulus; for they otherwise constantly endeavoured to spare the women and children from massacre, and

---

* Damboosa (or Zambooza) was Dingaan's chief *induna*, or "prime minister," and stood next under him. The other, Combizana, was the greatest chief under Damboosa; but, instead of Damboosa pleading for his life, as here related, the man resolved to die on his master's account. The Boers did not want to shoot him; but the man, faithful to his master, declared that, if they killed the master, the servant must die with him; separated they should not be. This statement I have received from a person who took part in these transactions.

have uniformly conducted their wars with as much discretion and prudence as bravery.

"A few days after this sad execution, the Zulu army under Panda encountered that commanded by Dingaan; whereupon a desperate engagement ensued, in the course of which one or two of Dingaan's regiments went over in a body to Panda; upon which two of Dingaan's best regiments, who fought bravely for him, were totally destroyed, the battle ending in his utter defeat and flight. The Emigrant Farmers, not having been engaged in this action, followed up this success (as soon as they heard of it) with great vigour. They drove Dingaan over the Black Umvoloos, and from thence still further to the banks of the Pongola, where, deserted by almost all his followers, he endeavoured, with about one hundred warriors, to find shelter amongst a small tribe living near Delagoa Bay, named the Amasuree, but who, it is supposed, (for I believe there is no actually authentic account of his death,) murdered him, to insure their own safety from his constant and fearful forays upon them and the adjacent tribes.*

"There existing, however, no doubt as to his death, and the dispersion of all his army, the Emigrant Farmers assembled in great state on the banks of the Umvoloos, on February 14th, 1840; and there, under the discharge of their guns, Andries Pretorius proclaimed Umpanda the sole and acknowledged king of the Zulus; and by a proclamation issued by him, and attested by the other commandants, they declared their sovereignty to extend from the Umvoloos Umfana, or the Black Umvoloos, and the St. Lucia Bay, to the Umzimvubu or St. John's river; and in fact, by their proceedings of that day, assumed a certain authority, or sovereignty, over Umpanda himself, from whom they received, as their indemnity, 36,000 head of cattle, 14,000 of which were delivered to those Farmers who resided

---

* It is said that Dingaan was about gaining the victory, when Umpanda's people, under Nonklaas, shouted, "The Boers are coming!" which dispirited the former, and inspired the latter with new courage. There is also some error in the account of Dingaan's flight, and of the manner in which he met his death, as will be shown in the volume upon the natives, where the circumstances of his flight and death are detailed. He had half the Zulu warriors with him, and was cut off by treachery; otherwise he might again have conquered Umpanda, and given the Boers more trouble.

beyond the Draaksberg, and had only come in as allies to their friends; and the remaining 22,000 (or, rather, the sad remains of them; for very many were lost or embezzled on the way) were brought to the foot of the Zwart Kop, near the town, where, at a spot still named the *Deel Laager*, they were distributed among such Farmers as belonged to this district, and had claims for losses sustained in the previous wars and engagements.

" A few days before the Emigrant Farmers started on their last and crowning victory over Dingaan and his forces, Sir George Napier, having been ordered to send the Seventy-second Regiment home, and finding that the secretary of state for the colonies still continued little inclined to support his policy of occupying this district, sent a vessel to the Bay, with orders to Captain Jervis to embark with his whole detachment; on which occasion he addressed a letter to the Landdrost Roos at D'Urban, which, after referring to some complaints of natives as to encroachments on their gardens, contained the following farewell address and peroration : 'It now only remains for me, on taking my departure, to wish you, one and all, as a community, every happiness ; sincerely hoping, that, aware of your strength, peace may be the object of your counsels ; justice, prudence, and moderation, be the law of your actions ; that your proceedings may be actuated by motives worthy of you as men and Christians ; that hereafter your arrival may be hailed as a benefit, having enlightened ignorance, dispelled superstition, and caused crime, bloodshed, and oppression, to cease ; and that you may cultivate those beautiful regions in quiet and prosperity, ever regardful of the rights of the inhabitants, whose country you have adopted, and whose home you have made your own.'

" From these expressions, enunciated by the officer commanding the forces on the eve of his departure, and from the general tenor of the intelligence received by them at the time from the Cape, there can be no doubt that the Emigrant Farmers became then fully impressed, that her majesty's government had determined, by no consideration to swerve from that line of policy which had already declared that nothing would induce her majesty to assert a sovereignty over these territories.   They therefore conceived that by this act of abandonment of the territory by her majesty's forces, and by their recent conquest and installation of Panda, as a chief set up by themselves, they had become both *de facto* and *de jure* the undisputed rulers of the country.   They saw themselves respected and dreaded by all the neighbouring tribes; every Farmer now had himself the opportunity of sitting down 'under his own vine and under his own fig-tree,' none making him afraid: and there is, further, no doubt that if they, as a body, had possessed sufficient intelligence to feel the exact position in which they were then placed, her majesty's government would then already have bestowed upon them all the advantages of self-government, consistent with a mere acknowledgment of their allegiance to her majesty and her heirs."

CHAPTER VI.

NATAL TAKEN BY THE ENGLISH FROM THE DUTCH.

IN closing the last Chapter, we left the Dutch in quiet and happy possession of Natal. Dingaan, the immolator of Retief and his party, the slaughterer of the Dutch families to so great an extent as to cause the name of *Weenen* ("Weeping," or "Suffering," or "Lost") to be given to the site, to perpetuate the record of this fearful tragedy, was no more. Umpanda was a king of their own making, and subject to their pleasure, holding his position between the Umslali and the Umvoti rivers by their permission, from which he was to move beyond the Tugela when circumstances were favourable; so that now, after their many wanderings and great privations and sufferings, they fondly hoped that a long course of repose and prosperity lay before them; in which they might frame their own laws, establish their own institutions, consolidate their power, bring up their families, secure their own possessions, and, as soon as possible, obtain their own ministers, worshipping God according to the dictates of their consciences. A church and minister's house at Pietermaritzburg were among the first and best buildings erected.

But how soon were these hopes to be blighted, and a dark cloud cover the horizon! How soon was their bright sunshine to be succeeded by shadows, and darkness, and death!

When they left the Old Colony, they did it in broad, open day, advertising their farms, and selling them by public auction or private contract, with the avowed purpose of going beyond the boundary, in order to be free from British rule, and establish their own Republic. The following copy of an advertisement, published in the colonial papers of the day, is taken from Chase's "Reprint of Natal Documents:"—

"MR. PETER Hendrick Kritzeuger, desirous of removing from

the Colony to join his friends at the new Dutch settlement, will put up at auction, for public competition, on Wednesday and Thursday, the 12th and 13th of August next, the whole of his landed and other property in this district; consisting of two farms; the *first* being his present residence, and now under complete cultivation, generally known as the 'Church Place,' distant about fifty miles from Port Elizabeth, on the Gamtoos-river side, along the main road to Cape Town, reputed healthy for sheep-grazing; has several convenient buildings, including a very superior over-shot mill, erected thereon; also possessing a productive garden, fenced by a strong wall. This property, in point of situation, too, (on a most pleasant eminence, embracing an extensive view of the surrounding country, and ocean beyond,) can scarcely be excelled.

"The *second*, a grazing farm, exclusively sweet grass, in the neighbourhood of the farm, known by the name of '*Drooge Kloof.*' A flock of fifth and sixth cross-breeding sheep, 150 head of Fatherland cattle, household furniture, farming implements, &c., &c.

"R. A. STRETCH, *Auctioneer.*"
"*Uitenhage, June 24th,* 1840."*

"It must not be forgotten that the Emigrants at Natal have strong claims to the country where they now are, which cannot be set aside, on any existing plea, without treating them with flagrant injustice. Let it not be forgotten that their removal from this Colony was not a covert act, done in darkness and in silence, or with a seditious or sinister object. Their intentions were openly announced; their march was performed in the light of the day; their destination was pointed out distinctly; and the whole of the facts connected with the case were recorded and published to the world, as they occurred, by the press of the Colony. What more could the government require? Did it prohibit their departure? On the contrary, the highest official authority—the representative of the sovereign—declared that it would amount to an act of tyranny, were measures adopted to prevent their removal. The emigration, therefore, took place, not

---

* "A Reprint of Natal Papers, Notices, and Public Documents. By JOHN CENTLIVRES CHASE," vol. ii., p. 138.

merely with the full knowledge, but with the publicly recorded sanction, of the executive government of this province."* The British government ought, therefore, to have acted with promptness and decision, and at once to have made suitable arrangements for preventing the emigration, or have pointed out clearly to the Boers their true position, and not have allowed them to be the dupes of delusion, and· afterwards have to undeceive them at the expense of so much blood and treasure to both parties. The weak and vacillating course pursued by the British government was highly censured by all parties at the time: it was specially reprehended and strongly exposed by the editors of the Cape and Graham's-Town newspapers.

For, although temporary military possession had been taken of Natal, by Major Charteris, in December, 1838, who was succeeded in command by Captain Jervis, who greatly assisted the Boers in making their arrangements with Dingaan, yet this officer was also removed in December, 1839. "The governor of the Colony, having received orders from England to send away the Seventy-second Regiment, determined to withdraw the detachment posted at Natal:—*a fatal measure*, the blame of which must be equally borne by the home government and by himself; for he was still left, as was his predecessor, Sir Benjamin D'Urban, without the least instructions, or any reply to the numerous dispatches forwarded to Downing-Street, relative to the rapidly accumulating embarrassments of the Natal question. On the 24th of December the 'Vectis' left that port with the troops; and the Farmers, thus released from their presence, and very naturally interpreting their departure as a final abandonment of the place and recognition of their own oft-proclaimed sovereignty, fired a salute, and *for the first time hoisted their new colours*, (similar to the Dutch, but placed transversely, instead of horizontally,)—the colours of the 'Republic of Natalia.' The Farmers and the troops parted with the same good feeling as had been mutually entertained, with a single exception, during the whole of their intercourse; which was mainly attributed to the conduct of Captain Jervis, the officer who had held the command." †

---

* "Graham's-Town Journal."   † CHASE'S "Reprint," &c., vol. ii., p. 115.

Captain Jervis appears to have been a man admirably fitted for the office he sustained. It was one of extreme difficulty and delicacy, with the fretted, angry Boers on the one hand, and the enraged despot Dingaan on the other; yet, by his moderation, firmness, and kindness, he softened the asperities of contending parties, controlled the agitated minds of the people, and restored a great degree of order out of confusion; so that, when he left, he carried with him the confidence, esteem, and respect of all parties.

In this open and entire abandonment of the country by the English, a tangible proof was given that they intended to occupy it no longer. The British flag being withdrawn, and the flag of republican independence being hoisted, the Dutch at once applied themselves to making such a government as best accorded with their views and wishes.

They now also began to pursue the peaceful occupations of life, in settling on their farms, erecting houses, cultivating the soil, and rearing flocks and herds; whilst they were encouraged and strengthened by additions to the numbers of their friends from different parts, and their enemies were in subjection around them.

But, lo! another storm arose, which might not be so easily dispelled as those which had gone before, but was destined to destroy their independence in Natal, probably for ever. The English government had at different times informed them that, notwithstanding military occupation of Natal, had ceased, yet it still regarded and claimed the Dutch Boers as British subjects, and should not release them from fealty to the British crown, and could therefore by no means allow a Dutch republican government to be established at Natal.

Attempts at an amicable arrangement by negotiation were for some time made; but, these proving abortive, recourse was at length had to force; and Captain Smith, being appointed military commander of Natal, was directed to march from the Umgazi post to Natal with the ridiculously small force of 200 men and two field-pieces, showing the inaccurate estimate which had been formed, both of the character of the foe, and of the task which had to be performed. Captain Smith left the Umgazi on the 31st of March, 1842, and arrived at Natal on the

12th of May following. A characteristic account of this journey cannot be better given than in the letter of the Bugler of the Twenty-seventh Regiment.

"*May* 12*th*, 1842.

"I RECEIVED your epistle on the south bank of the Umsacoola (Umzimkulu) river. It was after travelling eighteen miles, and the whole day raining on us; and then I had to mount guard the same night. I promised to send you all the particulars relating to our march; but I am sorry to state that opportunity will not allow me at present, in consequence of our sad situation.

"Our march was *long* and *fatiguing;* and we had a great many delays at rivers, and bad weather was the cause of detaining us likewise. I will just mention a few particulars on the occasion, and draw to a close unto Natal, as you will be somewhat surprised to hear how we came on since we came here. On the 1st of April we left the Umzimvubu river, after taking leave of Faku's kingdom and all its inhabitants, singing the song, 'We fight to conquer,' chorused by the men and officers, as we marched along. We were three days marching through Faku's territory. The same night Mrs. Giligan was delivered of a son; and the next day the commissariat issuer's wife was delivered of a beautiful daughter. On the morning of the 9th, we arrived on the sea-coast, where we took breakfast; and every man had a good swim in the salt water, and had great eating of oysters and many other varieties of shell-fish. On leaving this place, Fisher was nearly killed in crossing a river. He was jumping up on the gun, to pass over dry, and save the trouble of stripping; but he fell under the gun-wheel, and it went over his left shoulder, and, only for one of the artillery being so expert in drawing him from under the wheels, it would have gone over his head, and killed him on the spot. The doctor had great work to bring him to, and he complained for three or four days after of having a great pain in his chest and breast; but now he is quite recovered. You must understand that the three buglers were divided every day into three divisions,—one with the artillery, and one with the division, and one with the rear-guard.

"Our march chiefly was along the S. E. coast the whole way, until within a few days of Natal. We came across many pieces of wrecks belonging to unfortunate vessels, and skeletons of whales; and many curious shells, and many other things, were picked up by the men and officers, as we went along. The men caught three brown bucks, and gave them to the officers. We saw a great many sea-cows, and came across the *spoor* of lions and elephants in the woody parts along the coast. We suffered much from marching in the sand; it got into our boots, and cut our feet to pieces; and the sun, reflecting from the sand, burned our faces. In like manner, the men had many fatigues in repairing the roads every four or five miles they went along.

"Mr. Archbell, the Wesleyan missionary, and family, were in company with us the whole way. We never saw a sail the whole time on the water, until, the 29th morning, we beheld a small brig sailing from Natal harbour. We marched from the sea-coast the same morning, and continued on the inland the whole day, until we arrived at the east banks of the Umkomass river.

"I must draw to a close with the remainder of the march, in consequence of having other bread to bake at present. As I mentioned before, and at the same time informing you, that we crossed 122 rivers, and most of them we had to swim over; some of them extending across 600 and 700 yards in breadth: they are the largest and greatest rivers I ever saw in my life. We stopped two days and part of the third at the Umkomass river. During our stay here, we had to muster, parade, and Articles of War.

"The night before, James Devitt, of No. 2 Company, died, and was buried next morning with the usual martial ceremonies. Poor fellow! his death was occasioned from the fatigues of the march; and it is a wonderful mercy of Providence that a great many more did not share the same fate. The next day we departed from this river; and when the guns went over, they loaded with grape, and every company, according as they reached the other side, all loaded with ball, and every soldier on the expedition; for the captain did not know the moment the enemy might approach him. And due precaution was taken every night in pitching the camp: the guns and infantry were ordered to be kept loaded until further orders. The next day's march we came within twenty-five miles of Natal; and that evening there came four Englishmen out to meet us, all armed with swords, pistols, and double-barrelled guns.

"You may depend, it alarmed us very much to see them so well armed; but you would not believe how much they were overjoyed to see us. They stated to the captain that they were obliged to fly for refuge : the Boers threatened to hang them, and a good many more that stopped in the town. The next day's march we met the whole of the Englishmen coming out to meet us, all armed in the same manner as the first four. When they came up to us, they all shouted unanimously together, 'Welcome, welcome, boys! you are the brightest sight we saw this many a day : our lives are in danger this month past, since they heard of the troops coming up; and we were all obliged to make our escape from the band of ruffians, who said they would hang us all if we would not go in arms against the troops that were coming up; but we never would consent, and we had to fly, leaving our property and houses behind us, to get some protection from you; and, thanks be to the Almighty, you are at hand!' Now they told us many yarns about the Dutch barbarians, the ill-treatment they gave them, and how they made them pay heavy revenue and duties upon all kinds of goods they purchased out of different vessels.

"But, to draw to Natal: the last day's march, being the 4th of May, as we drew within twelve miles of the town, it was surely handsome to see all the pretty cottages and handsome villages belonging to the peaceable Dutch Farmers. The captain received word outside of the town about the enemy abandoning the town and port. We arrived in Natal about four o'clock in the evening, and pitched our camp on a projecting hill, about the distance of six miles from the town and harbour; for the captain thought that the enemy might give him a visit that night, and all preparation was accordingly made in placing the guns and waggons all round the camp. The English agent paid us a visit before we were long arrived; his name is Mr. Dunn. He has a magnificent house and premises, and a splendid garden, here on the hill. He wondered very much to see such a small force going to face the enemy as we were; and he asked the captain if there was not a force coming by sea; but the captain told him there was not, and that he was not the least afraid to meet as many more. The agent smiled to think he would face 1,500 men, armed in the manner they were, with swords, pistols, and double-

VIII.—THE BRITISH CAMP, HASTILY FORMED, NEAR CONGELLA.

barrelled guns,—the best-armed men in the Colony. They purchased all these arms, since they came up here, out of different shipping that came into the harbour. The evening we came in here, we saw the haughty Dutch banner was displayed on the fort at the harbour, as large as life. But next morning the captain and the engineer-officer, with all the Cape Corps, and a few of the Artillery, went down to the port, and hauled down the rebellious flag, and hoisted the British Union of Old England, and spiked their gun alongside of it,—a six-pounder. In the meantime the captain and engineer-officer planned out a place for our camp, alongside the town, but in an open plain. The captain and the remainder of them arrived at the camp about four o'clock in the evening.

"During our arrival here, for those two days, the enemy made no appearance about the town, but their chiefs sent in a great many letters to our captain. But when he found out that they were from the impetuous chief, he would not read them, and desired no person to attempt to take any letters from any of his followers; for, he said, he wanted to see himself, and not his letters. All this time the Boers were encamped about twenty miles from the town, at a place called the 'Long Kloof.' The next day we marched to our camp, where we were destined to remain, with fixed bayonets, and the officers with their swords drawn, and in full uniform. We passed through a small village, belonging to the Dutch, called 'Kongela;' but there seemed to

IX.—THE BRITISH CAMP, REGULARLY FORMED, ON THE ROAD TO UMGENI.

be very few inhabitants in it, as they were all out in the country. We marched through the town, and came to our camp-ground at eleven o'clock; but such a place for bad water I never saw in my life; it is as black as ink, and full of different insects, and stinks into the bargain. I am very much afraid it will make away with the whole of us before long. But, for Natal, I think it one of the handsomest places ever I saw in my life.

"Ever since our arrival in Natal, the whole of the men are obliged to wear their accoutrements the whole night, and keep their arms alongside of them, lying on top of their blankets and great-coats, ready at a moment's warning to turn out; and the artillery, in like manner, lying alongside their guns. The duty is very hard here; the men have only two nights in bed. We give thirty-six men and two officers, and a bugler every night for outline picket, and an advance picket of the Cape Corps. No person of our camp is permitted to go to town ever since we came here; we are locked up the same as if we were in a French prison. A great number of the Kafirs came here to our camp, and showed us by their backs the manner the Dutch so unmercifully flogged them; they are almost afraid to speak to a white man. On the night of the 8th, we were alarmed to hear waggons going the whole night through the woods northward of our camp towards the Dutch village. But news soon came to the captain next morning of all the Boers being assembled in town; and this day being Sunday, the captain made all preparation for action that night.

"The captain sent word to the Dutch chief next morning to come himself in person, and he would let him know the general's mission; but he refused coming. But the captain was determined to fetch him: accordingly he ordered out all the Cape Corps, one gun, with six rockets, and a hundred infantry. I and Blake were the two buglers; with them we marched away from the camp at ten o'clock, leaving all in the camp under arms during our absence, and to be ready, the first gun they heard fired, to proceed and reinforce us. We proceeded towards the village, and during our march we saw multitudes of armed parties galloping through the woods towards the village; and, drawing near the village, we could see the Boers all in the utmost confusion, running here and there; and we could hear their women and children roaring and crying, and the men exclaiming violently, they were sure we were going to have at them at once. When we drew nigh to the village, we saw the valiant chief coming out, and two more, to meet us. When the captain saw him coming, he halted us, and made us order arms and stand at ease. When he came up to the captain, he made a low bow, and took off his hat. We had a fine view of him for the first time, during the time he was speaking to the captain. He is about six feet high, and has a belly on him like the bass drum.

"The captain stated all the general's orders to him; but he seemed to decline them, and told the captain he did not want to meddle with the troops, but he nor his men never were to come under the English laws, and be subjects of England; and said he would trade to the harbour. But the captain told him this would not do, he must come to a resolution at once; and he gave him fifteen days to think about it. He parted with the captain here, and we marched home to our camp. They were peaceable now for two days; but the third morning they were seen brigading about the town in large parties as before; but the captain was rather vigilant for them, and ordered out a forlorn-hope party, the same number as before, and came down to the town, and sent word to the chief, if he did not soon disperse his men, he would burn, murder, and destroy all their property, and set fire to the village. They all dispersed in about an hour's time, and the troops marched home again.

"Nothing extra has happened since, only they are all in camp
at the village, within a gunshot of our camp, with all their
waggons round the camp, the same as ourselves: but we expect
some bloodshed at the end of the fifteen days which the captain
gave them to come to a treaty to become subjects of England.
I forgot to mention that the Boers bought up all the provisions
in the town before we came up,—flour and meal. Their foolish
idea led them to think they could starve us by so doing.

"To draw to a close with my small narrative, I wish to mention that the Boers were not far astray of us being starved; for
our provisions are out these four days past, and we are living on
one handful of rice. But, thanks be to God, a small brig arrived
in harbour this day with plenty of provisions, namely, biscuits,
salt beef and pork, and plenty of rum. She brought two long
eighteen-pounders with her, to put upon our battery. There
came also nine settlers in her, (Englishmen,) to stop here, from
Cape Town, and a canteen-man for the troops; but the captain
would not allow him to sell any liquor to the troops until all is
settled. As the town at present is under martial law, all the
Englishmen are doing their duty the same as our men,—mount-
ing guard over their property day and night, and relieving their
sentries correctly, and having a trumpet to sound every time they
require him. They are all mounted men: the Boers are all
mounted men, and have beautiful horses.

"I conclude now, and I hope you will excuse my hurried
epistle, as my time is short, and I am so much fatigued: for I
can assure you that I and many men of our expedition have not
closed our eyes to sleep since we came here; and this is the
ninth day since our arrival, and I am just the same as usual.

"JOSEPH BROWN, *Bugler, Twenty-seventh Regiment.*"*

The site of the camp then chosen is still the same; and during
the space of ten years no regular barracks have been built, the
present building being only wattle and dab, with thatched roofs;
but a rumour is abroad that regular barracks are at length to be
built. By referring to the Chart, the reader can see its precise
position, and measure its exact distance from the town and the
Congella.

* CHASE's "Reprint of Natal Papers, Notices," &c., vol. ii., pp. 207–212.

Fifteen days were allowed the Boers to come to a decision. During this respite, they had full time to collect their forces and make arrangements, which were done with all possible care and expedition; and all preparations were made for defence with the greatest skill and determination. I subjoin an account of the intervening transactions from Chase:—

"On the 4th instant, the troops arrived here, after a long, tedious, and arduous journey. A month was occupied in marching from the Umzimvubu. They entered the Natal country without the least opposition.

"Captain Smith" (the commander of the expedition) "took up a temporary position on the mound upon which stands the residence of Mr. Dunn; but, after due inspection of the ground around, he removed to the flat immediately in front of the town, and distant from it about a mile. The day after this movement, a few Farmers, about twenty in number, under the command of Pretorius, came to the old Dutch encampment, on the Congella, about three miles distant from the English camp, and took up their quarters there. During the night, the numbers were somewhat increased, and continued to increase by driblets until the 12th, when their number might amount to 150 or 200 men. This, I believe, is the utmost that Pretorius had, to that date, been able by any means to persuade to join him.

"The day after Pretorius's arrival at the Congella *leger*, Captain Smith, at the head of about 100 men, and a six-pounder, marched down upon them with the design of dispersing them; which seemed the more desirable in this embryo state of their proceedings, as their numbers were gradually augmenting, and as it had been reported that two cannons had been sent down from Pietermaritzburg.

"On the sudden appearance of the troops, the Boers were thrown into great commotion, and each ran to his gun and horse, though, had they intended to maintain their position, the latter would have been useless, as they could not have used them against an enemy on the ground. In a moment, however, two men were dispatched to meet Captain Smith, and to desire him to stand back. The reply to this was a message that he would talk with their leader in his camp. Finding that he continued his march, and was so determined, C. Landman and De Jagers, both men of

I

the best spirit, and desirous to adopt pacific measures, galloped forward, and, on meeting Captain Smith, entreated him to suspend his march, *as there were women and children in the camp.* To the entreaty of these men Captain Smith at once listened, but demanded an interview with Pretorius; who, after making many objections, was at length induced to come to a parley, which he evidently would, if possible, have avoided. On meeting Captain Smith, his eye glanced at the carabines of his escort; and, observing the hammer at half-cock, he requested that it might be let down upon the nipple, or otherwise they might shoot him. Captain Smith, in the course of the conference, gave him some very plain advice; and upon understanding that it was his intention to disperse his followers, he marched back his troops to the camp.

"The following day, instead of dispersing, the Dutch camp received some reinforcement; and, on the 11th, Pretorius, at the head of about 100 armed men, came towards the camp, on the plea, as he said, of visiting his friend, Jan Meyers. This movement brought out the English forces. They were drawn up in line directly before them, and the guns at the camp pointed accordingly. Observing this, Pretorius sent forward two men to explain to Captain Smith that his intentions were not hostile. Captain Smith would scarce hear them; but, enraged at the evident duplicity of Pretorius, and his breach of faith, told them that he thought he had said enough to him on the former occasion; but if he had not, he would tell him something more, in language too intelligible to be misunderstood. He concluded by ordering them immediately to disperse, telling the messengers that if any more of their number were sent to him, he would make them prisoners, and treat them according to martial law. They made no reply to this, asked for no further explanation, but at once retired.

"The day before the arrival of the troops, Mr. Boshoff left for the Colony, in company with the supercargo of the Dutch vessel which recently put in here, and whose visit has done incalculable mischief. The master, Captain Reus, gave the Boers to understand that the Dutch government would espouse their cause, and advised them not to offer actual resistance to the English, but to avoid collision, and by an evasive line of policy, which should determine nothing, keep them in play till his return.

"In accordance with this advice, they drew up a protest

against the occupation of the country by the English, but which Captain Smith refused to receive. In this document they declare allegiance to what they term 'the Dutch government,' and the king of Belgium!

"This display of turbulence on the part of the Boers is the result of two causes. The first is the evil interference of the Dutch skipper, Reus, by whose advice they are obstinately guided; and the second is *the weakness of the military force sent from the Colony.*"

"My last gave you an account of our affairs to the 17th of May; and little did I then think I should have to inform you so soon of actual collision between the Farmers and the troops; that is, between the latter and that portion of the Farmers who are known to be men of desperate fortunes, and who are capable of any thing. They had assembled in a force of about 300 men; and this, had Captain Smith not been bound to suffer any thing rather than proceed to extremities, he might easily have crushed in its rise or embryo form; for it was fifteen days in collecting: but, being tied down by his instructions, he was obliged to submit to observe an enemy raising a force before his eyes, and encamping within shot of the eighteen-pounders in his camp.

"This forbearance was construed by the Boers into fear; and this idea, added to the evil influence of the Dutch captain, Reus, brought matters to a most painful issue. On Monday, the 23rd, the first aggressive act was committed by the Boers. They commenced by seizing about sixty oxen, and then moved down upon the camp. On this, Captain Smith opened a fire upon them with one eighteen-pounder which he had just got mounted, and which had not been on its carriage more than three hours."*

The attack on the Boer camp at Congella was made by our troops on the night of the 23rd, near midnight; but, before giving an account of it, I desire the reader to consult the description of the Bay in the Chart, page 1. I have there had the path of the troops marked out by the dotted line drawn from the camp, near the road to Umgeni, through what is now called "Aliwal-Street," to the Bay, when a sudden turn to the left is made, and the troops march along the sandy beach, the right being lined with mangrove-

---

* "CHASE's "Reprint of Natal Papers," vol. ii., pp. 212–214.

trees, and the left by the Bay.   Let the reader now follow this
little company of British troops, as they thread their course along
the beach, often sinking ankle-deep in the soft sand and mud, or
wading knee-deep in water, but holding on in good order,—the
fair moon from the spangled heavens pouring her gentle rays
upon them, as, in the silence of night, they rush into the jaws of
death.   Borne onwards by dauntless courage, they march till
within a short distance of the Dutch camp.   They begin to think
that the enemy, unconscious of their movements, is about to fall
an easy prey into their hands; when suddenly, from the last
point of the mangrove range, a deadly fire is opened upon them.
Their assailants, being hid and protected behind the trees, were
able to point the muzzles of their long guns towards their helpless victims; and the Boers being dead shots, taking a long
range, and having the advantage of the bright moonlight, our
gallant troops became a target, into which they fired with fatal
effect.   Some of the draught-oxen in the gun-carriages being also
wounded, much confusion among the little army was created by
the detention of the guns, and by the oxen running into the
ranks, maddened by their wounds.   These beasts are difficult
enough to manage in the day-time, when nothing is amiss; but
when, in the night, they were thus fired at and broken, no wonder the gallant commander had to report in his dispatch that he
left his guns behind him, which, as a matter of course, fell into
the hands of the enemy.   Neither was Lieutenant Wyatt to be
blamed for not bringing his howitzer to bear; for it is only those
who have the management of boats in the Bay that can understand the difficulty of getting them to certain places at certain
times; for, if the exact height of tide is not taken, and other
things favourable, a large boat cannot be brought to Congella at
all.   But some living witnesses say that the howitzer was there,
and did great execution.

The remainder of the soldiers who were not killed or wounded,
returned in considerable disorder, with all possible speed, to the
camp, on the same line on which they went; and the greatest
expedition must have been used to get to it, and collect in such
a manner as to be prepared for its defence, when so quickly pursued by the Boers.   I shall allow the commander himself to state
his own case, having given these illustrations and descriptions.

CAPTAIN SMITH'S DISPATCH.

"PORT NATAL, *May 25th,* 1842.

"SIR,—IT is with feelings of deep regret I have the honour to communicate to you the disastrous result of an attack made by the force under my command on the Emigrant Farmers, congregated at the Congella camp at this place.

"In my last dispatch I detailed the various steps taken by the Farmers to annoy the troops, and my determination to abstain, if possible, from hostilities, if it could be done without detriment to the honour of the service, in the vain hope of conciliating these misguided people, and smoothing the way to a quiet settlement of their long-disturbed position as regards the government of the Cape. But the receipt of an insolent letter, demanding that the force I commanded should instantly quit Natal, followed up by the removal, by armed men, of a quantity of cattle belonging to the troops, rendered it absolutely necessary that some steps should be taken in order to prevent a repetition of such outrages.

"I therefore determined, after mature deliberation, to march a force and attack their camp at the Congella, (a place about three miles from our position, where they had been for some time collecting,) and set apart the night of the 23rd instant to effect that object. As the road leading to the Congella from the post the troops now occupy, lies for the most part through thick bush, I thought it best to cross the sands at low water, as by this means I could avoid annoyance from the Farmers, till within a short distance of their station. Fitting a howitzer, therefore, into a boat, under the superintendence of Lieutenant Wyatt, of the Royal Artillery, and leaving it under the charge of a sergeant of the same corps, I gave him directions to drop down the Channel to within five hundred yards of the Congella, and await the troops, in order that they might form under cover of its fire, aided by that of two six-pounders, which accompanied the force I took with me. This consisted of 1 subaltern and 17 privates, Royal Artillery; 1 subaltern, 1 sergeant, and 7 privates, Royal Sappers; 2 captains, 2 subalterns, 5 sergeants, and 100 rank and file, Twenty-seventh Regiment; and two mounted orderlies of the Cape Rifles.

" Having previously sent a picquet out to feel the skirts of the wood in front of our position, in order to prevent our movements being discovered, I put the whole party in motion at 11 P.M., (it being bright moonlight,) and arrived without molestation within nearly eight hundred yards of the place I proposed to attack. To my great mortification I found that the boat had not dropped down the Channel according to my instructions; but, as I considered it imprudent to await the chance of her arrival, I was forced to make the attack without the valuable assistance which a discharge of shells and shot from the howitzer would have afforded me. Giving the order to advance, therefore, the troops had just moved to where the termination of a range of mangrove bush opened to a level space in front of the Congella, when a heavy and well-directed fire from the bush was poured on them; upon which they immediately formed, and commenced a fire in return, while the two six-pounders were loading. Unfortunately, one of the draught-oxen being shot caused some interruption; but this being soon got over, a destructive fire from the guns silenced for a while our opponents: but several more of the oxen, becoming wounded, and escaping out of their *trek-touws*, rushed among the troops, upsetting the limbers, which caused much delay in re-loading, and some confusion in the ranks. This circumstance, added to the partial, and at length total, silence of the guns, being taken advantage of by the Boers, they again opened a heavy fire: (their long pieces carrying much farther than an ordinary musket:) a severe loss resulted to the troops in consequence. Finding, therefore, that I was not likely to accomplish the purpose for which I had put the detachment in motion, and that the men were falling fast, I thought it expedient to retire, effecting this object after some delay, the partial rising of the tide rendering the road difficult. The troops, however, reached the camp about two o'clock, in tolerable order, leaving behind them, I regret to say, the guns, which the death of the oxen rendered it impossible to remove.

" Thinking it probable that this partial success of the Farmers might induce them to make an immediate attack on the camp, I made such preparations as I thought necessary; and found my suspicions realized shortly afterwards, a large body of them opening a heavy fire on three sides of it. This was met by a spirited resistance on our part; but they did not finally retire until about an hour before daybreak.

"Such, I regret to inform you, has been the result of this attack, and the consequent loss has been severe; the total in both skirmishes being as detailed in the return enclosed. One great cause of failure I attribute to the mismanagement of the boat in which I had placed the howitzer, with the shells of which I had hoped the Farmers might have been thrown into confusion; but she dropped down too late to be of any use, and even then took up a position too distant for her fire to produce much effect.*

"Among the many matters connected with the subject of this report, and awakening the deepest regret, is the death of Lieutenant Wyatt, of the Royal Artillery, who, for the two previous days, had exerted himself much in making the necessary arrangements. He was killed early in the action. Of the zealous services of Captain Lonsdale and Lieutenant Tunnard, of the Twenty-seventh Regiment, I was also deprived, both these officers being severely wounded. In fact, under the trying circumstances in which the detachment was placed, I have only to regret, that, with such willingness to perform the duty assigned them, the result should have been so unfortunate.

"The loss on the part of the Boers it is difficult to estimate; but I am told it has been severe.† The whole of this day they have made no movement; but I have to give them the credit of treating such of the wounded as fell into their hands with great humanity. These, with the bodies of those who fell, they sent to the camp in the course of this afternoon; and to-morrow

---

* It is confidently asserted by living witnesses who were in the engagement, that the howitzer in the boat, under Lieutenant Wyatt, was brought to bear, lying in position some time before the troops arrived. I am unable to reconcile this apparent contradiction; but possibly it admits of explanation.

† A gentleman, an Africander, who was in the Boers' camp, says, that the number of Dutchmen on the rolls, on the day before the engagement, was 333, but that only about twenty-five were in the bush fighting at this time, the remainder being in the camp; and that not one was either killed or wounded, they being so effectually protected by the trees behind which they stood. He also states that the howitzer and two guns were worked with admirable precision, together with the firing of the troops, but without effect, on account of the peculiarity of the occasion.

the sad duty of interring our departed comrades will take place.*

"What steps the Farmers may subsequently take, I cannot at this moment surmise with any degree of certainty, though I think it probable they will again demand that I should quit the territory they call their own, within a specific time. I shall, of course, do what I can to maintain myself in my present position; but, considering the number of the disaffected, and the means they possess of molesting the troops, I beg to urge the necessity of a speedy reinforcement, as I scarcely consider the troops at present stationed here sufficient for the performance of the duty to which they have been assigned.

"I have the honour to be, Sir,
"Your obedient humble Servant,
(*Signed*)   "J. C. SMITH, *Capt. 27th Regt. Com.*"
"*His Honour Col. Hare, C.B. and K.H.,*
      Lieut.-Governor, &c., &c."

"RETURN OF KILLED, WOUNDED, AND MISSING, (MEN AND HORSES,) BELONGING TO THE DETACHMENT UNDER COMMAND OF CAPTAIN J. C. SMITH, TWENTY-SEVENTH REGIMENT, ON THE NIGHT OF THE 23RD AND MORNING OF THE 24TH OF MAY, 1842.

"PORT NATAL, *May 25th*, 1842.

"ROYAL ARTILLERY.—Killed: 1 subaltern, 3 rank and file; wounded: 2 rank and file.

"ROYAL SAPPERS AND MINERS.—Wounded: 2 rank and file.

"TWENTY-SEVENTH REGIMENT.—Killed: 12 rank and file, 1 battalion horse; wounded: 1 captain, 1 subaltern, 2 sergeants, 23 rank and file, 1 riding horse; missing: 1 rank and file, 1 troop horse.

---

* There was a slight breeze from the west, causing the smoke from the firing of the troops to collect between them and the mangrove-trees; so that, when the firing took place, a sheet of light showed exactly where the English were; and this was instantly followed by the darkness of the smoke, when the Boers fired, having marked their victims before; and, using guns with long range, they were able to do terrible execution. The wounded they carried from the field, or rather out of the water, (the tide having come in,) and showed them every kindness, sending them back to the camp on the next day, together with the dead.

"CAPE MOUNTED RIFLES.—Killed: 1 rank and file; wounded: 2 troop horses; missing: 2 rank and file.

"Total.—Killed: 1 subaltern, 15 rank and file, 1 battalion and 1 troop horse; wounded: 1 captain, 1 subaltern, 2 sergeants, 27 rank and file; 1 riding and 2 troop horses; missing: 3 rank and file, 2 Hottentot waggon-drivers killed on the morning of the 24th, 1 English driver wounded ditto.   In all, 34 killed, 63 wounded, and 6 missing." *

On the 25th, the melancholy task of burying the dead was performed.   The case, however, was not yet desperate, as some English residents and soldiers still kept the line of communication open between the camp and the Point; but, on the 25th, the troops were called into camp, and the English ordered to the Point, where the stores brought by the "Pilot" were deposited. These had been brought, for the special use of the troops, by Captain M'Donald.   But, on the morning of the 26th, about 150 Boers attacked and took the Point, as also the two vessels in the Bay, the "Mazeppa" and "Pilot:" both were ransacked, and the goods taken out, with all that the Boers could find in the town, and appropriated to their own use.   The following persons were taken prisoners: a sergeant and guard, Messrs. G. C. Cato, Beningfield, Ogle, Toohey, Douglas, Armstrong, G. Hogg, and M. M'Cabe.   These were marched first to Congella, put into stocks, and kept there eight days; then marched to Pietermaritzburg, for more perfect security.   On their arrival at this place, they were put in chains by day, and in the stocks by night, in which state they were kept six long weeks.   A German, named Stockhard, was afterwards taken, and added to the prisoners. After the Point was taken and plundered, a guard of about thirty men was stationed there, and the camp regularly besieged. Joseph Brown, the Bugler, had now full time to prove, that the idea of starving them out was not so foolish as he at first thought it to be; but I find no record of his views and feelings, during this long month, on short allowance and bad water.

Captain Smith and his devoted little band were now cooped up in their camp, with prospects as poor, and hopes as forlorn, as

* CHASE'S "Reprint," vol. ii., pp. 214–218.

ever fell to the lot of mortals; but there is a courage and power of endurance in British soldiers which is truly astonishing, as will be seen in the sequel, when these determined men were reduced to horse-flesh, biscuit-dust, and ground forage-corn, and yet were determined to hold out. Under these circumstances, Captain Smith had no other prospect before him than a surrender to a company of Farmers, unless he could communicate to the governor of the Cape the news of his unfortunate position, and obtain timely reinforcements. He therefore applied to Mr. G. C. Cato to provide the means of forwarding his dispatch overland to his excellency. On this difficult but urgent mission *Mr. Richard King at once volunteered to go*, and was conveyed across the Channel with two horses, in two boats, by Mr. Cato at midnight, in order to escape the notice of the Boers by taking the path along the shore of the Bluff.

There were six hundred miles to be traversed through the heart of Kafir-land, two hundred rivers to be crossed, and tribes of savages to be passed through,—many of whom were too ready to stop and plunder and murder a solitary traveller,—in order to convey information of their destitute and trying circumstances to those from whom alone relief could be obtained; the journey being enough to damp the courage and break the heart of any one except an Englishman. Such deeds of determination and of daring remind us of olden times, in which astonishing acts of valour were performed by our forefathers, whose soul is truly found among the settlers of Albany.

This Herculean task was successfully performed in ten days, two of which were spent in sickness and consequent detention, thereby leaving only eight days' actual travelling. Many of the rivers had to be swum from bank to bank; so that, taking the whole journey into account, it was one of the most wonderful performances ever recorded in the pages of history; which will be admitted by all who know the distance, the rivers, the country, and the Kafirs. Mr. King travelled the whole alone. I have received this information from himself; and it has been confirmed by others, leaving no room for mistake or falsehood. And so prompt were the measures taken by his excellency, that, in thirty-one days, succour arrived for the almost famished little force. But, before detailing their operations, it is needful to give an account of what transpired during the interval. For this purpose we quote the Dispatch of Captain Smith, and the Letter of Captain Lonsdale, completing the narrative from authentic information furnished by living witnesses.

"NATAL CAMP, *June 30th*, 1842.

"SIR,—I HAVE the honour to lay before you the following particulars respecting the position of the force under my command, from the date of my last dispatch until the period of their being relieved, on the 26th of this month, by the troops sent for that purpose from the Colony.

"Various reports having been brought to me on the 25th of May, respecting the intention of the Farmers to make a combined attack on the camp that night, I kept the troops under arms; but nothing transpired until a short time previous to daybreak on the following morning, when volleys of musketry, accompanied by the fire of large guns, were heard at the Point; which post, I regret to say, the Boers carried after a desperate resistance on the part of the detachment stationed there. By this untoward event, an eighteen-pounder, which there had not been time to remove, fell into their hands, as well as the greater portion of the government provisions landed from the 'Pilot.' Fortunately, all the powder, with the exception of a small portion for the eighteen-pounder, had been brought to the camp, in which I had caused a field magazine to be constructed. The engineer stores were also saved; but there being no place at this post wherein the provisions could be protected from the weather, I had been obliged to leave the greater portion at the Point, merely bringing up a few waggon-loads, from time to time, as required.

"Finding myself thus cut off from my supplies, I resolved to concentrate the remainder of my force in the camp, and there await the reinforcement which I made no doubt would be sent from the Colony, on the receipt of the dispatch forwarded by me overland on the evening of the 25th of May, and intrusted to the care of Mr. King.

"The Farmers having desired the captains of the 'Pilot' and 'Mazeppa' to write and express to me their willingness to enter into arrangements for the removal of the troops, which letter reached me the day after the Point fell into their possession, I accepted their proposal for a truce, being desirous of gaining time to strengthen the post as much as possible. During its continuance, they sent in terms so ridiculously extravagant, that although the quantity of provisions in the camp was extremely limited, I immediately broke off all communication with them, being fully determined, sooner than submit, to endure the extremity of privation. I therefore placed the men upon half allowance, destroyed a small post which I had caused to be erected between the camp and some buildings occupied by the English residents, and made my position as secure as I possibly could, with a view of holding out to the last.

"Their arrangements being completed, the Farmers, about six A.M. on the 31st, made a desperate attack on the camp, throwing into it, during the course of the day, one hundred and twenty-two round shot, besides keeping up an incessant fire of musketry. On the following day, (June 1st,) they slackened their fire of musketry, but threw in one hundred and twenty-four round shot, and, on the 2nd, opened a fire from the eighteen-pounder, which they had contrived to bring from the Point, while they still continued their discharges of musketry. During the course of this day, they sent the Rev. Mr. Archbell with a flag of truce, proposing to allow the women to quit the camp, and to send back two wounded men; but this was done merely to gain time to repair some works thrown down by the fire of our batteries. Here I think it right to observe, that they were incessantly employed every night in making approaches towards the post, which were constructed with considerable skill. This the nature of the ground enabled them to do with much facility; and from thence a most galling fire was constantly kept up, particularly on the two batteries, wherein I had placed the eighteen-pounder and howitzer.

"Finding that the few cattle remaining at the kraal were dying either from wounds or want of sustenance, I directed that they should be killed, and made into *biltong*, reducing the issue to half a pound daily. I had also a well dug in the camp, which gave good water, there being a risk in going to the *vley* at night, from whence we had hitherto procured it.

"In resuming my details of proceedings, I may state, generally, that the attacks on the camp were continued from day to day, with more or less spirit, by the Farmers, who, having soon exhausted their iron balls, fired leaden ones from their large guns, in some instances sending them with much precision. Our practice from the camp was excellent, a shot from the eighteen-pounder having dismounted one of their six-pounders on the 3rd instant, besides wounding several of those attached to it.

" On the night of the 8th, I sent out a party to destroy some works in our front, which was accomplished without loss. In a subsequent *sortie* made on the night of the 18th instant, we were less fortunate, although the duty was performed with great gallantry, the Boers being surprised in their trenches, and many bayonetted after a stout resistance. In this attack, which was headed by Lieutenant Molesworth, Twenty-seventh Regiment, I had to regret the loss of Ensign Prior and two privates of the same corps, who were killed, besides four others who were severely wounded.

" Upon inquiring into the state of the provisions this day, I found that only three days' issue of meat remained. I therefore directed that such horses as were living might be killed, and made into *biltong*. We had hitherto been issuing biscuit-dust, alternating with biscuit and rice, at half allowance. The horse-flesh, of which there was but little, we commenced using on the 22nd, and, by a rigid exactness in the issues, I calculated we might certainly hold out, although without meat, for nearly a month longer; for we had eleven bags of forage-corn in store, which I had commenced grinding into meal; and, by every one contributing what remained of private into the public stock, a tolerable quantity of various articles of sustenance was procured.

" On the night of the 24th, several rockets, apparently from a vessel in the Bay, assured us that relief was nigh at hand : these we answered. On the night of the 25th the many rockets from seaward assured us that not only was a vessel in the Bay, but that she was communicating with another in the offing,—a surmise corroborated, on the following day, by the landing of the party under Colonel Cloete, and their final relief of the post in gallant style, between three and four o'clock in the afternoon.

" To the dry detail of proceedings I have given, I beg to add a few remarks; and, first, with respect to our loss. Within the period embraced between the 31st of May and 25th of June,

651 round shots of various sizes had been fired at the camp, in addition to a continued and watchful fire of musketry; and yet our loss, during this period, was but one sergeant and two privates of the Twenty-seventh killed, and three wounded; one Cape Rifleman and one civilian killed, and one wounded, exclusive of the loss I have previously noted as occurring during the *sortie* on the morning of the 18th instant. The damage of the waggons and tents, and private as well as public property, was, however, great; for these it was impossible to secure in such a manner as to preserve them from injury.

"Among the serious disadvantages I had to contend with, I may mention that the numerous people attached as leaders and drivers to the different waggons,—many having large families, who required to be fed,—hampered me sadly in the trenches; whilst the vast number of cattle, originally with the waggons, were a very material encumbrance. These, however, were soon driven off; for nearly all the Boers (contrary to the opinion entertained in the Colony) were mounted, and thence enabled to move from point to point with a celerity which baffled nearly every movement that infantry could make against them.

"I have thus given a detail of the chief circumstances connected with the command intrusted to me. That it should have been so far unsuccessful, I regret: but the resistance on the part of the Farmers, since my arrival, has been universal, those few who professed themselves friendly having carefully abstained from giving assistance; in most cases using that profession as a convenient screen for the purpose of hiding their disaffection from observation. All the property of the English residents the Boers plundered and sent to Pietermaritzburg. They also took out the greater part of the freight of the 'Mazeppa,' (including the whole of my own property,) which they sent to the same place. The prisoners taken at the Point, English residents as well as soldiers, have also been marched thither; and the former have, I understand, been treated with great harshness. After being plundered, the 'Mazeppa' escaped from the harbour on the night of the 10th instant.

"In conclusion, I beg to state that nothing could exceed the patience and cheerfulness evinced by the troops under the privations they suffered; and I feel satisfied that, had it been necessary to have held out for a longer period, they would have endured their further continuance without a murmur.

"I have the honour to be, Sir,

"Your most obedient Servant,

"J. C. SMITH, *Capt. 27th Regt.*"

"*His Honour Colonel Hare, C.B. and K.H.,*

Lieutenant-Governor."

"P.S. I omitted to mention in its place, that a round shot, on the 8th instant, broke the carriage of the eighteen-pounder in two places; but we repaired it so as to be perfectly serviceable.

"J. C. SMITH."*

The deplorable situation of the troops in their intrenchment, their privations and praiseworthy endurance, are well told in the following extracts from a letter addressed by Captain Lonsdale of the Twenty-seventh Regiment to his mother. The letter is dated "August 6th," when he had arrived at Graham's Town.

This is his description of the Boers as an enemy: "Before proceeding further, I must tell you that the Boers' mode of fighting is much on the same principle as formerly in America,—not in a body, but in skirmishing order; they have the very best description of arms, that carry from eight to seventeen balls to the pound; they have, almost all of them, horses; they will ride within shot, dismount, fire, then mount and retire: they are most excellent shots."

After recounting the events up to the "untoward" night of the 24th of May, he proceeds:—"From the 26th to the 31st of May, every thing was quiet, during which time we did all we possibly could to fortify our camp. During this time, as you may suppose, I was not able to move, but was lying in my tent, with a good deal of fever. On the morning of the 31st of May, just before sunrise, we were saluted by a six-pound shot, which passed through the officers' mess-tent, knocking their kettles and cooking apparatus in all directions. Every one, of course, went to his station in the ditch. The Boers then kept up an incessant fire from four pieces of artillery and small arms, never ceasing for a moment during the whole day till sunset. During the whole

* CHASE's "Reprint of Natal Papers," &c., vol. ii., pp. 221–224.

day Margaret and Jane were lying on the ground in the tent close by me. Many shots, both large and small, passed through the tent close to us. James was lying in my other tent on the ground, with his legs on the legs of a table, and his dog with him, when a six-pound shot struck the legs of the table just above him, cut them in two, and struck him in the face with some of the splinters. You will say he had a very providential escape. When the attack of the day was over, all the officers came to our tents, expecting to find us all dead. During that night I said, if they attacked us the next morning, we should go into the trench. Margaret then got up, and put on a few things, and assisted me in putting on some clothes as well as I could. I had got my trousers on when we were attacked. Margaret and the children ran immediately to the trench, and I was carried into it; and we all lay down or sat up. The firing continued all the day, the same as the day before. About the middle of the day, the children were getting very hungry, as they had not had any breakfast. Jane said there was a bone of beef in the tent, and that she would go for it; but we did not wish her, for she might have been shot: but, before I knew any thing about it, she was there and back again with the bone, and James with some cheese and biscuit; but we were obliged to be very sparing with our provisions, as we did not know how long this was to last..

"We all slept in the trench this night; next morning we were awakened by a shot from one of the great guns passing just over our heads. The firing continued as usual till about twelve o'clock, when a flag of truce came to the camp to say that the women and children might leave the camp, and go on board one of the ships in the Bay. After a little consideration, Margaret consented to go with the children; for they could not be of any use in the camp; and how were they to live when we ran short of provisions? So they were escorted to the shore by some of the Boers. Part of the way they went in a large waggon: they were also very polite, and some of them wanted to know if Margaret was old Captain Smith's *vrouw*. I must also tell you that Margaret and the children were in the first attack the Boers made on our camp, May 24th. They went on board the 'Mazeppa,' which was at this time, as was also the other vessel, in the possession of the Boers, who used to go on board when they pleased.

" On the 10th of June the ' Mazeppa' slipped her cable, and put out to sea; but not before she received a salute from the Boers at the Point, but she did not receive any injury. After Margaret and the children left,—which they did in such a hurry that they had not a change of clothes,—the Boers con-

tinued the attack, and they made trenches all round us, so that no one could go outside the camp, or into a tent, without having a shot at him. We never returned the fire at random, but only when we had a chance of doing some execution. We sent out a party early on the morning of June 18th, to fill up some of their trenches; and when our party came to it, the Boers were alarmed. They fired one round, which killed Ensign Prior of our regiment and two men. Our fellows did not give them time to load again, but rushed into the trench, and bayonetted almost all of them. At this time nearly all our provisions were gone: we were living on our horses and biscuit-dust, six ounces

of the former, and four of the latter, *per* day: sometimes we had
a little corn. We dug a well in our camp, but the water was
bad. Sometimes it was difficult to cook our little provisions for
want of wood. The wounded suffered very much, as the doctor
had nothing in the way of medical comforts. I was lying in the
trench twenty-seven days, hardly able to move, and not so much
as a jacket on."*

X.—THE MAZEPPA LEAVING NATAL, TO OBTAIN REINFORCEMENTS.

During the short respite referred to in the preceding letter, a
number of families and individuals embarked on board the
"Mazeppa." It was in May, 1842, that this gallant little
vessel left the Bay under the fire of a four-pounder from the
Boers, besides small arms. Fortunately a gun most likely to do
damage (an eighteen-pounder) could not be brought to bear in
time. The woodcut gives a lively sketch of her having just
slipped her cable, and spreading her sails to the wind. But it
was a hazardous affair,—neck or nothing. She was 90 tons'

---

* CHASE's "Reprint of Natal Papers," &c., vol. ii., pp. 218–220.

burden; had on board 2 officers, 5 men, and 2 boys; and 28 passengers,—3 males, 7 females, and 18 children. The following account I obtained from Mr. Joseph Cato, who had charge of her :—

"June 10th, 1842, four o'clock P.M.—Slipped both our anchors, and made all sail to cross the Bar, before the Dutch guard placed at the Point could muster to oppose our departure. The wind failing us off the sand-spit," (see it laid down in the Chart by the same hand,) "gave the Farmers the advantage: eighty of them got down before we could round the Point, armed with muskets and a four-pounder. The tide making in strong flood, at about four knots an hour, with light winds, made our progress very slow, and we became quite a target for them to fire at. For a short time they did us great damage in the rigging and sails, their muskets being those used for elephant-shooting, some of them four balls to the pound, and our distance from them being not more than thirty yards. The breeze at length freshened, and we happily got out safely without any loss of life. We unfortunately lost our long-boat on the Bar, there being a very heavy sea at the time. After passing the Bar, we hove to, to repair damages; and were busily employed with our rigging until nine P.M., when we made sail and shaped our course to Delagoa Bay, in search of her majesty's cruiser, to relieve the detachment of the Twenty-seventh Regiment under the command of the much respected and gallant Captain (now Colonel) Smith. Our instructions, by flag of truce, were, that if we succeeded in getting out safely, we were to shape our course to Delagoa Bay. As our vessel had been entirely ransacked some time previously by the Boers, who had taken out her whole cargo belonging to Cato, and left her without ballast, it was thought by Captain Smith that it would be best for us to go to Delagoa Bay, as it would be a fine wind for us; and that being the cruising ground for her majesty's ships, we might most likely fall in with one of them to relieve him; at the same time, should we not succeed in falling in with one of the cruisers, to take ballast and make for Algoa Bay, allowing from twenty to twenty-seven days to the time when his dried horse-flesh would be consumed, the troops having only half allowance.

"We had, at the time of our departure from Natal, only four

days' water on board, short allowance; and, having on board twenty-eight people besides the ship's company, our condition was not enviable. We made all possible sail the ship could carry, and fortunately had a fair wind all the passage. We made Cape Inyack, off Delagoa Bay, on the night of the 13th, about twelve o'clock P.M.; brought up in two and a half fathoms' water, having a south-west swell, which continued all night, and increased as the tide fell; carried into port the only anchor we had left. We immediately shaped our course for Cape Corrientes, expecting to find some whaling-ship there: fortunately for us, about three o'clock P.M., we fell in with four American whalers at anchor: we signalized for a boat, when they sent their own boat to learn what we wanted. As soon as they ascertained our wants, the whole of the vessels' captains came on board, and offered us all the assistance they could render. We purchased an anchor from them before we could bring up, also a couple of casks of water; but they, having been here some time, could spare us no provisions. Therefore, on the morning of the 15th, about two o'clock A.M., we made sail for the Portuguese settlement in Delagoa Bay, to purchase provisions. We came to anchor about five o'clock P.M. The port-boat immediately boarded us, when we learned the town was in a state of blockade, the natives having had a battle with them the day before our arrival. On the 16th, we purchased a little corn, pork, and a few pigs, these being the only provisions we could get. We filled our water-casks, and took in a little fire-wood. On the 17th and 18th, we waited the arrival of the government boat, with provisions from Cape Inyack; but, she not arriving, we made sail on the 20th for Algoa Bay, not having fallen in with any of her majesty's cruisers.

"On the 27th, at five o'clock P.M., we made Cape Natal, and found her majesty's ship 'Southampton' at anchor. We brought up close under her stern, and were immediately boarded by one of her boats, from whom we learned the relief of the gallant Captain Smith and his small party, she having landed her troops the day before. As soon as the commander of the 'Southampton' found we intended entering the Port, he signalized us to wait for the ordnance belonging to the troops. We accordingly hung on: the breeze freshening from the N.E., and blowing hard, brought up a heavy swell with it, when our cable broke, and we left the only anchor we had. About twelve o'clock A.M., we ran for the Bar with what sail we could make, and got in all safe ; but, not having any anchor or kedge left to bring up with, we were obliged to lay the vessel on one of the banks inside the Harbour, where we unfortunately lay for nine days, the breeze freshening into a perfect gale. The 'Southampton' was obliged to slip her cable, and go to sea ; but, on account of the near position she had taken up in order to cover the landing of the troops, she had a very narrow escape of getting upon the rocks on the Bluff Point.

"On the 29th I visited the camp, and found the place in a most horrid state, the smell from the dead carcases of the horses being insufferable. Out of some sixty waggons forming the camp, not one was in a state to be moved; and the few tents that had been pitched at the commencement of hostilities were entirely riddled with shot, nothing but shreds being left."

The above is given nearly in Mr. Cato's own words, and vividly describes the difficulties, privations, and dangers to which this little company were subjected : but this is merely a general outline, whilst the every-day detail would be sufficient to fill many pages. So short of hands were they, that Mr. Cato had to be both captain and pilot, and, at particular times, had to convey a rope down into the cabin, so that men, *women*, and *children* might pull at it when the signal was given. That all were preserved, and permitted to return in safety, was a remarkable interposition of Divine Providence; and the success of Mr. Cato deserves to be recorded in the same chapter with the journey of Mr. King to Graham's Town, with Captain Smith's defence of the camp, and with the taking of Natal by the "Southampton."

Having thus broken the thread of our narrative to give an account of the "Mazeppa," we return to place before the reader the events immediately succeeding the departure of that vessel.

I know not what were the tunes which Joseph Brown the Bugler played during his thirty-one long days of half allowance on horse-flesh, or whether he laid his instrument aside till a more fitting occasion should arrive; but, if the idea of starving out was "foolish," the experiment was a painful one both to him and his comrades. But "the God who rules on high" interposed in their behalf. The dispatch of Captain Smith, and the letter of Captain Lonsdale, have spoken their own language on this subject.

On the night of the 24th of June, the hearts of Captain Smith and his companions in privation and suffering were gladdened by seeing rockets ascend from a vessel which they concluded must be lying in the roadstead, and which thus announced to these determined men that succour was at hand. Such was the case: the "Conch" was there; and the next evening they were signalized by the "Southampton" in the roadstead. The task of taking the Bay, and with it the Colony, of Natal was now to be performed; and, to those who know the difficulties connected with this service, it will appear surprising that so great an object was accomplished with so little real loss and suffering. It is difficult to conceive of a position in which the odds were so decidedly against the assailants, and the advantages so greatly in favour of the defenders.

The "Southampton" was some distance out; and the "Conch," with the boats in tow, (as will be seen from the woodcut, No. XIII.,) had to cross the Bar,—a difficult thing at all times, but especially so when exposed to the fire of the enemy. The "Conch" landed a few men on the rocks of the Bluff, and attempted to land men on the Back Beach, but failed in this latter service. In this position, a few Dutch on the Bluff, and a few more at the Point, might have driven the boats back to the ship with great loss; but, fortunately for the English, and fatally for the Dutch, the latter had no expectation of such an attack from such a quarter, and therefore were not prepared for it. They had one field-piece on the Bluff; but a shell from the "Southampton" silenced it at once; and those who worked it thought it the better part of valour to run away with all convenient speed; and, as there were only a few Boers at the Point, their strength being mostly at the mouth of the Umgeni and on the Back Beach, they made little resistance. Many of the Dutch were away from the Port, having made sure that Captain Smith would be starved out before succours could arrive, and would be obliged to submit to such terms as they might dictate.*

---

* This is the account current among the Dutch now residing near us, who took part in the events of the times. Probably the numbers of the Boers had been considerably lessened since the commencement of the siege: and the residents are speaking *comparatively*, while the language of the dispatch was intended to convey nothing more than that the whole available force of the Dutch opposed the landing.

XIII.—LANDING OF BRITISH TROOPS FROM THE SOUTHAMPTON.

Under these circumstances, the "Conch," commanded by Captain Durnford, and piloted by Mr. Bell, (now Captain Bell, the harbour-master,) came on with her line of boats, filled with those who, by their courage, were to take possession of Natal in the name of her Britannic majesty; and who, after landing, at once tore down the republican flag that was flying at the Point. The particulars of the manner in which this service was performed are given by Colonel Cloete, in his dispatch to his excellency Sir G. Napier, and are as follow:—

"PORT NATAL, *June 28th,* 1842.

"SIR,—ON the 27th instant I availed myself of a Kafir messenger to report to your excellency, in a few words, that Captain Smith was extricated, and Port Natal in our possession.

"It is now my duty to give the details of my proceedings.

"Her majesty's ship 'Southampton' arrived, and anchored off Port Natal, on the night of the 25th instant. Here was found at anchor the schooner 'Conch,' with Captain Durnford, of the Twenty-seventh Regiment, and a detachment of one hundred

men, two small howitzers, and some stores, dispatched by Colonel
Hare from Algoa Bay, on the 10th instant.

"Captain Durnford reported that the insurgent Boers had
refused him all communication with Captain Smith, who was still
holding his post; that the headlands at the entrance of the Harbour were armed with guns; and that the Boers had collected in
force to oppose our landing.   Signal guns and rockets were fired
from the frigate, to intimate our arrival to Captain Smith, and
every arrangement made for carrying the place as soon as the tide
served, and the frigate could be placed so as to cover our landing.

"At two o'clock P.M. on the 26th instant, the 'Southampton'
was in position; and the troops were embarked in the boats,
which, however, could only take eighty-five men.   Thirty-five
had been previously added to Captain Durnford's detachment on
board the 'Conch.'   The sea-beach being impracticable, the previous order of attack was changed; and I directed Captain Wells,
with a detachment of thirty-five men, to land on the first point
of the high Bluff within the Bar, and drive the Boers out of the
thick bush; whilst the 'Conch,' the launch armed with a carron-

ade, and the barge were to proceed direct into the Harbour, land, and take possession of the Port.

"A fresh sea-breeze fortunately set into the Harbour at the very time of our advance. The 'Conch,' taking thus the boats in tow, crossed the Bar at three o'clock. Captain Wells landed where directed, when a fresh fire was opened on the 'Conch' and boats from both shores,—that from the high, wooded Bluff within twenty yards of the boats; yet, in spite of the short range and cross fire under which the boats had to pass, so quick was our advance, aided both by wind and tide, that but little effect was produced from their fire. When opposite the landing-place, from whence the firing still continued, I ordered Major D'Urban to land, who immediately jumped on shore; and we rushed to the flag-staff, to pull down the colours, and give her majesty's frigate notice that we were in possession, and to cease firing.

"The Boers abandoned their strong ground the instant we landed; yet so thick was the bush, and so broken the ground, that though, from the smart fire kept up, they must have been in force, yet not half-a-dozen of them were ever seen; and, on the southern Bluff, so thick was the wooded covering, that nothing but the smoke from their firelocks was ever seen. I have since learned that the number of Boers who defended the Port amounted to 350 men: their loss it has been impossible to ascertain.

"Having thus seized the Port, and landed the men from the 'Conch,' the troops were immediately formed. Captain Durnford was ordered to enter the bush on the right, and drive the Boers before him, whilst I placed myself on a roadway in the centre; Major D'Urban taking the left along the Harbour beach. In this order we advanced through the bush, the character of which it is difficult to describe, and which might have been held by a handful of resolute men against any assailants. On reaching the open ground, we found the direction of Captain Smith's intrenched camp by the firing of his heavy gun; we marched upon the point. Captain Smith now threw out a party, and we joined him at four o'clock. Having thus executed your excellency's commands with all military promptitude, by extricating the brave detachment of troops under Captain Smith's command, I strengthened his post by Captain Durnford's detachment, and directed Major D'Urban to hold Stellar's Farm, (Cato's house,) returning myself to the Port, to arrange a post of defence with such of the troops as I expected would have been landed.

"The gallantry with which Captain Smith defended his post, for a whole month, under no ordinary circumstances of privation, having been reduced to horse-flesh for food, closely hemmed in by a desperate and vigilant foe, with no less than twenty-six wounded within his closely-confined camp, is highly creditable to him and his party.

"Thus was accomplished, within the incredibly short space of one month from the date of Captain Smith's report of his position, the relief of his party at the distance of fifteen hundred miles from Cape Town, whence the relief was dispatched, his communication having to pass through hostile bands and a savage country.

"I have now reported to your excellency the proceedings which have placed me in possession of Port Natal; and I have kept them distinct from any mention of the naval co-operation and assistance I received from H. M. ship 'Southampton,' feeling it to be due to Captain Ogle, commanding, to Captain Hill, and the officers and seamen of that frigate, that their services to us should be separately noticed, whether as to the cheerful good-will displayed toward us whilst on board, or subsequently in the more important service performed in covering our landing, by the admirable practice from the ship's heavy battery, and spirited assistance given us by Captain Hill, in command of the boats. In my order of the day I have inadequately endeavoured to express my thanks to those officers; and I should not be doing them justice without repeating it here in the strongest terms. If our success be not absolutely indebted to the opportune presence of the 'Conch,' to her protection must be mainly ascribed the very small loss we suffered in forcing the entrance.

"The troops conducted themselves with the greatest steadiness; and I am much indebted to Major D'Urban for his prompt landing, and the assistance he has afforded me throughout these operations.

"I also received the best support from every officer under my orders in conducting these operations, and particularly so from Lieutenant William Napier, who acted as my Aide, and has been of the utmost service to me, not only by his spirit in our active operations, but equally so by his attention to all details and arrangements so essential on such occasions.

"I enclose a return of casualties. I have the honour to be, Sir,

"Your most obedient humble Servant,

"A. J. CLOETE, *Lieut.-Colonel,*

"*Dep. Quart. Mast. Gen. Commanding.*"

"*His Excellency Sir George Napier, K.C.B., Governor and Commander-in-Chief, &c., &c., &c.*"*

It is stated that the report of the firing was heard as far as Algoa Bay on the west, and Umpanda's Kraal on the north-east.

The immediate consequences of taking the Port are fully set forth by Colonel Cloete in the following dispatch :—

"PORT NATAL, *July 3rd,* 1842.

"SIR,—THE immediate effect of taking Port Natal on the afternoon of the 26th ultimo, as reported in my dispatch of the 28th to your excellency, was, that on the same night the master of the 'Pilot' brig, who had been detained as a prisoner among the Boers, and four other persons, made their escape from Congella, during the panic caused by our advance movement on Captain Smith's camp, and joined me in this place. They reported to me that the Boers had abandoned Congella in the greatest haste, and had taken flight.

"On the morning of the 28th, however, we discovered with our spy-glasses that there were a number of horses about Congella; and I immediately determined to march upon it; for which purpose I collected from each of the out-posts one hundred men, and with this force and a howitzer I took the road to Congella. A small party of the insurgents' scouts were seen a little in advance of the place : on perceiving our approach, they retired under shelter of the bush; and we entered the village, consisting of about fifteen or twenty houses, without any opposition. Here we found some stores, merchandise, spirits in casks, and their curious establishment for moulding six-pounder leaden shot. I resisted the burning of the place, and prevented all

---

* CHASE'S "Reprint of Natal Documents," vol. ii., pp. 224–228.

plundering. As, however, the troops were still without any of
the provisions to be landed from the 'Southampton,' and with
only two days' provisions in hand, I directed such articles of
consumption as were necessary for the use of the troops to be
put into a waggon, which we found there, and conveyed these
supplies to the camp.

" Four persons, inhabitants of Congella, gave themselves up to
me : one, Gueinsius, a German naturalist; another, Scholtz,
practising as a doctor; and two others. I availed myself of
these people to convey to these misguided Boers the merciful
intentions of the government; placing in their hands a copy of a
public notice, which I affixed to one of the houses at Congella;
and, having liberated these people, I returned to the outposts
with the troops. I regretted my force did not permit me to
leave a guard for the protection of the property, the more so as I
felt every apprehension that the number of Kafirs who had made
their appearance as soon as we got into the place, would plunder
it the moment of our leaving it.

" I understood the Boers to have retired to one of their camps
about twelve miles off, where they were said to be four hundred
strong, with four or five guns.

" Without any of my provisions or ammunition yet landed
from the 'Southampton,' or any means of organizing transport,
I did not feel justified in entering on any forward movement,
which would tend only to lead me away from the more important
object of strengthening my posts, forming and securing my
magazines. Upon these objects I have since been engaged;
and, having required of the Kafirs to bring me in as many horses
and cattle as they could get, I have no doubt that I shall soon
be in a condition to take the offensive with some effect.

" The Boers will in the mean time have had ample time to
consider their position, and the terms of my notice; upon the
subject of which I received, on the 30th of last month, a letter
from Pretorius, their military commandant, asking me if I wished
to confer with them; and, if so, to appoint a place between Congella and Captain Smith's camp to meet him. I answered that
I could enter into no negotiation with him, without a previous
declaration of submission to her majesty's authority. To this I
have received no reply.

"Several inhabitants, fifteen in number, have come in and taken the oath of allegiance.

"On the 28th, 29th, and 30th, the weather had continued so boisterous that, on an attempt being made, on the last of those days, to send on shore some provisions, the men's packs, and our ammunition, the boats struck on the Bar, one man of the Twenty-fifth Regiment was drowned, the whole of the provisions were lost, all the men's packs thrown overboard, and eighteen thousand rounds of ammunition destroyed. The greater portion of the men's packs were fortunately picked up on the following morning; when we found that the frigate had been obliged to put to sea.

"I regret to be obliged to close this dispatch with a report that reached me last night,—that the Kafirs had begun to set upon the Boers, and that three had been killed by them. The enclosures explain the manner in which I have treated this subject, and upon the principles of which I propose strictly to act; for if England will not put down the Boers by her own legitimate means, it were better to abandon the question altogether, and submit even to the insult we have received, than to adopt the degrading process of enlisting the savage in our cause, or call upon the Zulu assagais to commit all the atrocities of indiscriminate bloodshed and spoliation.

"I have received such aid from Lieutenant M'Lean, Royal Artillery, and his services will be of such advantage to me in our forward movement, that I have not sent him back in the 'Southampton.' I hope to be able to send the sick and wounded by her.

"I have the honour to be, Sir,
        "Your Excellency's most obedient humble Servant,
                "A. J. CLOETE, *Lieutenant-Colonel.*"
"*His Excellency Major-General Sir George Napier, K.C.B., &c., &c.*"

"NOTICE.

"A REPORT having been brought in to me, that the Kafirs have killed three Boers, (Dirk Van Rooyen, Theunis Oosthuizen, and another,) the insurgent Boers are warned of consequences such as these, which it will be impossible to arrest, while they continue in arms against her majesty's authority; and thus bring all the evils and horrors of Kafir murder and devastation on themselves, their families and properties, in spite of every endeavour on the part of her majesty's troops to prevent them.

"A. J. Cloete, *Lieutenant-Colonel.*"

"Port Natal, *July 4th*, 1842.

"Sir,—Since writing to your excellency yesterday, I have received from Pretorius a communication, complaining that the Kafirs were committing fierce outrages upon the Boers; that we were receiving the cattle plundered from the Boers; that the destruction of the Kafirs must follow such proceedings; and that, anxious as the Boers were to put a stop to all this war and coming bloodshed, it was impossible for them to accede to the conditions of my notice, which required, as a first step, a declaration of submission to her majesty's authority: and he ends his letter thus:—

"'I must also acquaint you that we have already made over this country to his majesty the king of the Netherlands, and have called upon that power to protect us; so that we have every right to expect that our cause will be supported in Europe.'

"My answer to this letter is enclosed. (See below.)

"I have also been informed that Pretorius and his hostile bands have retired from this neighbourhood, to within fifteen miles of Maritzburg. This sudden move I ascribe to the rumour that has just reached me,—that Panda and the Zulus are marching against the Boers.

"All this is a melancholy state, but unavoidable when dealing with such elements.

"I have the honour to be, Sir,

"Your most obedient humble Servant,

"A. J. Cloete, *Lieutenant-Colonel.*"

"*His Excellency Major-General Sir George Napier, K.C.B., &c.*"

"P.S. The detachment by the 'Maid of Mona' has been landed.—A. J. C."

"(Copy.)

"Port Natal, *July 3rd*, 1842.

"Sir,—I have received your letter of this day's date; and no one can lament more than myself the melancholy prospect

before us, of seeing the savage engaged in a murderous onset
of extermination against you and your fellow-countrymen; but it
is an evil so unavoidably consequent upon the events which you
and your unfortunate misguided people have brought about by
your acts of determined hostility against her majesty's government and troops, that it ought not to surprise you; and in spite
of all my efforts to prevent, and my determination to arrest as far
as in me lies, these excesses, (as you will have seen by my public
notices of yesterday, which I have sent to you,) you must be
perfectly well aware that, beyond such positive prohibition, and
the having employed persons to explain my determination to the
Kafirs, I have no power over these people.

" I have certainly required the Kafirs to bring into my canton-
ments all the horses and cattle they can get, so as to enable
me to act with vigour, and put down the state of war and
bloodshed which you have spread over these districts: and to
expect that I should deprive myself of the only means I possess
of equipping myself, and that, too, in the face of your having
cut off the whole of Captain Smith's cattle, to the amount of
some seven hundred oxen, besides causing the destruction of his
horses, and having further seized all the stores of those inhabitants who are peaceably disposed towards her majesty's government, is to suppose me incapable of reasoning and acting.

" You have caused the horrors of this state of things; and you
must bear the consequences to yourselves, your properties, your
wives, and your children.

" You say you would still be disposed to avert the evils of
this coming bloodshed, which you are aware will lead to extermination. If you are sincere in this, there can be nothing
degrading, in so great a cause to humanity, in your giving in
your submission to her majesty's authority, as an indispensable
and preliminary step to a final adjustment, which, you may be
very certain, the government has every disposition to settle with
justice and leniency towards the Emigrant Farmers; and in the
favourable interpretation to your interests, you will find in myself
a friend, rather than one inimical to your unhappy countrymen.

" I regret much that you should have allowed yourselves to be
so grossly deceived with regard to the intentions of the king
of Holland, by a person totally unaccredited; and that you

should have been urged to act as you have upon the vain supposition that any of the European powers would lend an ear to
any question arising between England and her Colony of the
Cape of Good Hope, of which you cannot be so ignorant as not
to know that Port Natal has always been a dependency.

"I shall be happy to lend my best efforts to arrest any general
rising or partial acts of violence of the Zulus or Kafirs; but
I feel my incapacity to do much in this respect, while your
people continue in arms against her majesty's authority, and thus
lead these tribes to think that whatever injury they do you, must
be pleasing to the government.

"I have the honour to be, Sir,
     "Your most obedient humble Servant,
          "A. J. CLOETE, *Lieutenant-Colonel.*"
"*To Mr. Pretorius.*"*

The particulars of Lieutenant-Colonel Cloete's *pacification* at
Natal are thus related by an individual on the spot; whose
remarks, making allowance for the bitterness of spirit which
they display, appear to be in the main correct :—

"A provisional settlement of Natal affairs has been made by
Colonel Cloete; but the terms have not yet been complied with.
The treaty with the Boers is most dishonourable to the British
government; and the circumstances attending upon it are most
humiliating to the troops, and to the loyal subjects of the queen
here.

"The Boers, by the loss of the engagement at the Point,
on the arrival of the 'Southampton' and 'Conch,' were so panic-
struck that they never recovered themselves; many returned
home; and the remainder retired to a very respectful distance,
where they halted for a short time, but ultimately fell back to
near Pietermaritzburg. They were, in short, completely routed
and broken up, and must have submitted to any terms the British
commander might have chosen to exact from them. He did not,
however, avail himself of the advantage thus afforded him; but
demeaned himself, and compromised the British flag, by going to
meet them at a place of their own appointment; and, when there,

---

* CHASE's "Reprint of Natal Papers," &c., vol. ii., pp. 224–233.

allowed them very nearly their own terms, which, when afterwards verbally explained, were found to mean nothing.

"The terms of the treaty are :—1. That the Boers should acknowledge themselves British subjects,—but not requiring them to swear allegiance to the queen. 2. That the pieces of ordnance be given up. 3. That all public and private property be restored. 4. That all prisoners be liberated.

"On the first I shall say nothing. The second, in respect to the ordnance, is a part of the treaty which all felt to be of the greatest importance to the future preservation of the public peace. How much, then, were we disappointed to find, that Colonel Cloete, after stooping to wait upon the Boers, accompanied by only three or four attendants, at Pietermaritzburg, had allowed Pretorius—a man whom at first, when the terms of the amnesty were signed by the deputation, he found it requisite to exclude from the hope of pardon—to retain his brass gun, a four-pounder, which, more than any other, annoyed the camp during the siege!

"The third clause of the treaty refers to the restoration of property, in respect to which the following verbal understanding was given ; namely, that the treaty merely had reference to the property then in their hands, and not to that which had been consumed, destroyed, or conveyed away. This, of course, left them an opportunity of withholding the greatest part of the property which had been taken ; and the Boers were heard to say, at the close of the conference, ' We will take care that the English shall have little enough restored to them.'

"Though Colonel Cloete leaves us to-morrow, not any of the property has yet been received, nor do we expect to recover a tenth part of what we have lost, while that which is returned will be greatly depreciated in value. This, you will say, is great injustice to her majesty's subjects, who, on account of their loyalty, have suffered in common with the troops ; some of them having endured imprisonment, accompanied by insult and cruelty. Those who have not been deprived of their liberty, have had to submit to the most degrading inequality.

"But the worst part of the story is yet to be told. Colonel Cloete, on his arrival, sent for the Kafir chiefs, and desired them to go out and bring to the camp all the cattle and horses they could find, and that for all brought they would receive payment.

L

'But mind you,' he added, 'do not kill the women and children.'
This was a thing just suited to the Kafir taste. They set off
immediately, and the following day brought in a small lot of
cattle, a tithe of Dirk Van Rooyen's large herd, first having
murdered Van Rooyen himself, together with Marthinus Oester-
huisen and his son. The Kafirs stripped the wives of the murdered Boers naked, cut and mangled them, and then drove them
from their homes in that hapless condition. These men had not
been engaged in the war, but, on the contrary, had early tendered
their allegiance to Captain Smith.

"The following and succeeding days, the Kafirs brought in Landman's, Raat's, Cowie's, Gregory's, Old Kemp's, and Laas's cattle,
or, rather, a small number from each, the greater part having been
driven another way. Now these men were all peaceable and
well-disposed British subjects, who, on account of their loyalty,
were inapprehensive of danger. When their cattle were taken,
they instantly complained to the head of the troops, but soon
heard sufficient to convince them it was as great an evil to be
defended as to be attacked. They were told that he must have
cattle; that he would not pay for what were used; but that when
he had done with them, those which might be left would be
returned to their owners: as to those which the Kafirs had
taken, but not brought in, he had nothing to do with them; and
that the owners might be thankful they had escaped with their
heads.

"The property of the few English here, and of the well-
disposed Dutch, being in this way swallowed up, the one half
by their foes, and the other by their friends, they have no alternative but to remonstrate with the higher authorities, and plead
for that justice to which, by the British constitution, every
British subject is entitled. This remonstrance will be sent in at
the proper time; and in the mean while it will be well to allow
a good deal of reservation, in giving credit to the glowing
accounts which it is thought will be given of affairs here on the
arrival of Colonel Cloete at the Cape. With regard to the men
who were excluded from the general amnesty,—the heads of the
insurgents were told they would not be demanded; and that if
they kept out of the way, no one would be at the trouble of
looking for them. Two of them, Burghers and Prinslo, had the

audacity to wait upon Colonel Cloete at Pietermaritzburg, and were told that he would speak favourably of them to the governor. The two Bredas sent in their names, but were refused an interview. To the question, 'Could they go to the Bay to fetch their goods?' the reply was, 'No; they must not go themselves, but might send for them.' One of these men, the younger Breda, is the principal in the piracy committed on the 'Mazeppa' and 'Pilot;' and yet he is not only allowed to escape, but is aided in doing so!

"You will hear more on this subject soon; but I send you this now, as Colonel Cloete is leaving, which is the only thing he has done since he has been here which has given perfect satisfaction.

"The Boers say, his treaty is too good to be true; and they are making up their minds for an explosion. They say they have not been called upon to acknowledge themselves British subjects, but merely to allow the establishment of British law. In short, they do not know in what position they stand to Great Britain, nor does Colonel Cloete appear to have any clear perception of this subject himself. They are, he says, British subjects; but yet he allows them an independent executive! and we have now, therefore, two governments here."

I subjoin an extract from another letter, dated, "Port Natal, July 21st:"—

"After the camp was relieved, and the Point taken, by the arrival of the 'Southampton,' had the advantages been followed up, a very large amount of property would have fallen into the hands of its proper owners, while the cause of the rebels would have been irretrievably lost. Even two days afterwards, when Congella was in possession of the troops, much property might have been saved: but no steps were taken to subdue hostilities, or to protect or remove the property already taken; and the rebels ventured to convey it away from the mouths of the British guns.

"This supineness rendered strong measures imperative, and paved the way for the introduction of Kafir assistance; to which Colonel Cloete's predecessor, in his greatest extremity, refused to have recourse. He perceived the lawless disposition of such allies, and that he might raise a storm which it might be impossible to govern. His successor, it appears, had no such fears;

and the Kafirs were accordingly authorized by him to seize cattle and horses, with but one injunction, which was intended to preserve the women and children from the violence of their unrelenting hands;—a measure this fraught with the most disastrous results.

"The Kafirs, elated with this authority, instantly proceeded to exercise it; and, in accordance with the measures of Colonel Cloete, treating friend and foe alike, occasioned the most grievous reverses of fortune, and committed the most appalling cruelties upon peaceable and loyal British subjects, who, conscious of unflinching integrity, were unapprehensive of danger, until the unsheathed sword was bathed in the blood of those unsuspecting victims to Kafir cupidity.

"One part of the story, not less sanguinary, remains to be told. The treaties having been signed, the Boers applied for the cattle taken by the Kafirs, who were desired to restore them. Before, however, any arrangement for this could take place, the Boers fell upon the Kafirs, who were left to defend themselves the best way they could. While I am writing, report says that, on the Umgeni, a whole kraal or village, tolerably large, has been massacred.

"With regard to the treaty obliging the restitution of property, it really means nothing; and hence the Boers refuse to restore any thing but what they, in mercy to the sufferers, think proper. Not more than a third of the cattle known and acknowledged to be in their hands have been sent down; and the whole restitution as yet made by them does not amount to three *per cent.* of the lost property."*

The following is the official account of the termination of hostilities:—

"Lieutenant-Colonel Cloete left Port Natal on the 21st ult., on board her majesty's ship 'Isis,' and arrived in Simon's Bay yesterday afternoon, accompanied by a portion of the troops sent to reinforce the detachment under Captain Smith; and has reported to his excellency the governor the final cessation of hostilities between her majesty's troops and the insurgent Boers,— no further hostile demonstration having been shown by them

---

* CHASE's "Reprint of Natal Papers, Notices," &c., vol. ii., pp. 233–236.

after the troops under Lieutenant-Colonel Cloete's orders were landed.

"The Emigrant Farmers having made a solemn declaration of their submission to the queen,—having released the prisoners, whether soldiers or civilians,—having given up the cannon captured, as well as those belonging to themselves,—and having restored all public as well as private property seized by them:—the lieutenant-colonel, acting under the powers vested in him by the governor, granted a general amnesty or free pardon to all persons who might have been engaged in resistance to her majesty's troops and authority, with the exception of JOACHIM PRINSLO, A. W. PRETORIUS, J. J. BURGHER, MICHAEL VAN BREDA, and SERVAAS VAN BREDA.

"He further declared that all private property should be respected;—that the Emigrant Farmers should be allowed to return to their farms, with their guns and horses;—that they should be defended from any attacks by the Zulus;—that the tenure of their lands should not be interfered with, pending the determination and settlement of her majesty's government;—that, beyond the limits fixed for the military occupation, their existing administration and civil institutions should not be interfered with, till the pleasure of her majesty should be made known;—that the Kafirs should not be molested in the occupation of the lands on which they were settled at the date of the arrival of her majesty's troops;—subject to such future arrangements as may be made for general security by her majesty. And, by a subsequent article appended to the conditions of this surrender, the lieutenant-colonel, in consideration of MR. A. W. PRETORIUS having co-operated in the final adjustment of the articles of surrender, and of his personal humane conduct to the prisoners, and his general moderation, included him in the amnesty which he had extended to all, with the exceptions above named.

"Major D'Urban and a second detachment of the Twenty-fifth were to leave Port Natal on or about the 25th *ultimo*, leaving Captain Smith in command of the post, with a force of 350 men."*

---

* CHASE'S "Reprint of Natal Papers," &c., vol. ii., pp. 236, 237.

. Many and bitter complaints were made by the loyal English and Dutch against this settlement. They had been plundered, imprisoned, and otherwise shamefully treated by the Boers. Biggar was shot at the Bushman's River as a spy, and others were in danger of being cut off in the same way. Yet these afflicted and robbed people obtained no redress whatever; for the part of the agreement which professed to secure the restoration of property, was no more than a dead letter; whilst the few Dutch who had been loyal had their cattle stolen and their persons butchered by the Kafirs, who were sent out by Colonel Cloete to bring in cattle, &c., where they could find them. The loyal Boers had supposed that their persons and cattle would be safe; and they thus suffered both in life and property. The feeling of dissatisfaction is still deep and strong among the old settlers. When asked what compensation they obtained, their answer is,—£0. 0s. 0d.

Ten years have passed away since the events above recorded transpired. During that period most of the Dutch families that were on the coast have removed upwards, and occupy the range of country betwixt forty miles from the coast and the Quahlamba Mountains. Many of this number still reside in Pietermaritzburg; this tract of country being better suited to their pastoral habits than the coast.

Some have also crossed the mountain, and have joined their friends in the Sovereignty or the Vaal-River districts; and during the late serious commotions in that country, in which English, Dutch, and natives have been involved, and which threatened consequences of a very alarming kind, the two commissioners, Major Hogg and Mr. Owen, who were lately sent there by his excellency Sir H. Smith, have arranged to allow a Dutch Republic in the Vaal River, which, if approved at home, will place these Emigrants in possession of that for which they have contended so long. This arrangement has been sanctioned by his excellency, and appears likely to become law. For fourteen years last past has this severe struggle been continued, until it is at length crowned with success; and the very same Andries W. J. Pretorius, who was commanding at Natal when it was taken by the English, is head and representative of the VAAL-RIVER DUTCH REPUBLIC. This man's head was worth £2,000 in 1848, which amount was offered by Sir H. Smith; but in 1852, four years later, he first treats with her majesty's commissioners in the Sovereignty, and concludes with them a treaty, in which the existence and future independence of the Dutch Trans-Vaal Republic are acknowledged, and then, as the representative of that Republic, visits Natal; and many of the gentry of Pieter-maritzburg and D'Urban go to meet him on his approach, and escort him into their respective towns.   Consultations are held between the republican chief and many of the leading English colonists, with a view to the promotion of commerce between this Colony and the Republic, and to the cementing of the bond of friendship so auspiciously established, by ties of common interest. As a commencement, a number of waggons come down to the Bay, bringing articles for export: their owners buy goods of English manufacture, and return gratified with the whole transaction.   At D'Urban the representative of the Republic is invited to a public dinner, and takes the seat of honour, being the guest of the evening: her majesty's representative, the magistrate, takes the next place below; and sentiments of friendship are recipro-cated, the whole proceedings passing off with considerable *éclat*. I extract the report of this meeting from the "Natal Times" of May 21st, 1852.

"PUBLIC DINNER TO A. W. J. PRETORIUS, ESQ.

"The dinner given to the veteran commandant of the Trans-Vaal Republic by the inhabitants of D'Urban, took place at M'Donald's Hotel, on Monday evening, the 10th instant.   The long room was very tastefully decorated with the foliage of the palm-tree; the dinner was on the table in Mr. M'Donald's usual profuse and excellent manner; and above eighty gentlemen of D'Urban sat down to the good cheer, with evident fraternizing participation in the joyous event that had brought them toge-ther.

"E. Morewood, Esq., occupied the Chair, and A. W. Evans, Esq., ably confronted him as Vice.   Mr. Pretorius, who was accompanied by two of his fellow-countrymen, occupied the seat of honour on the right of the Chairman; H. J. Meller, Esq., resident magistrate, supported the left.   Mr. Herbert acted as interpreter.

"The usual loyal toasts having been warmly responded to, MR. MOREWOOD gave the toast of the evening:—'Mr. Vice-President and Gentlemen,—It is now my pleasant duty to propose the toast of the evening. Your kindness has placed this in my hands; and if I do not do justice to it, I can assure you, Gentlemen, that it arises solely from the novelty of my position. For years have I known Mr. Pretorius: in times of discord and danger I was with him; in good times also I am near him, and but too proud to have been chosen to congratulate him, in your name, on his success. Gentlemen, to dilate upon Mr. Pretorius's character and career would be questioning the interest you take in the current history of this our adopted country. It must be in the knowledge of you all,—his exertions, his exposures, his defamation, his triumphant rise from the many difficulties and perils that surrounded him. He is here, however, in his own proper person, to proclaim those sentiments of peace, those wishes for a free and uninterrupted intercourse between the Trans-Vaal Republic and Natal, which I am sure is the wish of you all, as sincerely as it is of Mr. Pretorius. I am convinced, Gentlemen, that the feelings which I have tried to express are the same which the majority of you, or, I hope, all of you, entertain; and I will, therefore, not trespass longer on your forbearance, but, as this has been thought a fitting opportunity to communicate to you his reply to the address which many of you presented to him last Tuesday, I shall have great pleasure in reading it to you:'—

"'GENTLEMEN AND FRIENDS,—It was highly pleasing to me to witness the hearty good-will which so generally exists among the inhabitants of Port Natal towards my brethren on the other side of the Vaal River. Such a feeling has likewise always existed among the Trans-Vaal inhabitants towards all of you. Although a misunderstanding took place during some time, still it was proved by mutual visits, which continued uninterruptedly, and by the friendly receptions, that the Christian brotherly love between one another had not suffered the least interruption.

"'Not through my management alone is it that we at present enjoy the privileges of self-government: numerous friends assisted me in the severe struggle; but with the deepest veneration I own that it is only through the help and assistance of the Almighty, who has settled every thing according to his wonderful dispensations.

"'That unity and true friendship may always exist between the Vaal-River Republic and the inhabitants of Natal, is my most heart-felt wish; and as I am convinced that the good understanding between neighbouring people cannot be promoted by better means than by commerce, I can give you the assurance, Gentlemen, that I shall not fail to use my utmost influence to promote this commerce between my brethren on the other side of the Vaal River and D'Urban.

"'The influence which Providence has given me over my brethren, I have used, as far as it lay in my power, to procure for them and myself what you with so much truth call, the invaluable privileges of self-government; and also to preserve peace among the tribes and nations which surround us, and particularly with the Colony of Natal; and I am very happy to hear that my conduct meets with your approbation.

"'For the great signs of respect with which you received me on my arrival here, as Representative of the Vaal-River Republic, I return you my most hearty thanks; and I accept the same as a happy pledge of our everlasting and constantly increasing friendship.'

"MR. PRETORIUS, on rising, was received with a storm of hearty applause. He said, he could not but feel highly flattered at the way in which he had been received. He could assure them, his sole reason for coming among them was to express his good feeling towards them, and to cement the bonds of amity and brotherhood which should always exist between the two people. Do not let themselves believe evil reports; let nothing but good prevail between them : he had joined heartily in drinking the health of the queen, and of all who held authority. The queen had now accorded to them (the Trans-Vaal Boers) their rights; and it was to their mutual interest that both countries should flourish; we were so bound up commercially, that the interest of the one was the interest of the other. He regretted that he could not express all his heart felt towards them ; but he regarded it as one of the pleasantest duties of his life, to return thanks to the men of D'Urban, not only in his own name, but in the name of his friends over the Vaal. (Great applause.)

"A. W. Evans, Esq., then rose and spoke as follows:—'I cannot but consider the present one of the most interesting, peculiar, and, in many respects, most important meetings I have attended in D'Urban:—*Interesting*, because we are come to acknowledge what our government has already done: the existence of a free and independent people, of European origin, in the interior of Africa, and of a people who stand in the position in which they do, must be interesting. *Peculiar*, because it is the first Republic that ever was established in South Africa, and created under peculiar circumstances. *Important*, inasmuch as such a community cannot but have a most important influence on the future prospects of this Colony, and of South Africa in general. It would not be interesting for me to enter into a detail of the migration of the Dutch Farmers from the old Colony; the privations and hardships of so many years' expatriation; of the treacherous murder of Retief and his brave followers, whose fall was so gloriously revenged by him who is our guest this evening; nor of subsequent events, to the 16th of March, when they were acknowledged a free and independent people:—as most of them must be familiar to you, from the perusal of the Lectures of the honourable the recorder. But do not these things indicate an energy of character, an indomitable courage, an adherence to principle, which, whilst it made them formidable to us as enemies, renders them no less valuable now that they are our friends and allies? and is it not a matter for self-congratulation on our part, that we can look upon these people as our allies and friends, and a shield and protection to us from the thousands of barbarous nations who surround us? Yes, Gentlemen, we have on our borders a Republic composed of those whose sufferings we have sympathized with, and whose bravery we cannot but admire; and can we doubt that such men, now that they are enjoying the blessings of self-government, will become as great as they now are free? I have it on good authority, that, since they have become a free people, two towns have been commenced building, the foundations of two churches have been laid, gardens have been laid out; showing that the man who, in troublous times, could tread the wilderness, fearing neither the assagai of the savage, nor the spring of the lion, can now, with equal ability, hold the plough or the tool of the workman, and that he only wanted the blessings of peace to make his new home equal to what the one was ere he commenced his wanderings.—I have no hesitation in saying, that this people will be powerful and prosperous beyond our present conjectures.   Let the blessings of peace continue, and we shall see schools established, civilization advancing, riches in flocks and herds increasing, and, I trust, a beneficial influence extended to the surrounding tribes.   I cannot but think that we see in this one of those signs which tend to show that the white man must people the whole of this Southern portion of Africa.   In the few years that I have known this country, I have seen the white man penetrate hundreds of miles further into the interior, and possess himself of portions of the land that once were occupied by the native : and, in the case of our own Cape frontier, do we not perceive, in recent events, that the black is to recede before the white ; and this irrespective of the policy, be it inclined to be peaceful or otherwise, which may regulate intercourse between the two ?   For years have we acted on the principle that we should treat with the uncivilized as we do with the civilized,—that all men are equal : and what has been the result of this line of conduct ?   Why, far more bloodshed, more misery, more desolation, than ever would have followed a less mild and less erroneous policy.   As a proof of the injurious effect of these principles, look at the probable fate of the Gaika and T'Slambie tribes.

"' The capabilities of the Vaal-River country are great, and only require time and the blessings of peace to develope them. We shall see large quantities of wool coming from that country, when it recovers itself from the effects of its late losses.   Very much depends on the state of the roads, which now makes it almost impossible for loaded waggons to travel.   We must urge upon our government to put them in order.   A desire to open a most friendly and profitable intercourse is manifested by our Vaal-River friends, and we must show that we appreciate it by doing our part.   I do trust that no time will be lost by his Honour in forwarding that on which so much of our commercial prosperity depends.   Scores of waggons get supplies from other quarters, which would come to Natal if the roads were not so bad ; and it

is in vain that we expect to derive much benefit from the advancement of the Trans-Vaal Republic, or they from us, unless a
better communication be made.

" ' But let us not forget to whom has been committed the grave
responsibility of exercising a powerful influence in the management of the affairs of this new community. You, Mr. Pretorius,
have obtained for your countrymen an independence almost without bloodshed,—at all events, with an ease unprecedented in the
annals of history. You can use your influence for the weal or
woe of your countrymen. You have laws to be made; justice to
be administered; education to encourage; religion to honour and
disseminate. Without peace there can be no prosperity. We,
the people of D'Urban, wish to see you in the possession of those
privileges which, as Englishmen, we ourselves enjoy. We wish
to see you an educated, a prosperous, a happy people. We bear
no ill-will : we cherish no feelings of animosity. We give to
you and to every honest Boer the right hand of fellowship.
We wish to cherish the principle of doing unto others as we
would be done by, and, as citizens of the world, peace and good-
will to all our fellow-creatures.'

" Mr. Evans then proposed the toast, ' The social and commercial intercourse between ourselves and our friends of the Vaal-
River Republic,' and sat down amidst loud cheers.

" G. Gain, Esq., in proposing the health of the resident
magistrate, said,—' It becomes my peculiar pleasure on this
occasion to rise to propose a toast to which I know you all will
pledge with me in full bumpers. It will not be necessary for me,
in the proposing of this toast, to detain you by many observations. In D'Urban, Mr. H. J. Meller, in occupying the position
of resident magistrate, is the representative of government for
this division; and it is meet in that respect solely, on such an
occasion, to testify our public regard and respect to him. But
when, apart from that representative capacity, I observe, as I
have the opportunity of closely doing, the great zeal and
strenuous exertions used by him for benefiting the Colony in
general, and this place in particular, it behoves us to bestow that
degree of applause and approbation which so deserving a character merits. The infantine position of our institutions, and the
natural results of an unsettled course, consequentially place diffi-

culties in what otherwise would be a smooth path. To watch with eagerness the actions emanating from a public man for the purpose of misplacing constructions, and contriving to accomplish some sinister object, has been the plot of parties :—these petty doings warrant nought but contempt. Fanatics and disappointed adventurers may disclaim my sentiments, but in my estimation Mr. Meller is above the reach of such attacks; therefore, Gentlemen, I pledge you all in full bumpers to Mr. H. J. Meller, the resident magistrate of D'Urban.'

" H. J. MELLER, ESQ., who was received with general acclamation, said, that, on an historic event like the present, he did not think it becoming to say any thing about himself. He would therefore briefly express his sincere thanks for the kind way in which they had received him.

" J. F. KAHTS, ESQ., proposed the health of Mrs. Pretorius and the ladies of the Vaal-River Republic; which was most rapturously received, and was followed by a glee :—'Here's a health to all sweet lasses !'

" M. PRETORIUS, ESQ., returned thanks on behalf of the Trans-Vaal ladies, and gave the health of the ladies of Natal; to which MR. W. DACOMB responded, in his position of 'chronic' representative of female beauty.

" S. BENINGFIELD, ESQ., proposed, 'The homes we left behind us,' and urged the company to have no other thought than that of making Africa their home. ' God forbid that we should ever have to fight for our homes, as our guest and his compatriots have had.' If the time should come, he for one was not afraid but that the English would know what to do : but let them heartily unite in bonds of brotherhood with their friends across the Vaal, and they might snap their fingers at the whole coloured population of Africa. (Loud cheers.)

" H. J. MELLER, ESQ., then said, the pleasing duty devolved on him of proposing the health of their chairman; and he congratulated them on the excellent spirit and order of the company under Mr. Morewood's able presidency; and alluded to the chairman's enterprise, perseverance, and industry, in proving the fact,—a great fact,—that SUGAR could be grown in Natal. (Thunders of applause, which ended in the chorus of musical honours to the chairman's health.)

"E. MOREWOOD, ESQ., briefly thanked the company for their kind support, and vacated the chair, accompanied by Mr. Pretorius, Mr. H. J. Meller, and several gentlemen.

"JOHN BROWN, ESQ., J. P., was then voted into the chair, and the company did not break up till an early hour in the morning. Too much praise cannot be awarded to the several gentlemen who volunteered songs on the occasion, contributing as they did to the real harmony and conviviality of the evening; and we think the results must have been such as realized the desires of the philanthropists, whether Dutch or English, ' to the top of their bent.' "

The author is not responsible for any of the sentiments expressed on this public occasion, but gives the report as the closing of one of the most remarkable historical-records ever penned. How altered the circumstances of A. W. J. Pretorius on this festive night, from those in which he was placed ten years before, when contending in strife and blood for that liberty which he and his countrymen have at length obtained! How wonderful are the vicissitudes of human life! and how far beyond all human foresight are those events which are brought to pass by the providence of "Him by whom kings reign, and princes decree justice!" Much of the preceding record would appear as a leaf of fiction,—

> "Which, like the baseless fabric of a vision,
> Leaves not a wreck behind,"—

were it not that certain fact and stern reality invest the whole with a practical character, and furnish no mean matter for the historian's pen or the inquirer's eye.

CHAPTER VII.

ESTABLISHMENT OF THE ENGLISH GOVERNMENT IN NATAL, WITH
ITS LAWS AND REGULATIONS, DOWN TO THE PRESENT TIME.

IT cannot be doubted that both the Home Government, and
the authorities at the Cape, were most anxious to give to Natal
an enlightened, liberal, and efficient Government; and, for this
purpose, persons of acknowledged skill and ability in colonial
matters were selected.

Martin West was the first person appointed to the onerous
and responsible office of Lieutenant-Governor of Natal. This
gentleman had long filled the post of Magistrate of Graham's
Town, with great credit to himself, and satisfaction to the public
of the Eastern Province; and he left that important function
followed by the regrets and best wishes of the inhabitants.

Mr. Moodie, who had displayed deep acquaintance with
colonial affairs, and especially those relating to South Africa, by
the publication of the "Records of the Cape of Good Hope,"
was chosen as the first Secretary to Government, and still (1852)
remains in office, having at present leave of absence.

Dr. Stanger was appointed first Surveyor-General, who, from
his connexion with the Niger Expedition, his acknowledged scientific attainments, and his unswerving integrity, was regarded as a
very suitable person to fill this important post. He has for some
time been in England, but his return is (1852) daily expected.
John Bird, Esq., has ably acted for him during his absence.*

---

* Since the above was written, Dr. Stanger has departed this life. We can
give no better tribute to his talents and worth than the following account, extracted
from the "Athenæum" of June 17th, 1854:—

"Natal papers record the death of Dr. Stanger, the Government Surveyor-
General of the Port Natal District, on the 14th of March. Dr. Stanger was only
in his forty-second year, and seems to have fallen a victim to an ill-judged application of the so-called hydropathic treatment. He had travelled from Maritzburg to
Port Natal on horseback; and, in order to relieve the fatigue he felt, was induced

T. Shepstone, Esq., was called upon to take charge of the native department,—an office of no ordinary importance and responsibility, when 100,000 Kafir barbarians had to be managed, their disputes settled, and judgments awarded. These duties, however, he has fulfilled with the greatest ability, and to the entire satisfaction of the parties, whilst securing the general approbation of the white population. For such an office he was well fitted by his long residence at Fort Peddie, as diplomatic agent, and his intimate acquaintance with the Kafir language and character.

Major Smith, of Her Majesty's Twenty-seventh Regiment, was Military Commandant for a short time. When Captain (now Colonel) Smith began hostilities with the Boers, he was very reluctant to come to fighting, and did all he could to avoid it. The following testimony is from a living witness: "A day or two afterwards, the Boers took the oxen from the waggon-train; and, finding that none of these insults were revenged, they con-

---

to submit to the application of the 'wet sheet.' The next day inflammation of the lungs took place, which carried him off in one week.

"Dr. Stanger was born at Wisbeach, in Cambridgeshire, and educated at Edinburgh, where he took his degree of Doctor of Medicine. He subsequently visited Australia, and returned to England, and settled in London, where he commenced the practice of his profession.

"His knowledge of natural history, and his enterprising character, recommended him to those who were engaged in fitting out the Niger Expedition, which turned out so disastrously in 1841. During the voyage up the Niger, Dr. Stanger was one of the few who were not prostrated by the terrible fever which raged on board the ships; and it was mainly owing to his energy, in conjunction with Dr. M'William, that one of the steamers was brought down the river. Although not attacked with the fever, his strong frame never wholly threw off the effects of exposure to the pestilential swamps of the Niger. The scientific results of this expedition were small; and nobody regretted this more acutely than Dr. Stanger, who had anticipated a rich harvest along the banks of the river. On his return to England, he obtained the appointment of Surveyor-General to the New Colony of Natal. Here his services were of great importance to the Colony; and perhaps there is no individual in that community whose loss could have been so deeply felt. Dr. Stanger performed the duties attached to his office laboriously and conscientiously, and had little time afforded him to reduce to form his numerous observations on natural history. One of his last contributions to this science was the discovery of a plant belonging to the family of Cycads, possessing characters differing from any hitherto found in that family. This plant has been named after him, *Stangeria*; and a very interesting specimen is now producing its peculiar fruit in the Royal Gardens at Kew."

strued forbearance into fear on the part of the brave commander. But time taught them a different lesson; and he afterwards left Natal, bearing with him the greatest respect, for his bravery and gentlemanly conduct, from both friends and enemies, rich and poor, and under the cognomen of the 'Lion of the Hill,' on account of his fire-eating qualities."

Lieutenant-Colonel E. F. Boys, of the Forty-fifth Regiment, succeeded Major Smith as Military Commandant of Natal.

The Honourable Henry Cloete, LL.D., was selected to fill the office of Recorder; and for nearly ten years has occupied the Judge's chair with distinguished ability and general approval.

The Honourable W. P. Field was appointed Collector of Customs.

The Honourable W. Harding was made Crown Prosecutor.

On the death of His Honour Martin West, His Honour Benjamin Chilley Campbell Pine was appointed Lieutenant-Governor.

The Roman-Dutch law has been the code used in the Colony; but some alterations have recently been made by the Legislative Council, who have adapted some parts of it to the altered circumstances of the Colony, and thus removed great inconveniences which were found to exist.

Much dissatisfaction prevailed, for a long time, in reference to land-claims and titles; but these appear now to be satisfactorily arranged, after a long course of litigation and complaint.

PRESENT GOVERNMENT.

CIVIL ESTABLISHMENT.

His Honour BENJAMIN CHILLEY CAMPBELL PINE, Lieutenant-Governor. Salary, £800 a-year and £100 for house rent.

S. B. GORDON, Esq., Captain in the Forty-fifth Regiment, Private Secretary.

Lieut.-Colonel E. F. BOYS, Forty-fifth Regiment, Military Commandant.

EXECUTIVE COUNCIL.

His Honour the LIEUT.-GOVERNOR, President.

The Hon. Lieut.-Colonel BOYS, Commander of the Forces.

The Hon. D. MOODIE, Secretary of Government.

The Hon. S. B. GORDON, Acting Secretary in the absence of D. MOODIE, ESQ.

The Hon. W. Stanger, Surveyor-General. (Lately deceased.)
The Hon. John Bird, Acting Surveyor-General.
The Hon. W. S. Field, Collector of Customs.
The Hon. W. Harding, Crown Prosecutor.

LEGISLATIVE COUNCIL.

His Honour the Lieut.-Governor, President.
The Hon. S. B. Gordon, Acting Secretary of Government.
The Hon. W. Harding, Crown Prosecutor.
The Hon. J. Bird, Acting Surveyor-General.
W. J. Dunbar Moodie, Esq., Clerk of the Council.
(The Queen reserves to herself the power to increase the number of the Council.)

COLONIAL OFFICE.

The Hon. S. B. Gordon, Acting Secretary to Government in the absence of the Hon. D. Moodie, on leave.
The Hon. J. Shepstone, Secretary to Government for Natives.
The Hon. W. Harding, Acting Treasurer-General.
Mr. C. Behrens, Clerk.
John Hawthorne, Esq., Acting District Auditor.
George Macleroy, Esq., Acting Registrar of Deeds.
The Hon. John Bird, Acting Surveyor-General.
John Mylne, Esq., Resident Engineer, D'Urban.
W. J. Dunbar Moodie, Esq., Chief Clerk; Mr. D. H. M. Moodie, Second Clerk; Mr. J. Hawthorne, Temporary Dispatch Clerk; Mr. W. Hamilton, Messenger.

JUDICIAL ESTABLISHMENT.

DISTRICT COURT.

The Hon. H. Cloete, LL.D., Recorder; the Hon. W. Harding, Crown Prosecutor; J. N. Boshoff, Esq., Registrar and Master. J. E. G. Cloete, Esq., Clerk.
J. P. Zeitzman, Esq., Sheriff; J. R. Wood, Esq., Deputy Sheriff for D'Urban.

RESIDENT MAGISTRATES' DEPARTMENT.

Pietermaritzburg: Hon. W. Harding, Magistrate; J. P. Steel, Esq., Clerk of Court.
D'Urban: H. G. Meller, Esq., Magistrate; — Roberts, Esq., Clerk of Court; — Shuter, Esq., Clerk of the Peace.
Klip River (Ladysmith): J. H. M. Struben, Esq., Magistrate; J. P. Griffiths, Esq., Clerk.

MAGISTRATES OF NATIVE LOCATIONS.

Inanda : L. E. MESHAM, Esq.
Umvoti : J. CLEGHORN, Esq.
Impafani : G. R. PEPPERCORN, Esq.
Klip River : J. H. M. STRUBEN, Esq. (Acting.)
Zwart Kop, and Pietermaritzburg : J. SHEPSTONE, Esq.

It is expected that the number of Magistrates and Justices of the Peace will be greatly increased in a short time, and their powers will be augmented. This will be a great boon to the Colony, as it frequently happens that petty offences cannot be punished because of the distance of the officer, or the limited power which he possesses ; so that a great amount of annoyance, disorder, and loss, is the result. The population of the country is scattered ; and if two or three days are required before offences can be punished, the farmer prefers sustaining loss rather than the expense of leaving his establishment for so long a time.

FIELD CORNETS.

Messrs. D. J. PRETORIUS ; C. F. LOTTER ; G. D. GREGORY ; J. ROCKERNOOR ; G. POTGIETER.

JUDICIAL COURTS.

The resident Magistrates' court in this and other divisions of the district has jurisdiction in civil cases up to £15, and in criminal cases can fine up to £10, or imprison as long as three months, and inflict corporal punishment up to twenty-five lashes. In a few special statutory cases its jurisdiction goes further. The fees for taking out and serving a summons, are in ordinary cases 7s. 6d. ; but they are higher according to the distance of the defendant from the court-house, the number of the defendants or witnesses summoned, &c. Appeals and reviews from this court lie to the district court at Pietermaritzburg, which has unlimited jurisdiction in all civil and criminal cases, whether original, or on appeal, or review ; but from its decision appeals lie to the supreme court at Cape Town.

Circuit courts at D'Urban, April and October.

By the law of this Colony, no Englishman can by will dispose of his property contrary to the Roman-Dutch law. Englishmen marrying in the Colony can avoid the operation of this law, by the precautionary measure of making an ante-nuptial contract. In the Cape Colony, settlers are protected by Special Ordinance, which, however, is not in force in this district.

An Ordinance, an outline of which is given in page 171, has since been passed, to extend the jurisdiction of the Magistrate's court at D'Urban, which was felt to be a great boon.

CUSTOMS' DEPARTMENT.

Hon. W. S. FIELD, Esq., Collector of Customs.

J. R. SCOTT, Esq., Clerk and Warehouse-keeper.

L. NEWTON, Esq., Tide-Surveyor, Searcher, and Landing-Waiter.

Mr. G. PRESTWICH, Tide-Waiter and Locker.

Mr. J. GREY, Acting Tide-Waiter and Weigher.

IMPORT DUTIES.

Port Natal is a Free Warehousing Port.

Coffee, (British Possessions,) 5s. per cwt.

———— (Foreign,) 10s. per cwt.

Flour, Wheaten, (Foreign,) 3s. per Barrel of 196℔.

Flour   „   (from Great Britain,) 5 *per cent.*

Gunpowder, 3d. per ℔.

Stamp Duty on importation of Gunpowder, 3d. per ℔.

Meat, (British,) salted or cured, 1s. 3d. per cwt.

———— (Foreign,)   „   3s. per cwt.

Oil, (Foreign,) £3 per 252 gallons, imperial measure.

———— Sperm, £7. 10s. per ditto.

Pepper, 4s. per cwt.

Rice, 1s. 6d. per cwt.

Sugar, not refined, (British Possessions,) 2s. 3d. per cwt.

——————————— (Foreign,) 4s. 6d. per cwt.

———— Refined or Candy, 3s. per cwt.

————   „   (Foreign,) 6s. per cwt.

Spirits, proof, 2s. per imperial gallon.

Tea, 4½d. per ℔.

Tobacco, unmanufactured, 12s. per cwt.

———— Manufactured, £1 per cwt.

Cigars, 5s. per 1,000.

Wine, (Cape,) 9d. per imperial gallon.

———— (Foreign,) bottled, 6 to the gallon, 4d. per dozen.

Wood, unmanufactured, Mahogany, Rosewood, and Teakwood, 3d. per cubic foot.

———— all other Foreign, 2d. per ditto.

British Goods (inclusive of British Possessions) not enumerated, 5 *per cent. ad valorem.*

Foreign Goods not enumerated, 12 *per cent. ad valorem.*

PORT-OFFICE.

Port-Captain, W. BELL, Esq.

Pilots, Messrs. G. ARCHER, W. HODGE, and W. VIONNEE.

Pilotage, 4s. 6d. per foot, draught, into the harbour, and the same charge out.

A flag-staff is placed on the Bluff to communicate with vessels, and a semaphore to communicate with the Port-Office. The house erected for the signal-man will be lighted up, as a guide to the outer anchorage, at night.

G. C. CATO, Esq., Lloyd's Agent.

It is of very great importance for parties in England to know that, in shipping goods to Natal, they must pay duty on entrance, even though duty has been *paid on the same goods before at either the Cape or Algoa Bay*: so that those who ship goods should do so *direct*, if possible; but, if they are obliged to ship to either of the above-named ports, great care should be taken that the goods are put in the *Queen's Warehouse*, being bonded, —a course which would obviate the necessity of paying duty a second time. If this is not done, duty must be paid twice. This subject occasioned much dissatisfaction and litigation some time ago; and the Home Government was memorialized to alter it, but in vain.

PROPOSED ORDINANCE FOR THE IMPROVEMENT AND BETTER REGULATION OF THE HARBOUR OF PORT NATAL.

WHEREAS it is expedient to provide for the improvement of the Harbour of Port Natal, and also for the better superintendence and regulation of the said Harbour; and whereas these objects can be more effectually accomplished by means of a Board of Commissioners, resident on the spot, than they can be by the general Government of the district:

Be it therefore enacted by the Lieutenant-Governor of Natal, with the advice and consent of the Legislative Council thereof, as follows :—

I.—CONSTITUTION OF A BOARD OF COMMISSIONERS.

1. The following persons shall be constituted a Board of Commissioners, for the purposes of this Ordinance; namely,—

The Lieutenant-Governor;

The Surveyor-General;

The Collector of Customs;

The Resident Engineer of the Harbour;

The Municipal Officer of the town of D'Urban for the time being;

Two Merchants, or Ship-owners, resident in the town of D'Urban, to be appointed from time to time by the Lieutenant-Governor.

The Port-Captain.

The Agent for Lloyd's.

2. For the purposes of this Ordinance, the said Commissioners shall be and are hereby constituted a Corporation, by the name of "The Commissioners of the Harbour of Port Natal," and by that name shall have perpetual succession, and shall sue and be sued, enter into contracts, and take lands and other property to them and their successors for ever, for the purposes of this Ordinance.

II.—POWERS OF THE COMMISSIONERS.

III.—MEETINGS OF THE COMMISSIONERS.

IV.—APPOINTMENT OF COMMITTEES.

The whole of this document contains twenty-one sections. The demand for Harbour improvements is very great, and calls for the most serious consideration of the Government and of the public. Such measures ought to be at once vigorously adopted as shall greatly lessen the evils connected with the Bar and entrance, if not entirely remove them. The complaints against the delay—not to say, neglect—of the Government on this subject have been loud and long. Various suggestions have been made, and some works on a small scale have been constructed; but nothing effectual has yet been accomplished.

It is said that two small steamers are about to be put on, to ply betwixt Natal and the Cape,—the "Sir Robert Peel" screw-steamer, of 320 tons, and the "City of Rotterdam" screw-steamer, of 272 tons. The "Sir Robert Peel" is expected in the beginning of next month, (July, 1852,) with the English mail to the 15th of May. The establishment of a regular line of steamers on the coast will be of the greatest service to the Colony, bringing into, and taking out of, the Bay sailing vessels, and conveying the mails from Natal to Cape Town, to meet the steamers from London; and from the Cape to Natal, on the arrival of the English mail. In this manner Natal would be brought a month nearer England in correspondence than it has hitherto been.

Great loss and damage are often sustained by vessels being

ready for sea, but unable to get out for want of a westerly wind; and, on the other hand, by vessels outside not being able to get in for want of an easterly wind. They are often obliged to go out to sea again, or be wrecked on the Back Beach or Bluff rocky point: but steamers will remedy this evil.

HARBOUR ORDINANCE.
(FROM THE "NATAL TIMES.")

As we intimated last week, Tuesday's "Gazette" contains a Draft Ordinance, "For the Improvement and better Regulation of the Harbour of Port Natal."

Its provisions appear to us simple, yet effective for the purposes contemplated; and although we apprehend some difference of opinion will arise as to land-reserves, as a source of future revenue, we doubt not that more specific explanations will satisfy all reasonable persons that no unnecessary infraction is contemplated of the land-rights of the future Municipality of D'Urban, nor any powers vested in the Harbour Commission, that are incompatible with the interests of the community at large.

It will be seen (from the constitution of the Board) that four out of the nine (members) are unofficial persons; who will form a *majority* of the *resident* Commissioners. So far as we can at present judge, the constitution of the Board seems fair and liberal.

The above are the views of the "Natal Times" upon the proposed Harbour Ordinance; but it is likely that it will not meet with the acceptance of the public, and remedy the wants of the case, as nearly the whole list consists either of Government officials, or of individuals under direct Government control. The probability, however, is that the Ordinance, after having been discussed, will be somewhat altered.

POST-OFFICE.

J. M. AITCHISON, Esq., Postmaster, Pietermaritzburg.

Letters are transmitted to and from D'Urban and Pietermaritzburg, also some of the principal settlements in the Colony; the charge for which is, when pre-paid and not exceeding ½oz., 4d.; under 1oz., 8d.; and for every ounce or fraction of an ounce, an additional 8d. If not pre-paid, the charge is one-half more. Newspapers, 1d. Letters for England, or beyond the sea, are 8d., without reference to weight; pre-paid in all cases. Newspapers, 2d.

GENERAL POST-OFFICE, D'URBAN.

F. SPRING, Esq., Postmaster-General.

NEW POST-OFFICE ORDINANCE.

Daily Post between D'Urban and Pietermaritzburg.

POSTAGE.—Every letter not exceeding ½oz., 3*d.* prepaid, 4*d.* unpaid.

Every additional ½oz. .... 3*d.* „ 4*d.* „

Newspapers ½*d.* each.

To England, all pre-paid.

Every letter not exceeding ½oz., 6*d.*

Every additional ½oz., 6*d.*

Newspapers, 1*d.*

A post to the Sovereignty from Pietermaritzburg every Tuesday.

A private post from the following stations of the American Missionaries is received every Wednesday, and returns the next morning, from the Rev. Mr. Butler's, *D'Urban:—Inanda,* Rev. D. Lindley; *Umvoti,* Rev. A. Grout; *Umsunduzi,* Rev. L. Grout; *Esidumbini,* Rev. J. Tyler; *Mapumulo,* Rev. A. Abraham; *Itafamasi,* Rev. S. D. Marsh; *Umlazi,* Rev. D. Rood; *Ifumi,* Rev. W. Ireland; *Amahlongwa,* Rev. S. M'Kinney; *Ifafa,* Rev. S. D. Stone; *Umtwalumi,* Rev. H. A. Wilder.

TABLE OF STAMP DUTIES.

District Court original sentence 3*s.*	Petitions to District Court 1*s.* 6*d.*
All copies or extracts .... 9*d.*	Affidavits in ditto .... 1*s.* 6*d.*
Summonses .... 9*d.*	Arrest of person or property 1*s.* 6*d.*

Acceptances, promissory notes, or private bonds, filed in the District Court, half the amount directed to be paid for bonds executed before a Notary.

Transfers passed at the Registry Office.

	£.	s.	d.	£.	s.	d.			£.	£.	s.	d.
From £1 to	7	10	0...0	.0	3	From £300 to		375...0	15	0
	18	15	0...0	0	9			500...1	2	6
	37	10	0...0	1	6			750...1	10	0
	75	0	0...0	3	0			1250...2	5	0
	187	10	0...0	6	0			1875...3	0	0
	300	0	0...0	12	0			2500...3	15	0

Upwards, £4. 10*s.*

Bonds passed before Notaries.

	£.	s.	d.	£.	s.	d.			£.	s.	d.	£.	s.	d.
From £1 to	7	10	0...0	0	3	From £75 to 187	10	0...0	4	6
	18	15	0...0	0	9	375	0	0...0	9	0
	37	10	0...0	1	6	750	0	0...0	18	0
	75	0	0...0	3	0	Upwards 1	10	0

Deeds for securing the Portions of Children by former Marriages.

£.	s.	d.	£.	s.	d.	£.	s.	£.	s.	d.	£.	s.	d.
From £1 to 37	10	0...0	0	6		187 10 to 375	0	0...0	3	0			
75	0	0...0	0	9			750	0	0.. 0	6	0		
187	10	0...0	1	6		Upwards..............0	12	0					

Pre-contracts of marriage under £75, 4s. 6d.; £76 to £375, 9s.; £375 to £750, 30s.; upwards, £3. 15s.

General power of attorney to persons not residing in the district, 15s.; ditto special, 1s. 6d.; ditto within the district, 4s. 6d.; ditto special, 9d.

Protests of bills, notes, &c., 3s.; sea protests, 6s.

Repudiation of inheritance and deeds of consideration, 9d.

Inventories of intestate estates without valuation, value under £500, first sheet, 1s. 6d.; each subsequent sheet, 9d.; ditto, above £500 value, double the above.

Accounts of the administration of estates by last will, except insolvent estates, when the receipts and expenditure jointly amount to more than

£.	s.	d.	£.	£.	s.	d.	£.	£.	s.	d.
7 10 0 and under	30	...0	0	3	1,500 and under 2,000	...1	10	0		
	75	...0	0	9	2,500	...1	17	6		
	150	...0	1	6	3,000	...2	5	0		
	300	.. 0	3	0	4,000	...3	0	0		
	500	...0	6	0	5,000	...4	10	0		
	750	...0	9	0	7,500	...6	0	0		
	1,000	...0	15	0	10,000	...7	10	0		
	1,500	...1	1	0	Upwards 12	10	0			

Contracts of apprenticeship, 1s. 6d. Copies of ditto, 9d.

Sale of movable or immovable property same as bonds executed before Notaries. Copies, half ditto.

Charter parties for a ship under 200 tons' burden, 15s.; above, £1. 10s. 0d.

SURVEYOR'S TARIFF.

	£.	s.	d.
For the measurement of any piece of land up to 10 acres .	1	0	0
For every acre above 10 up to 100	0	0	3
For 100 acres	2	2	6
For every acre above 100 up to 250........................ ...	0	0	2
For 250 acres	3	7	6
For every acre above 250 up to 500	0	0	1½
For 500 acres	4	18	9
For every acre above 500 up to 1000	0	0	1

	£.	s.	d.
For 1000 acres	7	0	5
For every acre above 1000	0	0	0½
For 2000 acres	9	2	1
For every diagram	0	6	0
For every figure on general plan	0	4	0

CURRENCY.

British money is now current in Natal. The following is the proportionate value of Dutch money and British currency:—

> 1 stiver is equal to $\frac{3}{8}$ of a penny.
>
> 6 stivers   =   1 schelling = $2\frac{1}{4}d$.
>
> 8 schellings   =   1 rix-dollar = 1s. 6d.

WEIGHTS AND MEASURES.

The proportion generally made use of, in comparing Dutch with English weight, is 92℔. Dutch, to 100℔. English; the true rate is considered to be $\frac{9180}{100}$ Dutch, to 100℔. English, or avoirdupois. Dutch weights are the only legal weights used in this Colony.

The muid is the principal measure used as a corn measure, which is equal to 3 imperial bushels; 4 schepels are a muid.

The weight of a muid of oats is 104℔.; wheat, barley, beans, peas, &c., 140℔.; mealies, (or maize,) 180℔.

Liquids are measured by the old English wine measure; which, as compared with the imperial measure, is 24 gallons wine measure to 20 gallons imperial measure.

The legal interest at Natal is six *per cent.*; but for cash a much higher rate is ordinarily obtained, probably from ten to twenty *per cent.*, and sometimes from twenty to fifty, since great scarcity of cash generally prevails, especially as the military force is small, and consequently the commissariat drafts very limited.

LICENCES, &c.

	£.	s.	d.
Auctioneers'	3	0	0

Bonds also required to the amount of £2,000; the Auctioneer £1,000, and two others £500 each. Auction duties, four *per cent.* on movable property, two *per cent.* on immovable property, by custom payable by the seller.

	£.	s.	d.
Butchers'	3	0	0
Bakers'	3	0	0

	£.	s.	d.
Retail Shop	1	10	0
To trade beyond the Boundary of the Colony	10	0	0
To sell Gunpowder	20	0	0
Marriage, without Publication of Banns	3	10	0
Wines and Spirits, 1 year (retail)	75	0	0
„ 6 months „	40	0	0
„ 3 months „	25	0	0
Malt Liquors, Ginger Beer, &c., for 1 year (retail)	10	0	0
„ „ 6 months „	5	0	0
„ „ 3 months „	2	10	0
Wines and Spirits, 1 year (wholesale)	20	0	0
„ 6 months „	11	0	0
„ 3 months „	6	0	0
Billiard Table, each	7	10	0
Admission of a Notary	7	10	0

TRANSFER OF LANDED PROPERTY.

When parties agree about the purchase and sale of land, the first step to be taken is, for each to make a declaration before a Magistrate of the amount of the purchase money : and upon that amount a transfer duty of four *per cent.* is levied by Government, which must be paid within six months from the date of the purchase; if not paid within ten days of this time, a *further* charge is made of two *per cent.* for the first month, increasing one *per cent.* each month after; if unpaid for twelve months, ten *per cent. per annum* is charged above the four *per cent.*, or fourteen *per cent.*   The next step is, for the seller, if living out of Pietermaritzburg, to execute a power of attorney in favour of some one there, to pass transfer to the buyer; and the Registrar thereupon registers a deed of transfer, upon which a stamp duty is payable, according to the amount of the purchase money. Including this and the Registrar's, Surveyor's, and Conveyancer's fees, the whole expense of transferring property in town is generally about £5, besides the transfer duty to Government, as above stated.

An Ordinance has recently passed the Legislative Council for extending the powers of the Magistrate's Court at D'Urban, so that £100, instead of £15, should be the *maximum* value of the cases tried therein; the Governor having power at the same time to extend the provisions of the Ordinance to other places, if he thinks it desirable.   This law is now in operation, and has rendered the settlement of cases much more simple than before.

Besides, when the parties had to take them to Pietermaritzburg, it was attended with great expense and loss of time, making the damages amount to a very serious sum.

Another Ordinance, for establishing trial by jury in civil cases, has also lately passed the Legislative Council. The number of Jurymen is seven; and their decision must be unanimous. The sum sued for must exceed £15. The applicant must deposit thirty shillings with the Registrar on application, to pay the Jurymen, which sum shall constitute the costs for them: but if both the parties to a trial prefer taking the decision of the Magistrate or Judge, they are not obliged to have a jury.

Trial by jury in criminal cases was previously in practice, and continues to be so, in the Supreme Court at Pietermaritzburg.

Another important measure has been enacted recently: it is an Ordinance to facilitate the arrest of debtors, by giving the resident Magistrates power to grant a warrant of arrest of a debtor, on proof of his intention to leave the Colony, in concurrent jurisdiction with the Recorder, who previously was alone authorized to issue such a warrant. On the old plan, many debtors contrived to leave the Colony before the creditor had time (after he had reason to suspect his debtor's intentions) to obtain from the Recorder, at Maritzburg, in the centre of the Colony, the necessary power to detain him.

It may not be out of place to state here, that when persons have entered into engagements with their masters in England, this agreement is not binding when they arrive in this country, unless they appear before a Magistrate or Justice of the Peace, and have it confirmed: and if either of the parties depart from the agreement, in the absence of this precaution, no redress can be obtained.

The first trial by jury in civil cases in this Colony, took place on June 24th, 1852. The case was " Smerdon *versus* Jacques," and the verdict was given in favour of Smerdon, after the Jurymen had been locked up for two hours. The defendant was not satisfied with the decision, and appealed to the District Court at Pietermaritzburg, when the decision was reversed: consequently litigation, in the first case, has not been prevented by the new arrangement.

Great dissatisfaction has also been felt and expressed against the present constitution of the Legislative Council, as it consists of only four individuals, and those four are all government-men; the voice of the people being thus excluded altogether from the councils of the Colony. This cannot be either a correct or a healthy state of things; and surely the time is not far distant, when this law-making Council shall be placed on a basis much broader and more liberal. Until this is done, dissatisfaction must and will prevail.

A native force, consisting of Kafirs, was, for a while, organized under T. Shepstone, Esq., who was Captain and Commandant, and whom they implicitly obeyed; but these warriors have now for some time been disbanded.

The British force in the Colony has hitherto been small, as, since the country was taken from the Dutch, there has been continued peace. Sometimes rumours of the natives rising have been circulated, but without any sufficient foundation.

Were the vast bodies of natives in the Colony to rise, with the Amampondas to the west under Faku, and the Zulus on the north-east under Panda, I fear the Colony would be found in a very defenceless state. The native force under Mr. Shepstone, as just stated, is disbanded: of British troops there is but a handful; and although the English population is now considerable, yet there is no military organization amongst them; the corps which some time ago existed at Pietermaritzburg having been allowed to dissolve from want of interest, whilst at D'Urban there has never been one formed; and the many English scattered through the Colony are without any principle of cohesion or means of self-defence.

The Lieutenant-Governor has recently been bringing forward a measure for the civilians to be taken under military discipline, and made into a disposable force, in case of emergency; but hitherto he has not succeeded in carrying out the project. The chief ground of safety which at present exists is, that Panda is afraid that his people would desert if a commotion arose, whilst within the Colony the petty chiefs and tribes have great jealousy of each other. Let, however, any thing occur to ignite the train of combustible materials existing, and there may be an explosion which will be very terrible in its results.

I thus write, not as an alarmist, but with a knowledge of the native character, and with a vivid remembrance of the melancholy scenes which have transpired in three desolating wars on the frontier of the old Colony. I seek to point out the true state of the case. One cause of such a large amount of blood and treasure being expended by the English in South Africa has been, either gross ignorance of the enemy with whom they had to deal, or holding their foes in too much contempt. They have greatly underrated the power of the hostile chief, or the Boer; and, by small forces and ill-digested measures, have tempted him to put forth his energies with well-grounded hopes of success; so that in the end the results have been most disastrous. Witness Captain Smith, with two hundred men and two guns, sent to conquer the Boers, and to establish British supremacy in Natal, with the results of the expedition,—needless suffering, and additional outlay !

In this Chapter I have sought to give a general and comprehensive account of the Government of Natal; endeavouring, on the one hand, to avoid entering into those minute details which would not be of general interest; and, on the other, to escape the charge of being so meagre in statement as not to afford such information on all subjects of importance as the public in general wish to obtain.

It may be thought by a few persons, that some things are here introduced which might have been omitted as unnecessary; and by others, that topics which ought to have been mentioned, are not here touched upon : yet I venture to hope that I have so far succeeded as to meet the *general wishes and wants* of my readers upon the subject.

COLONIAL CHRONOLOGY.

CHAPTER VIII.

THE ENGLISH GOVERNMENT OF THE NATIVES.*

THE professed object of the English, in taking possession of Natal, was the protection and preservation of the Natives; and for the accomplishment of this. profession all their measures were framed and operations conducted.

For this purpose, Theophilus Shepstone, Esq., (son of the Rev. William Shepstone, Wesleyan missionary,) was selected; who, having for some time honourably filled the office of diplomatic agent for the Kafirs at Fort Peddie, and possessing a thorough knowledge of the Kafir language, and an extensive acquaintance with their laws and usages, was thought the most suitable person for filling the important office of taking charge of the large native population of Natal.

The plan of government devised was, to preserve the Natives distinct from the whites; and, for this purpose, large tracts of country were set aside, under the designation of "Locations for the Natives." On these Locations the Natives were to be collected, and governed by their own laws, through the medium of their own chiefs; Mr. Shepstone being the great chief, trying all cases, settling all disputes, and inflicting all punishments. It is astonishing to what an extent peace was preserved amongst them, the losers in the various suits generally having cause to be satisfied; whilst the influence which Mr. Shepstone acquired over them was very great; and, had the principles on which the

---

* The figures in Plate No. XI., facing this page, are Koffyan and his chief wife, with Adonis, his *induna*. The drawing is very correct, and will convey as accurate an idea to the English mind as though the observer were on the spot, and saw for himself. Koffyan is a chief of some importance, living on the Little Umlanga river, about ten miles from the Bay, and has many people under him; but he is not of the royal line, having been constituted a chief within the last few years, probably by John Cane, who was his chieftain, and on whose side Koffyan and Adonis fought at the celebrated battle on the Tugela, as detailed in Chapter IV.

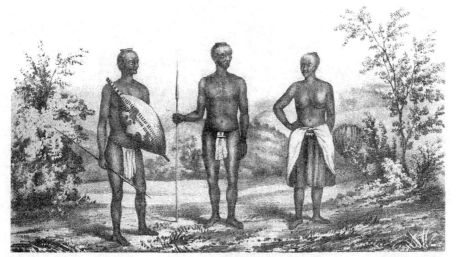

XI. KAFFYAP A KAFFIR CHIEF, HIS PRINCIPAL
WIFE AND ADONIS HIS INDUNA.

A.La Rovere litho 95.Paternoster Row

government of them was based been sound, the ultimate and permanent benefit to the Natives and the Colony would have been of the most gratifying kind.

The persons employed to assist Mr. Shepstone in locating the Natives were,—Dr. Stanger, the surveyor-general; Lieutenant Gibb, of the Royal Engineers; with the Rev. Newton Adams, and the Rev. Daniel Lindley, of the American Mission. The number to be provided for was about 100,000. These gentlemen did their utmost to set aside such lands as were suitable for the Natives, and to make that provision which was regarded as needful. The large tracts of country, thus selected, were such as Natives alone could use, being exceedingly rugged and mountainous, and only fit for such people to occupy: but, in the more open parts, if a farm happened to be claimed by a Native, the claimant was to have another farm given in some other suitable place by government, so as to allow the Locations to remain entire. The Kafirs were then all ordered off from private lands, and the neighbourhood of towns, where no squatting was to be allowed. These orders were given in 1846.

The unsoundness of some parts of this mode of proceeding was pointed out by the writer of this volume to some of the members of the commission in 1847,—especially those parts which applied to separation from the white population, instead of amalgamation with them. He thought that, as a natural consequence of such a system, the want of labour would be severely felt; and this foreboding has been very sadly fulfilled,—a result which induced him, in 1850, to publish a pamphlet, of which the following is the substance:—

THE KAFIR LABOUR QUESTION, &c.

THIS is pre-eminently the question which at the present time affects the Natal Colony; and upon the right settlement of which depends its future prosperity.

The subject of Kafir Labour has never yet been placed on a satisfactory basis; but, during the last few months, not only has great inconvenience been felt, but much loss sustained. The farmer has not been able to carry on successfully his agricultural operations, or the merchant to obtain the assistance required, whilst household labours have fallen chiefly on the master and

mistress of the establishment.   Many of the Europeans have had
to perform the most menial services, and could proceed no further
in any undertaking beyond what they were able to accomplish
by their own efforts; or they had to pay for the white man's
labour.   The consequence is, that all parties are greatly dissatisfied, many are utterly discouraged, and some are leaving the
Colony in despair and disgust.   A few, who had capital, and had
commenced farming operations, are abandoning them; whilst
others, who would invest capital, are prevented from doing so
by seeing no reasonable hope of conducting their operations successfully, for want of labour: and thus a fine Colony is seriously injured, and the developement of its resources indefinitely
postponed.

But what aggravates the evil is, that no one appears to know
how to correct it; and government either cannot or will not do
it.   All parties speak and complain; but none appear to have
penetration enough to see the mode by which the evil is to be
remedied, or to have any fixed principles to guide their proceedings in treating upon it.

Amongst the many plans which have been recently devised, is
the one of importing Coolies from India or China.   What! and
is it really come to this?   Is this the consummation of British
enterprise, of British legislation, and of British philanthropy,—
thus deliberately to hand over one hundred thousand Kafirs to
irreclaimable heathenism and barbarism, until they shall be annihi-
lated before the face of the white man, or driven back into the
depths of the interior, or only a few scattered fragments of them
be left remaining?

Suppose the importation of Coolies can be successfully conducted, what will be its probable results?   The remedy will
quickly be worse than the disease.   In a short time many of
them will be abandoned drunkards, and quickly die in large
numbers from the diseases thereby entailed, as was the case in the
West Indies; adding the vices of other countries to those which
are already so prolific amongst the black races; and thus making
the whole a mass of corruption and idleness, which must eat out
the heart of the Colony, or hang as an intolerable weight upon
the wheels of its advancement.

But thoughtful, well-meaning people ask if this is quite needful.   They admit that government has tried for six or eight years, and that things have only got worse, until the case has become desperate; but they ask, "Did the government commence on right principles? and has it proceeded according to the dictates of a wise and correct policy?" They answer, "No!" There are those who, years ago, saw and said that such was the case, and that the results which we now witness would transpire; but they were looked upon as persons who knew nothing about the matter, and were told that the result would be far better than was prognosticated; indeed, that it was a grand experiment upon a large scale, and its consequences would be of the very best character!

I do not hesitate to state my conviction to be, that the original plan for the government of the Kafir tribes was *false* in its *principles*, and injurious in its consequences.   It was, to govern them according to their own laws and usages, through the medium of their own chiefs; and, in order that this might be the more effectually done, they were to be collected together in great masses upon large locations, thus to be kept a separate, distinct people, enjoying their own heathen rights and immunities.

That the British nation should seek to preserve and benefit these people, was kind, and just, and right; and I judge that there never was a more favourable opportunity than this for making a successful experiment, had it been commenced in a proper manner.   The raw material was the very best to work upon.   Unlike the bold, independent, warlike frontier Kafirs, given to mischief and plunder, the Natal tribes were scattered, broken, powerless, and honest, and thus disposed to submit to any form of government under which the English might be pleased to place them; being thankful and happy to live in peace and security, saved from the terrible devastations and slaughters of the Zulu chiefs and warriors; so that, had right methods been adopted, they might at this day have afforded one of the finest spectacles that the world ever witnessed,—that of a vast concourse of human beings rising from the darkness, degradation, and cruelty of heathenism, to the position of civilized and Christianized men.   But the means selected, unhappily, were calculated to produce only an opposite effect.

Many of the native laws are not only grossly impure, but are also contrary to the dictates of humanity, and the usages of all enlightened and civilized nations, and especially of the English by whom they are surrounded. For example, take the glaring cases of *polygamy* and *witchcraft*, with their consequences,—idleness and cruelty.

It was an impossibility that two nations, guided by laws so opposite and practices so contrary, should ever proceed peacefully and prosperously together.

If the Kafirs were occupying a tract of country beyond the limits of the Colony, or upon the extreme borders of it, the case would be different; but for them to be in the very heart of a British Colony of limited extent, with the white man pressing upon them on every side, is a state of things in which the weak must fall before the strong, unless amalgamation can be effected: yet amalgamation there cannot be, where the laws and usages of the two nations are at the antipodes of each other.

But it was supposed that by the influence of Christian missions the Kafirs would be quickly Christianized and civilized, and so elevated and preserved. None can attach more importance to the labours of Christian missionaries, or wish them greater success, than I do; and, doubtless, much good has been already effected, and much more will be accomplished. But the success of Christian missions is most seriously retarded by the operation of those laws and usages which prevail among the Kafirs. Polygamy and witchcraft are so directly opposed to Christian institutions, that these two evils alone have placed the Kafirs in a position of the greatest hostility to the Gospel; and the most systematic persecution is arranged, consolidated, and practised; so that at this moment this vast mass of heathens stand boldly confronting the only instrumentality which is brought into operation for their improvement and advancement. Those who embrace Christianity have to do it in the face of an amount of suffering and provocation which is known only to the parties concerned.

The astounding result is, that there are a hundred thousand heathen Kafirs in the heart of a British Colony, for whose improvement the government has done absolutely nothing.

Besides this, by the system of preserving to them their own laws, governing them through the medium of their own chiefs, and placing them together in large bodies upon vast tracts of country, the Kafirs have had an opportunity of quietly collecting under their own chiefs; and the chiefs have had a favourable occasion afforded them of gathering their people around them, and consolidating their own power; until they are now become so formidable as to be in a position to resist the requisitions of government, and assume a hostile attitude towards the Colony. This has recently been done, when they were called upon to go to the assistance of Sir H. Smith, in the war now (1851) raging on the frontier of the old Colony, and at the same time causing alarm throughout this Colony; so that many left their homes to seek security in the towns, whilst the course of labour and business was grievously interrupted,—besides the unfavourable effect which must be produced in England by the report of these things taking place, by which many will be prevented from coming out, who would have greatly advanced the interests of the Colony, by investing capital in its various landed and mercantile speculations.

This unfavourable state of things is generally admitted and regretted; but what remedy can be found?   Not attempting to import Coolies,—not attempting to compel the Kafirs to wear clothes, which they will never do in their heathen state,—not attempting to reduce them to slavery, &c.   But let the government begin at the beginning, where the commencement ought to have been made years ago, and by delaying which the difficulties will now be much greater; let the government state in plain and distinct terms, that the Kafirs are British subjects, under British law, and subject to British institutions.   Let the head of the Kafir department change his name from " diplomatic agent," to " chief Kafir magistrate :" let him administer British law as far as possible, and use every practicable means to make the Kafirs acquainted with it.   Let the Kafir magistrates in the different localities do the same thing; and not resort to the wonderful plan of trying English cases, or the cases of Englishmen, by Kafir law; but, on the contrary, reduce Kafir to English law, and decide accordingly.

There are those who say that it is impossible that Kafir law can be set aside, and English law brought into operation.   We do not deny that it will require time and effort to produce this radical change in the administration of law among them; but we do maintain that this may be gradually done, and that upon *this*

principle legislative measures and magisterial acts should be based,
and the transition effected as fast and extensively as is safe and
practicable. But if there is no fixed principle upon which to
proceed, weakness and vacillation must attend every step, and
produce the worst consequences.

Let, also, the number of magistrates and justices of the peace
be *greatly increased.* Let care also be taken to select the most
suitable persons for these important offices,—not men whose only
recommendation is a letter from the foreign secretary, but,—men
of *correct moral habits,* of general good sense, having some knowledge of colonial matters, and some acquaintance with the native
character.

Let the Kafir chiefs be *set aside altogether ;* and let the Kafirs
know that we acknowledge no chief but the queen of England,
and that we cannot set a black heathen Kafir chief on a throne
by her side, for him to govern his subjects in her majesty's
dominions by *his* laws, and for her majesty to rule only her
white subjects by *her* laws. England is too small for two sovereigns, and Natal for two chiefs. Let it be known that her
majesty is chief alone ; and if the Kafir likes her laws, he can
come and sit quietly under them ; but if not, he can select another chief in a distant locality, whose laws he likes better. Let
witchcraft be punished, instead of its professors being allowed to
inflict cruelty and death, as is the case at present. Let polygamy
be put aside, not violently, but by stringent regulations, by which
it shall become difficult, and all but impossible, for a man to
get more wives than one,—until, at length, polygamy becomes a
condition nearly extinct, and punishable by the law.

" But how will this affect the labour market ?" Why, it will
send thousands to work who are at present supported in independent idleness by their wives. When a Kafir gets a wife, she
is to maintain him ; and, as she generally finds this rather hard
work, both he and she are clamorous for a second, so that the
labour of the first wife may be less, and her husband's supply of
food greater. Then he becomes rich and independent, and needs
to work no more. Nearly the whole of the money which the
Kafirs now get from the English goes to buy cattle, that those
who have them may obtain more wives. But let the Kafir
have only one wife, and he will be obliged to work. This is one

of the objections urged by them against Christianity,—that, as it allows of only one wife, the husband will be obliged to work; and therefore, they say, he is "a great fool" who embraces it!

Let the tax on each Kafir hut be limited to the *Locations and government lands,* but not levied upon those who are living on private property: so that it will be for the Kafir's own interest to obtain a place for his kraal upon private property, and he will be disposed to enter into arrangements with the proprietor to supply him with labour upon fair and reasonable terms. Every thing has hitherto been done to remove the black man from the white, instead of bringing them together, and making them reciprocally beneficial. At present, when the owner of land goes to the Kafirs on his estate to request them to work, they say, "No!" and present their tax-receipt, to show that they have paid what was demanded, and that nothing more is needful; and, when urged to labour, they independently answer that they shall move to some other place, where nothing will be required. But, if the plan here recommended was adopted, they would become respectful, and anxious to please; and, in a short time, every small farmer would have at least one Kafir kraal on his own estate: and, the people being to a great extent under his control, he might gradually encourage them in civilized habits, and induce them to attend a school or place of worship on the sabbath-day. This by some has been thought of little importance, but such is not the fact. Only the other day, when I was in the country, a large number of Kafirs being assembled, they said that the proprietor of the farm had just been to collect the payment for their houses, (five shillings each hut,) and that about the same time the government agent had been to collect seven shillings a hut as the government tax; and that as both came together, they were unable to pay; so that it would be needful to remove to those parts where there was only the government tax to pay, and thus the proprietor of the land would be deprived of that which ought to be to him a fair and reasonable source of income, either in money or labour.

There are some who say that they cannot get either taxes or labour from the people upon their lands. To such I would answer, that if this is the case, it is their own fault; and they, by allowing it, actually do their part to increase the evil against which they so loudly complain. But it is urged, "If we attempt to remove them, they will resist."   Yes, if the present Locations are broken up, and no others provided. But, if the subject is treated in a righteous manner, (as set forth in another part of this Chapter,) there need be no fear on that ground.

But, when they do pay or labour, let the white man proceed towards them in a proper manner. Let him, on the one hand, avoid being tyrannical, not beating them and destroying their houses for slight provocations; and, on the other hand, let him allow no undue familiarity; for, when this is permitted, (which in many instances has been the case among newly-arrived emigrants,) it is most injurious. It at once destroys all due respect, and induces them to take liberties which ought never to be conceded, making them regardless of their employer's commands, and careless in the performance of that which is done; in short, causing them to become bold, forward, idle, and impudent. Let the Kafirs be treated with *kindness* and *firmness*. Let the master give only such orders as his servant is capable of fulfilling; but, when the order is given, let him firmly insist on being obeyed. The Kafir will always try this point; and if he finds he can overcome his employer, he is worth nothing afterwards; but, if the master resolutely insists on being obeyed, the servant will soon learn to respect and obey him.

When a man begins his farming operations, he should first look over his estate; and having determined upon the site for his own residence, let him assign a spot for his Kafirs, where they may not inconvenience him, and yet may at the same time have a suitable home. Often they may be located so as to clear away needless bush, whilst the manure, &c., will be very serviceable to the parties on whose land they reside.

Every one who intends to do any thing in farming pursuits in this country, ought not to leave the subject of Kafir labour to the "chapter of accidents," but be as much concerned to secure a proper supply of Kafirs, and to manage them well, as he is to acquire cattle and farming implements.

Then, I think it a decidedly bad plan for the master to require labour *gratis;* such as, the women to work one day in the week, or the men two months in the year, for nothing. It produces only discontent and quarrels. The Kafir will do his utmost to avoid fulfilling his engagement, and the proprietor will have a ceaseless source of annoyance and trouble. But, having taken their names and numbers, let the latter make an agreement with them to this effect:—First. That if at any time he is short of labourers, he shall be supplied with as many boys, women, or men, as he may want, who are to be paid at the same rate as others. Secondly. That if any of them want work, they shall in every instance ask him first if he requires their services; and if not, then they can go to what other master they like, but on no account without offering their labour to their own landlord.

Let the agreement be properly made,—*before a magistrate, if possible,*—but certainly by some person who knows the Kafir language, and will make them understand the nature of the contract into which they enter. For want of this precaution many are brought into serious difficulties. It may be a little more trouble at first, but this will be amply repaid in the end. Some say that these regulations cannot be carried out; but many have made them, and have had as large and steady a supply of labour as they have required, and that of the cheapest kind. Let the proprietor be also as considerate as possible, in not requiring more labour than is quite needful just at the time at which the Kafirs are busy upon their own lands, when, if called away, they would themselves, to a great extent, be deprived of the means of subsistence.

But what has been hitherto written, has related chiefly to the country, and does not at all apply to the towns, where the want of labour is almost as bad. This must be the case, as a matter of course; for there are *no native towns,*—the government and colonists thus *tacitly avowing that they do not need native labour,* and consequently have made no provision for it. The inhabitants, too, have made no provision for any thing, beyond the accommodation of a few ñaked Kafirs, in huts of the worst description, upon their own premises. In the towns there is scarcely an instance to be found where the master has prepared a small cottage, or a decent room, in which his servants can live; nor would they be of any service for naked Kafirs, who prefer the hut to the cottage.

But the heathen Natives are not the only people in the employment of the white man; there are also clothed Christian Kafirs, and a considerable number of Hottentots and ex-slaves, who speak the Dutch language, and who have been almost the only people in service during the last few months; but, instead of the white man trying to raise them in civilization, (about which many talk so much, and do so little,) now that they are raised so as to drive his waggon, thatch his house, wear clothes of British manufacture, and use the same kind of food as himself,—spending the money they earn, not in buying wives, but in purchasing that which the merchants and store-keepers sell, and thus making their money beneficial to the community, &c.,—they have no place in which to live but the most wretched hut, not fit for human beings to inhabit; and they can have no other, the master not being willing either to build a cottage, or to allow his people to do it; so that, whilst his horse must have a stable, his servant may sleep in a hovel, or in the kraal or the bush.

Besides, most of the settlers are not willing to have these native establishments upon their premises, because of the company that they have in the evenings; so that young people who have been brought up in the towns, and know how to work, when they get married, *are obliged* to leave and go to live upon some mission-station, or somewhere else, where they can build their houses and dwell securely. Then many begin to cry out against these stations, as being the resorts of the idle, &c.

This is not theory, but fact. Many Natives have thus left; and more, that are now in the towns, will soon follow, if something is not done to prevent it.

Take the case of my own servant-boy, Luke, who has been in my employ for three years, is well clothed, talks a little English, reads the Kafir Scriptures, performs all the work of our kitchen, sets out our table, cleans our shoes, knives and forks, grooms my horse, &c. He is about to be married to a Kafir girl, who speaks English, is well clothed, performs all sorts of household work, and is in every way a most valuable household servant. In a few weeks they will be married, and then they will have to leave the town in the same way. Twenty or thirty more instances I might adduce. Young women from the country stations should not be brought into the towns, because they are in danger of being quickly seduced and ruined. Men may talk in folly as they please about these people being on their own master's ground; but the solitude they will not endure: besides, they look upon it as next to slavery.

But how may this be remedied? Why, in the first place, let there be a tract of land selected for a native town, in connexion with each English town.   Let it be at a short distance from the English settlement, and yet sufficiently near for the people to be at their employment at an early hour.   Let the land be sub-divided into small allotments, large enough for a small cottage and garden.   Let a few plain rules be made, and the whole be placed under the care of the magistrate, or some other suitable person.   Let the people *not become actual possessors of the land by gift;* but, if they are able to purchase, let them do so at a reasonable rate; if not, let them have the land on loan, so long as they comply with the regulations of the place.   If this was done, it would soon be found that a large number of persons would be collected together, who would be *dependent* for their *subsistence upon their labour in the service of the white man;* and, instead of respectable English families being obliged to have naked heathen Kafir men to nurse their children, or to nurse themselves, they would have girls decently dressed for that pur-pose.   The price of labour would also quickly be reduced.

How is it in the old Colony, where labour is not either so scarce or so dear as in this? the common price of clothed female servants (coloured) being about six or seven shillings a month, and of male servants from seven to fifteen shillings *per* month. The reason is, that, in most cases, they are allowed to squat about the towns; and the English would rather permit this, than be placed in the painful state of destitution which exists in Natal. There are hundreds, if not thousands, of these squatters about Graham's Town, the capital of the Eastern Province; and one of the first acts of Sir H. Young, the last lieutenant-governor, was, to reduce these to order, and bring them under wholesome laws; and had not that valuable officer been so quickly removed to govern another Colony, he would doubtless have conferred one of the greatest boons upon that Colony, in this particular, which it was capable of receiving.   Whilst the present war has been raging, thousands of these natives, Fingoes and others, have been amongst the most efficient supporters and defenders of the British government.

The squatting system has many evils, arising from the fact of
so large a number of natives being promiscuously collected together
without being placed under any proper control, whereby they may
do much mischief, as well as some good.   But let there be native
towns, placed under the regulation of a few wholesome laws, and
the effect will soon be most beneficial to all the parties concerned.
These native servants have been represented as the worst characters, and guilty of the gravest crimes.   Doubtless, many evil-
disposed persons have been among them, and crimes have been
committed; but, at the same time, many of the best servants
have been found in their ranks; and, they being adjacent to the
towns, justice could, in most instances, be quickly obtained, and
punishment inflicted upon the guilty.   Not only so, but these
are proper objects for the government to bestow care upon, and
it should not leave them to work evil without law, order, or
restraint.   This is a vital subject to the prosperity of a Colony,
and to the comfort of all classes of the community.

I am aware that various objections and difficulties will be
started; but what of that?   Was ever any thing great or good
accomplished without exertion?   Will it not require much effort
and expense to import Coolies, &c. ?   Certainly it will.

The government will object to the taxation being limited to
government lands, as it will affect the revenue; but I have
always thought that—in theory, at all events—the government
existed for the benefit of the Colony, and not the Colony for the
support of the government.   True, the government must be
supported; but surely there are ways of doing so without
stopping the progress of the Colony.   A country prospers when
the governor and the governed proceed harmoniously together;
but when they clash, the worst consequences follow.

Against a native town it will be objected, that the natives ought
to buy land, &c.   But this is impossible at the present high rates
at which *erven* are selling.   Besides, it would soon be objected
that the property of the white man was depreciated in the neighbourhood where the Natives were residing.   But if land could be
bought at reasonable rates in the native towns, there would be an
inducement for the people to become landed proprietors; and,
before many years had passed away, not a few would be found in
the possession of their own houses and their own land.

Other difficulties will present themselves; but there is not one of them which may not be overcome, and that, probably, with less effort than might at first be supposed.

The subject is of vital importance; and every one who has the least desire for the advancement of the Colony ought to put forth his energies, and do his part,—not fold his arms in cold supineness, finding fault with every body and every thing, whilst he is himself helping to make bad worse. Natal, as well as " England, expects every man to do his duty!"

In the preceding pages I have called attention, First, to the great want of certain labour; and, Secondly, to the anomaly and impropriety of governing the Natives by Kafir law, through the medium of Kafir chiefs, with its consequent dangers and evils. I have endeavoured, Thirdly, to show that, whilst we have no righteous authority to compel the Aborigines to labour, and form settled and industrious habits, there are certain plans which, if adopted, may work powerfully towards such a desirable end, as offering to the Natives a great inducement to engage in steady labour. One of these plans is, to take off the tax which is at present levied on the Natives living upon a farmer's lands, by which he is deprived of a fair and legitimate source of income, either from the labour or rent of the Natives. By such a remission of taxation the relative position of the two parties would be so altered, as to render it the *interest* of the Kafir to place himself under the control of the white man; while his disposition would be strengthened to submit to steady labour, and adopt orderly habits, detaching himself from his Kafir chief, and by degrees acquiring an interest in the white man's prosperity, which would become identical with his own, and cause the white to amalgamate with the black. Fourthly, I have pointed out, that this result would also be greatly accelerated by the removal of witchcraft, and the gross evil of polygamy, with as little delay and in as effectual a manner as possible. By the abolition of polygamy the male portion of the Kafirs would be obliged to work, instead of being supported in independent idleness by the severe labours of their oppressed wives.

Then, in reference to the towns, it has been shown that every thing has hitherto been done to *drive labour from the towns,* instead of *bringing labour into them.* But let native towns be formed, and placed upon a proper basis, in connexion with the English towns, and it will quickly be seen that, instead of the present uncertain supply of naked Kafirs from the country, a sufficient number of civilized and clothed coloured persons will be at hand, not only to supply labour, but to do it on reasonable terms. But let us not blame the Native for that which is the result of our own folly and selfishness.

Let it not be supposed that evils which have been growing for five or six years will be removed in as many hours or days. No; things must first be placed on a proper basis, and then have time to work out their own legitimate consequences. Nor will it happen that every individual case will be met; but the general state of things will be such as to allow the public in general to obtain the labour that they require for the purposes which they wish to accomplish.

The fact, however, must not be overlooked, that there are probably, upon an average, taking the whole year round, not less than four or five thousand Kafirs in the employ of the white colonists: the evil mostly consists in the *uncertainty* of labour, and in its not being of the *kind* frequently desired.

Since the publication of these statements in my Pamphlet, important changes in the government of the Natives have taken place. The authority of the native chiefs has been greatly lessened, and the power of the English magistrate increased; which is a very valuable change. Kafir law has also been placed in abeyance, and English law brought into greater prominence and better operation. Witchcraft has been less tolerated, and polygamy, as a crying evil, has attracted attention, which will lead to the adoption of measures for its removal.

By these important and great changes in the management of the Natives, the governor has manifested his desire to remove existing evil and prevent future danger, and is so far entitled to the thanks of the colonists. It is also stated that a general plan is in course of preparation by which to make still greater alterations, especially with reference to the Locations: but what this plan may be, is not yet fully known, and therefore it is not before us as a proper subject of public investigation and discussion. We can only, for the present, treat upon such parts of the plan

as have been stated privately and officially to different individuals.

It has been alleged in private circles that it was the intention
of government to give *five acres* of land to "each Kafir." I
know not whether children are included, and whether there would
be given a title to the land, and power to sell if the party pleased.
It has been stated officially by the lieutenant-governor to a
deputation of American missionaries,—who waited upon him to
ascertain what were the intentions of the government on this
subject,—that the Locations would be cut up, and the Natives
scattered; that there were only about thirteen thousand who had
any proper claim to land, and their claim would be regarded; and,
further, that he could not engage that the Location land should
not be taken from the Natives, and appropriated to other purposes, to within fifty rods (one hundred yards) of the mission
premises.

Before entering upon the discussion of these propositions, I
shall extract some passages from official records made by the
local government, at the time when the different claims of
respective parties were being considered and settled by the
government, and when the English took possession of the
country.

In order that the number of Natives might be correctly ascertained, and their claims equitably considered, a Commission for
Locating the Natives was formed, consisting of Dr. Stanger, the
surveyor-general; T. Shepstone, Esq., diplomatic agent for the
Natives; Lieutenant Gibb, of the Royal Engineers; with the
Rev. N. Adams, and the Rev. D. Lindley, of the American
mission.

The Instructions to these gentlemen were furnished by His
Honour Martin West, the lieutenant-governor, in a public
document written in 1846, which was partly based upon the
Instructions given by the Cape government to Colonel Cloete,
her majesty's commissioner for considering the various claims for
land, in May, 1843, and reporting upon them; and in which it
is stated "that the first duty of the commissioner there appointed
was to inquire into and report upon the number of farmers and
others holding land in the district of Natal, and of the extent of
it, with a view to their receiving grants of it from the crown."

Section VII. of the same Instructions sets forth, "The preamble of the same Proclamation (of his excellency in 1843) declares that the object of her majesty's government was the peace, preservation, and salutary control of all classes of men settled at and surrounding that important portion of South Africa;" and both in the Instructions and Proclamation it is laid down as an "absolutely essential and absolutely indispensable condition," "that there shall not be in the eye of the law any distinction or disqualification whatever formed on mere distinction of colour, origin, language, or creed; but that the protection of the law, in letter and in substance, should be extended impartially to all."

Section IX. states, "The commissioner was, at the same time, instructed to make it known that her majesty's government and the colonial government will spare no pains to secure protection and justice to the native tribes around Natal; and that they are not to be restricted in locating themselves to any particular spot or district; nor are they to be excluded from occupying any land whatever which remains at the disposal of the crown. The government will neither disturb them, nor allow them to be disturbed, in their occupations or selections." "It is not probable that the Natives will apply to government for grants of the land they now hold, or may hereafter occupy. The advantage of such titles will not occur to their ignorant minds; but if they should, or government should consider that the issue of these will afford greater enjoyment and protection to the Native in his possession, they will undoubtedly receive them, precisely as would the farmer or any other persons."

Section XI. declares that, as to "the claims of the Natives to lands they either held or occupied, (in May, 1843,) it does not appear that it was intended that those claims should be the subject of requisition, with a view to the issue of titles; and, consequently, no requisition appears to have been made by the commissioner of the claims which the Natives had either acquired by occupation previous to May, 1843, or of those arising from selection subsequent to that date."

In Section XIII. it is said, "These people, perhaps to the number of from 80,000 to 100,000, are scattered over a territory which seems to afford an abundant space of most fertile country for them, as well as for a dense European population."

In Sections XX., XXI., and XXII., it is stated that "the public has also been pledged to protect these claimants (farmers) in the occupation of their particular lands." "The public has also been pledged to the Natives not to disturb them in the selection and occupation of any lands remaining at the disposal of the crown." "It is the chief object of your appointment to see that the public faith is kept with both parties; and, where any difficulties may present themselves, from the isolated position of the selections which have been made, either by Europeans or Kafirs, to propose to government, by way of compromise, such an exchange as shall be satisfactory, especially *to the parties removing*." "His honour is of opinion that the total removal of the Kafirs to the east and west, as proposed by the late *Volksraad*, is neither desirable nor practicable; but he is disposed to concur with Mr. Cloete in the general expediency of separate locations, in the best disposable situations, providing they are well defined, and not too distant from the present abodes of the Natives who may be induced to occupy them, and that they afford sufficient space for such a number of Natives (from 5,000 to 10,000) as may be hereafter conveniently superintended by one magistrate, and placed under the pastoral care of one or two missionaries."

Here, then, in these extracts, we have set forth before us some fundamental principles, and government acts and pledges of public faith, with respect to the Natives of the Natal Colony.

But before making remark or comment upon this important subject, we wish to premise that what is written is not on the ground of *philanthropy*, but of right. I shall not discuss the subject as a missionary, who might be regarded as a special pleader, but as an English farmer or a Dutch claimant,—on the ground of actual right. These parties have not thought it out of place to carry on years of discussion and strife in the local papers and with the local government, in great numbers, and with untiring perseverance: let them not, then, be displeased, and use hard names, if an individual should raise his feeble voice, or use his silent pen, not to deprive the one party of what they think they righteously possess, but to place the claims of the other in a correct light; and the more so, as the latter have not the means of doing it for themselves.

Let it, then, be distinctly borne in mind, that the position I take is public ground,—the first law of nations,—the rights of men and duties of governments. Let it not be said that the righteous settlement of the question of native land-claims has nothing to do with the government of the Natives. Have not both the English and the Dutch in this Colony urged, again and again, that the interests of the Colony and of the inhabitants have been most seriously retarded by the long non-settlement of their claims? And now that they are met and satisfied, have they not, again and again, declared that it was for the benefit of all parties, and that the government has only done a slow and tardy duty in setting this important question at rest? I would not find fault with them for the course they have adopted, nor take away one "iota" from the value they have received; but I maintain the same right to set forth the claims of one hundred thousand Natal inhabitants, who have been *bonâ fide*, to all intents and purposes, the party chiefly concerned in these transactions, and have been treated as such in all the arrangements of the government, yea, and whose claims must be equitably settled, or the curse of Heaven and the damage of the Colony must be the inevitable result.

Let not a fair, manly, earnest, and faithful treatment of the subject, in stating facts and engagements, and reasoning upon them, be placed to the account of anger, bitterness, opposition to the government, or disloyalty to the queen. I entirely disavow all intention to indulge in any expression which would convey any meaning of this kind, and will yield the palm to no man in loyalty to the queen and the government of my country.

Having thus cleared my way by stating distinctly the position which I take, and the manner in which I propose to treat this subject, I proceed to observe, First, that when the commissioners had received these instructions from their government, they proceeded to select such tracts of country as they thought most suitable for the Natives, taking care to choose, as far as possible, all those lands which were the most barren and rocky, and which were not suitable for the use of the white man. These, of course, must and did include some fertile spots, as they ought to do; but the rule which guided the commissioners was, I believe, to take in, whenever and wherever they could, all the worst land, (that is, the worst for the white man,) and such as must have been the resort of wild animals,—elephants, lions, tigers, and wolves, which would have acted as a scourge on the Colony and farmers. The general boundaries of the lands thus selected were defined, submitted to the local government, and afterwards to the home government, and approved; and were again confirmed by the land commission appointed by his excellency Sir H. Smith, in 1848, which sat for one year to consider the claims of the Dutch Farmers, and reported and decided upon them. Their recommendations have been carried out, and titles are now issued to these claimants. This commission had not the slightest connexion with the one for locating the Natives, which was dissolved for the purpose of removing every impediment out of the way of settling the claims of the Farmers. Being thus unfettered, they not only confirmed the recommendations of the previous commission for locating the Natives, with some slight alterations, but proposed that, in addition, two other small Locations should be fixed for the Natives.

We have, therefore, First, the instruction of his excellency, Sir G. Napier, when governor of the Cape, to the commissioner, Colonel Cloete, that "the commissioner should make it known, that her majesty's government and the colonial government will spare no pains to secure protection and justice to the native tribes around Natal; and that they are not to be restricted in locating themselves to any particular spot or district; nor are they to be excluded from occupying any land whatever which remains at the disposal of the crown." "The government will neither disturb them, nor allow them to be disturbed, in their occupations or selections;" and if either the Natives should think proper to apply for titles, or the government to give them, "they will undoubtedly receive them,—precisely as would the farmer, or any other person." "There shall not be, in the eye of the law, any distinction or disqualification whatever formed on mere distinction of colour, origin, language, or creed; but the protection of the law in letter and in substance shall be extended impartially to all." And further: "The public has also been pledged to the Natives not to disturb them in the selection and occupation of any lands at the disposal of the crown." Such were some of the instructions to the first commissioner appointed by the Cape government.

Secondly. The commissioners for locating the Natives were appointed in 1846, with these instructions before them, as the basis on which they were impartially to act towards all claimants. What words can be plainer and stronger than these?—" It is the chief object of your appointment to see that the public faith is kept with both parties; and, where any difficulties may present themselves, from the isolated position of the selections which have been made, either by Europeans or Kafirs, to propose to government, by way of compromise, such an exchange as shall be satisfactory, especially *to the parties removing.*"   " His honour is of opinion that the total removal of the Kafirs to the east and west, as proposed by the late Volksraad, is neither desirable nor practicable; but is disposed to concur with Mr. Cloete in the general expediency of separate Locations, in the best disposable situations, providing they are well defined, and not too distant from the present abodes of the Natives who may be induced to occupy them; and that they afford sufficient space for such a number of Natives, (from 5,000 to 10,000,) as may be hereafter conveniently superintended by one magistrate, and placed under the pastoral care of one or two missionaries."

Thirdly. The number for whom provision is to be made is fixed.   " These people, perhaps to the number of from 80,000 to 100,000, are scattered over a territory which seems to afford an abundant space of most fertile country for them and a dense European population."

Fourthly. With these instructions before them, the commissioners proceeded to select tracts of country; on the coast, three, which are designated the Umlazi, the Inanda, and the Umvoti locations; and near to Pietermaritzburg, the Zwartkops; to which has since been added a small one on the Ilovo.

These were to be increased to the number of ten. But the Impafana, the Umzinyati, and the Quahlamba Locations, as marked on Dr. Stanger's map, and also on the map of the Colony appended to this volume, have never been given out to the Natives at all; or, if so, in so indefinite a manner as to be of no, avail. On these three large tracts of the Colony not a single missionary has yet been placed; and, for the whole of the upper division of the Colony, only one magistrate for the Kafirs has been appointed; whilst two more Locations advised by the commissioners are not yet fixed upon at all.

Fifthly. The provision being thus given, the Natives were informed of what was done, and directed by government authority to leave the lands on which they were living, and take possession of those assigned them; receiving assurance that "the English government would neither disturb them, nor allow them to be disturbed in their occupation."

Sixthly, follows the land commission appointed by his excellency Sir H. Smith in 1848; when, the previous commission being dissolved, they for one year hear the different claimants, and determine upon their merits, confirming the decisions of the former commissions, with some slight alterations; and recommending that two additional Locations should be formed in the upper division of the Colony for the Natives, whilst they decide upon the claims of the Boers and others.

Seventhly. The present governor paid a visit to the Zwartkops Location, in company with the bishop of Cape Town, on June 26th, 1850; and the latter observes, in his Journal:—"A neighbouring chief, with his tribe, came to greet the governor. He complained that the white man was daily encroaching upon his location, and that he was uncertain whether he would be allowed to stay on his land. The governor told him that, so long as he and his people did well, they need not be afraid of any; that he was to remain upon his location, and would not be disturbed. Upon inquiry of Mr. Davis, he stated that the land commission had given farms to individuals within the limits of the location, the boundaries of which had been fixed, by proclamation, by the late governor. It appears absolutely necessary that some steps should be taken to secure to the Natives the lands which have been assigned them."*

And again: "I should here observe, that the local government, acting under the instructions of Earl Grey, who takes a deep interest in the welfare of the Natives, is about to fix the whole coloured population in ten Locations. This had been decided upon for some time; but it has never yet been carried out, and the Natives are quite uncertain as to the proper bound-

* "Journal of the Bishop of Cape Town."

aries of their reserves.   The Report of the committee appointed
for locating them, dated so far back as March, 1847, strongly
recommends that all lands set apart for the Natives should be
vested in trustees for their use.   I believe this to be a point of
great importance.   Unless it be done, the Natives will be gradually deprived of their lands.   No local government will be able
to withstand the restless and insatiable demands of the white
man, even if its own wants did not tempt it to sell, from time to
time, under various pretences which will always be forthcoming,
property which has no legal owner, and is in the hands of government.   The question is one which demands immediate attention,
and should not be postponed."*

Eighthly. Then comes emigration, and a tremendous stir is
made about these "leviathan Locations and Zulu refuges;" and
the commissioners for locating the Natives are loaded with abuse.
A proposition is then made to appoint a commission to inquire
into their conduct.   The public mind is inflamed, and missions
are scandalized.   Location commissioners and Christian missionaries, civilized Kafirs and black savages, are all held up to execra-
tion; and the man who dares to speak a word in their favour at
once loses caste among his fellows.

Ninthly. At length we arrive at the last disclosure,—the
climax,—the consummation :—13,000 Kafirs are entitled to lands,
and shall have *five acres* each; and the remaining 78,000 are to
be scattered to the winds or the wolves; the Locations are to be
cut up, and the mission-grounds pared down to within fifty rods
of the mission-house !   This was the grand consummation of a
long course of misgovernment.

There has ever appeared to the writer to have been an error
on the part of the commissioners in making the Locations so
large, and consequently so few.   Had they been smaller and
more numerous, and placed at greater distances from each other
through the whole Colony, I believe it would have been decidedly
better.   But it is not now too late for this to be done, and it is a
thing which ought to be done immediately.

His Honour Martin West (the then lieutenant-governor)
concurred with Mr. Cloete as to the "expediency of separate

---

* "Journal of the Bishop of Cape Town."

Locations in the best disposable situations, providing that they are well defined, and not too distant from the present abodes of the Natives, who might be induced to occupy them; and that they afford sufficient space for such a number of Natives (from 5,000 to 10,000) as may be hereafter conveniently superintended by one magistrate, and placed under the pastoral care of one or two missionaries," with an *industrial agent*, (as we have in another place advocated,) to assist in the civilizing process.

But the notion, that the quantity of land proposed to be allotted to the Natives is too large, is totally unfounded, as will appear from the following computations :—The commissioners proposed that the three large coast Locations, which are those mostly complained of, should contain about 1,240 square miles, and a population of about 30,000 souls. This would give a fraction more than 24 persons to the square mile, which is a population to the square mile of 21 persons more than the Cape Colony averages,—greater by 20 than that of North America,— greater by 22 than that of South America,—greater by 19 than that of Africa,—and greater than the average of any other in the whole world by 8 souls to the square mile. This average, of course, is less than that of Europe, or of many European states ; where the people are crowded to suffocation, and where many live not upon the soil, but by their trades, their capital, or their commerce. But it must be remembered that the habits of this people are agricultural and nomadic. Of trade, commerce, and mechanical arts they know nothing; neither have they the means of following them, had they the requisite knowledge. For the present, until they can be gradually raised to these pursuits, they must live as they do, by their cattle, and by cultivating the earth. They have certainly a right so to live, and to the means necessary for so living, at all events until they are acquainted with other modes of obtaining a livelihood, and of their own free-will choose those modes. Twenty-four persons to a square mile will give about 26⅔ acres to an individual. It must not, however, be thought that all of these 26 acres is adapted for either cultivation, pasturage, or any thing else. *It is not :* much of it, as we have said, is barren, broken, precipitous, and rocky; fit only for the owl and the eagle, the baboon and the jackal. "A great part of them" (the Locations) "are only fit for the residence of Kafirs, from the unevenness of the country; and, were they not inhabited by them, would soon become such a den of wild beasts as would be a great scourge to the adjacent farms."* All those lands, as well as others, are occasionally visited with severe drought, and by destructive swarms of locusts, to say nothing of other wasting insects, and animals, of various kinds. To attempt, therefore, to shut up this agricultural and pastoral people to the narrow limits of such land, would be merely an attempt to shut them up to death, or to mutual contention and destruction, and drive them to plunder the cattle and horses of those about them, and thus to seal their doom, in annihilation, as a people.

But the above allowance of 26⅔ acres to each Native does not give a fair view of the state of things which is the subject of present consideration. The amount of population on the three coast Locations, for which no other provision has been made, is now about 50,000. But while the population has been thus increasing in numbers on the Locations, the Locations have been diminished; and some of the best parts of them, as proposed by the original commissioners, have been cut off and made over to white emigrants. We know not the exact sum of these reductions, though we are well acquainted with the parts of land cut off, and suppose they may amount to 150 square miles. This would make the present extent of the Locations something less than 1,100 square miles. But 1,100 square miles for 50,000 inhabitants, give a population of about 45 souls to the square mile for the Natives in Natal; while the population of the Cape Colony, both East and West, is only 2½ to the square mile, including coloured and white. That of Africa, as a whole, is only 5 to the square mile; North America, 4; South America, 2; Asia, 28; the Chinese Empire, only 43; Sweden and Norway, 13; Russia and Poland, 28; and that of the whole habitable globe, only 16 to the square mile. That is, the Kafir population allotted to a square mile in the Natal Locations is three times as large as that of the average throughout the entire world! Surely too much land is not set aside for the Natives of Natal.

As matters at present stand, notwithstanding all that has been said about these " gigantic," these "leviathan Locations," the pro-

---

* " S. D. J.," in the " Natal Witness," February 9th, 1849.

bability is, that—taking the proportion of white and black population, and including in the white all the emigrants that have
come out—there are in the hands of the white man one hundred
acres of land to one acre of land occupied by the Kafir. No
"petting" the Kafir here, or giving him land at the expense of
the white man! nay, it is the black that gives it to the white;
or rather, it is the white who helps himself.

We now come to consider the governor's proposition of cutting
up the Locations, and giving the 13,000 Kafirs titles to five acres
of land, whilst the remaining 78,000 or 100,000 are to be scattered abroad without any allotment. We have shown from
official records, 1. That both Dutch and Kafir were admitted as
claimants for land, by the British government, *on equal terms*.
2. That there was to be "no distinction or disqualification in the
eye of the law, arising from colour, origin, creed, or language."
3. "That the claims of 80,000 or 100,000 *were admitted*." 4.
That they were to receive the titles to their lands in the same
way as the whites, if they desired it, and if it would give them
more enjoyment and security. 5. That, in the absence of these,
a commission was appointed, who first selected and defined the
lands, and then directed the people upon them. 6. That "*the
public faith is pledged*" to the fulfilment of these engagements.
We do not again quote in this place from existing public records;
but if doubt on these points exists in the mind of any one, let
him consult for himself the documents and quotations already
given, (pp. 192, 195,) and he will find there recorded all that is
here stated, and much more.

We come now to place the Boer and the Kafir side by side at the
door of the Colonial Office. The former is interrogated, "What
do you want, Sir?" "O, *only a six-thousand acre farm, Sir*, as
I lived *twelve months*, Sir, on yonder hill, and am thereby entitled
to it." "Yes, Sir, your claim shall be considered; and if fully
made out and supported, you shall receive it."

The poor Kafir waits long to get a hearing; but at length the
opportunity is given, and the question is asked, "Well, what is
it? What do you want?" "Only that piece of land on the
Ilovo or Umtwalumi river, where I was born, and where my
father and friends lived, until Tshaka came and conquered us,
and drove us away; but I have now been sitting there for many

moons. My father was murdered by Tshaka, and his bones lie
by such a river; and my friends, who were taken into Zulu-land,
have now returned," *(alias,* are "Zulu refugees," as some falsely
name them,) "and we wish to sit down in peace." "Yes, yes! Your
claim shall be considered; and if you make out a good case, you
shall have *five acres* of land:"—a princely grant, when compared
with that made to his fat friend, who has got six thousand acres
of land, which belonged to the father and friends of the Native,
and of his brother, who, perhaps, is now fighting for the English
in the Frontier war! This proposition, under the peculiar circumstances, and carried out as shown in the previous remarks on the
quantity of land, is so bad, that I must not allow myself to designate
it in suitable language. Does not a noble, manly Englishman feel
himself dishonoured by the proposition? and must not our good
queen feel that she is put to shame by some of her servants?

Give a Kafir five acres of that land to which he has an hereditary right; (as I shall prove elsewhere;) and what is such a pit-
tance to him, or to the Boer, both of whom have been accustomed
to look around, and feel that they were "monarchs of all they
surveyed?" Pin the man down to five acres of land, who has
been accustomed from time immemorial to walk through the whole
country as the rightful possessor of it, and to claim it for himself
and fathers,—preposterous! As well might you attempt to fix
the Englishman on five yards of his own land, and forbid him to
move; or tell the Boer, as he walks in state over his six thousand
acres, and feasts his eyes on the extent of his possessions, " *Five
acres* are all that you are entitled to."

As to "titles," what do the Natives know or care about them?
Nothing at all; they are like so much waste paper. But I have
lately heard of an exception to this general rule: I have been
informed, on good authority, that Umnini has made application
for a "title" to land. This is the hereditary chief of the large
Amatuli tribe, which was distinguished by the name of *Ama-
fengu,* on account of their living near the sea, in the bushy
and rocky parts to the west of the Bay, hiding themselves here,
and feeding upon shell-fish, roots, &c., during the invasions of
Tshaka, who was never able to subdue them. When I first
visited him in company with the Rev. John Richards, formerly
the Wesleyan minister at Pietermaritzburg, we found him, even

in this time of peace, in a large kraal in the middle of a dense bush, where we might have searched for him in vain at a period of warfare and danger.   His title to his lands, which he has occupied, with his fathers and people, from "moons" untold, was fully admitted by the British government; but since emigration has set in, his lands have been looked upon as too valuable for the black man, on account of their proximity to the Bay and town, and he has been obliged to move his quarters; whilst a portion of his land has been knocked down under the auctioneer's hammer, and Mr. Ogle, an old English settler of Farewell's time, has a farm of 6,000 acres close by.

The following extracts are from the Journal of the Bishop of Cape Town :—

"June 9th, 1850. I have heard to-day, from a lady who lives in the neighbourhood, that the chief Umnini, of whom I have before spoken, removed from his lands on the Bluff last Friday. He came to bid her farewell before he left; for they had been kind neighbours to each other. 'It was not without sorrow that he quitted his birth-place, where he has resided all his life, and withstood in his fastnesses the victorious troops of Tshaka, who conquered the whole country, and brought into subjection all the native chiefs, except this one and another. But now we want his land. It is important for our growing settlement at D'Urban that it should be in our possession; therefore he must go.   He is weak, and we are strong.'

"If we are to pursue the system which we have already in some degree adopted towards the Native tribes, the same judgments from a just God which have already overtaken the Boers for their cruelties and injustice to the poor heathen, will assuredly come upon us. I fear we are treading in their steps."*

And, when leaving the Colony, the Bishop again writes :—

"July 1st.—One most important question is that of the coloured population. It is essential for the sake of the whole Colony, white as well as black, that well-considered and well-digested plans should be adopted for the moral, religious, and social improvement of the Natives; and should the present time be allowed to slip by, there will be no possibility of redeeming it."

---

* " Visitation Tour," p. 58.

Umnini, with his people, has now moved thirty miles lower down the coast, betwixt the Ilovo and Umkomazi rivers; and a gentleman of great respectability has informed me that he has applied for the title-deeds for his land. But if he obtains them, on *what scale* are they to be given, whether *for five acres or for five thousand?* The tribe of which he is chief once occupied nearly the whole country from the Umgeni to the Umkomazi, and, some say, as far inland as Pietermaritzburg; the great chief living near the present site of New Germany. Is this man, then, who is the only natural and lawful heir to the whole of these parts, to be pared down to five acres of land, and his people in the same proportion? or, when he has occupied his present locality awhile, is he to be driven still further back, and his land to be brought to the auctioneer's hammer? Would this be English justice or liberality? I trow not.

We would not say, Give him 6,000 or 3,000 acres of land; but, Give him and his people a block of land of *ample space* for them to live upon, to grow their corn and graze their cattle; so that they may not, from the pressure of narrow limits, be tempted to steal the white man's cattle or goods. When the Colony was taken by the English, this chief had about fifty large kraals; and, during these ten years of peace, the number of his people must greatly have increased. Allowing ten huts to a kraal, and four persons to a hut, this would give 2,000 people at that time; to whom must now be added all who have returned, together with the natural increase of population, making possibly 5,000 people at the present time. These would constitute a small Location, such as the late Martin West contemplated, which could be efficiently and conveniently managed by one magistrate; to whom should be added an industrial agent; whilst the Christian churches would supply one or more missionaries. *The whole of the boundary-lines ought to be definitely fixed, and the title-deeds made out, and held sacred and inviolable;* a copy being placed in the chief's hands, or deposited with trustees, and the original in the Colonial Office.

What is thus done in this case should be done in other places, and these small Locations be multiplied through the Colony; whilst the large ones should be reduced in size, and brought into manageable dimensions. Let magistrates of good character, and suitable industrial agents, be appointed; let the census of the population be annually taken, crimes be punished, and contracts enforced: the magistrate then becomes the acknowledged and authorized head or chief of the tribe or people, and British law the guide and rule of conducting business and punishing crime; so that, being reduced to order, the native tribes may become a useful and happy people.

If this land question is not satisfactorily settled, *faith is broken with the people*, and the government has no fair basis on which to work. If a just settlement is not made speedily, the people will be provoked and chafed, and will say that the white Englishman is Tshaka in another form. The savage Zulu took their country, and scattered and destroyed the people: the civilized Englishman now does the same thing in another way. " He has taken our country, and the country of our fathers, so that we have not now a foot of land on which to live; and we may therefore as well die fighting against him, and wreaking our vengeance upon him, as be forced into exile, or starved into slavery."

But let the English government take the fair and honourable ground here advocated, and they at once attach the Natives to their nation and government. Give the Kafir an interest in the country and soil, which he will defend, and for which he will die; and this large number of Natives then becomes a strong wall of defence against the Zulu on the east, and the Amaxosa on the west, instead of a source of continual danger and alarm. Better feed them with just and lawful grants of their own land than with English powder and shot,—with British treasure and blood. Better make them a body-guard of defence around us, than a race of plunderers and murderers in our midst. Let it not be forgotten that in the last three Kafir wars on the frontier of the Cape Colony, thousands of these people have fought our battles and braved danger with us; have been part of our best and most efficient armies, and, by hundreds, if not thousands, have died in our cause.

But it is objected that these are " Zulu refugees." The fallacy and incorrectness of this assertion I shall not attempt here at length to point out, but will do so in a subsequent volume, on the Natives, where the historical and statistical information will be given, and this legitimate ground of right to a full share of the

soil pointed out.   I will only adduce in this place a statement of
what has already been ascertained upon the Inanda Location.
The whole number of kraals belonging to this Location are
1,176 ; the number of huts, 5,214 ; besides 17 belonging to those
who have received the truths of Christianity, and are professed
Christians.   Of the above 1,176 kraals, 929 *belong to the Natal
tribes, and fragments of tribes,* all here *long before* Natal became
a British Colony.   This leaves 247, mostly of an unknown origin,
probably belonging to tribes of Aborigines who were here before
Tshaka's invasion ; thus allowing only very few who can have
emigrated from Zulu-land, and proving to a demonstration that
those who have been coming into the Colony for some time past,
and have been represented as "Zulu refugees," were none others
than those who had been before driven from it by Tshaka, and
are now returning to the land of their fathers, the only place in
this wide world to which they can be considered as having any
legitimate right or title.

The Kafir has a very strong attachment to the land which he
looks upon as his own, where he was born, and where his father
lived before him.   Let him be wherever he may, he never forgets
it ; and, if he has an opportunity, he will return to it.

But setting this altogether aside as irrelevant to the question,
we state, First. That this whole country was formerly the property of the Kafir, and not of the English.   Secondly. That
though Tshaka, by his desolating wars, has scattered most of its
people, yet as soon as they could again collect, they did so ; and
that most of those now in the Colony are the collected fragments
of tribes once scattered.   Thirdly. That, omitting all reference
to this, it was stated by the commissioners for locating the
Natives, that there were 100,000 to be provided for, and the
arrangements were made on this admission.   Here, then, whatever was or was not before, the claims of 100,000 to British
protection and provision were fairly and fully admitted by the
British government.   A committee was appointed to select the
lands ; and they did select ; and the order was given by the
British functionaries for the Kafirs to move from other parts,
and take up their abode upon the lands assigned them, with the
assurance that those lands were set apart for their sole use.

This was done in 1846.   When, in 1852, it is asserted that

there are only 13,000 to be provided for, by what process of fair argumentation such a conclusion can be arrived at, I cannot tell : for, as most affirm, the number of Natives has been increasing, and not diminishing, since that time; and no overt acts of violence, theft, or war, or refusal to pay taxes, have taken place, by which they might have forfeited what was then allowed and given. We have, therefore, no open way whatever of taking from them what was then given, except on the ground of, " Might is right."

Now I maintain that, setting philanthropy and religion aside, the English government is bound, in honour, and justice, and truth, to carry out its own engagements. It is bad for a private individual to break faith with a Native; but for a great Christian nation to break faith with 87,000 Natal Kafirs, is an offence of such fearful magnitude, that honour and justice stand abashed before it. Surely our beloved queen will never allow the records of this great nation to be darkened and polluted by a deed of such wholesale wrong!

I have ever believed that the Locations were too large for the well-working of the interests of Natal: but if they are lessened, others should be provided, as the case may require. Meanwhile, let the demand be made as small as possible, by every facility being given to the Native to enter into the industrious relationships of civilized life. If the present Locations are to be greatly diminished, land should be given for Native Towns near the English towns, or in the midst of an English population; by which means amalgamation may go on. But it is wrong, in every aspect, to drive them back into the interior, where no elevating process can be in operation, and where, like the wild beasts, they must ultimately melt away before the face of the civilized white man. The sons of Japheth have entered into the tents of Ham: let it not be to destroy, but to save.

Whilst writing on this subject, I would point out another glaring act of wrong and injustice, which is proposed to be inflicted, in connexion with missionary operations. When the American and other missionaries commenced their operations on the Locations, it was with the full understanding that they should *not be disturbed* in them; that, although titles might not be given, they should not be interfered with, so as to retard their efforts ; and that they might therefore select their own sites, and erect such buildings as were needful for the efficient performance of their benevolent duties. Upon the faith of this they have proceeded ; and two Wesleyan, fourteen American, and three Berlin missionaries have chosen their localities, built their houses, chapels, out-houses, &c., relying on the British government honourably to fulfil its engagements. " The public faith was pledged not to disturb the Natives." What must, then, have been the astonishment of the American missionaries, the other day, when, a deputation from their body having waited on his honour the lieutenant-governor, to know the intentions of government upon this important subject, they were told that the Locations would be cut up, and the Natives scattered ; the claims of about thirteen thousand would be admitted ; but the remainder must either leave the Colony, or make arrangements with private parties to reside upon their lands ! In answer to the question whether the mission-premises would be given into the hands of any claimants, they were told, " No ;" but that he (the governor) could not engage that the land, to within five rods (fifty yards) of the house, should not be appropriated,—an act which would be equal to the entire removal of the mission-stations.

They had good reason to make these inquiries, as, within a few weeks previously, nearly twenty thousand acres had been surveyed off the Umvoti Location, for three farms, allotted to different claimants. And, only a few weeks later, another person, visiting one of the stations, congratulated the missionary on the improvements he had made upon *his farm ;* that is to say, the improvements made by the missionary upon the farm of the person who had now come to *claim all !* and thus the care, and toil, and expense of the missionary for years are swallowed up at once by the congratulations of a needy settler. This farm has since been surveyed to within a short distance of the house ; so that it will be with difficulty that the cattle can graze in one direction without committing trespass.

A still more recent instance of this kind of justice has occurred at the station of the Berlin Missionary Society, under the Drakenberg, which was formed in June, 1847. This was a six-thousand acres Dutch farm, with buildings thereon erected ; and was given to Usikali, on the condition that the Berlin Missionary Society should pay £37 to the farmer for the buildings on the spot. This money was paid, and the farmer was to receive compensation from the government by land allotted to him in another place. The diplomatic agent for the Natives, in company with Dr. Stanger, the surveyor-general, then gave it over to this said Usikali. The land-marks of the boundary were pointed out by the diplomatic agent to the chief; and every thing was supposed to be settled according to "the law of the Medes and Persians, which altereth not;" when, lo! in 1852, the governor comes, and says that the government had not power to do what it did before, and which we have proved from official records to have taken place; and now the farmer must be paid for the farm; and, if this feeble mission will not pay £150, he (the governor) must buy it as the seat of a magistracy. So now this small mission is put to the last extremity, either to raise the money, or to prepare to leave the place. How grievous the effects of such vacillation,—doing and undoing! one governor having power to do one thing, another denying it; one giving, another taking away; the dispirited missionary and faith-broken Native going to the wall! The beginning of such proceedings we see; but the end, if they are persisted in, may be written in tears and blood.

I would say here,—as I have said elsewhere,—*Begin at the beginning:* do *not* put the *first* last, and the *last* first. It is admitted, on all hands, that the Locations were set apart for the Natives; and the missionaries were encouraged by the government to go upon them, with the prospect of £50 *per annum* towards their support, one of them (the Rev. Aldin Grout, on the Umvoti) being actually appointed by the government. This gentleman was on his way to America, in January, 1844, when he was stopped at Cape Town by his excellency Sir G. Napier, who inquired if he was willing to become a government missionary at Natal. Sir Peregrine Maitland arrived at this time, and engaged Mr. Grout as *government missionary,* paying part or all of his salary *out of government funds.* Upon his return, he was directed to select a site which would not be claimed by the farmers; and the present recorder assured him that the site which he then selected on the Umvoti would *not* be thus claimed. But he is now told that ten rods from the house may be the utmost extent of his allowance; by which curtailment his missionary enterprise would be utterly frustrated.   Now, as the primary object on the Location was the good of the Natives, and, in connexion with them, of the *mission;* so, in all truth and honour, their interests should be settled first, and that in a manner which will not put our queen and country to shame.   A Dutch Farmer gets his six thousand acres of land, who has resided on it *twelve months,* in order to claim it; whilst devoted missionaries, who have lived for years on the stations, giving all their time and labour and property to benefit the Aborigines of the country, are to be pared down to one hundred square yards. I shall not pass those strictures and censures on these transactions which they merit, being satisfied that the bare mention of them must call forth the indignation of every honest man.

But alarming representations have been made of the danger of missionary institutions, taken from the scenes which have recently transpired in the old Colony.   The cases, however, are by no means parallel.   *There* the people went to reside upon the stations, collected from different parts, without any claim, but were *not trained for rebellion: here* the masses have never been under engagements, and are the *proper claimants of the soil,* to the number of one hundred thousand !

From what has taken place in the war of the old Colony, the trumpet of danger has been loudly blown, sounding an alarm against the treasons taught on mission-stations: but this has been done to serve a purpose; whilst the facts are destructive of the calumny.   A few Hottentots and others, connected with some institutions in the old Colony, have unhappily been betrayed *into* either actual hostility or neutral inactivity; but this by no means applies to *the whole.*   And why keep the eye continually fixed upon these, dwelling only on the partial evils which may have arisen from mistaken views on the part of some ?   Why not look on the opposite side a little ?   Who is it that has assisted Sir Harry Smith in the present war,—keeping open his outlet at East London, (the Buffalo Mouth,)—preserving his posts along the whole line of frontier,—escorting his waggons,—conveying his dispatches,—presenting a breakwater against the terrible flood of Kafir-land Proper, which would have poured down, and either have swept the English into the sea, or besieged them in

their chief towns?   Who?   *Kafirs trained on mission-stations,*
—PATO, KAMA, UMTIRARA, and other chiefs and their people,
who have nobly resisted the many and powerful temptations
which have assailed them, have fought under our banners and
against their own countrymen, and for our defence and preservation.   The good behaviour and brave help, also, of multitudes of
Fingoes, Hottentots, and ex-slaves, who have resided near the
colonial towns, and been members of Christian churches and con-
gregations, throughout the Colony, add another proof that Native
towns near the English may be made a great auxiliary in defending the Colony; whilst the evils which have incidentally arisen
may, in future, be guarded against and prevented, at the cost of
a little prudence and fair dealing.   Why, then, should a desperate attack be made upon missionary institutions?   In this
instance it must certainly recoil upon those who have made it;
laying open *the malice,* or *the interested views,* which have called
it forth, and showing that the parties against whom it has been
directed are grossly calumniated.

This representation and statement I have made, *not in Exeter
Hall,* but in the largest public meeting ever held in Natal, in
the face, and on the chosen ground, of the champions of mis-
representation and wrong towards missions.

But it is objected that, on some of these stations, magisterial
functions, &c., have been performed.   How so?   Were there no
magistrates in the country?   If there were, why did they not look
after the usurped exercise of those functions, and prevent it?   Let
suitable magistrates be appointed, who will attend to their duty;
and, depend upon it, there will be no complaint on this ground.

I cannot leave this subject without stating that, in my opinion,
there ought to be a *government industrial agent* in every suitable locality.   Industrial institutions for the Kafirs will be of no
use; but a proper person might and ought to be appointed to
take the oversight of this department; whose business it should
be to search out and encourage the most deserving amongst the
Kafirs, distribute seed, give instruction in raising the crops,
encourage them to grow cotton, ginger, arrow-root, &c., give the
highest price for the produce, so as to make these and other
export articles pay better than growing maize and pumpkins; also
to bestow a reward on the most successful and deserving.   Let

these agents be multiplied to as great an extent as possible; and over them place an *overseer*, who shall carefully look after the whole business, and report to the government. This agent might also collect the taxes; as it is rather an anomalous affair for magistrates to be the tax-gatherers general of the country, and may place them in circumstances very unfavourable for the right performance of the other duties of their office. This industrial agent would then be able to press upon the people the necessity of bringing produce instead of money, especially that kind which was not bulky; and in this manner they might be stimulated to action.

It will be objected that Mr. Shepstone gave cotton-seed, and requested the Natives to pay their tax in produce, but the plan failed. Mr. Shepstone, however, could not divide himself into a hundred parts to look after it; and, without some attention and care, it were preposterous to expect great things from naked barbarians.

It will be further objected that the mode will be expensive; but I would ask, in the name of humanity and right, What is done with the £8,000 *annually collected from the Kafirs?* Is this to be swallowed up by the English officials, without any reference to those from whom it is taken? To the present time, only £50 *per annum* has been directly paid for the benefit of those people,—a sum which has been allowed to the Rev. James Allison towards the support of his manual-labour school. What becomes of the large remaining balance, extracted from the sweat of 50,000 poor Kafir women? Is it to be expended in employing men to rob them of their land, and drive the inhabitants out of the country? What! is this British honour and justice in the middle of the nineteenth century? Nay; every particle of nature in a just and honourable man repels the proposition as an insult and a wrong, setting aside the " bray of Exeter Hall," and the " morbid philanthropy of the religious public of England."

Betwixt the barbarian Kafir and the civilized Englishman, there is a great chasm, a mighty gulf. The cold, stern Englishman stands on the one bank, crying, " Civilize! civilize!! civilize!!!"—but lends no helping hand to convey the poor Native across. The devoted missionary stands on the opposite bank, exclaiming, " Christianize! Christianize!! Christianize!!!"—at the same time taking by the hand as many as he is able, and landing them safely at the English settler's side, amid a thousand discouragements, some of which are laboriously placed in the way by the " civilizer " himself.   But let the government thus do its part, and improvement will advance at a rapid rate.   There will then be, on each station, *the missionary,*—the representative of God and the church ; *the magistrate,*—the representative of the queen and Great Britain ; and *the artisan,*—the representative of the great commercial and civilized world.   The progress may appear slow for a time, but it will increase as years advance ; and each year will add its link to the chain which stretches across the gulf, and joins the white man to his coloured brethren, until a nation of barbarous savages rises to bless the people which has made them great and good, and puts a brighter crown upon Britain's head than the lovely queen of England ever wore.

It will be said, " Yes ; this is all very plausible upon paper ; but it is only the production of a hair-brained theorist, and can never be practically carried out."   No ; certainly not,—if the attempt is never made.   It is always easier to fold the arms in cold supineness, and to utter loud and long complaints, than to put forth effort, especially if it is attended with labour and expense : but let this attempt be fairly made, or some better plan be carried out,—since I have no desire to be dictator on the subject,—and then with some show of grace and propriety may it be said that "it is all in vain."

Some have talked and others have written about making the Kafirs half slaves or apprentices.   On this point I would ask two plain questions : 1. Can they do it ?   2. Have they a right to do it ?   If so, from whom is the right derived ?   Most assuredly this scheme is chimerical ; for if the British government and people had the full guarantee as to the right both from earth and heaven, both from man and God, they have *not the power* to do it.   No ; they may drive the Kafir back into the wilderness, but they will never bind him, except in fetters ; they will never confine him, except they lodge him in a prison.   The right, also, to carry out this scheme, in the name of reason, honour, justice, and religion, I deny.

But in order to anything being permanently and effectually done, the second great measure, after righteously settling the land

claim, must be, *to establish a thoroughly efficient English government over them.* This is absolutely essential. As set forth in
another part of this Chapter, Kafir chieftainship must be utterly
abolished. Good and efficient magistrates must be appointed,—
not one magistrate for 20,000 or 30,000 people, scattered over a
wide extent of country; but the number must be so far increased
as to enable each to take the strict oversight of all within the
limited circle of magistracy.

Offences must be clearly proved and severely punished; the
people being made to feel that the strong hand of a strong
government is upon them, and that they *must* submit, they *must*
obey.

A census of the people in each magistracy should be annually
taken and carefully kept. None should be allowed to come
within the bounds of the magistrate's jurisdiction without reporting themselves, or to leave without permission, and its being
known whither they have proceeded. Every facility for detecting crime should be adopted; and no crime should be allowed
to go unpunished, upon any consideration whatever.

Contracts for service should be strenuously enforced; and, in
order that this may be done, means of detecting the breaches of
engagement should be contrived, so that these wild creatures
should not be the sport of their own whims and inclinations,—
engaging one day, and leaving the next,—losing the oxen on
the journey, and then running away and leaving master and waggon in the lurch, thus occasioning great delay, damage, and loss,
—or, when at home, being sent for the oxen, and walking away,
to return no more. The English have, in these and other ways,
been greatly provoked; and it is no wonder that they should
utter loud and bitter complaints; but the fault has been with the
government, and not with the Kafirs. The government ought to
have adopted wise and vigorous measures, so as to have prevented
these things; and instead of this being hard for the Kafir, it
would have been the greatest benefit that could have been conferred upon him, and the contrary line of proceeding has been the
greatest curse.

Let justices of the peace be placed on private lands, at suitable
distances from each other, with or without salary, and possessing
the power of punishing petty offences; whilst greater ones should

be referred to the magistrates, who should decide upon them; and the whole should be submitted to the revision of the chief magistrate.

But let not those who are invested with a little brief authority use it in playing all sorts of fantastic tricks, or something worse. A Kafir has a sharp sense of justice; and whilst he will respect and reverence the officer who will give him just punishment for his misdeeds, he will abhor the man who does him wanton wrong, and may be tempted to settle accounts in his own way.

The Kafirs must be treated like children. If a man has a large family, and leaves them without restraint or control, his children become a plague to himself and a scourge to the community. The Kafirs are children of a larger growth, and must be treated accordingly,—*children* in knowledge, ignorant of the relationships of civilized society, and strangers to many of the motives which influence the conduct of the white man. But they are *men* in physical and mental powers,—*men* in the arts and usages of their nation, and the laws of their country; and the great difficulty in governing them is, to treat them as men-children, teaching them that to submit and to obey are essential to their own welfare, as well as to that of others.

Some kind-hearted Christians will say, "This is much too severe;" but my firm conviction, after many years' experience, is, that it is not merely the best, but also the only, way to save the Native races from ruin and annihilation; and that had the Kafirs on the Frontier of the old Colony been treated with more apparent severity after the first war, a second outbreak would not have taken place. Who, I would ask, is their best friend,—the man who would save them by apparent severity, or the man who would destroy them by mistaken kindness? I presume, the former.

Besides, it should not be forgotten that what appears to be severe to us, is not so to them, since many of them have lived under the iron rule of cruel, capricious despots, with no security for life or property, and are consequently unable to appreciate or understand our excess of civilized kindness, being strangers to those refined feelings which operate in the breasts of the Christian. The result of too mild a policy is, that in a few years they are changed from crouching, terror-stricken vassals, to bold, lawless, independent barbarians.

By these and other methods a systematic, well-regulated, power-ful control should be exercised over them, by which they would be rendered unable to plot schemes of mischief, or to arrange plans for war. Let it be remembered that these remarks apply to British subjects in a British Colony, and not to independent Native tribes in the interior; and that the measures proposed are needful for their benefit and preservation, as well as for our peace and prosperity, being calculated to prevent mischief and to promote virtue.

The following remarks, by a correspondent of the "Watchman" newspaper, from the Eastern Province, are so appropriate that I introduce them here. Speaking of the Frontier tribes, the writer says, " *What, then, can be done?*   Why, in sober truth, you can do nothing in this matter *per saltum*. What I have indicated above with regard to the Gaikas, would perhaps be the best mode of recommencing a series of quiet and well-considered measures for gradually counteracting the evil influences often exerted by the chiefs. A good deal was effected in this way during the three years 1848, 1849, and 1850. Similar measures, improved by the suggestions of experience, should continue to be employed. A regular system of government should be constructed for British Kaffraria, adapted to the peculiar circumstances of its population. The British functionaries should, in their several districts, be paramount, and only responsible to the chief commissioner. The chiefs in these districts should not be allowed publicly to exercise any *independent* authority; whatever it may be requisite for them to do, should always be understood to be done with the concur-rence and sanction of the chief British authority of the district, or otherwise to have no force. But while the chiefs of British Kaffraria should not exercise any independent authority, every favourable opportunity should be embraced to engage them to support and carry out the views and measures of government. They should be taught by every means that their good faith and co-operation will always be acceptable, and meet with substantial reward from the government."*

In the last page of my pamphlet, the following passage is found: "Having already trespassed so far upon the reader's

----

* "Watchman" newspaper, April 21st, 1852.

time and patience, I must forego what I would have otherwise disclosed of what is transpiring around us, especially in connexion with the revolting system of female slavery which exists. Supposing about one hundred thousand Kafirs to be in the Colony, about one-half of them are females, who are as fully articles of merchandise, in being sold for wives to the highest bidder, as the horses and cattle and goods which are brought to the auction-mart, and knocked down to those who will give the best price. Our nature recoils with indignation and horror at the fact of there being fifty thousand female slaves in the Natal Colony, under the government of our beloved queen, and amongst the free institutions of honoured Britain."

I am happy to hear that the government has resolved to put an end to this revolting practice; but, in doing this, the greatest caution will be required. If violent hands be laid at once on this complicated and powerful machinery, it will break into a thousand pieces, and do not a little damage to those that stand by. One hundred thousand Natives are not a plaything. The Boers made light of them; and they did it to their cost, some of their best men falling the victims of mistaken and presumptuous conduct. The English settlers of Natal thought little of the Natives, when they entered Zulu-land in the early part of 1838; but, leaving the bodies of two thousand of their people (Kafirs) on Zulu hills, and in the Zulu gorges, to be eaten by the beasts of prey, and their bones to whiten in the suns of many years, whilst only a few scattered remnants returned to tell their tale of woe and slaughter,—they were taught to measure their foes better. No; this mode of depreciation will not answer; but laws must be made which will cause the evil gradually to work itself out, and which must be administered under the best and most efficient management of *British agents.* I know not what the plans of the government are, or whether it has any at all; but I make these statements as the convictions of my own judgment, and am not led by the theories of any class of men.

Two very simple laws would greatly check the evil; and more stringent ones could be adopted, as the case might require. The *first* is,—not to allow more than *five* head of cattle to be given for a wife. This would put a stop to the *auction* part of the business at once; and young women would be able to take young men whom they liked, instead of being taken by old men whom they hate, but whom they are obliged to marry, because they can give the most cattle, and so the father of the girl, looking upon her as a marketable commodity, says, "I shall take the highest bidder; and I shall make her take him; if willingly, well; but if not, I shall inflict torture until she does."

A *second* law I would suggest; namely, to make the *first wife free from taxation,* but to levy a heavy tax or fine on every succeeding one. Some might say that this would be licensing the transaction. I would say, "Yes, in the same manner as that in which you license foreign corn, when you place a high import duty upon it."

Let these two simple regulations be fairly worked into the system of Kafir government; and then, others more stringent being applied, the evil will be likely soon to work itself out, and come to an end.

The affairs of South Africa are now become all-absorbing to the British nation, taxing the energies and calling forth the resources of the land. Three terrible Kafir wars in the old Colony, the last of which has only just come to an end, attended with so large an expenditure of English blood and treasure, invest the subject with no ordinary importance, and afford an opportunity for the exercise of all the power which England possesses. This is admitted to have been one of Lord John Russell's "great difficulties;" and not his alone; for the ablest statesmen, and the warriors that have won the highest honours on other battle-fields, have scarcely been adequate to the task of subduing and governing the Kafirs in the old Colony. Three governors and three lieutenant-governors have been appointed and recalled, in a comparatively short space of time; and those who before thought and spake lightly of a Kafir war, have proved to their sorrow, that it is a serious affair; and now allow, that if it can be avoided on honourable terms, no means should be left untried to prevent it.* Natal is inhabited and surrounded by vast numbers of Natives, (Kafirs,) and has a solemn admonition before its eyes, in the old Colony. Let, then, the warning voice be heard, and a

---

* See the end of this Chapter, page 226, for more recent observations on the third Kafir war, now happily terminated.

policy, not timid, but cautious, just, and firm, be adopted and pursued. Under these circumstances we look with some concern upon the journals of the day, the editors of which must be regarded as, to some extent, the exponents of prevailing public opinion.

The colonial papers have not, upon the whole, appeared inimical to the cause of the Natives; but occasionally articles of great warmth and severity have been published, which probably were, to some extent, called forth by the passing events connected with the Frontier war, but which will be discontinued when the immediate and temporary cause has passed away.

The same may also be said of some of the English papers, when discussing the same subject. From the "Times" we quote the following: "We consider that our insular position compels us to colonize; that colonization implies contact with savages; and that contact with savages involves the suffering of the inferior race. We consider that colonists are as morally entitled to protection as the Aborigines; and that when these interests clash, *as clash they must*, the weaker must go to the wall. No territory, not even an entire continent, has ever yet proved spacious enough for Europeans and savages together."

On this paragraph we remark, that its chief recommendation is its plainness; its purport being simply, in plain English, "Colonize with European or English emigrants, and exterminate the Natives." " We consider that colonists are as morally entitled to protection as the Aborigines," &c. So say we; but we ask, Does the writer mean by "colonists" those who were in the country when the English took possession of it, or those who have since emigrated to it, or may emigrate at any future time? and does he mean by the "protection" of the colonists, exterminating the Native, and *taking his lands as a lawful prize?* I think that the latter will be allowed to be the fair and natural deduction from the paragraph, where it is stated, as a very consoling fact, that "the weaker must go to the wall!"

So far as concerns the colonists who were at Natal when the English took possession of it, I think they have no reasonable ground for complaint of want of protection in the distribution of land, since, upon proof of twelve months' occupancy, they had 3,000 or 6,000 acres given,—no small or mean allowance, surely;

whilst the Aborigines have received nothing approaching to the same proportion. The first claimants having been thus dealt with, we come to the second class,—more recent emigrants; and, in order to understand the subject aright, let us change the position of the parties, placing them *vice versâ*, and ask, whether the Aborigines of England or America would admit the soundness of the proposition,—that the Natives of South Africa should be at liberty to enter their country; and, because their skin was of another colour, and their habits superior, should, on the ground of *might*, lay their hands upon the goodly homesteads and rich farms of the inhabitants? Neither Englishman nor American would consent to any such mode of reasoning; but both of them would consider that they, as the original possessors, were doing "morally" right in exerting their utmost strength to repel the outrage, and to punish the wrong-doers; and, until this was done, would maintain the direst hostility.

But because I thus take the writer upon his own ground, and reason on the subject of "moral" right, let no one say that I would, for a moment, instil these views into the mind of the Native. I most solemnly repudiate the thought, and fully believe that no missionary in Natal has so acted.

I should not have deemed it needful to notice these extreme views, were it not for the fact, that they are either forming or feeding public opinion on this very grave subject; and these notions are not confined to Natal or the Cape, but fly on the wings of the wind to all parts of the world. But I, for one, am not at all inclined to relish the idea, that our great nation should become the public executioner of the Natives of South Africa. No; I would say, If England finds it needful to exterminate, let it be *the last fearful resort:* nay, it were far better not to colonize at all.

Under these dark and saddening views, it is most gratifying to find that there is, at least, one pleasing exception to what is here set forth as a universal rule; proving that these painful results of colonization do not take place as a matter of necessity. This exception is in the case of New Zealand. We quote from the "Watchman" of May 5th, 1852, where the writer says, in reference to the subject of Sir J. Pakington giving a constitution to New Zealand, " In these and other places, the English settlers, it will also be remembered, have been thrown among a native race, which, by its aboriginal attributes, appears to be the most formidable, and most capable, of all uncivilized tribes of man, but which, by the beneficent influence of Christianity, has been reclaimed, within a single generation, from savage habits, (notoriously including cannibalism,) to such a condition of amelioration,* that government now judges these native Christians to be as deserving of the privilege of local self-government as their European neighbours.

" Each " chamber " will have its legislative council, all the members of which will be freely elected; and the franchise for that purpose is given alike to the Native and to the European : the property test being, in its lowest form, the occupation of a house worth £10, if situate in the towns, or £5, if in the country.

" Without entering further into details, while we have only an outline before us, we recur to the great and gratifying fact of the witness borne in the British House of Commons to the success of Christian missions in New Zealand. The missionary preceded the merchant in these islands, and civilization was taught by Christianity, and not by commerce or by government. The present governor, Sir George Grey, tells us of the Maories, that ' nearly the whole nation has now been converted to Christianity; that they are fond of agriculture; take great pleasure in cattle and horses; like the sea, and form good sailors; have now many coasting vessels of their own, manned with Maori crews; are attached to Europeans, and admire their customs and manners; and that they are extremely ambitious of rising in civilization, and becoming skilled in European arts.' He adds that ' many of them have also now, from the value of their property, a large stake in the welfare of the country. One chief has, besides valuable property of various kinds, upwards of £500 invested in government securities; several others have also sums of from £200 to £400, invested in the same securities.' It would appear that such a race could easily be incorporated into any British settlement, with mutual

---

* For the most ample and interesting account of this great triumph of Christianity, consult " Remarkable Incidents in the Life of the REV. SAMUEL LEIGH, Missionary to the Settlers and Savages of Australia and New Zealand. With a succinct History of the Origin and Progress of the Missions in those Colonies. By the REV. ALEXANDER STRACHAN."

advantage to Natives and settlers. In fact, the process of the incorporation of the native population into the European settlements 'has, for the last few years, been taking place with a rapidity unexampled in history. Unless some sudden and unforeseen cause of interruption should occur, it will still proceed; and a very few years of continued peace and prosperity will suffice for the entire fusion of the two races into one nation.'

"The aboriginal population of whom such things are spoken, displayed, forty years ago, their pre-eminence over other savages chiefly in a greater ferocity, and superior daring and accomplishment in the arts of war. Only seven years ago, they were in rebellion against the British government, and in arms against those new neighbours whom now the New-Zealander copies, emulates, and unites himself to, in one allegiance, in one religion, and in domestic relations. He, in return, will be acknowledged by the imperial legislature as a fellow-subject, possessing the rights of a common citizenship. 'For this part of the measure Colonel Thompson could not refrain from offering to the colonial secretary his warmest congratulations; and in it believed that he saw the recognition of a principle, which was capable of carrying forward this country to as much of the empire of the world as the ambition of an honest patriot should desire.'"

This is precisely what I contend for in this Chapter. Whether it is wise or not to give the New-Zealander the franchise, I do not pretend to determine; but I do contend that it is not needful to exterminate the aboriginal savage, according to the doctrine set forth by the "Times," and warmly advocated by unscrupulous adventurers in our Colonies. The great moral and civil amelioration which has taken place in New Zealand may take place in Natal, and amongst the vast tribes of the great continent of Africa; and it is the duty of every honest man to try to bring about this desirable result.

But I am happy to find that the policy of extermination does not accord with the general sentiments of the public at home. I will give another extract from the "Times" of April, 1852: "We do not deny that the evil has been greatly increased by the insanity of our territorial encroachments. Doubling our dominion—which has positively swelled from 110,000 square miles in 1842, to 230,000 in 1850—doubled our dangers; but the principles in operation would have been the same wherever our frontier line was drawn. What we have now to do is, to relinquish with the best grace, and in the best manner practicable, our untenable positions, and confine ourselves to a frontier more easily defensible." This forms part of a long article in the "leading journal" of Europe upon South African policy. I know not how the English can relinquish any of the territory acquired in the old Colony, with either good or bad "grace;" for it would be without "grace" at all, so far as I can see: but there are some matters relating to Natal which stand entirely on another footing, and which I shall now detail.

The boundary of the Natal Colony, as originally fixed, on the west, was the Umzimkulu river; but, a short time ago, this boundary was extended to the Umtafuna; thus taking in nearly one hundred miles of additional coast range, and reaching inland, in a parallel line with the old boundary line, to the Quahlamba Mountains; by which alteration a large portion of additional territory was added to the Natal Colony, and taken from Faku, the Amamponda chief.

But on what ground was this large extent of additional territory annexed? Was it because the present Colony was filled up, and families were pressing so closely upon each other, that more ample space was requisite? No; beyond the Isipingo, as far as the Umzimkulu, there is scarcely a family located. Was it because the country was an unoccupied waste, untenanted by man? No; along the whole line of coast, at least, it was possessed by Natives. Was it because Faku had broken faith with the Colony, and stood in hostile array against it? No; the assagai and the kerrie were lying bloodless on the ground, or used only for the more laudable purpose of spearing bucks, or knocking down birds.

The alleged cause was, that, Faku having become responsible for such cattle, stolen by the Bushmen, as should be traced into his country, and many having thus been traced, he must now make restitution for the stolen property; and the modest total of so many thousand acres of territory was allowed to be an equivalent. But, according to the "Times," did it not *really* arise from the "insanity of territorial aggrandizement," or from the notion of making way for the *future possible* wants of the white man at the expense of the black?

But how came it to pass, after all was supposed to be settled, signed, and sealed, that the same official who had accomplished his task so successfully before, was found again at the court of the Amamponda chief, demanding one or two thousand head of cattle on the same score as before? These were also given, but with what grace I must leave honest men to judge. The cattle were brought to Maritzburg, and advertised for sale by public auction; but, I suppose, serious misgivings began to work in certain quarters, and it was thought that some very inconvenient questions might be asked by and by; and therefore, to make the best of a bad matter, it would be well to send them back again, and thus to "relinquish, with the best grace and in the best manner possible," this unrighteous acquisition. But both the "grace" and the "manner" were bad enough to make an English government hang down its head with shame before the barbarian monarch, who had never done them wrong, but was a friendly ally. Such an act of restitution would, by him, be put down to weakness on our part, rather than to a desire to render tardy justice to him. With such tricks it is much easier to rouse the lion than to tame him; but, though fretted and angry, he has not sprung upon our little Colony, nor revenged the wrong in blood.

But here is the point of the evil:—if, at any time, there should be an outbreak, all the blame will fall on Faku and his people, and perhaps upon the missionaries; and it will then be regarded as a fair and legitimate ground on which to take away his life and those of his people, and add his country to " our territorial aggrandizement." But let the recollection of these acts of provocation offered to him soften our resentment in such a case, and modify our measures.

I must leave it for politicians to determine whether it is well to make Faku responsible for the Bushmen's depredations; but, according to my opinion, such an arrangement is both impolitic and unjust.

Then, on the north-eastern frontier of this Colony, how stand matters at present? For some time past Umpanda has removed his people to a distance of about sixty miles from the Tugela river,—the boundary of the Colony,—in order that they might not escape, and cross the boundary into the Colony; but in this vacant space an English trader has now taken up his abode, stating that Umpanda has given him a large tract of the frontier land. Report says that it is the reward of having handed over a large quantity of arms and ammunition to his Zulu majesty; and certainly this is a very favourable place for him to occupy, in order to carry on this suicidal traffic.

It is now a fully admitted fact, that Umpanda has a large supply of arms and ammunition, and would be able to bring many armed warriors into the field. Some parties must have been employed in trading in these deadly weapons; and strong suspicions are entertained concerning particular persons. But they are still allowed to trade; and I would ask, Have those searching investigations been made by the authorities into these matters, which might and ought to have taken place? And if so, have the best means been adopted to stop such unpatriotic traffic?

I HAVE in this Chapter entered very fully into the subject of the English government of the Natives in Natal. I have adduced facts, principles, and engagements: I have reasoned upon them, drawn inferences from them, and established certain positions. I have done this, not as a philanthropist, but as a man of honour, taking the first principles of the laws of nations as the basis of my remarks and conclusions. If any man is disposed to find fault, let him disprove my facts, or point out the illogical cha-racter of my reasoning, and the fallacy of my conclusions. But let him not make a bluster, and use hard names, because I have sought to set forth " the truth, the whole truth, and nothing but the truth."

If the policy advocated in these pages were carried out, I believe that the native population of this Colony might be made a great blessing to it. If a contrary course is pursued, they will be made a great scourge; but the blame and guilt of it will lie at the Englishman's door.

I should not have bestowed so much labour upon this subject, if I were not convinced that it is one of transcendant importance to South Africa. It will soon be a vital question on the Frontier

of the old Colony,—when the claims of the Kafirs between the
Fish and Kei rivers have to be considered and settled,—whether
England is to be the great destroyer of the South African races ;
or whether she will, by proper government, raise and save them.

I have sought to place the whole matter in a clear, just, and
convincing light ; and, having had to manage Kafirs, Hottentots,
and other Natives, for thirteen years, I believe that I understand
what I have been writing about; and that what I have written
is worthy the serious consideration of those who may be intrusted
with the management of South African affairs, and who are
responsible, not only to the colonial and British public, but to
Almighty God, for the right discharge of their duties.   May He
impart " the wisdom that is at his right hand " to those who
have to govern South Africa !

CLOSE OF THE KAFIR WAR.

When the former part of this Chapter was written, the Kafir
war was raging ; and it was expected that this work would have
passed through the press before its close ; but circumstances
have occurred to render delay needful, and thus allow an opportunity for making a few observations upon that important event.

The *third* Kafir war is now among the things that were, but
are not : it is now matter of history, and is thrown into the
general summary of human affairs.   But its effects are not dead :
these are still deeply, painfully felt on every part of the Frontier
of the Cape Colony ; and only those who have witnessed the disastrous consequences upon property and life, the order and well-
being of society, and the temporal and spiritual interests of the
inhabitants, can form any thing like a correct idea of the dreadful reality.   These sad results, too, bring again to mind the two
millions of British treasure cast into this whirling vortex, and
cause us again to lament the fact that much of the best blood
which flowed in the veins of British soldiers should have been
spilled in such an inglorious way.

The past cannot now be recalled, or its effects prevented : but
wise and thoughtful men look anxiously into the future, and

earnestly desire that this may be the last tragic scene of the kind that shall be acted along this fine Frontier.

No wonder, then, that every act of each government functionary, and every measure of the imperial legislature, should be watched with feverish anxiety, and sifted with searching care; and that the nature of the peace made, and of the acts subsequent upon it, should be looked upon with tremulous concern. Every person is gazing into the future with deep emotion, and asking if it is to be peace or war, life or death.

When the treaty of peace concluded by Sir George Cathcart, the governor, was first published, there was much dissatisfaction felt at the terms of it; and general fears were entertained that only a few years, at most, might pass, before the same melancholy scenes would be again presented to view. But I am happy to find that the course subsequently pursued by his excellency has done much to allay fear and inspire confidence.

Having driven the Kafirs from the Amatolas, and otherwise dislodged them from most of their strongholds along the entire line of Frontier, he is giving out farms, and establishing villages, through the whole of the vacated territory; thus occupying and intersecting those parts which were before the fortresses of the treacherous foe, and preventing them from returning to, and settling in, their old haunts. The importance of this measure does not so much depend upon the extent of country assigned, as upon the fact, that it is those particular parts which were the *rendezvous* of plundering, murdering freebooters; and to follow them into these fastnesses could only be done with a strong force and at great expense,—a system attended with much delay and danger, and so defeating the ends of justice, and preventing the detection and punishment of the worst offenders.

One of the conditions upon which farms are here given out, and village allotments made, is, that the parties shall do military duty when called upon, holding themselves in readiness, with a certain number of mounted men, well armed, to be called out upon any sudden emergency by the commandant, to repel the inroads of the Kafirs, or quickly follow stolen cattle; and thus, by having a sufficient force at hand, small depredations may without delay be detected and punished. The extent to which this measure is receiving the favourable consideration of the colonists, is astonishing; many farmers and others having boldly come forward to place themselves in the front of danger, and receive the first and warmest brunt of the enemy. The result is, that the inhabitants appear as though they were recovering breath, and as if new impulses of stirring life were being infused; the air of dejection and the tone of despondency are, to some extent, passing away; and the sturdy farmer is beginning anew to seek the recovery of fortunes lost, and to apply himself with vigour to the peaceful operations of industry.

The task of beginning the world again, for the third time, is, to some of the hard-working settlers, saddening and sickening in the extreme. Having been for two or three years cooped up with their families in inconvenient rooms in towns or villages, whither they had fled for safety, supported by a waggon or waggons in government employ, they again begin to collect their small effects together, and return to their homestead that was: but O, how changed is all! The substantial house and commodious outbuildings are lying in ruins; and the roofless and blackened walls, and scattered wrecks of furniture, present melancholy mementoes of the comfort that before reigned, and declare how complete has been the work of destruction effected by the hand of the ruthless destroyer. Before, there was the busy hum of active life, the lowing cattle, the bleating sheep, the labouring plough; all presenting an air of contentment and prosperity: but now, alas! the whole has disappeared; and the long grass, the over-grown bush, the hardened ground, and the unsightly garden, all concur in proving that the hand of the industrious owner has not been there.

In such a scene there is enough to damp the most ardent spirit, and to cripple the most determined energy: but the worst complaint is this: "Ah! we begin again, but we do not know whether the Kafirs will not soon come back and sweep the whole away. We have lost all our cattle; half the sheep are dead, and the remainder are so poor that they can hardly live; and poor John was shot as the waggon went up out of the Ecca, and William was killed by the side of yonder hill," &c., &c. There is something so truly sickening and heart-rending in these simple tales, and the stubborn facts by which they are corroborated, that the visitor *feels* that it is a hard case, and wonders how the parties can muster courage to begin again.   Hope, thou bright and morning star! how much do these tried, afflicted, bereaved people owe to thee!   This country *needs not* the thousands and millions of English treasure pouring into it for Kafir-war expenditure.   If it could only enjoy peace and security, it has resources of prosperity, wealth, and happiness in itself, which require no foreign aid.   Its *wool* alone is its fortune and salvation.

In spite of all these discouragements, the farmers are now moving to their former places of abode, hoping for better times and happier days.   There are, however, two new sources of perplexity rising up before them.   The one is *an unsuitable Constitution*, with the prospect of the speedy withdrawal of the troops, or having the whole expense of the military establishment saddled upon them, as the very small return for a privilege so great!   The other is *the abandonment of the Sovereignty*, with the not distant prospect of the giving up of British Kaffraria also.

1. Wonder will be felt by many, especially in England, at the granting of a Constitution, and the establishment of self-government, being regarded as evils, or thought premature, such privileges being ordinarily looked upon as the greatest of boons.   Were the country in a state prepared for that particular kind of Constitution which has been chosen for it, and sent out to it, this privilege would doubtless be a boon: but residents in the Colony are in a better condition to form a correct opinion upon matters amongst themselves, than are others at a distance.   If the Colony was a connected and compact one, where the interests of all parties were the same, and where the dangers and losses of all parties were equal, and where the sources of profit and emolument were open to all alike, there would be very little difficulty in the case: but in South Africa the opposite of all this is the fact.   There is no central place in which a Parliament can be assembled.   The two great moving bodies are at the extreme points of the Colony, with local interests so different from or opposite to each other that they cannot agree; and the majority of the Frontier inhabitants are so perfectly dissatisfied with the arrangement, that, if they knew how to avoid it, they would have nothing whatever to do with the Parliament.

Besides, the franchise being fixed at £25, every person who has a small dwelling but little better than a hut, with a little ground attached, is entitled to vote. This arrangement is designed to embrace the whole of the coloured population, and to make provision for their voting; and doubtless was made with the best intentions.

Let the reader distinctly understand that the remarks which I now make are not upon the abstract merits of universal suffrage; what I write being rather a statement of facts, and the record of an historian, than containing the discussion of the abstract merits of the Constitution; and being designed to impart to English legislators and general readers correct information, not to promote any party purpose. From all that I have witnessed, I am therefore bound to say, that I think the Natives or coloured inhabitants of this Colony are not yet in a state either correctly to understand, or rightly to appreciate, the privilege of the franchise. Not only have they less knowledge concerning our modes of government than the most illiterate Englishman, but all their notions, modes of thought, and forms of government are of a *contrary* nature, and mixed up with their former state, which, in many instances, was that of the most arbitrary despotism or pitiless tyranny; and their increased knowledge of our modes of administration has not kept pace with their information upon other subjects. Take, as an illustration, the following expression of their views upon this point. From my peculiar position, it became my duty to inquire, the other day, after the nature of the Constitution had been explained to them by others, if they really understood the subject. If they did, I had nothing to say; but if not, I would endeavour to explain it to them. They unhesitatingly replied, *"No!* they did not understand it." One of the number, an elderly man, stood up, and gravely asked, "*What has the Queen done amiss*, that the government of the country should be taken out of her hands?" Another positively declared that, "in their country, the old chief died before they made a new one; and they could not understand why a number of new chiefs should be made at Cape Town, *whilst the old chief was living;*" at the same time frankly and honestly avowing, that they "did not want another chief, being quite content with the old one." A third, an old man with grey hairs, stood up, and said, " We hear they are going to make us all slaves again : our old masters are to be among the Members of Parliament; and we are afraid they will soon make laws to make us slaves again." This last statement is the expression of the views and fears of a very large portion of the late slave-population, who, with the Hottentots, are almost the only coloured people that will be entitled to vote. They look upon it as a thing which they have great cause to fear, rather than a boon for which they should be thankful.

But some will say, " They will soon learn." Forcing unnatural political growth upon them is, however, perhaps the most injurious, the very worst, line of policy that can be adopted towards them. I presume, the greatest politicians among them before the war, were those who became rebels. Having learnt a little about their rights and privileges, as they thought, and not getting them quite so fast as they, in their self-conceit, supposed they ought to do, they were determined to take the matter into their own hands; and, combining in unlawful and wicked rebellion, have caused a most frightful amount of destruction, suffering, and death; and the few poor fugitives who remain are seeking a wretched and precarious subsistence in Kafirland, near the mouth of the Kei, where the notorious Brander has lately died, and been buried with military honours, about three hundred of his wretched comrades attending his funeral, and a salute being fired over his grave. In this situation they may do still more mischief, by poisoning the minds of the Kafirs by whom they are surrounded, and possibly hurrying them on to their own ruin.

Being most anxious for the preservation, improvement, and prosperity of the native races, I am deeply and fully convinced that the greatest evil which a well-meaning, but mistaken, English government can inflict upon them is, to treat them like political men, whilst they are the veriest children, and then to load the missionaries with opprobrium, as having been the cause of their waywardness. At present, and for some years to come, they are only prepared to be governed, *not to govern.* Give them moral and religious training, lead them forward in the arts of industry, prepare them to take a respectable place in civilized society,—to obey law, to revere the magistrate, to fear God, and to honour the king or queen; you then raise them in the scale of being, and confer upon them that which is above the price of rubies; and then, when they have attained an elevation at which they can understand political privileges, let such rights be awarded.

2. The second great calamity which the Frontier inhabitants complain of, is the abandonment of the Sovereignty. My views upon this step will be found in the Appendix. The settlers augur that this is only a preparatory step to giving up British Kaffraria, or to throwing the whole burden of the military establishment upon them; and that, now the Constitution is given, they must govern their Colony in their own way, and pay for its government out of their own resources. This, they think, is already indicated by the large reduction of troops, and the instructions sent to the governor, that the colonists must take the posts on the Frontier line into their own hands.

They maintain, first, that, in the present state of the country, they cannot do without a large military force on the Frontier: secondly, that they are not able to bear the support of it. That the Colony should, as soon as possible, support its own military establishment, and bear its own military expenditure, and thus relieve the mother-country of a burden, is a proposition so reasonable and just, that it must commend itself to the approval of every honourable mind. But to require this at once, or for some time to come, is regarded as being both unreasonable and unjust. What would be said of a parent who would place his child before the mouth of a devouring lion, and say, that it must defend itself against his furious attacks? All would declare this conduct to be unnatural, unjust, cruel; but such is the position in which the colonists would regard themselves as being placed, by the precipitate withdrawal of the troops. They say, "You have first brought us to the country, and placed us by the side of these fierce savages, and now you cry, 'Defend yourselves!' Further, you have supplied our enemies with arms and ammunition, and trained them in the art of war; and now you exclaim, 'Defend yourselves!'"

There are those who will answer, that this ought to be the case; the Natives ought to stand on equal ground, and maintain an equal contest, in the use of equal arms, especially when the encroachments of the white man are continually made upon the black.   But, in order to make the parallel complete, the Natives should possess an equal amount of honesty.   Had the colonists been from time to time making aggressive inroads upon the Natives, and provoking acts of reprisal from them, I should feel bound in truth and honour to place these attacks on record in this place, just as I have done in the case of Tshaka in Natal, and of the Dutch in the interior; but I am bound in truth and honour to state, that if there has been a single act of the kind, *I am perfectly ignorant of it.*   As far as I know the facts, had the Kafirs been as honest as the colonists, there would have been no stealing, no murders, no wars.   I have lived eight years on the immediate Frontier, and six at Natal, and have been acquainted with all that has been going on; but I know not of a single instance in which the colonists have entered Kafirland to commit depredation, or evoke anger.   The colonists have had to act on the *defensive*, and, with their best efforts, in connexion with the troops, have only just been able to avoid being "driven into the sea."   But had the Kafirs been quiet, so far as I am able to judge, the Fish river, instead of the Kei, would have been the boundary, as heretofore.   Therefore, when these Natives are now well armed, mounted, and trained to war, the sudden reduction of the British force, or its entire removal, is an act against which the colonists have a right to protest, and, if it should be committed, they possess a just ground of complaint.

Again: another reason for objecting to this measure is, that the colonists will be called upon to do this at a time when the imperial government has brought upon them the destructive results of *two* desolating wars.   At the close of the first war, Sir Benjamin D'Urban took-in the country from the Fish river to the Kei; that clever statesman regarding such a measure as essential to the peace and preservation of the colony, and taking that step with the cordial approval and warm concurrence of many of the colonists.   But no sooner was this known in England than that able governor was recalled, and this tract of country abandoned, just as we are now abandoning the Sovereignty; the result of which is, two more dreadful wars have been forced upon the Colony.

Thus, on the one hand, the English break forth into loud and bitter complaints against these deadly and ruinous wars,

with their frightful expenses, and say, " You must support yourselves;" and the colonists as loudly and bitterly complain of
the wars being forced upon them by the imbecility and folly
of the imperial government. They say, " *We* are the sufferers;
and *you* are the cause. We told you plainly, at the time the
neutral territory was abandoned, what would be the result. You
would not hear nor believe us, but acted contrary to the dictates of reason and common-sense; and you have your reward.
But we have enough to endure in the burning of our houses, the
destruction of our property, and the slaughter of our sons on the
battle-field, without having thrown upon us the burden of maintaining a large military array, which *you have forced upon us.*"
I place these representations and facts plainly before the mind
of the reader: he must form his own views upon them, and draw
his own conclusions.

Some may ask how I reconcile these views and representations
and details with the conduct of the whites against the blacks,
as recorded in the Appendix, when treating upon the Sovereignty
and the Boers. In doing this there is no difficulty. If I were
a party-man, writing for party purposes, such a thing might be
difficult; for then I must labour so to explain facts, and record
events, as to make them accord with my own predilections or
party views. But as I endeavour to hold the scales with an
equal hand, and represent things as they are, the difficulty
vanishes. What I ask is, that the reader will not confound or
jumble together things that are widely different; but as
Natal, the Sovereignty, the Frontier of the old Colony, and the
Trans-Vaal Republic, are each treated upon according to their
respective merits,—as the English, Dutch, and Natives are also
presented to view under their individual phases and separate
aspects,—so let the distinctions of country and class be clearly
formed in the reader's own mind. For want of observing these
distinctions, some of our ablest statesmen and best writers occasionally make the most egregious blunders, and call forth astonishment at their not being better informed upon the great questions and subjects concerning which they write or speak with
such confidence.

There is, however, one consideration more which ought to have
great weight in regulating the conduct of government, in reference

to the withdrawal of the troops; and this is, that by weakening the defences too much you prepare a trap, and offer a bait, to the Natives to destroy themselves. An article in the "Times" of February 14th, (if my memory serves me correctly,) speaking upon this point, represents that so long as governors can have a large military force supported by Great Britain, they will never want an enemy against which to fight. Yet so far from this being the case, the last Kafir war was hurried on by Sir H. Smith having reduced the Frontier forces too greatly. The Kafirs, finding *that* a favourable opportunity, rushed on at once; and so crippled was his excellency, that for many months he was actually confined in his Frontier posts, not daring to take the field at all, until he obtained re-inforcements from home. Then he was blamed for having weakened his defences,—a course which previously the secretary for the colonies had done all in his power to induce him to adopt. The fact was, Sir H. Smith was mistaken. He thought he could defend the Frontier with less troops than were really adequate for the purpose. Now, no sooner is the war over again, than the secretary for the colonies is moving heaven and earth to reduce the forces. Before people have even had time to get upon their farms, or erect a hovel on their desolated homesteads, they must prepare for militia duty,— be ready to take the field; and nothing but the steady, decided tone of his excellency's dispatches in reply will prevent the Colony from being again menaced with danger and destruction. I would ask, Is it not the consummation of weakness, folly, and wrong, thus to place before the naked savage the temptation to seek his own destruction, to open a volcano into which he may precipitate himself, and find his end amidst the burning lava?

I know not how statesmen and editors in England may think and feel, but to those who are in the midst of the great life-and-death struggles of this Colony, it appears wondrous strange, that, at the close of a three years' devastating war, the abandonment of the Sovereignty, the withdrawal of the troops, and the bestowal of an unsuitable Constitution upon the Colony, should all be attempted at once. Any one of these three great measures, in the time of peace, is enough to shake the fabric of society to its foundation; but to try the whole at once, at the close of a cala-

mitous war, appears madness; and people on the spot ask, if our
legislators are really of sane mind.

Let England pause and reflect. Africa is a fine country, and
worth very much more to England than she is aware of. She
would learn its value to her cost, if it was at the price of its loss.
Africa is not only the key to England's vast colonial empire in
the East, but is the *depôt*, the victualling mart, the repairing
dockyard, and the life-preserving country to her navy and merchant ships in the Indian Ocean; and without it the whole of
that great empire would be damaged, and thrown into disorder
and embarrassment.

Whatever has been gained or lost in these three Kafir wars,
much knowledge and experience has been obtained, and that
of the most valuable kind. Let, then, the home government
do nothing rashly. If England is in debt, I suppose she is yet
solvent; and a few more pounds for the military department, (the
civil requires none,) for a few years, will not sink her in the
midst of the waters by which she is encompassed, or cast her
bankrupt upon the old or the new world, suing for pity.

Give Africa a suitable and strong government; send into her
most fertile provinces a healthy stream of emigration from
England's best blood; foster her people, and govern her
Natives; and in a few years no one will sigh for the gold-fields
of Australia, or pine for the treasures of the Indies.

On the subject of the Kafir wars, I would refer my readers to
an able article in the Edinburgh Review, (July, 1854,) in which
the true policy to be observed towards the native tribes of South
Africa is shown to be that of according to them their just rights,
and treating them, whether Christians or heathens, in the spirit
of Him who has commanded us to love our neighbours as ourselves, and to do unto others as we would have them do unto us.
Though on some points the writer differs from the opinions
expressed in this volume, his main conclusions are the same; and
he recommends, as the grand preventive of future warfare, that our
governors and commissioners should exercise that kind consideration towards the dark chieftains in South Africa which has lately
been shown to an European potentate, before rushing into battle.
He also quotes the statement of Colonel Maclean, chief commissioner of British Kaffraria, that "the whole of the Mission popu-

lation, (numbering 2,523,) with the solitary exception of one Kafir, remained faithful throughout the war, and in many instances realized considerable property by their industry; and their conduct has given universal satisfaction."

To show in what estimation the Kafirs are held by the Reviewer, and that they are worthy of a little care and kindness, and of more extensive missionary and civilizing efforts, I cite the following passages from this interesting article :—

"Yet, compared with other savages, African or Indian,—compared even with our own barbarian ancestors,—the Kafirs cannot be called especially cruel or revengeful. All the Missionary Journals are full of touching proofs of the heroism, kindliness, and generosity of their converts; and even as heathen, they not seldom set an example which their Christian neighbours would not do ill to follow. Notwithstanding all the outcry that has been made against Kafir treaties, Sir George Cathcart tells us that 'in justice it must be admitted that this remarkable people have a strong sense of the moral obligation of good faith, and, if they enter into any agreement at all, are seldom found to promise one thing and do another;'* and a missionary, for many years a neighbour of Sandilli, the head chief of the Gaikas, lately told us, that he never knew him break his word, or try to exculpate himself at the expense of another. Almost all travellers inform us, that, however openly they may have professed stealing cattle from the colonists, as did the Gael from the Saxon, yet that if property be placed under their protection or care, they preserve it with honourable fidelity. Their habit of begging for small presents of Europeans gives an unfavourable impression of them at first acquaintance; but if they beg, they also give; almsgiving being, according to Mr. Backhouse, the Quaker Missionary, so much their custom, 'that a man's wife and children often go to work in the garden, that the begging stranger may be supplied.'

"Their martial qualities of skill, activity, daring, and endurance, our soldiers have only too well proved; and our officers tell us, that another campaign or two of lessons would teach them our tactics almost as well as they have already learnt from us to ride on horseback, and to use fire-arms instead of assagais.

---

* "Parliamentary Papers, Kafir Tribes, 1853, p. 107."

Indeed, their intellectual powers generally seem good; a perusal
of the Blue Books would prove to any one that a Kafir chief is
in diplomacy no bad match for an English general; and we have
the testimony of Mrs. Ward, no friendly witness, that 'they
are the cleverest logicians in the world, and have always an
answer more suitable to their own purpose than we could
possibly anticipate.'

" There is, however, one most striking and all-important peculiarity in which they differ from almost all the aboriginal tribes
with which our colonists have come in contact.   To the Red
Indians and New Zealanders, the Australians, and even their
own Hottentot neighbours, Christian civilization has been as an
upas-tree, destroying them by its diseases, or still more fatally
poisoning them by the infectious contamination of its drunkards
and debauchees : but the Kafirs have shown that they can live
on the borders of a civilized community ; and, unless killed off
by war, or by famine caused by war, they keep up their numbers.

" The history of European civilization has, indeed, but too plainly
proved how hard it is for a strong race to do more for a weak
race than to bestow upon it its vices ; and, too quickly deducing
from the sad facts of this history the conclusion, that that which
is hard must be impossible, there are many persons who advocate
severe measures against the Kafirs, as against all savages, on the
principle that it is more humane to kill them quickly with powder
and shot than slowly by drink or disease.

" The Boers, we are told, are great readers of the Old Testa-
ment ; and, comparing themselves to the Israelites, as did the
Puritans of New England, they shoot a Native on the strength of
a text out of Joshua.   In like manner, not a few of our present
political *doctrinaires* justify injustice and atrocity by their interpretation of their gospel,—'the theory of human progression.'
The interpretation is in both cases equally at fault ; but even
granting its truth, as regards the Kafirs the facts are against
them.   They are not a drunken people : they make, it is true,
a mild, almost harmless, beer among themselves, and some of their
chiefs have become drunkards from disappointment and from the
temptation of Europeans ; but Mr. Backhouse, himself a zealous
teetotaller, who complains greatly of the drinking habits of many
of the Hottentots, tells us, as the result of his keen observation,

that 'few of the Kafirs, even on the frontier, drink intoxicating liquors,' a statement confirmed by the testimony of other missionaries. Even more important is the jealous care with which they preserve themselves from the effects of European profligacy, so fearfully fatal to the South-Sea Islanders.

"In a word, the Kafir race has in itself strong elements of continuance, and a power of co-existence with civilization, which ought to add strength to the efforts to civilize, inasmuch as it makes these efforts more hopeful; missionaries and philanthropists not being among them, as they often are, haunted by the conviction that death dogs their footsteps; while, if they really be the 'irreclaimable savages' they are so often called, there is little hope of exterminating them except by the old-fashioned method of fire and sword. How far, with what success, and on what grounds, this method has been tried, it will be needful, in order to understand our present relation with them, briefly to consider."*

These are the calm and dispassionate reflections of an able British statesman, and harmonize most completely with the views to which I gave utterance, six years ago, in the Colony.

---

* "Edinburgh Review," No. cciii., pp. 118–120.

CHAPTER IX.

TOWNS, VILLAGES, AND SETTLEMENTS.

THE chief towns in the Natal Colony are D'URBAN and PIE-TERMARITZBURG. The former is the Port, and the only entrance for shipping to the Colony. The latter is the seat of government.

It is probable that other entrances for shipping will soon be discovered, especially for small craft; and thus a large amount of expenditure will be saved in the item of land carriage.

D'URBAN.

THE reader will observe, on consulting the "Chart" of the Bay, (page 1,) that a plan of the town of D'Urban is given; also the site of the Camp, situated on the flat at a short distance from the town.

The site of the town is above the head of the Bay to the north; and its position, being on a low flat, is more favourable for business than conducive to health. It is skirted by the Berea Hills, at a distance of about two miles, where the range curves, running to the Umgeni river on the north-east, and the Umbilo river on the west. A plain, some parts of which are swampy, and covered with a tall, broad-leaved grass, extends along the base of these hills, on a part of which the town of D'Urban is built.

The name "D'Urban" was given to this place by the early English settlers, in honour of his excellency Sir Benjamin D'Urban, the highly esteemed governor of the Cape.

There is much bush and wood about the town, which at once contributes to the beauty of the scenery, and supplies poles and laths for the erection of those houses which are not built of brick. Of fire-wood there is a good supply; and it may be easily obtained. Of water there is abundance, but often not of the best quality, except it can be fetched from the Umgeni river, —a mode of supply which is both troublesome and expensive. This defect will be fully remedied if that river can be brought through the town, as already contemplated.

Indeed, the probability is, that the town would be decidedly unhealthy, were it not for the sea being so adjacent, the breeze from which usually rises about ten o'clock in the morning. As strong winds also occasionally prevail, the atmosphere is kept pure and clear.

When the white man first trod this plain, it was a beautiful green sward, covered with grass, and interspersed with clumps of ever-green trees; but now, in the town, the streets are long beds of deep sand, through which it is very difficult to walk; and, indeed, a march through it is a heavy task for the pedestrian to perform. A municipality is likely soon to be formed, when this evil will probably be removed in whole, or in part, and the swampy parts will be drained.

When the author arrived in the Colony, upwards of five years ago, there were only few houses, and those mostly of a very inferior description, being of wattle and clay. There were, also, at that time few inhabitants, some of whom were going away; the coasting vessels being full of passengers when leaving, and bringing none on their return voyages. Some of the houses were falling down; and these were said to be fit emblems of the place itself, which "could never rise;" for it was confidently predicted, that in a few years Natal would be amongst the places that had been, but which no longer existed. Advertisements might be seen in the papers, that houses could be had, without payment of rent, merely for keeping them in repair; but even on these terms occupants could not be found, and diviners said the place would soon be abandoned. The writer, however, was quite aware of that not being the time when such a catastrophe would take place. There was too much enterprise abroad in the world for such a country to pass long unnoticed; and, when known, it would assuredly become a point of interest and attraction to the civilized world.

Some years have since passed away, but how changed the scene! Instead of a solitary house here and there, hid in thick bush, and with difficulty found, dwellings now (1852) thickly stud the ground in every direction. Instead of a town whose highways could only be traced on paper, there are now streets well filled up, many of the building allotments having been subdivided to meet the wants of numerous applicants. Instead of a settlement only to be seen on the surveyor's Chart, you now find busy multitudes surrounding you on all hands. Instead of wattled huts falling to ruins, pole after pole of which bore unmistakeable marks of decay, there are now many buildings erected, both substantial and handsome.

The Plate No. XII. presents to view the large store of Middleton, Wirsing, and Acut, who occupy the whole of the ground-floor, with the exception of one room to the right, which is used by government for the post-office. Here, on the arrival of the mail, people may be seen pressing one upon the other, and anxiously seeking letters from their friends in England; and, having waited long, and inquired often, they return disappointed and downcast, not having received the remittance which they hoped for, nor heard from the friend most dear to the heart. The upper rooms of Middleton and Co.'s house are hired by government for the magistrates' court and other offices, for which they are very suitable. The low thatched house to the left in the illustration is the residence of Mr. Kahts, an old inhabitant, and one of the present landing-agents. This is a specimen of what the houses were in days gone by, only that it is now neatly dressed with a coat of thatch recently put on. The other buildings exhibited to view are of a similar kind, and need no description.

The waggons, the oxen, the drivers, the leaders, and the accoutrements are all correctly given, and may convey a just idea of South African life. The Kafir figures, also, unlike most of those in other books, show what these people in appearance really are. The old woman with the pumpkins on her head, her large breasts hanging down, and her leathern dress tied round the loins, is just what the reader would see if he beheld her in person instead of seeing her in a pictured representation. The young woman with the basket on her head, her round breasts and entire nudity, with the exception of a small strip of calico round the middle,—and the tall man, *without any load*, holding his assagai or stick in his right hand, and pointing with the left, and pro-

XII. THE MARKET SQUARE, D'URBAN, NATAL.

bably vociferating to the females, with his rings of leather or brass on the arms, his bands of beasts' skins with long hair round his ancles, and his ornaments dangling in front tied round his loins,—both are perfectly true to the life. The two Kafir boys with the hand-barrow, and all the *et cæteras* of Englishmen, horses, dogs, &c., make this a good description of what is stirring in Port Natal.

Amongst the public buildings are, a neat new Wesleyan chapel, in which the English congregation worships, and an old one, formerly used by the English, but now by the Natives. This last-named building was the first chapel used for public worship in D'Urban. There is a government school-room, in which the Episcopalians conduct divine worship on the Sabbath-day ; and also a large room fitted up for religious worship, which is used by the Congregationalists.

There are no barracks, the old Camp still being used for the soldiers. At the Point there is a large substantial Custom-House, and a Block-House, with a few soldiers and artillery, to guard the entrance to the Bay.

There is also a prison, which looks more like a neat cottage than the place in which convicts are to be incarcerated. In days of yore this building was without occupant, save and except the gaoler himself; but the good old times have passed away, and, with an increase of population, there has been an increase of crime.

Of religious bodies, there are Episcopalians, Wesleyans, and Congregationalists. The two former have regular ministers : the service of the latter is chiefly conducted by lay agency. A Roman Catholic priest was also officiating for a time ; but I know not that he has any regular ministration in the place.

A Literary Institution and a Library exist here ; but do not appear to be in a flourishing state, for want of more general encouragement and support. There is a public school, conducted by a teacher paid by government, besides several private schools of a respectable character ; so that the religious and educational wants of the community are, to a favourable extent, provided for.

An Agricultural and Horticultural Society (the names of the members of which are given elsewhere) adds a little zest to the

pursuits embraced within the range of its operations, and is of
the greatest importance to the prosperity of the Colony, since, if
wisely and vigorously conducted, it will greatly conduce to the
full developement of the resources of the Colony.   Mr. M'Ken,
the manager of the Gardens, is an able and suitable person for
accomplishing the object contemplated.

Of " stores," or what in England are called " shops," there
are more than enough; and, instead of each being restricted to
one kind of goods only, as in England, it generally has a
little of all sorts; so that a customer need not divide his favours
by going to more shops than one for all that he requires.

There are also some very respectable merchants' houses in the
Bay, which transact a large amount of business, and whose trade
appears likely to increase, as the export of wool, ivory, &c., from
the Sovereignty and the Vaal River, is beginning to come this
way, instead of going by Algoa Bay in the old Colony as heretofore.   The beneficial effect of this is already being felt.

The number of inhabitants in July, 1851, was,—

Men	629	
Women	404	
Children	541	
		1,574
Soldiers in Camp	100	
Ditto, at Block-House	20	
		120
Total Population		1,694

This statistical account was taken at the time when emigration
was at the highest, and is probably considerably above the present
number; some having left the Colony, and others having removed
into the interior.   If in round numbers we call it at present
1,200, this will allow a decrease of nearly 500, which is probably
more than the reality.   These numbers are not founded on guess;
the name of the head of each family having been taken, with
a statement of the inmates of the house and members of the
family, which insured this aggregate.   The probability, however,
is that some were overlooked, from the great fluctuation of the
population at that time, and the uncertain place of abode of many.

PIETERMARITZBURG.

THIS is the metropolis of the Colony. It is distant from the Bay about fifty-two miles in a north-west direction, as may be seen on consulting the Map. It is the seat of government, the officers of which reside there; and is also the head-quarters of the Forty-fifth Regiment, Colonel Boys being in command.

The town is situated on a sloping belt of land, with the Bushman's River flowing on one side of it towards the south, the high peak of the Zwart Kop Mountain bounding it to the west, and another range of mountains to the north. It is thought that these mountains, being so near the town, are the cause of the terrific thunder-storms which sometimes visit this place, and are occasionally attended with fatal consequences. The country around is almost entirely destitute of wood, except in some of the mountain kloofs, giving to the whole neighbourhood a wild, yet monotonous, appearance. The scarcity of wood makes fuel very dear in the town, this article being an item of some consideration in household expenditure. There is an abundant supply of fresh water, which runs through the town, and by which most of the *erven,* or building allotments and gardens, can be irrigated; and by the planting of trees, many of which have now grown to a considerable size, an air of freshness and variety is being given to the whole.

The streets are long, and intersect each other at right angles; but they are not yet by any means filled up with the habitations of man, although the number of dwellings has greatly increased during the past two years.

Of public buildings, there are the colonial offices, the court-house, and a prison, with a hospital in contemplation. Not any of the above are either great or grand, but serve the purposes to which they are appropriated. The barracks stand on a hill above the town, and are good brick buildings, being, I presume, every way convenient for the use of the military.

There is also a church, or chapel, built for and used by the members of the Dutch Reformed persuasion; with two Methodist chapels, one for the English, and the other for the natives; an Independent chapel; a government school-room, which is used by the Episcopalians for divine worship; and a church, in course of erection for the same religious Body. The Presbyterians are also hoping shortly to erect a chapel, having obtained considerable contributions towards this object.

Seven different religious denominations are here found,— enough, certainly, one would suppose, to meet the diversified creeds, tastes, and desires of the inhabitants. These are,—Episcopalians, Dutch Reformed, Wesleyans, Presbyterians, Independents, Lutherans, and Roman Catholics. Four of them have regularly ordained ministers; and the remainder are dependent upon lay agency, with the occasional services of regular ministers.

There is an efficient government teacher, and some private schools are carried on in the town; also Sabbath-schools, connected with most of the places of worship.

Pietermaritzburg was selected as a site for a town by the Dutch, and is in a favourable position, both as the seat of government, and for mercantile transactions; being central, and on the direct road from D'Urban to the Sovereignty. There are some good stores in it, and considerable business is connected with them. Much has been said about a new line of road to the Sovereignty, which would pass by the Ilovo River, near Richmond, direct to the Bay; but this will not be favourable to the interests of those who have invested capital in Pietermaritzburg, and consequently is not likely to be strongly advocated by them. Some, however, say that the road would come by Maritzburg.

LADYSMITH.

This place is also the seat of magistracy for the Klip River division of the Colony. It is situated about one hundred miles beyond Pietermaritzburg, being nearly on the direct line of road to the interior and the Sovereignty. There are not many houses in the town itself; but several Dutch families occupy farms in the neighbourhood. This locality is regarded as favourable for the production of corn and butter, both of which are likely to become abundant. The advancement or neglect of this place will be greatly affected by the trade of the interior.

WEENEN.

" Weenen " signifies " Weeping," or " Suffering," in Dutch, and derived its name from the terrible slaughter of the Dutch Farmers by Dingaan's army in the early part of 1838, when six

XIV.—VIEW OF VERULAM, ON THE RIVER UMHLOTI.

hundred human beings were ruthlessly massacred by the assagai of the savage Zulu; and the name, "Weeping," fitly perpetuates the remembrance of that day of sorrow and tears. This place is situated on the Bushman's River; and the inhabitants of these parts are mostly Dutch. It has not yet risen to much note; but as it is in the centre of a rich agricultural district, the probability is that it will increase in importance.

VERULAM.

THIS rising town and settlement is the result of Mr. Irons's emigration scheme, which was merged in the greater one undertaken by Messrs. Byrne and Co. The first occupants came to Natal in the "King William," which arrived on January 23rd, 1850. They had many trials to endure in the commencement of their new settlement, which were greatly aggravated by a delay of nearly three months before they could get possession of the land upon which they are now located. This so discouraged most of them, that they seriously contemplated abandoning the idea of forming a new settlement, considering their almost exhausted means; but, following the advice of one or two friends whom they consulted, and who took an interest in their welfare, after long delay they made the attempt; and the accompanying drawing shows part of the result. (Plate XIV.)

The site of the town is on the Umhloti river, about five miles from the sea, and about twenty miles from D'Urban, on the proper route to Zulu-land, the high road passing directly through it. The drawing shows most of the houses erected on the site of the town or village, without embracing a number of others built in different parts of the settlement. The reason why there are not more houses in the town is, that many of the people are occupying their country holdings, in order to cultivate land more extensively than would be practicable upon the limited space allowed in the town itself. The river, and hills, and surrounding scenery, interspersed with trees and bush, and covered with grass, with the sea opening at the mouth of the stream, present a beautiful and varied prospect to the admiring eye of the spectator, and invite the skill and energy of man to develope their resources.

Many of the inhabitants are members of the Wesleyan church;

and one of the first buildings erected was a chapel for the worship of their God. This is seen in the drawing, with its tiny
bell by the side of it, and the chapel for the use of the Kafir
congregation just above.

How gratifying is it to the mind of an English Christian, thus
to find the intelligence, the enterprise, the energy, the language,
and the Christianity of England transplanted to an African soil,
and becoming the nucleus of an important and prosperous
Christian community! May God smile upon them, and speed
their undertakings!

RICHMOND.

Richmond is situated on the Ilovo River, at nearly a right
angle from D'Urban and Pietermaritzburg, to the westward;
being about at an equal distance from both in a straight line, but,
by the circuitous route, being further from the Bay than from
Pietermaritzburg. From the latter place it is distant about
thirty-five miles.

This little settlement and town in embryo is likewise the result
of Mr. Byrne's emigration scheme; a few families from different
vessels taking up their abodes on the lands assigned them by the
emigration agent, and making, in the aggregate, an interesting
community, the number of whose members I cannot accurately
state. This town is in a fruitful part of the country; but there
is little wood near, and the scenery is not picturesque.

YORK.

This great English name distinguishes the place where the
emigrants by the " Haidee," under the late lamented Mr. Boost,
have fixed their residence. It is about twenty or twenty-five
miles to the east of Pietermaritzburg, in the upper part of the
Umvoti division. It is said to be a good country for cattle and
corn; and the people are beginning to make the effects of their
industry felt, in producing various articles for the consumption of
man and beast.

Many of the inhabitants of this town are Methodists, and have
had divine worship regularly conducted from the commencement
of their settlement.

Strong indications of copper ore have been met with in this

locality; but nothing certain or definite has yet been done to ascertain whether this valuable metal is actually there to be found or not.

PINE TOWN

Is about thirteen miles from D'Urban, on the direct road to Pietermaritzburg. There are a number of families in the neighbourhood; but only few in what is called "the town." Here is a chapel built, in which the Presbyterians and the Wesleyans conduct divine worship alternately.

NEW GERMANY is close by, which contains some forty families, who are greatly benefited by the zealous labours of the Rev. W. Posselt, from Berlin.

In addition to the places already enumerated, there are several more that have the names of towns, and are laid out upon the surveyor's chart; but they can establish no fair claim to this pretension, having probably but from one to six houses erected upon them. Whether they will ever attain to any importance, is still problematical. ALBERT (or COMPENSATION) I except, how-

ever, and shall treat more directly upon its importance in the Chapter upon Emigration. This being the place where sugar has been successfully cultivated, and where other valuable tropical productions have been raised, it has solved the difficulty, and answered the question, whether, or not, Natal is suitable for the cultivation of these valuable export articles.

SETTLEMENTS.

Of these there are a considerable number in the Colony; and they are still on the increase: but it is not needful to enter into any particular description of them; the bare enumeration, with a few passing remarks, being sufficient.

The Woodcut No. XV. shows the settlement on the Drift of the Umgeni river, three miles from D'Urban, towards Zulu-land. The largest buildings there shown are Mr. Morewood's emigration barracks, whither those who came from England in connexion with him were at once conveyed, and thus placed beyond the temptation to drink, and to acquire those idle and dissolute habits which so greatly abound in the town, and into which those who have been so long cooped up in an emigration vessel are in the greatest danger of falling.

XV.—THE UMGENI RIVER, AS SEEN FROM MR. MOREWOOD'S DRIFT.

Milkwood Kraal, the estate of Mr. Henry, has now a number of families,—say twenty or thirty. In the immediate vicinity of it, a small Wesleyan chapel is erected, and divine worship is regularly conducted on the Sabbath. Further on in the same direction,—passing through Verulam and by Compensation,—on the Umhlali River, a small community is established.

To the west of D'Urban is Congella, three miles distant,—the original Camp of the Dutch Boers. There are a few English families at present living there. On the Umbilo River, and near Sea-View, probably twenty more families reside. Beyond the Umhlatusan River is Claremont Town *in name*, and Wentworth, which together contain, perhaps, twenty families. Still further, after passing the Umlazi River, in the vicinity of the Isipingo River, may be thirty families more. Seven parties here are growing wheat, as an experiment, with confident hopes of success. These, with others settling in different localities near the Bay, give a large aggregate population along the coast.

There are some additional settlements around and beyond Pietermaritzburg; namely, Byrne Town, Lidgetton, Shafter, and others; but in these parts the inhabitants are more scattered, rather occupying farms than collecting in villages.

Some have doubted whether, all things considered, the Colony has been benefited or not by the result of Byrne's emigration scheme. Doubtless much evil has existed, and much suffering has been endured, and many have left the Colony in disgust, speaking all manner of evil of it, and retarding its progress. But, upon the whole, there are now probably thousands of emigrants, who are already incomparably better off than they had any reasonable prospect of being, had they remained in England. Their first difficulties are surmounted, and a course of honest industry, if persevered in, will yield a rich reward.

Towns, villages, and settlements are rising up in all directions, founded and raised up by British enterprise, skill, and labour, which will probably increase, until a hardy, prosperous, and happy people cover these fertile lands; and if they pursue the path of virtue and piety, the blessing of Jehovah will rest upon them. "Righteousness exalteth a nation," whilst "sin is a reproach to any people." The civilization, the arts, the language, the institutions, and the religion of the British nation, being planted here, will produce their legitimate consequences, until this portion of the Anglo-Saxon race shall rival, if not exceed, the greatness and glory of their forefathers.

TABLES OF DISTANCES FROM D'URBAN TO PIETERMARITZBURG AND LADYSMITH.

252

HISTORY OF NATAL.

[CHAP.

D'Urban to Pietermaritzburg (mls. yds.)

To	D'Urban, from Cato's	Top of Berea	German Hotel	Pine Tn. Hotel	Field's Bush	Botha's Hlf. Way	Bottom Stony Hl.	Sterk Spruit	Uitkomst	Fisher's Hotel	Rolfe's Hotel	Luscomb's Hotel
Top of Berea.	2 1,529											
German Hotel.	8 464	5 695										
Pine Tn. Hotel.	12 541	9 772	4 77									
Field's Bush.	14 1,488	11 1,719	6 1,024	2 947								
Botha's Hlf. Way.	20 1,817	17 1,548	12 853	8 776	5 1,589							
Bottom Stony Hl.	22 1,568	20 39	14 1,104	10 1,027	8 80	2 251						
Sterk Spruit.	27 456	24 687	18 1,752	14 1,675	12 728	6 899	4 648					
Uitkomst.	33 456	30 687	24 1,752	20 1,675	18 728	12 899	10 648	6 —				
Fisher's Hotel.	37 18	34 249	28 1,314	24 1,237	22 290	16 461	14 210	9 1,322	3 1,322			
Rolfe's Hotel.	38 757	35 986	30 293	26 216	23 1,029	17 1,200	15 949	11 301	5 301	1 739		
Luscomb's Hotel.	44 —	41 231	35 1,296	31 1,219	29 272	23 443	21 192	16 1,304	10 1,304	7 —	5 1,003	
Colonial Of. P.Mtzburg.	52 128	49 359	43 1,424	39 1,347	37 400	31 571	29 320	24 1,432	18 1,432	15 110	13 1,131	8 128

Pietermaritzburg to Ladysmith (mls. yds.)

To	P.Mburg.	Umgeni.	Mooi River.	Bushman River.	Blue Krantz.	Tugela.
Umgeni.	13 1,300					
Mooi River.	41 952	27 1,412				
Bushman River.	60 642	46 1,102	18 1,450			
Blue Krantz.	78 1,194	59 1,654	32 242	13 552		
Tugela.	81 1,570	68 270	40 618	21 928	8 376	
Ladysmith.	100 356	86 816	58 1,164	39 1,474	26 922	18 546

CHAPTER X.

ON EMIGRATION AND THE CAPABILITIES OF NATAL.*

THE subject of emigration has, for some time, occupied the serious consideration of the British public; and both political economists and the community in general have had their attention specially directed to it.

Amongst the different places which have been represented as favourable for the purpose of emigration, Natal has lately held a prominent place; the result of which has been that in the course of the last six months six vessels have arrived, bringing about one thousand British subjects to our shores. These have mostly been under the arrangements of Messrs. Byrne and Co., and the parties have had portions of land allotted to them. About a fortnight ago, the "King William" arrived, with upwards of two hundred on board, forty of whom were, more or less, connected with the Methodist Society, under Mr. Irons. Most of the emigrants that have hitherto arrived, have been of the poorer class of honest, industrious Englishmen, and have got employment without going upon the lands at all. Tradesmen and mechanics have obtained wages from 5s. 8d. to 7s. 6d. per day, and others at a lower rate. But the wants of a small Colony are soon supplied, when numbers so large are poured into it in so short a time. Consequently, for the future, most of those who come will have to be supported from the resources of the soil; and it is therefore of the utmost importance to them to have correct information on such matters as concern them. Amidst the multiplicity of writers and talkers on Natal affairs at the present time, I should not attempt to put my pen to paper, if it

---

* The substance of some of the early pages of this Chapter was written by me about two years ago, (1850,) and published in the "Watchman" newspaper. It is here introduced partly for the purpose of comparing the past with the present, and also as containing much that is of permanent interest.

were not for the fact that great misapprehension exists about the true state of things here, arising from the contradictory statements which are put forth.

Parties wishing to promote emigration to Natal, give the most glowing description of it. On the other hand, when emigrants arrive, they say the country is not what they were authorized to expect; and after a few days spent in their new and discouraging circumstances, they are disposed to give the most unfavourable account of every thing.

Now it appears to me that both parties err;—the former, in not accompanying their high recommendations with a statement of the difficulties which must necessarily be connected with emigration, and starting life under new and untried circumstances;—and the latter, in not sufficiently calculating upon the discouragements and privations which must inevitably be endured for a few months, and perhaps years, in a new country. Hence some of them directly exclaim that "they have been deceived; the country is not what they expected to find it, nor are its capabilities at all such as they were represented to be;—the ground is bad; the cattle are small, and do not give much milk; this plant will not grow, and the other crop has failed." Such language does not surprise us; but we think that before people make use of it, they should know a little more about the country and its capabilities; and then, in many instances, their sentiments would be much modified, or entirely changed. They certainly are not able to form an opinion concerning that of which they speak so positively: not one in fifty has yet been upon the land assigned them; and the few who have been, did not remain sufficiently long to give it a fair trial.

The other day, one gentleman said he had been round to look at what was doing, and had found a few persons who were cultivating; but, even there, only two sorts of seeds had grown; that the country was altogether too dry and arid to produce any thing, &c., &c. So would old England also seem at Midsummer, and especially in an unusually dry and hot summer, such as has been at Natal this year; but Midsummer is not the time for sowing in Natal, any more than it is in England. Another gentleman said, that the land had been represented as flowing with milk and honey; whereas it would produce nothing but trees, and grass, and Indian corn. The fact is, that it is one of the finest countries in the world. Milk-wood trees there are in it, but not yielding such milk as is used for the ordinary purposes of life by human beings. Rich fruits and nutritious plants grow in abundance; but the ground does not *spontaneously* produce wheat, oats, barley, potatoes, cabbage, beans, peas, &c., &c.: so that those who expect to find things after this fashion had better not come; for 'they will certainly be disappointed, as these esculents can only be obtained by the exercise of skill and labour. But if they want to know what they may rely upon, as to the condition of this country, I will state the following facts, without fear of successful contradiction:—

1. *The climate* is delightful, approaching nearly to a tropical one, without superinducing the enervating and sickening effects of the tropics. Even the newly-arrived emigrants have worked out of doors during the warmth of this summer, without any particular ill consequences. In winter, frost and snow are unknown along the coast; but at fifty miles inland both commence, and the heat of summer and the cold of winter increase, as you proceed farther. The snow lies on the Drakenberg Mountains for a considerable time in the winter. The country is exceedingly healthy.

2. *The seasons.*—Two crops a year may certainly be grown, unless there happen at some time to be a particularly dry season, when a crop may possibly be lost; but five crops out of six may be calculated on. Sometimes, also, a crop may be destroyed by locusts; but I think this may be prevented when the proper time for sowing and reaping is more certainly known. Two crops a year may be ordinarily calculated upon.

3. *The soil.*—This, most of the new-comers say, is bad; while the old colonists declare that these detractors know nothing about it. I believe I may safely affirm that, if well cleared and manured as the English lands are, it will produce two crops a year, each of them quite as abundant as the single one in England. As for grass, I am quite satisfied that the same quantity of land which will support five cattle in England will feed twenty in this country. All the cattle which both white men and black men have yet been able to keep, have scarcely made a perceptible difference in the grass; and it has to be burnt off the ground every year. In autumn and winter the country is lighted up with fires burning in all

directions, some of them from one to three miles long, raging fiercely before the wind, and curling beautifully along the hills. The sight is pleasant to the eye, but saddening to the heart of the philanthropist, when he thinks of the thousands pining in squalid misery in England, who might be deriving a comfortable subsistence from this soil under proper cultivation and management.

4. *Cattle* are in good condition, being fat; "but," forsooth, "they are very small, and give but little milk." Indeed, to an eye accustomed to the fine cattle of England, the colonial ones look contemptible. But this statement is correct only concerning those along the coast; the cattle fifty or one hundred miles inland being larger, and giving more milk. But then most of these complaining gentlemen lose sight of the fact, that one cow in England costs as much as four at Natal; and, to say the worst of it, four here will give as much milk as one of the best in England; whilst the man gets four calves in the year, instead of one; and, if he happens to lose a cow by death, the loss is but £3, instead of £12, which would be its amount in England. "But," the objector says, "if I should be fortunate enough to rear the four calves, they still are only worth £12;" forgetting that, as a consequence, he pays but 2½d. *per* pound for his beef, instead of 6d., as in England; and that, if a small party are located together in the country, they can slaughter a beast occasionally, which would be utterly impossible on the English scale of prices. Besides this, by importation an improved breed may be obtained more advantageously than in almost any other country. The present cattle on the coast are small Zulus; but, if crossed with a good English breed, they would be amongst the best for yielding milk and enduring labour. These cattle are obtained at the cheapest rate. A trader goes into Zulu-land with a few blankets, or sends a trusty Kafir, who gets for a twelve-shilling blanket a young beast, which, being kept two years, is either having a calf and giving milk, or is a fine young ox, ready for the yoke or for the butcher. I think I do not exceed the truth when I say, that thousands are annually brought out in this manner, so that the herds along some parts of the coast are now becoming exceedingly numerous.

It must not be forgotten either, that in England a man must

be at some expense to keep only one cow. He must hire a field of grass in the summer, and buy hay in the winter. But here he keeps a large herd for the same or less expense than one there; nay, the more he keeps, the better : for then the cattle eat the grass, and manure the ground; whereas otherwise the grass must be burnt off, which is an injurious practice, when long-continued, as it makes the surface of the ground very hard, and, for a time, difficult of cultivation. On some parts of the coast where cattle could not formerly live, they now do well, owing to the grass being *eaten*, instead of being *burnt* : at least, such is the opinion of the best judges.

5. *Productions.*—Concerning agricultural pursuits and developement, I am sorry to say that every thing is so far in a state of infancy here, as to make it exceedingly difficult to speak with certainty. There is only one place to which I can refer, where any thing like a fair attempt has been made at cultivation; and that is upon the estate of Jung and Co., where cotton has been grown; but the situation is unfavourable, the land being poor and too far distant from the coast for the fine cotton-plant to flourish. I have been informed that a large quantity of upland cotton has been raised there; but this is worth only sixpence *per* pound in the English market, whilst the fine cotton obtains one shilling.

Cotton was the great engrossing article of cultivation at one time; but it is now by some pronounced to be a failure. In coming to this conclusion, however, I think the parties have been much too hasty. Those who have resided the longest in the country, and have instituted experiments in the mode of rearing the plant or tree, are only now possessed of sufficient information to enable them to *commence* its cultivation *in a proper manner.*

I believe it is found that the upland cotton yields only a small profit; but if the fine Sea-Island cotton can be successfully cultivated, it will yield a large return. This was partly tried on the estate of Messrs. Jung; but it was found that the land was too weak, and too far from the coast, so that the cold winds cut it off. Consequently the fine plants were removed, and the indigenous put in their place. It is generally believed, however, that the rich lands along the coast, which are now chiefly covered with bush, will produce the fine cotton very abundantly. I am

s

sorry that hitherto the experiment has not been tried; nor can it be, until a little capital is invested in the attempt.

Sugar is now beginning to attract attention, and it is thought that it may be grown advantageously. One gentleman has planted several acres; and I am informed by two competent judges that the plants are looking well. These persons have been in the West Indies, and are therefore able to form an opinion on the subject. Two years ago I purchased a few plants, which were brought to this place from the Isle of Bourbon. I planted them in two different situations: one failed; the other brought forth abundantly, producing canes six feet long, and six inches in circumference, which, by proper care, might have been even much larger. The quality of these canes was pronounced to be equal to West Indian, and the saccharine matter was good in flavour and abundant in quantity. If the canes look well this year, which is one of drought, then in the rainy seasons the probability is that they will be incomparably better. Gentlemen from the Mauritius are here for the purpose of ascertaining whether sugar can be profitably cultivated; but their report I have not heard.*

Amongst other articles spoken of, but not tried, are indigo, coffee, arrowroot, ginger, turmeric, &c., &c.

Fruits.—Of these, the orange, pine-apple, banana, guava, &c., flourish luxuriantly along the low lands; the apple, pear, peach, fig, &c., &c., inland.

Grain.—Oats flourish upon the coast; wheat, barley, and oats, further inland. It is the opinion of some that wheat and barley will flourish also on the coast; and some farmers, who have sown a little this year, are preparing to sow much more largely next.

Vegetables.—Potatoes, cabbage, beans, peas, carrots, pumpkins, Indian corn, &c., may be grown twice a year in almost all parts of the country.

Timber.—There is no large timber along the coast for general building purposes, but much thick bush, with large trees interspersed amongst the small underwood, which may be used advantageously in the construction of waggons, boats, furniture,

---

* For an account of Mr. Morewood's successful trial of sugar-growing, see Chapter XI.

&c.; but the timber for building is either imported, or brought from beyond Pietermaritzburg.

In order that emigration to Natal may be mutually beneficial to the Colony and the emigrant, there are a few things which are necessary to be observed.

The prosperity of the Colony, and the consequent advantage of the emigrant, depend on the exports raised; and these, as far as is at present known, must be chiefly drawn from the soil. *Wool*, which is the chief article of export from the old Colony, and actually the source of its wealth, has not had a fair trial in this Colony; and, I think, will not for some time be largely grown, the native grass apparently being too rank and abundant, and thus either killing the sheep, or filling the wool with seeds and weeds. What may be done in the course of time it is impossible to say. Some parts, where formerly horses and cattle could not live, have now thousands living upon them, and every year are becoming more healthy, and less infested with annoying insects. By some change in the class of grasses, pasturage may be greatly improved, and so managed as to allow wooled sheep to thrive. If so, then this will become an exhaustless source of wealth.

Cattle.—These are numerous, and are exported to the Mauritius; but this export, while valuable in the abstract, has been carried out only to a very limited extent; nor is it on the increase, or likely to improve.

Wheat flourishes in some parts, and may be grown in almost an unlimited quantity: but the demand for it in this Colony is only very small; and then the only market open for it is the Mauritius; but, before it can be exported thither, the parties exporting must be able to supply it at a lower rate than the Cape merchants can. By the time this is brought about, the price will be so low as to make it barely remunerating. It is true that, at present, large quantities of American fine flour and Cape coarse flour are imported into the Colony, which must be stopped by the growth of wheat upon a large scale. But this will doubtless be done in the space of a few years. Not only are the English farmers beginning to be producers, but many of the Dutch Boers have returned from beyond the Drakenberg, and are now settling upon cattle-grazing and wheat-growing farms, from

which great quantities will soon be produced; and bread, one
of the dearest articles in the Colony, will then become one of the
cheapest.

Peas and *beans* may also be largely produced, and exported to
the Mauritius; and *butter* will doubtless be exported, in great
quantities, to the same place, as well as to the Cape. But, to a
reflecting mind, it will be apparent that these all relate only to
local markets, and can be carried on, at best, only to a small
extent; whereas, for the Colony really and permanently to pros-
per, there must be some exports for the English market. If this
can be managed, then whatever is produced will every year be
increasing in value; whilst the most successful modes of producing will be gradually discovered. In order to obtain this
result, the resources of the soil must be developed. The coast
range of land appears at present to be the only land available for
this purpose. If the soil further inland be suitable for some
things, yet the cold of winter is too severe for tropical productions; whilst, along the coast, frost and snow being unknown in
the severest winters, those plants are not cut off which require
more than one year for bringing them to perfection.

The only two articles that are now the objects of experimental
farming, are cotton and sugar. These I have already noticed;
and there appears every probability that they may be extensively
grown. The apparent failures which have taken place in the
growth of cotton have arisen mostly from ignorance as to the
mode of cultivation, and the proper sites to be selected. Parties
have been in too great haste. Before the ground could be properly prepared, they have, in many instances, put in the seeds;
and, as the ground was far from being in a proper state, they
have not done well: whilst others have begun the cultivation
of cotton, to the exclusion of other things; so that when
the returns have not been so quick and so large as they had
fondly anticipated, they have either entirely abandoned their
lands, or grown upon them other things upon which they
could more certainly calculate. Being persons of small capital,
it has been impossible for them to wait long for a return. It
now appears evident that persons of small means must grow those
articles *first* which as far as possible will supply their own wants;
and then gradually introduce other things, as opportunity occurs;

—not grow cotton first, and then look for something else to lessen their expenses or support their families.

Another evil has been that of people being too anxious to bring a large quantity of ground under cultivation in a short time, instead of seeking to do it *well;* so that, instead of the plants being fine and strong, and producing largely, they have been poor and comparatively unproductive. One thing is quite certain,—the climate and soil are well adapted to the growth of cotton. The plant grows like a weed, and only requires pruning, and the ground to be cleaned ; the same plant growing six or seven years without needing to be replaced ; as may be seen in those about the mission-house, which were growing when I came three years ago, and, although allowed to remain wild, are hanging with pods at the present time,—some of them having their roots washed with sea-water when the tides are high. But there must be capital invested, before a fair attempt can be made.

Besides these occasional failures in the successful growth of cotton, a few others may be expected to await those who, in the genuine spirit of enterprise, venture to engage in similar experiments on different articles of produce. Until men obtain practical knowledge of the best modes of production, want of success may sometimes be expected; but when they have acquired the requisite information, and have adopted the proper means, my opinion is that ultimately every tropical production will be raised without the distressing sickness and frightful mortality which occur in most of the places from whence these articles are at present derived.

Having pointed out the necessity of some great staple article of export being raised in Natal for the English market, I now proceed to show how this may best be done, so as most effectually to benefit both the emigrant and the Colony, as well as the parent country. In order to such a result, there must be some capital invested. It will be evident to every one, that if twenty or one hundred families were placed down in the finest part of England, and told that they must get their living from the land as best they could, the reply would be, " Yes, but how are we to live till the first crop is produced ? And suppose, from our ignorance or some other cause, the first should fail, how are we to live until a second can be obtained ? And perhaps that may not be half enough for our support," &c., &c. This is precisely the case with those who have come here : very few have yet been on their lands at all ; and, of those few, some have speedily left them, being disappointed and discouraged, and have sought employment elsewhere, which they have generally obtained at good wages. But this system cannot long continue. The two towns, D'Urban and Maritzburg, will soon be more than full; so that, unless other towns and villages can be quickly formed, embarrassment and suffering must arise.

To prevent such disasters, people of small capital, from £100 to £2,000, should come out, either on their own private account, or in connexion with an emigration company. If this were done, then a vessel bringing out two hundred families would bring one hundred who, having a little capital, might go upon the land assigned them, and commence the cultivation of the ground, being able to wait, say two years, before they received a remunerating crop ; by which time they would have gone through all the preparatory stages, *acquired knowledge*, brought the ground into a producing state, and obtained a few cattle, oxen, &c. The other hundred families might be farm-labourers, or follow their respective trades. This is the country for the enterprise of small capitalists, but not for having thousands of the poor labouring population of England poured into it. There are Natives in abundance on the land, and these are employed in a manner and upon terms which make all parties prefer hiring them to employing European labourers. One white man may have from two to twenty Natives under him. Under these circumstances, the parties might also be able to employ from one to three English labourers, paying them a moderate salary. By this means a community will be formed : employment will be found for tailors, shoemakers, storekeepers, smiths, carpenters, builders; and after two or three years a prosperous town will be produced. In process of time, as agriculture advanced, and the immediate wants of the people were supplied, they might then grow articles of export, with the certainty that, as they were suitable for the English market, there would always be a demand for them.

"But what would be the advantage in this case over England?" It would be, that *there* the small capitalist must run a sharp race, in order to avoid losing what he has got, and being reduced to poverty in his old age, as has been the case with many : whilst *here,* after struggling two or three years, he becomes actually independent.   He has his own ground, produces his own vegetables, butter, poultry, &c. : his cattle go on increasing without cost.   He raises articles for sale, and then purchases for himself those articles which he cannot produce.   As for the labourer in England, he must labour on to the end of life, with the prospect of spending his days of sickness or age in a poor-house : whereas here he would obtain wages, with food and lodging ; get by degrees some cattle ; and in a few years be able to occupy his own land, and become a small farmer.   Yes, in the old Colony there are many in affluent circumstances, who came out as labouring men twenty years ago : and twenty years hence such will be the case here also.   But I do not think that there will be the same opportunities for parties to rise very rapidly in Natal which have sometimes occurred in the old Colony ; especially as there is but a small military establishment maintained here, whilst there is a large one there.   I have travelled over nearly the whole of what is called "the Eastern Province" of the old Colony, and for three years over this Colony ; and my impression is that Natal will bear a very much larger population than the adjoining country.   Such is the arid character of that land that it produces only *karroo,* and other small herbaceous plants : sand and stone cover much of the ground, and water is very scarce ; so that many of the sheep-farms are of necessity very large, in order to secure water and pasture ; and often a man must have both a summer and a winter farm.   I do not mean to intimate by this that these farms are not valuable : they are, many of them, very much so ; but, under the peculiar circumstances of the case, instead of six thousand acres being capable of being divided into allotments of sixty or one hundred acres, and supporting as many families as there are allotments, they cannot be made smaller.   The opposite is the case here ; and I think it will be found that a family may be supported with comfort on a farm of one hundred or two hundred acres.

Parties intending to emigrate to this country should always keep in mind the different kinds of farming which may be most suitable to them.   If they wish to follow out English farming, growing wheat and rearing cattle, then they should buy a small farm up the country: but if they design cultivating the soil for export, they should get one hundred acres, or upwards, along the coast.

It has been said by some that the lands up the country which have been given to some of the emigrants, are not worth more than 1s. *per* acre. Perhaps they are not, if they are to be cut up into twenty-acre allotments; but, for small farms, they are worth very much more. However, the coast seems to be the tract which can be best divided into small portions, on account of its growing exports, and being intersected with numerous small and large rivers, on the banks of which crowds may live; and then, instead of beholding tens of thousands of acres of dense or scattered bush, the covert of elephants, tigers, &c., there will be seen one vast garden, giving subsistence and wealth to thousands of human beings,—an object most desirable to be accomplished.

Intending emigrants, when leaving England, should not expend their money in purchasing what they think will be useful on their arrival, with the exception of absolute necessaries. Money can be packed into a little compass, and is very useful on arrival at this place. But if the parties are breaking up a small business at home, and cannot dispose of their things without great sacrifice, then, rather than do that, let them bring out with them what is least bulky, and likely to be most profitable.

All who come out should be prepared to endure a little privation and hardship for a few months or years, having before them the prospect of future advancement and comfort, if they adhere to sober, industrious habits. I have been upwards of ten years in different parts of South Africa, but have not yet seen a poor-house, or the necessity for one. I have not seen a street-beggar, or the necessity for one. Individuals and communities have occasionally been involved in loss, and even temporary poverty, by unexpected calamities; but these instances form exceptions to the general rule, which is the gradual attainment of lasting prosperity.

———

The greater part of the preceding statement was written by me two years ago, (1850,) and inserted in the "Watchman" newspaper, and has been as widely spread as that paper has been circulated; but I am not aware that any of the assertions therein contained have been either denied or questioned. I insert them here in order to show the progress of events, and the manner in which the resources of the country are being developed; and also as they contain information which may be of service to intending emigrants at all times, and in going to any part of the world.

There may appear to be a little confusion in mixing emigration up with the capabilities and productions of the country: but these matters are so closely interwoven, and depend so much upon each other, that to combine them, giving a connected view in one general outline, appears better than treating each separately. In order to shorten what would otherwise have been a long Chapter, I have taken the growth of sugar and coffee, with a description of Mr. Morewood's estate, and placed them in a separate Chapter; by this means enabling myself to give a more full account than would have been convenient in connexion with the particulars enumerated in this Chapter.

In the early part of this Chapter I have stated that, although many things would grow and apparently flourish, yet agricultural pursuits had not been conducted on such a plan, or to such an extent, as to enable any one to speak with certainty upon them. The only thing which had then been tried was cotton; and it had not proved so profitable as many at first sanguinely expected, but may yet be produced on a large scale, unless it is superseded by other things that yield a better return.

It is gratifying to be able to state, that now the subject of the capabilities of the country and of its powers of production is set at rest, as will appear in this Chapter; and the great question must be,—What is the best and cheapest mode of bringing forth the dormant wealth of the soil?

As cotton was the first article which brought Natal into notoriety, and was the original cause of calling the attention of the mercantile world towards its capabilities, I shall treat upon it first in order.

Cotton.—Some remarks upon this shrub, written two years ago, will be found again inserted in the preceding pages. The chief causes of failure, as here set forth, are corroborated by the article which I now give from the " Natal Observer," of January 9th, 1852.

"COTTON AND OTHER CULTURES.

"In a late number we gave it as our opinion that the cultivation of cotton cannot be pursued with profit in this Colony in its present condition: but, in saying this, we entirely excluded from our calculations such a cultivation as might be carried out here by means of a large and really wealthy company; for we will not venture to affirm that such an undertaking might not, under judicious management, be made to return a moderate interest on the money invested by moneyed men in England.

"Hitherto success has not attended any attempt that has been made to grow cotton in Natal; but many circumstances must be taken into consideration, as connected with these efforts; and the following may be given as the chief reasons of failure:—

"1st. The land and localities chosen as cotton-lands were, in every sense of the word, unsuitable and injudicious.

"2nd. The managing men were not possessed of an amount of practical experience sufficient to guarantee success to so important an undertaking.

"3rd. The great want of cheap and abundant labour.

"4th. The paucity of means embarked in the speculation; quite insufficient to bear up against those losses which may have arisen from the above-mentioned causes.

"In dealing with the first reason, namely, choice of soil and locality, it may be held as an established fact, that, although the cotton-plant will grow in a vast variety of soils, and even in most uncongenial situations, yet there are few plants more sensitive to a change of *habitat* than cotton, which is abundantly evidenced by the great changes wrought thereby in the appearance of the shrub itself, as also in the quantity and quality of its produce.

"We are led to believe, from the concurrent testimony of many competent judges, that the true and natural *habitat* of cotton in Natal is near the Umkomaaz, where it flourishes with a vigour and with a fruitfulness totally unknown in these divisions of the Colony.

"If, then, this be the case, it is quite evident that it would be sheer folly to attempt cultivating the plant in or near D'Urban; but, as a matter of course, the very best position should be

chosen whereon to establish the cultivation of this valuable production, with a view to its becoming a great staple commodity.

" Grown on good soil, and in a favourable locality, an acre of
cotton-plants will yield 600 to 800 pounds of cotton; whereas
200 pounds only is not unfrequently the crop off poor land in
bad situations.

"Take 1,000 acres, each yielding 500 pounds of cotton, worth
(say, on the spot) 5*d.* *per* pound, or £10 *per* acre; equal to
£10,000 from the whole 1,000 acres. From the first year's
crop there certainly could be little or no profit, although succeeding crops might yield a moderate interest for the money invested.

" Now, contrast this with the usual return to be had from land
planted with other crops. Take potatoes for instance, and allow
8 tons to the acre, or 96 *muids* at 5*s.* *per muid,* equal to £24
per acre. And this may be had twice in one year, making £48
per acre !

"Potatoes are quite fit to dig in four months after planting.
The farmer's calculation may, therefore, be thus:—First crop,
full four months; after which an intermediate growth of clover,
lucern, or other fitting plants, which should be ploughed into the
ground as a *green-soiling,* whilst quite green and succulent;
occupying in all, say, three months (in summer), and then one
month more for the same to lie and rot. Second crop, potatoes;
taking four months again; thus making up the twelve months,
for *two crops of potatoes and one green-soiling.*

" Many other crops might be enumerated, which would yield
as large returns to the farmer; and it is absurd to say that good
potatoes will not always meet a ready sale, either for local consumption, or for exportation to the Mauritius.

"None therefore but large capitalists would think of quitting
these more lucrative cultures to take up cotton-growing, unless
some patriotic mania were to affect our agriculturists; more especially as expensive machinery is required in the latter, but not in
the former."

There are some things here stated as to which I beg respectfully to differ from the writer. Of the desirableness of large
companies for this one particular article of produce, I have some
doubt. I think that at least another commodity should be con-

nected with it, which, from the variety of climate, situation, soil,
&c., might yield a good return if the cotton sometimes failed, and
which would call forth the labour of a large establishment at
alternate seasons of the year. I would add, that little farmers
or tradesmen might grow much cotton on their small allotments,
which might be picked by the children of the family, without
any other labour at all; and by the addition of two Kafirs, a
large quantity might be reaped. Indeed, if the plan which I
have recommended in the Chapter on the English Government
of the Natives were adopted,—that of having an industrial agent
among them, to watch over and assist them in the cultivation of
cotton,—the probability is, that in a few years many ships might
be freighted with this valuable export.

But what is wanted is, dealers or brokers, to buy up the small
quantities which might be produced by persons with limited
means. I have heard that Mr. Leyland Fielden intends doing
this, which I highly commend; and think that, had it been done
before, much would have been produced by this time. As to the
profitable growth of potatoes, this year has shown the precarious
nature of that crop, since sometimes the growers could scarcely
sell, at any price, those which they brought to market, and a
large quantity which had been shipped had to be thrown overboard, because the potatoes would not keep until they arrived at
their destination.

Tea.—I should not have thought of introducing this plant into
this work, had it not been for the following most important
article in the "Natal Observer" of October 24th, 1851, from
the same hand as the preceding extract. This article must stand
upon its own merits, as to whether Natal is the place for tea to
grow and flourish, so as to become a valuable and *paying* production. I am not aware that any attempt has yet been made to
cultivate it. If so, I am ignorant of the fact, and of the progress
made. According to the writer quoted below, Natal is specially
adapted for the plant; and I doubt not that, before long, the
experiment will be made, and a good result shown. If it can be
successfully and profitably cultivated, the great advantage will be
self-evident.

"ON THE CULTIVATION AND PREPARATION OF TEA.

" IF there be one plant more than another particularly adapted to the soil and climate of Natal, and calculated to form in the course of years an important article for export, then that plant, in my opinion, is the TEA-PLANT.

"If we notice the geographical position of the present tea-growing countries, we shall find that although China, as the chief, (taking a range from Macao, in about 22° N., to Pekin, in about 40° N. lat.,) comprehends a great variety of climate; yet that part in which the best tea is principally grown, lies in and about the 30th degree of latitude; in which range much hilly and elevated land is found, and a climate not very dissimilar to that of Natal, situate in about 30° S. lat.

"Again, we have the tea-districts of Assam, in about 27° N., and those of Kumaon and Gurwahl in 29° and 30° N.; the climate of these latter very nearly assimilating to that of many parts of Natal.

"I am much inclined to think that, in point of climate, Natal has a decided advantage over Assam, Kumaon, and even China itself, for the cultivation of the tea-plant; for in many parts of China tea can only be grown successfully by the aid of a vast amount of labour, painful labour, expended in irrigation. This may seem a very random assertion; but to any one who studies the subject, its truth must become quite apparent.

"It would be no easy matter to describe the numerous varieties of soil in which the tea-plant is now thriving very luxuriantly. There can be little doubt that certain peculiar conditions in the formation of the soil tend very greatly to produce fine-flavoured teas; but what these peculiarities are, has never yet been correctly ascertained.

"It is beyond all dispute certain, that it will thrive well in stiff clay, and in very free soils, containing a large proportion of sand, so as almost to merit the designation of 'sandy' soils. We may therefore safely say, that any description of fertile soil will suit its growth.

"Tea-plants, like coffee, should enjoy the benefit of the morning's sun; but I scarcely think it is of so much consequence, although still desirable. It is, however, necessary that they be not exposed to the action of violent winds, which would greatly injure them; but they should be planted in sheltered situations, where they can have a good circulation of air, in the shape of moderate breezes. Otherwise the trees are liable to grow rank, and their leaves coarse and harsh-flavoured.

"Having selected a suitable spot, the first important step is to make a good and permanent fence, so as to exclude cattle and other destructive depredators. This must be attended to. The next step is, to attend to the drainage, so that the plants may not suffer; and in this regard the gently sloping sides of hills form advantageous sites. If the land be well ploughed and thoroughly pulverized, it is in the best condition to receive both the tea-plants themselves, and those which may be used as a shelter to the young plants.

"The land should be laid out in regular lines, so that each shrub be four feet apart; and spaces should be left at distances, to form paths and roads.

"Wherever a young plant or seeds are to be placed (in the field), holes should be dug, of about eighteen inches' diameter and two feet deep; into which good mould, enriched by well-rotted manure, is to be put. The seeds or young plants, being placed in the centre of these prepared spaces, would thereby exhibit a wonderful vigour of growth. The same effect would be attained by running trenches, of eighteen inches' width and two feet depth, every four feet apart, and filling them up again with prepared mould, so that the tea-shrubs or seeds might be planted along it at four-feet distances.

"Having advanced thus far in the choice and preparation of the land for tea-culture, let us now take a glance at the shrub itself.

"The tea-plant is of the genus *thea*, belonging to the order *terstræmiaceæ*, and is so nearly allied to the camellia species as to have led to many mistakes, even by acknowledged botanists. There are three, or perhaps, more properly speaking, two, generally recognised varieties, namely, *thea viridis* and *thea bohea;* of which latter there appear to be two kinds, exhibiting a marked difference from each other. *Thea viridis* is known by its leaves being of a pale green colour, thin, almost membranous, broad lanceolate, serratures or edges irregular and reversed, length from three to six inches. The colour of the stem of newly-formed shoots is a pale red, and green towards the end. It is also marked by its strong growth, its erect stem, and the shoots being generally upright and stiff. The flowers are small, and its seeds but sparing. It is considered by the Chinese as an inferior variety for making tea.* *Thea bohea* is characterized by its leaves being much smaller, and not so broadly lanceolate; slightly waved, of a dark green colour, thick and coriaceous, edge irregular, length from one to three-and-a-half inches. In its growth it is much smaller than the former, and throws out numerous spreading branches, and seldom presents its marked leading stem.

" The second kind is only a marked variety of *thea bohea*. Its leaves are thick, coriaceous, and of a dark green colour, but invariably very small, and not exceeding two inches in length, and thinly lanceolate : the serratures, too, on the edge, which are straight, are not so deep. In other characters they are identical.†"

Rice flourishes, and, I presume, may be grown to an indefinite extent. It has been before stated that Mr. Morewood had raised and sent to market five *muids ;* and it is affirmed that its growth was luxuriant, and the crop abundant. The same may also be said of Verulam, where there was some looking as fine as possible, but which the birds reaped ; showing that in its cultivation it must, when approaching ripeness, be guarded against these winged depredators : but this precaution is no more than is required in the wheat-fields of England. Mr. Wilson (called " Scotch Wilson ") had also a piece of wheat, growing about ten miles nearer in this direction, the fine crop of which was destroyed by the locusts. I mention these accidents to show some of the drawbacks to which early emigrants are exposed, and which often produce the most saddening effects on their spirits, and sometimes the greatest difficulties in their circumstances ; but many of which will be guarded against and prevented, as their knowledge and experience increase.

Wheat has been grown to some extent this year up the country, in the Klip-River division. Two years ago 12 *muids* were

---

* " DR. JAMESON'S Report in 1847."   † "*Ibid.*"

grown; last year, 300; and this year it is stated that it has increased to 1,300 *muids*, equal to 500 quarters. At the Isipingo, on the coast, seven parties are growing small quantities this year; and in some other places it is produced on a small scale.

Arrowroot.—This beautiful plant flourishes admirably in Natal. The Report of Mr. M'Ken shows that its yield must be very prolific. Mr. Morewood has reaped several bags full; Mr. Reynolds on the Umlazi is cultivating it very extensively; and Mr. Kahts of D'Urban has manufactured one of the finest specimens ever seen, which was grown in his own garden.

Having thus treated specifically upon a few particulars which I consider of leading importance, I now proceed to give a more general account of the whole. The first document of which I shall avail myself, contains a valuable " Report of the Agricultural and Horticultural Society" of Natal for 1851,—together with a list of the prizes awarded,—taken from the " Natal Times," of September 5th, 1851.

" SECOND ANNUAL REPORT OF THE AGRICULTURAL AND HORTICULTURAL SOCIETY, 1851.

" YOUR Committee, in presenting this their Second Report, at this your annual Meeting, see great cause of gratulation not only to the Society, but to the Natal public generally, inasmuch as their appeal to their agricultural and commercial friends in their last Report, issued in December, has been responded to in a spirit of energy and liberality far exceeding the expectations of the Committee; the contributions having since been increased from an income of £25 *per annum*, to £102. 1*s.* 6*d.*, which amount, your Committee feel assured, will not diminish, but may be fairly looked upon as an increasing annual income; and they trust that the efforts of their friends will be continued towards the steady increase of this fund, that the Society may be placed in the position which it should occupy in promoting the general interests and welfare of the Colony. And your Committee trust the energy and exertions of all well-wishers to Natal will be unremitting in endeavours to increase this fund, as a large proportion of its annual income must be expended in the salary of their curator. Whilst on this subject, your Committee cannot but congratulate the Society on their having procured the services of Mr. M'Ken, late of Jamaica, as curator, who has kindly placed his valuable services at the disposal of the Society, at the very inadequate remuneration of £50 *per annum*, with a view to meet the limited means of the Institution at the present time.

" The Committee are also happy in being able to state to the subscribers, that they have succeeded in their application to the government for the removal of the site of the Society's Gardens to a spot more accessible to the inhabitants of the town, and equally eligible for the purposes of the Society, and which has been duly surveyed to the extent of twenty-five acres by Mr. Upton, government surveyor, who gratuitously performed this service.   The title is in course of preparation by the government.   A great portion of this has been already fenced in, at a small cost to the Society; and a permanent quick fence will in less than twelve months surround the Society's Gardens.

" It is matter of congratulation to the Society, that many valuable plants have been introduced into the Colony by Mr. M'Ken, and are in course of removal from Mr. Beningfield's garden, where they have been kindly preserved, to the Society's Gardens.   They have also to tender their warmest thanks to their worthy President, Mr. Morewood, of Compensation, for his valuable present to the Society of six cases of mulberry trees. They have also to thank their Vice-President, Mr. Beningfield, for his kind present of coffee-plants, and other plants and seeds. And your Committee would, further, in general terms, express their obligations to the various contributors who have enriched their Gardens with their donations.

" Your Committee see great hopes of the Society soon assuming its true position, from the general interest manifested yesterday by the public at the Gardens; and they trust that at each succeeding show a great increase of produce will be exhibited.   In awarding their prizes, the Committee have been actuated by the desire to stimulate small producing farmers to become in future amongst the number of competitors. Turnips and mangel-wurzel, for their uses in the foddering of fat and of dairy cattle, —potatoes and sweet potatoes, as a nutritious food for man,— have been considered as worthy of prizes of £1 each.   Other produce shown has also had sums awarded, as deserving notice, although no competing samples were exhibited.

"THE PRIZES

have been awarded for the following articles:—

"£1 premium for the finest turnips, shown by S. Peel, Esq.

"£1 prize for the finest mangel-wurzel, shown by Mr. Brown.

"10s. prize for the finest sweet potatoes, shown by Mr. Henry.

"£1 premium to Mr. Kahts, for showing turmeric, arrowroot, and ginger.

"£1 prize for the finest potatoes, to Mr. Stockill.

"£1 to Mr. Brooker, for showing bacon.

"£2 do., for showing two bales of cotton, none other being at the Show.

"£1 premium to Mr. Terrason, for showing rice grown on high land.

"£1 premium to S. Beningfield, Esq., for showing the greatest variety of vegetables and fruits.

"£2 do., for the production of coffee-plants and coffee.

"£1 do., for the production of pine-apples and yams.

"10s. to Mrs. Hawthorne, for the production of cheese.

"Total amount, £13.

"We, the judges of the ploughing at the Agricultural Show to-day, award the prize to No. 1; but, at the same time, we are unanimously of opinion that No. 2 is deserving of high commendation, considering the circumstances under which they were respectively placed.

"*(Signed)*   H. J. BARRETT.
                                              ROBERT BABBS.
"D'URBAN, *August 1st*, 1851.   JOHN GRICE.

"VEGETABLES EXHIBITED.

"MR. BENINGFIELD.—Drum-head lettuce, cabbage do., dwarf beans, 2 sorts turnips, 3 sorts cabbage, carrots, cole rabbi, cassava, Scotch kail, peas, 3 sorts chillies, mountain spinach, broccoli, leeks, onions, cauliflowers, 2 sorts eschalots, watercress, mustard and cress, radishes, endive, 2 sorts celery, parsley, sage, thyme, cucumbers, sorrel, Kafir beans, parsnips, sweet potatoes, red beet, yams, broad beans, guavas, pine-apples, lemons, coffee-plants, (a box,) coffee, bananas, 3 sorts potatoes, bacon, pork, tomatoes.

"Mr. Brown.—Mangel-wurzel.

"Mr. Henry.—Sweet potatoes, underground nuts, pistachios.

"Mr. Kahts.—Turmeric, arrowroot, ginger.

"Mr. Peel.—Turnips.

"Mr. Terrason.—Mangel-wurzel, pistachio nuts, cambarns, rice, tobacco.

"Mr. Garrod.—2 samples wheat.

"Mr. Stockill.—4 sorts potatoes, white mealies.

"Mrs. Hawthorne.—Cheese.

"Mrs. Bowen.—Papaw.

"Mr. Bottomley.—Bamboo.

"Mr. Brooker.—1 bunch bananas, lemons, 1 bale of cotton, 1 do. do., 1 white mealies, 1 do. mealie meal, side bacon, yams.

" Rev. Mr. Lloyd.—Mauritius beans, 1 sample potatoes.
" Mr. Edmondstone.—Potatoes.

" MISCELLANEOUS.

" Mr. Sanderson.—1 plough, 1 harrow, 1 grubber, 1 Scotch cart, cottage cotton-gin, 1 drill harrow, 1 double mould-board plough convertible into drill harrow, 1 scarifier or horse-hoe.
" Mr. T. P. James.—2 lion skins, 1 rhinoceros horn.
" Mr. West.—2 water-colour drawings, views of D'Urban.

" In retiring from office, your Committee trust you will elect such gentlemen officers of the Society for the ensuing year, as are likely to devote their energy and attention to forwarding the interests of the Society, which are so completely identified with the only true interests of the Colony.

" By order of the Committee,

" J. R. GOODRICKE, Secretary."

" <i>August 1st,</i> 1851."

Being anxious to make this part of my work as complete as possible, I have applied to Mr. M'Ken, who has kindly furnished me with a highly valuable report of the Gardens to the latest date; and I take this occasion of thanking that gentleman for his assistance in this particular and in others, and for the readiness with which the favour was granted.

It will be evident that the Gardens are still in their infancy, supported by voluntary contributions; and it is hoped that the influence and support awarded will go on with accelerating force, until this embryo Society will become great in size, perfect in its proportions, and mighty in its influence for good upon the Colony.   It is certainly worthy the strenuous support of every well-wisher of the country.   Mr. M'Ken's report is as follows :—

" In the month of June, last year, 1851, a grant of twenty-five acres of land was obtained from his honour the lieutenant-governor, for the purpose of forming an experimental Garden in connexion with the Natal Agricultural and Horticultural Society. Operations were immediately commenced, and the land fenced in. Six acres out of the twenty-five were grass land on the D'Urban flat, and the remainder hill-side bush-land.   It was thought advisable to clear a part of the latter for the reception of those plants which were already in possession of the Society, the flat requiring considerable working before it could be in a proper condition for the reception of crops.   Accordingly about one and a half acres of the hill-side were cleared, prepared, and laid out; and one hundred and twenty white-mulberry plants, *(morus Indica,)* presented by E. Morewood, Esq., were planted there.   They have grown luxuriantly; and I have propagated upwards of fifteen hundred from them, which are now ready for distribution.   One thousand pine-apple plants, presented by Mr. Kahts, have also succeeded well.   They are now strong, vigorous plants.

"From a single plant of the arrowroot, *(maranta arundinacea,)* which I procured, with other valuable plants, from the Royal Gardens at Kew, I have now sufficient to plant at least the third of an acre.   From its abundant produce and easy cultivation, I have no doubt but it will soon become an important article of export.   I have also another plant, a species of *canna*, which yields a *farina*, called 'tous-les-mois,' said to be equal to that made from the *maranta*.

"Ginger and turmeric are both growing in the Gardens, and have yielded most satisfactorily.   China grass, *(corchorus sp.,)* a plant from which a fine silky fibre is prepared, grows luxuriantly, and appears quite at home.   This article is in great demand for the manufacture of textile fabrics, and commands a high price.   A small piece of cotton, part Sea-Island, and part New-Orleans, is growing well, and producing abundantly; thus clearly proving that the red hill-land is admirably adapted for the cultivation of cotton.

"The pistachio nut, *(arachis hypæga,)* which forms an extensive article of export from the West Coast, is growing very strong, and yields most abundantly.

"In addition to the plants mentioned above, I have been enabled to introduce and procure from different sources the following; but as they have only been a short time in my possession, I am unable to speak decidedly respecting their adaptability to the country :—

" *Garcinia Celebica* (Mangosteen) ; Do. *Cochinchinesis: Eriobotrya Japonica* (Loquat) : *Anona reticulata* (Sweet-sop) ; Do. *muricata;* Do. *cherimalia: Spondias dulcis* (Otaheitan apple) : *Psidium pyriferum* (Guava) ; Do. *Cattleianum: Persea gratissima* (Avocado pear) : *Tamarindus Indica* (Tamarind) : *Theobroma caccoa* (Chocolate nut) : *Carophyllus aromaticus* (Clove) : *Artocarpus integrifolia* (Jack-fruit) : *Carica papaya* (Papaw-tree) : *Elæocarpus serrata: Sorindeia Mada-*

gascariensis: *Sambucus niger* (Elder) : *Acer negrindo* (Maple) : *Olea Europæa* : *Encalyptus pulverulenta* (Blue gum) : *Casuarina Indica* (Club-wood) : *Solanum esculentum;* Do. *undatum* (Garden-egg) : *Iatropha manihot* (Cassava) : *Ceratonia siliqua* (St. John's bread) : *Andropogon schœnanthus* (Lemon grass) : *Anatherum muricatum* : *Discorea stativa ;* Do. *aculeata* : *Hibiscus esculentus* : *Citrus limonum* (Lemon) ; Do. *limetta* (Lime) ; Do. *decumana* (Shaddock) ; Do. *aurantium* : *Bixa orellana* (Arnotto) : *Acacia Libbeck* : *Cactus coccinilifer ;* Do. *opuntia* : *Mangifera Indica* : *Larus cinnamomum* (Cinnamon) : *Coffea Arabica* : *Cytisus Cajan.* : *Melia Azedarach ;* Do. *sempervirens* : *Poinciana elata* : *Brugmansia arborea ; Ipomœa quamoclit. ;* Do. *bona nox ;* Do. *coccinea.*

"A small piece of land sown with lucern, in October, is thriving well. This valuable artificial grass is deserving of particular attention from the agriculturists of this Colony, as its roots penetrate so deep into the soil, that the plant is not affected by ordinary droughts; and, as fodder for cattle, either dry or green, it is unequalled.

"In the preceding statements, I have only taken notice of those plants which are not yet generally cultivated throughout the Colony; but I may state that I have tried Madagascar hill-rice, sweet potato, common ditto, maize, or Indian corn, forty-day maize, Guinea corn, buckwheat, banana, beans and peas of various kinds, grenadilla, pomegranate, sugar-cane, coffee, tobacco, &c., &c., and a great variety of European vegetables; the whole of which *thrive exceedingly well.*

"Although the Gardens now cover nearly four acres of land, I regret that I have not been able to make greater progress. In consequence of the limited funds of the Society, much has been left undone that would otherwise have been done; but, with the growing importance of the Society, and the general acknowledgment of the value of a public central repository, from which all useful plants and seeds may be disseminated throughout the Colony, I doubt not we shall receive increased support, which will enable us to carry on operations on a bolder scale, and, at the same time, multiply our means of serving the community at large."

The last two quotations, with the very interesting and able report of Mr. M'Ken, prove, beyond the possibility of dispute or denial, what *has been* produced. The following will show what is expected to be exhibited at the forthcoming D'Urban Agricultural Show, in August next, (1852,) from which it will be evident at once to every observer, that the prizes are not for vegetables or fruits, so much as for *grain* and *tropical produce,* which may become articles of export.

"THE NATAL AGRICULTURAL AND HORTICULTURAL SOCIETY.

"NOTICE is hereby given by the Committee of the Natal Agricultural and Horticultural Society, that the following Prizes will be awarded by them, at the ensuing Show in August.

"COTTON, £20, to be awarded as follows :—

	£.	s.	d.
"FIRST PRIZE.			
For the finest sample of Cotton produced from the best cultivated plot of five acres and upwards	10	0	0
Next best sample ditto, ditto	3	0	0
"SECOND PRIZE.			
For the best sample of Cotton produced from the best cultivated plot of one acre or upwards to five acres	5	0	0
Next best sample ditto, ditto	2	0	0

"Both quantity and quality will be considered in awarding the above prizes; and [the samples must be accompanied with] a paper containing full information respecting the mode of culture, extent of land in cultivation, the yield *per* acre cleaned, &c., and such observations on the seasons for planting, pruning, and gathering, as may have been within the observation of the producer.

	£.	s.	d.
For the best acre of Coffee under cultivation	4	0	0
For the best sample of 1 cwt. of Tobacco, known in the trade as unmanufactured	5	0	0
Second best sample 1 cwt. of Tobacco, ditto, ditto	3	0	0
For the best *muid* of Wheat	3	0	0
For the best 1 cwt. of Flax	2	0	0
For the best 1 cwt. of cleaned Rice	2	0	0
For the best bale of Wool	1	0	0
For the best 1 cwt. of Arrowroot	1	0	0
For the best sample 25℔. of Green Ginger, with 7℔. of the same growth preserved	1	0	0

"All competing samples shown must be the growth or produce of Natal, and must be accompanied with a paper containing the mode of culture, extent of land in cultivation, the yield *per* acre, and such other statistical information as may be within the knowledge of the exhibitor.

"None of the above prizes will be awarded where there shall

not for each prize be two competitors; but it is in the discretion of the Committee to award an honorary premium for any praiseworthy and successful individual effort.

"By order of the Committee,

"JNO. R. GOODRICKE, *Honorary Secretary.*"*

Side by side with the preceding may not unfitly stand the report of the Pietermaritzburg Fair, which was held on May 14th, 1852.

"PIETERMARITZBURG FAIR.

"FRIDAY last was a 'fair day' in every sense of the word. A bright, but not hot, sun; crowds of well-dressed spectators on horseback and on foot; several tents pitched on the Market Square; the horse and ox waggons from the country; the band of the Forty-fifth Regiment, and the British Union-Jack floating in the breeze,—contributed to give the town a gayer aspect than we remember having ever before seen it wear. In the show-tent of the Society was a goodly display of indigenous productions; among which we particularly noticed pine-apples, oranges, lemons, the egg-plant, ginger, arrowroot and turmeric plants, black and white turnips, carrots, celery, cabbages of very large size, potatoes in variety, radishes, mangel-wurzel, sugar-cane and the sugar produced from it, brandy from figs, vinegar, pumpkins, butter, lard, bacon, biltong, beef-hams, &c., &c. The live stock comprises fat cattle, horses, mules, sheep, and pigs of unwieldy dimensions.

"A list of the prizes will be found in another part of our columns; and, besides these, the judges bestowed especial commendation on,—Mr. King's cheese, jam, and raspberry-vinegar; Mr. Beningfield's pine-apples; Mr. Slatter's potatoes, 12 sorts; Mr. Parnaby's and Mr. Wakefield's sows; Mr. Keyter's boar; Mr. Murdock's hog.

"PIETERMARITZBURG AGRICULTURAL SOCIETY.

"THE DINNER.

"ABOUT 170 guests assembled to a cold dinner at four o'clock in a temporary building attached to Florey's Hotel; the Hon.

---

* From the "Natal Times," June 25th, 1852.

H. Cloete in the Chair, Messrs. Otto and Moreland, Vice-
Presidents.

"The Chairman proposed 'the Queen,' 'Prince Albert and the
Royal Family,' 'the Governor-General of Southern Africa,' 'the
Lieutenant-Governor of the District,' 'the Lieutenant-Governor
of the Cape Colony,—Mr. Darling,' and especially 'the interests
of Agriculture in this District,'—toasts which were drunk with
great enthusiasm.

"The Chairman observed that to agricultural societies were due
most of the improvements in agriculture ; and he trusted that the
beginning already made here had proved we were not entirely
unsuccessful. The townspeople invited the co-operation of the
rural population, not merely by the small prizes that could be
given, but also for the merited applause of their fellow-colonists ;
and he hoped they would respond to the call in the public papers
for this purpose. He thanked them for the astonishing specimens
(considering all things) of live stock and vegetable productions ;
the former of which were very creditable to a rising community,
and the latter second to none in the world ; proving, what he
had long ago asserted, that this would prove one of the first gems
in her majesty's crown. He hoped they would still persevere ;
and as they had sent home for a twenty-five guinea cup for the
farmer who had housed the most wheat in his barn, he trusted
they should have the opportunity of worthily bestowing that prize
another year.

"The other speakers on the occasion were Messrs. Archbell,
Otto, W. Uys, Moreland, Fannin, Pretorius, Ferreira, Beningfield,
Walker, and Vanderplank.

"THE PRIZES.

Mr. HENDRICK Boshoff, for the best imported stallion, (a bay horse, six years
    old,) £3.
Mr. Carl Prellar, for the best imported bull, (three years old,) £3.
Mr. Wade, for the best imported sow, (no competition,) 10s.

"COLONIAL PRODUCE AND STOCK.

Mr. Kritzenger, for the best two-year old colt, £3.
Mr. Wessel Uys, for the best two-year old filly, (no competition,) £1.
Mr. P. R. Otto, for the best gelding, £1.
Mr. A. Keyter, for the best mule, £1.
Mr. P. R. Otto, for the best bull, £2.
Mr. A. Walker, for the best cow, £2.

Mr. Landsberg, for the best heifer, £1.

Mr. William Baker, for the best ox, £1.

Mr. P. R. Otto, for the best sow, £1.

Mr. Bentley, (of York,) for the best boar, £1.

Mr. Clayborne, for the fattest pig, £1.

Mr. Clarence, for the best half-dozen fowls, 10s.

Mr. Henderson, for the best half-dozen geese, (no competition,) 5s.

Mr. P. R. Otto, for the best specimen of wool, (no competition,) £2. 10s.

Messrs. Rothwell and Stanton, for the best specimen of mealies, 10s.

Mr. Steabler, for the best specimen of wheat and oats, (no competition,) 5s.

Mr. Clarence, for the best specimen of barley, (no competition,) 5s.

Mr. Bottrill, { for the finest specimen of beans, 10s. / for the finest specimen of potatoes, 10s.

Mr. William Allerstone, for the finest vegetables, 10s.

Mr. Rawlinson, for the finest show of fruit, 10s.

Mr. Ralfe, for the best specimen of bacon, 5s.

Mr. Mason, { for the best hams, 5s. / for the best beef, (salted,) 10s.

Mr. Smith, (of York,) for the best butter, 10s.

Mr. H. Boshoff, { for the best specimen of tobacco, £1. / for the best grass hay, (no competition,) 5s.

Mr. King, for the excellent specimens of cheese, butter, ham, native raspberry jam, jelly, and vinegar, which he was prevented from showing in time by an accident to his waggon, £1.

Mr. Rawlinson, for the best specimen of pickled fish, for exportation, 10s.

Mr. Hendrick Boshoff, for a pen of wethers, (not produced in time through accident,) 10s."*

The following statement is of a highly satisfactory nature, showing how, and to what extent, the Colony is already supplying its own wants, and becoming less dependent upon other sources for support and greatness.

"PROGRESS OF PRODUCTION IN NATAL.

"WE leave the following facts to speak for themselves; and shall continue to report similar ones, as they transpire.

"Messrs. Hartley and Handley lately received about 4 cwt. of molasses, manufactured by Mr. Morewood, at Compensation, which were sold off in an incredibly short time. From 8 to 10 cwt. more are daily expected, besides a large quantity of sugar from Mr. Morewood's estate.

"100℔s. of arrowroot, of excellent quality, have been received from Messrs. Reynolds Brothers, grown at Compensation; also samples of ginger from the same quarter.

---

* From the "Natal Standard and Farmers' Courant."

"Two pigs, salted and cured by Mr. Coward, of Compensation, were lately received by Messrs. H. and H., and met with an immediate and highly remunerative sale. These, we understand, are but the first-fruits of a *porcine* harvest.

"The consumption of mealie (maize) meal in D'Urban has increased from *four* muids weekly, a year ago, to *four hundred* at the present time; and the mills at this place are not sufficient to supply one-fifth of the demand; the greater part coming from Maritzburg, and the mills in that neighbourhood. This wholesome article of home-production has entirely superseded the use of Cape meal, of which none, comparatively, is now imported, though, a year ago, the importation averaged 200 bags monthly; and it has also, to a very great extent, superseded the use of rice, the importation of which has dwindled from 400 or 500 bags monthly to a very small quantity. The variety of modes in which maize-meal can be prepared as nutritious and agreeable food, the cheapness of its production, and the indefinite extent to which it can be grown in this district, justify the confident expectation that it will shortly become an extensive export."*

The only remaining distinct subject upon which I shall dwell is,—*horned cattle.* On these something is said in my communication to the "Watchman," before cited. I now give, in addition, the remarks of a writer in the "D'Urban Observer" of January 9th, 1852 :—

"THE HORNED CATTLE OF NATAL.

"THERE is, perhaps, no portion of the earth better adapted to the rearing of cattle than the *whole* district of Natal, although the coast-lands are peculiarly unsuited to the health of other than those born and bred in those parts.

"The *breeds* to be found here are somewhat numerous, in consequence of the difference of choice in the importers, whose various tastes or prejudices lead them to select the particular breed which may chance to suit their fancy. There are, however, three or four recognised breeds now common in the country; namely, the Fatherland, the Africander, the Zulu, and the bastard Zulu; which may be described as follows :—

---

* "Natal Times," June 11th, 1852.

" The *Fatherland*, as the name betokens, is the pure European breed, without cross or admixture. They are a large-sized, small-headed, light-necked, and well-made breed, noted as furnishing the best milch-cows in the Colony; whilst the oxen not only exhibit great pluck as draught-animals, but likewise fatten kindly, when put to pasture with that object.

" This breed has always struck us as being no other than the large marsh-ców of the Elbe, so common in Holstein and in Holland; and the very slight difference in form that may be detected between them, seems nothing more than might reasonably be expected from the great change of climate and pasturage. But a real difference, and one very material to the farmer, which is perceptible between these imported cattle and their descendants, is in their qualities as milch-kine,—the marsh-cow often yielding, in the dairies of Holstein, as much as from thirty to forty quarts of milk a day; whereas, in this Colony, twelve quarts a day are considered to constitute an extraordinary yield. It must, however, be remarked, that whereas seventeen quarts of milk from the former are required to make one pound of butter in Holstein, only ten quarts of the milk produced here are necessary for the same quantity of butter.

" This breed of cattle will not thrive down on the coast-lands of Natal, but abound some twenty miles up the country. Their price usually varies from £3 to £4 a head for oxen, and from £3 to £5 each for milch-cows.

" The *Africander* is a very tall, ponderous, large-horned breed of cattle. Some of them are exceedingly large and massive. They make excellent draught-oxen; but the cows are not much esteemed as milkers. The former sell at from £3 to £4, and the latter at much the same price.

" The breed appear to be the descendants of a large, coarse description of cattle, introduced very many years ago into the Cape Colony, from Holland, by the Dutch settlers; but much crossed with the English breed since that period. They, likewise, do not thrive well near the coast, but are in great perfection fifteen to twenty miles up the country.

" The *Zulu* breed, though generally held to be a distinct race, appear to us quite otherwise. We consider them to be a cross between the Spanish and the East-Indian breeds, long established in the country, and now quite acclimatized. The Spanish breed were introduced from Rio Janeiro and Valparaiso by the Spanish, but more particularly by the Portuguese, who likewise introduced, from Calcutta, Goa, and other ports, the East-Indian breed, from which latter the marked peculiarity of the hump is doubtless derived.

"From these two breeds a cross has been obtained, combining many excellent qualities, amongst which their extreme hardiness and great powers of endurance are remarkable, and render them peculiarly valuable both to the native tribes and to the European colonist settled near the coast.

"These are the only kinds of horned cattle that can, at present, be bred near the coast; but Zulu cows, crossed by Fatherland and Africander bulls, produce an excellent breed, usually termed 'bastard Zulus,' which inherit much of the hardiness of the Zulu, and the higher qualities of the sire. Bastard Zulus, again crossed by well-bred bulls, produce a greatly improved breed, which would, we imagine, stand the climate of the coast-lands almost as well as the original Zulus.

"Zulu cows give little or no milk, therefore cannot be termed 'milch-cows;' but, crossed with the Alderney or Devon breed, in three or four generations their progeny would be nearly equal to the original imported Alderney and Devon breed. This is a plan which might be adopted with every prospect of success, and with great benefit to the Colony at large.

"The price of Zulu oxen varies from £1. 10s. to £3, and of cows from £2 to £3.

"The Bastard Zulu has already been treated of: it therefore only remains to say, that the price of oxen and cows is usually from £2. 10s. to £3. 10s. each, and that the breed is much esteemed for draught-cattle."

The wonder is, that the cows give any milk, or the oxen do any work, in winter; for, whilst in England the cattle are carefully housed and fed at night, at Natal they are put into an open kraal, or fold, without covering, and kept the whole night without a particle of food. Surely English farmers will shortly improve upon this Kafir practice.

Butter has been largely exported this year. One captain

stated that he alone had butter to the amount of £400; and the supply will doubtless greatly increase.

Gold.—It seems probable that some amount (whether small or large, remains to be proved) of this valuable metal is to be found in the mountain-range which separates Natal from the Sovereignty. For some newspaper extracts respecting its discovery near Smithfield, I must refer the reader to Chapter XII.

From the preceding observations and quotations it will be apparent that my object has not been to present plausible theories, but certain facts; not to point out merely what Natal may do, but what it has done and is now doing: and if we are to judge of the future from the past, its progress is likely to be very rapid and certain.

But if I had to give advice to intending emigrants, I should say most emphatically,—*Have nothing to do with Emigration Companies*, whether conducted by private persons or government arrangement. They may make fair offers, but I am persuaded the result would be bad; for, setting aside every thing else, they have no land to give within a reasonable distance of any town; this being already in private hands, and requiring *filling up*, before any attempt to go beyond can be made. When an emigrant lands, and finds his location far away, the first expense of land-carriage appals him before he starts. Coming from "the city full," and being called upon at once to be the solitary occupant of the wide wilderness, with all his endearing recollections of home and friends left behind, he becomes enervated and sad; every thing looks dark and dull and profitless; and he quickly wishes himself back again.

No; Natal wants only two sorts of emigrants,—*agriculturists with capital*, and *farm-labourers*. These agriculturists should come and *look round for themselves, make suitable inquiries, select the land which they like best, and purchase just as much as they will require for their own purposes; take possession of it with as little delay as possible, and then set to work, exercising their reason and using their energies.* If possible, they should also be able to have one labourer at least, either with or without a family. This secures at once both company and assistance. When there is only one man upon a farm, he finds so many things to do that he becomes distracted and discouraged; but when he has one or two with him *who will work*, in a short time he becomes master of the work, instead of the work getting the mastery of him.

A man may buy land at a very reasonable rate, so as to meet all his demands. A small quantity of land in a suitable place is, of course, worth more than a large quantity in an unsuitable one. A great mistake into which most fall on coming is, that they fancy they must work so many acres, instead of determining, "We will do it well;" for land here is not like it is in England, where it can lie fallow for a time, and be the better for it. No; when the land at Natal has rain, *it will produce;* so that, if it has not a crop of vegetables or corn, it will produce a very large crop of weeds, and that in a very little time. It ought therefore to be a rule, that, as soon as one crop is off, the ground should be ploughed or dug, and manured, if it requires it. If this is not done, it takes as much labour and expense to clear it again, as preparing and putting in a fresh crop would do. This is a fact which is becoming every day more apparent to those who are employed in agricultural pursuits.

If in this manner Natal received about a thousand emigrants a year for a few years to come, and these were of the right kind, it would advance with rapid strides: but if an attempt is made to push it unnaturally, it will recoil with disappointment and loss upon the parties concerned.

In the natural world, trees are not produced by putting heavy branches on a slender stem, with only a few small fibres for roots; but all the parts grow together, and thus secure symmetry, strength, and beauty. If this is not the case, the tree becomes top-heavy, and must either bend or break; and the attempt to prop it, or repair it, only makes it ugly, and effectually prevents its becoming healthy and useful. In like manner, if a forced growth is attempted at Natal, it will be followed by loss, disappointment, and, in some cases, ruin.

I would not be understood to say, that a large number of those who came under Byrne's scheme have not done well. Many of them *have* done well, and are to-day in better circumstances than they had any probability of enjoying, had they remained in England. But, at the same time, many have not succeeded, and have left the Colony in disappointment and disgust, in this way inflicting a real injury upon the Colony, whilst they have endured much distress personally. The object of my present remarks, therefore, is to prevent such scenes from recurring, as they need not take place if a wise and vigorous course is pursued.

Some may say that in this Chapter I have taken the position of a compiler rather than that of an author: but this I deny, though I have not egotism enough to suppose that "I am the man, and wisdom must die with me;" but, on the contrary, whilst I have expressed my own views, I have sought to compress and confine my remarks in as small a space as possible, in order to give place to others, whose views and efforts are entitled to the greatest consideration and respect.

The actors on a lively and exciting stage are but ill-prepared to give a fair and impartial representation of their own performances: a calm, uninterested spectator is much better fitted for the task. So in Natal, I have taken no part in the living drama of political, or emigration, or land operations; but I have been a close observer of others, and think I have noted their dimensions with tolerable accuracy, and understand pretty correctly their physical and mental stature. But there have been a number of gentlemen of first-rate mental and moral respectability, who have spoken, and written, and acted the part of honourable men, and whose views are entitled to the respect of all who may desire to know any thing upon the highly interesting topics under consideration. I have, therefore, endeavoured to lay my hand upon their various powers and productions, and to press them into the service of this Chapter; in doing which I think I rather do them honour than lower their standing amongst their fellows. I have in this manner sought to collect into one focus the different rays of light, emanating from various sources, and to present to the earnest inquirer a truthful account of that which is desirable to be known about NATAL.

I shall close this Chapter by appending a list of the emigrant vessels which have arrived at Natal to the end of 1851, with the places from which they came, and the order in which they entered. This list is extracted from the "Almanack" of Mr. Cullingworth, printer and publisher at D'Urban :—

IMMIGRANT VESSELS.

Name.	From.	Arrival.	No. of Immigrants.
Beta	Bremen (Germans)	March 23rd, 1848	189
Sarah Bell	London	Nov. 17th, 1848	13
Gwalior	London	Dec. 25th, 1848	26
Elizabeth Jane	London	Feb. 9th, 1849	22
Lalla Rookh	London	May 9th, 1849	24
Wanderer	London	May 14th, 1849	108
Washington	London	July 18th, 1849	74
Henry Tanner	London	Oct. 10th, 1849	152
John Gibson	London	Oct. 27th, 1849	35
Dreadnought	London	Nov. 2nd, 1849	103
Aliwal	London	Dec. 10th, 1849	104
King William	London and Plymouth	Jan. 23rd, 1850	188
Ina	Glasgow	March 8th, 1850	120
Sovereign	London and Plymouth	March 24th, 1850	195
Edward	London and Plymouth	May 2nd, 1850	207
Lady Bruce	London and Portsmouth	May 9th, 1850	207
Hebrides	London and Plymouth	May 10th, 1850	129
Herald	London and Plymouth	May 27th, 1850	48
Conquering Hero	Glasgow	June 29th, 1850	118
Minerva	London	July 3rd, 1850	276
Henrietta	Liverpool	July 5th, 1850	169
Ballengeich	London	July 26th, 1850	95
Sandwich	London	July 27th, 1850	12
Henry Warburton	Liverpool	Sept. 4th, 1850	10
Globe	London	Sept. 7th, 1850	21
Unicorn	Liverpool	Sept. 17th, 1850	258
Nile	London	Sept. 25th, 1850	102
British Tar	London and Plymouth	Sept. 27th, 1850	98
Haidee	Hull	Oct. 7th, 1850	246
Tuscan	London	Oct. 9th, 1850	19
Emily	London and Plymouth	Oct. 10th, 1850	177
Choice	London	Oct. 12th, 1850	43
Devonian	Liverpool	Oct. 31st, 1850	84
Justina	London	Nov. 10th, 1850	102
Pallas	Hull	Dec. 11th, 1850	18
Amazon	London	Jan. 1st, 1851	60
Wilhelmina	Liverpool	Jan. 8th, 1851	13
Dreadnought	London	Feb. 17th, 1851	64
Bernard	London	Feb. 18th, 1851	54
Vixen	London	March 13th, 1851	10
Ceres	London	April 2nd, 1851	4
Albinia	Glasgow	April 28th, 1851	3
John Line	London	May 3rd, 1851	130
John Bright	London	May 12th, 1851	55
Balley	London	May 13th, 1851	1
Lady Sale	Glasgow	May 14th, 1851	2

IMMIGRANT VESSELS—*continued.*

Name.	From.	Arrival.		No. of Immigrants.
Ceres	Liverpool	May 21st,	1851	
Harlequin	London	May 26th,	1851	1
Jane Green	London	July 9th,	1851	54
Jane Morrice	Liverpool	July 11th,	1851	44
Cheshire Witch	London	July 28th,	1851	2
Urania	Leith	Aug. 25th,	1851	4
Borneo	London	Oct. 2nd,	1851	
Bellona	Liverpool	Oct. 3rd,	1851	33
Isle of Wight	Glasgow	Oct. 6th,	1851	13
Killermont	London	Nov. 27th,	1851	2
Devonian	Liverpool	Dec. 2nd,	1851	30

CHAPTER XI.

ALBERT, OR COMPENSATION. CULTIVATION OF SUGAR AND
COFFEE, &C. EMIGRATION.

ALBERT (or Compensation) is situated about thirty-six miles from D'Urban, and sixteen beyond Verulam, to the north-east, being on the direct line of road along the coast towards Zululand. It is about five miles from the sea, in a large plain of some thousands of miles in extent, with hills rising in the distance. The scenery is beautiful, and continues to increase in loveliness, until you arrive at the Tugela, the northern boundary of the Colony.

The estate of Mr. Morewood at Albert has lately attracted great attention, and excited much interest, amongst the Natalians, from the fact that the sugar-cane has there been successfully cultivated; and, although the works for making sugar have been very imperfect and incomplete, still a considerable portion has been manufactured and sent to market; thus giving unmistakeable proof of the suitability of Natal for the production of that staple article, and making it now only a question as to whether it can be produced so cheaply as to compete with other exporting countries. The general impression is that it can thus compete, except, perhaps, in the case of slave-growing countries.

Having heard and read much about Mr. Morewood's estate, and not relying upon all reports until I had seen for myself, I visited the place a short time ago, in order that what I wrote on the subject might be derived from personal observation; and I must candidly confess that the reality far exceeded my expectations. Having been disappointed in many instances, in which glowing descriptions had been given of other estates, my anticipations were not of the highest order; and so I had the pleasure of finding more than I had calculated upon.

Of the buildings there were not many; but the sugar manufacturing house (as shown in wood-cut No. XVIII.) was a respectable building, substantially built, and covered with galvanized iron. This stands on the right of a large open ground, as you enter the premises from the Bay; and on the left is Mr. Morewood's small residence, almost hid in the trees, as presented to view in wood-cut No. XVI.

XVI.—SKETCH OF MR. MOREWOOD'S ESTATE, NEAR VERULAM.

On dismounting from his horse, after a rather fatiguing ride through a beautiful country of rich and varied scenery, the visitor goes to the door in the gable of the house on the left, and meets with a cordial, though not a fulsome, welcome from the host, who invites him in, and directs his horse to be taken to the stable, or "knee-haltered," and turned out to grass. As the good gentleman of the house is a bachelor, the internal arrangements of the apartments indicate the absence of female taste and female art; but, this apart, generous hospitality is displayed.

On entering the garden below the house, the eye is at once gratified by beholding as splendid a plot of pines as perhaps were ever exhibited to view. These are regularly planted in rows, being full of life and strength. The square of dots, as seen in illustration No. XVI., marks them out.

As soon as the visitor has passed these, and turned to the right, a thick forest of sugar-canes runs along on his left hand, which are growing so thickly together as to prevent the eye from penetrating beyond the first or second row. These are shown in

Plate XVII., where two white men and five Kafirs are at work, cutting; and three more are drawing the canes on a truck towards the boiling-house.

On the right, the kitchen-garden is neatly laid out, intersected with walks; the beds being covered with almost every variety of culinary productions, in their different stages of growth, from the first-born, tiny blade of the smallest plant, to the plump turnip or large cabbage; the whole being clean and neat, and fresh watered. It lacks, indeed, the showy walks and flowers of an English gentleman's promenade; but these are more than compensated by the utility displayed in the growth of numerous profitable vegetables, or rich tropical plants. On proceeding a little further, a deep, thick bed of reeds, growing in some low

XVII.—CUTTING THE SUGAR-CANE ON MR. MOREWOOD'S ESTATE.

ground in which a stream of water is running, stops your progress; but, on turning to the left, the garden continues, about
thirty yards wide, with the sugar-plantation above, in which are
canes of all sorts and sizes.

When we were walking along this path, the secret of the garden being kept so clean and neat was explained. An old Dutchman, with his knife in his hand, pruning the trees, and two
Kafirs working with spades by his side, gave certain proof that
the garden was indebted to them for its order and fruitfulness.
But the eye of this old man is becoming dim, and will soon
refuse to perform its part in distinguishing objects, pruning trees,
or training plants: he was nearly blind. May his soul have a
place in the garden of the heavenly paradise! He stands, in the
drawing No. XVII., before the sugar-cane carriage, directing the
Kafirs.

But pines, and sugar, and vegetables were not the only things
growing here. There was arrowroot, three bags of which had
just been taken from the ground; also ginger-plants in great
numbers, which would soon be producing; and mulberry trees,
of the most luxuriant growth, with leaves as green and bright,

in the middle of winter, as any imagination could picture them. Five muids of the finest rice had also been sent to market and sold for seed. In addition to these, turmeric, yams, manioca, and papaws were found. Fruit-trees also were growing, including the fig, guava, plum, apple, pear, orange, lemon, apricot, peach, cherry, vine, &c., &c. The whole of these may not flourish, as not finding soil, situation, or atmosphere suited to their wants; but the probability is that most of them will.

Those productions which must be regarded as constituting the staple articles of subsequent exports, and determining the future character and standing of Natal,—as sugar, rice, arrowroot, &c.,—were here displayed in as great perfection as in other tropical countries.

On leaving the part of the premises now described in the drawing No. XVI., and crossing the ground, you enter the sugar-manufactory, at the back of which four Kafirs are seen turning the crushing-mill, (No. XVIII.,) each being at the end of a long arm, to which it is designed to attach a creature with four legs instead of two, when the works are more complete. One

XVIII.—SUGAR MANUFACTORY ON MR. MOREWOOD'S ESTATE.

man also appears putting the canes into the rollers, and a boy is taking them out after they have been pressed. From these rollers a spout is placed, through which the saccharine flows into a vessel inside the house, and is thence taken to the boilers, where, after having passed through its various processes, it is placed in the coolers, the molasses are run off, and a beautiful crystal sugar remains behind, which is pronounced by all competent judges to be of superior quality. Some old experienced West Indian planters may smile at the rudeness of some parts of the process, and the simplicity of this sketch; but let them remember that this is the *first attempt at Natal,* and not the result of a long course of operations, with great wealth at command, in the West Indies or the Brazils.

The whole of the manufacturing apparatus was on a very limited scale, and is still very incomplete in its operation; yet it was stated that a ton of sugar *per* week would be produced, giving four cwt. of molasses; and were the means greater, five or six tons might as well be produced as one, the quantity of cane ready for use being great. In other countries this would quickly be spoiled; but the probability is, that in Natal it will preserve its vigour some months longer than in hot countries, thus giving so much more advantage to the grower.

The ground shown in illustration No. XVI., with the plough and oxen at work, is being prepared for fresh cane-plants. This land is not by any means the richest in Natal; yet a gentleman who resided for some time in the West Indies, has stated that there the canes, being planted four feet apart in the rows, allow room enough for a person to go in betwixt them to hoe; whilst here the canes grow so close and thick as to render such an operation impossible. I have heard that Mr. Morewood intends in future to plant them eight feet apart, instead of four. The plough can also be used for planting to any extent at Natal; whilst in the West Indies ploughing is in some parts impossible, and in others difficult and expensive.

As I am merely a general observer, and do not pretend to any professional skill upon the subject under consideration, I shall here give the results of the investigations of professional men upon it, who, combining scientific knowledge with practical skill, and long residence in sugar-growing countries, are enabled to speak with authority, and whose statements bear the weight which must be attached to the possessors of such qualifications.

These opinions are taken from the "Natal Times," (published by Mr. Cullingworth,) and, being public documents, which on the spot call for denial if any can be given, and having met with no contradiction, they must now stand as authentic judgments upon the points which they determine.

REPORT ON EXPERIMENTAL SUGAR MANUFACTURE AT COMPENSATION.

"GARDENS OF THE NATAL AGRICULTURAL AND HORTICULTURAL SOCIETY, D'URBAN, *June 2nd*, 1852.

"GENTLEMEN,—IN compliance with your desire, I visited the sugar-plantation of E. Morewood, Esq., at Compensation, on the 29th ult., where I remained three days.

"The canes in cultivation are known as the Bourbon, Ribbon, Otaheite, Batavia, and Creole; 40½ acres being plants,* and one acre of first ratoons;† there are, besides, 42 acres of prepared land, part of which has been planted. 20½ acres of the above canes are seventeen months old, and fully ripe. The remaining 20 have been only about three months in the ground; but the whole are healthy and luxuriant, equalling any I have observed in Jamaica, where I resided in the Plantain-Garden River district nearly ten years; and I have no hesitation in saying, that they ought to produce at least three tons *per* acre.

"Mr. Morewood having kindly placed the boiling-house under my control, I was occupied two days in it, and manufactured a considerable quantity of sugar from the Creole cane. The density of the liquor I got was shown to be 11° or 20 *per cent.*, by Beaumé's saccharometer; and from 100 gallons of this I produced 110℔s. sugar, and 50℔s. molasses, besides skimmings.

"The Bourbon cane yielded, from 100℔s. weight, two quarts more juice than the Creole, but the density was only 10 or 19 *per cent.* I, however, have no doubt but the former, if cut when properly ripe, would yield even more than I have just named.

"The above statements show the canes to be very rich: still

---

* "Plants are the first cuttings of the canes."
† "Ratoons are the second year's cuttings."

the result was arrived at by actual experiment; and I feel confident that if the canes were thoroughly trashed and cleaned, the yield would be even more.

"I may mention that the mill at Compensation is very small, the rollers not being more than eighteen inches in length; and I do not think it could grind more than 250 gallons in ten hours,—that is to say, with the power of four Kafirs which I had. The driving gear has, however, been altered by Mr. Alfred Beningfield, so that horses or cattle can be used, which will expedite the work considerably.

"The boiling-house is a neat building, and roomy enough for all that is required; but the manner in which the three iron boilers have been set, wastes a great quantity of fuel, and at the same time does not give that brisk fire so essential to sugar-boiling. The other necessaries about the works for sugar-making, are mostly of a temporary nature; and the lime which I was obliged to use for clarifying, is very unsuitable for that purpose. But, on the whole, I have great pleasure in saying that, considering every thing, I succeeded beyond my most sanguine anticipations; and I beg to repeat, as my decided opinion, that the cane-fields on Compensation, if properly attended to, would produce a profitable return, both soil and climate being peculiarly adapted for the growth of the plant.

"In conclusion, I beg leave to add, that my best thanks are due to Mr. Morewood for the facilities he afforded me in the various experiments I made, and I will be truly glad if this Report meets with your approbation.

"I am, Gentlemen,
"Your obedient Servant,
"M. J. M‘KEN, *Curator.*"
"*To the Committee of the Natal Agricultural and Horticultural Society.*"

"ABSTRACT STATEMENT.
"(All Weights and Measures are English Standard.)

"CREOLE CANE.

Weight of Cane.	Yielded Juice.	Density by Beaumé's Sacc.	Cured Sugar Produced.	Molasses Produced.
1,600℔s.	100 gals.	11°	110℔s.	50℔s.

BOURBON CANE.

100℔s.	27 quarts.	10°	Experiment not concluded."

" Mr. Griffith's testimony to the peculiar adaptation of the land for the sugar-cane, and the greater luxuriance of its growth in Natal, as compared with Jamaica, is highly satisfactory, and cannot fail to stimulate the progress of this important enterprise.

"'In my letter which appeared in the 'Natal Times,' dated February 10th, I stated that 'no molasses appeared' in Mr. Morewood's manufacture. But at that period he laboured under every disadvantage, having only a small iron pot, containing about three gallons, for boiling the juice; but since his three boilers have been set up, he has succeeded in making a much finer quality of sugar, and a considerable amount of molasses, which he boils over again; and a darker description of sugar, with a large crystallized grain, is the result; a sample of which I enclose. In Jamaica all the molasses is distilled into rum: it would, however, be a question whether rum, or the description of sugar enclosed, would pay the best.

"'The land in the neighbourhood of Compensation appears peculiarly adapted for the sugar-cane. Those now growing on the farm, are much more luxuriant than any that I have seen in Jamaica, although the rows are the same distance apart (four feet) as in that island, which *there* allows ample space for the negroes to hoe between. At Compensation, the density of the canes is such as to preclude the possibility of such a thing, owing to a greater number of canes springing from the stock. No manure has been made use of; and another proof of the quality of the land is, that the ratoons before referred to are equal in luxuriance to the original plants.'"

PUBLIC MEETING ON THE CAPABILITIES OF NATAL.

" A PUBLIC MEETING of the inhabitants of the recently-formed village of Albert, and the neighbourhood, on the estate 'Compensation,' was held on the 29th of May, 1852, at which ALEXANDER GIFFORD, ESQ., presided.

"The Meeting was very numerously attended, and the subjects discussed included the general capabilities of the Colony as a field for immigration, with special reference, however, to sugar-planting and tropical agriculture; which naturally occupied a large share of the attention of a Meeting held, as this was, on the scene of Mr. Morewood's successful enterprise.

" We are unable to give the whole of the speeches at length,

and must content ourselves with reporting those of four gentlemen, whose statements and opinions carry great weight, from
the circumstance of their having had extensive personal experience as sugar-planters, in the East and West Indies, Mauritius,
and Egypt. In the other cases, we can only give the Resolu-
tions, with the mover and seconder of each; though all the
speeches in the Report furnished us by Mr. Moreland, contain highly interesting illustrations of the varied resources of
Natal.

"THE CHAIRMAN called upon Mr. Marcus to move the first
Resolution.

"MR. MARCUS commenced by stating that he had been in
the East and West Indies, and in Egypt; had been engaged in
sugar-planting for several years; and in this Colony had resided
for upwards of two years. It has been his opinion, from his first
arrival, that this country is admirably adapted for the growth
of sugar. The seasons are more propitious than in any other
country he has visited; and this is a great advantage. The soil
is capable of producing most of the tropical plants; and he had
no doubt that when its capabilities become better known, capital
will be employed extensively in developing its resources. Some
people say that it is not favourable for wheat; but his opinion is,
that not only wheat, but every other cereal produce, may be
realized. People ought to know that the land, when first brought
into cultivation, is not fitted for a wheat-crop, and no experienced
English farmer would attempt such a thing. For two or three
years the land should be cropped with other produce, before an
experiment could be fairly made. He had seen very fine samples
of wheat grown on the coast. Maize in America is more extensively grown than any other grain, and is a most valuable pro-
duct. It is impossible that it could be grown better or at less
cost there than in Natal, if so cheaply. Cattle also thrive well.
Of the successful cultivation of cotton, he could not express a
doubt:—the only thing wanting was labour. His opinion of the
Colony generally was most favourable, and that it offers peculiar
advantages to an industrious settler. Persons must expect to
rough it here for a time, as all others have done in new colonies;
but with such a beautiful and mild climate, no dangers or insurmountable difficulties are to be dreaded. The Resolution which

he had to propose was one which he had no doubt would meet
with their approval :—

"RESOLUTION I.—'That the soil and climate of Natal particularly adapt it for the growth of a great variety of products; the
coast-lands having already proved themselves admirably suited
for the growth of sugar and other valuable tropical plants; while
the interior is peculiarly well adapted for the English farmer and
grazier: and, as a whole, the Colony presents to the enterprising and industrious emigrant very superior advantages, and
promises, ere long, to become one of the most valuable appendages
of the British crown.'

"MR. THOMAS LEWIS seconded the Resolution. He had been
engaged as a sugar-planter for upwards of eighteen years in the
parish of Trelawny, Jamaica, principally on Tharp's Estate.
There were seven estates belonging to the same proprietor: each
estate might have, on the average, two hundred acres of cane,
and an overseer to each;—he had been one of the seven over-
seers. He had now been some time in Natal, having landed
from the 'British Tar' in 1850; had travelled the coast in every
direction from D'Urban to the Tugela, and beyond; and was
convinced that it is a fine country for the cultivation of the
sugar-cane and other tropical plants, such as ginger, arrowroot,
coffee, cotton, &c. The cane-field of Mr. Morewood, at Compensation, is as good as any fall-plant cane that he ever saw in
Jamaica. It will produce from $2\frac{1}{2}$ tons to 3 tons per acre; and,
with proper machinery, judicious management, and cheap labour,
great profits must be realized. The canes which he had seen
crushed within this week have yielded a large quantity of juice,
at least 65 to 70℔s. to 100℔s. of cane; and the sugar produced
is of a very superior quality.

"THE CHAIRMAN invited Mr. M'Ken, the curator of the Agricultural Gardens at D'Urban, to give the Meeting the benefit of
his experience, and more particularly his observations during the
experiments now being carried on by him on the quality of the
sugar-cane produced by Mr. Morewood.

"MR. M'KEN said that, from the experience he has had in
Natal, he could speak positively as to the suitability of both soil
and climate for the growth of various tropical plants. He had
been engaged for the last eleven months superintending the

Gardens of the Natal Agricultural Society; and during that period had introduced, or cultivated, several plants successfully, as ginger, turmeric, arnotto, pine-apple, arrowroot, *tous-les-mois*, or French arrowroot, China grass, &c. The latter has grown most luxuriantly, and, he believes, could be cultivated profitably. It is from the fibre of this plant that the celebrated grass-cloth is made; and, at present, the fibre is valued at £60 a ton in England. New-Orleans and Sea-Island cotton promises an abundant crop; and as this plant grows so vigorously, the cultivation could be carried on with success, provided the colonists could depend on continuous labour during the picking or gathering season. The white mulberry was introduced last year by Mr. Morewood, from whom we received 120 plants, which have grown remarkably well, and already produced him nearly 1,000. On pruning they shoot out again vigorously, and, in fact, appear so healthy and strong that he feels assured a good crop of leaves might be depended upon throughout nearly the whole year, which is a great *desideratum* in the cultivation of silk. Those growing on Mr. Morewood's estate at Compensation are still more promising. The pistachio-nut, which yields abundantly in the Gardens, is also worthy of attention. These nuts form a valuable article of export from several of the settlements on the western coast of this continent; and, as they require but little culture, certainly deserve the attention of the colonists.

"He fully agrees with the observations of Messrs. Marcus and Lewis, regarding the cane-fields here. They appear to him equal to the best he has observed in Jamaica, where he resided for ten years, on an estate in the Plantain-River district, considered the finest and most fruitful part of the island; and he was sure any superintendent there would estimate the yield of such a field (at least) at three hogsheads *per* acre. He does not think that all tropical plants would succeed here; for such as are truly so will thrive nowhere else, except within the Tropics; as any one acquainted with the geographical distribution of plants must know. He had been engaged here at Compensation, for the last two days, in the manufacture of sugar; but as that made is not sufficiently cured, he could not speak positively as to the quantity of sugar produced.* The density of the cane-juice

---

* "110lbs. of sugar, 50lbs. of molasses, besides skimmings, from 110 gallons of juice, were afterwards obtained by Mr. M'Ken."

proved by Beaumé's saccharometer, was 11°; which would
indicate 20 parts of sugar contained in 100 parts of liquid.
This may be considered rich.   From 100℔s. of canes he
found they yielded 6¾ gallons of cane-juice.   He might add that
the results of his investigation, so far, are most satisfactory; and
it is with the greatest pleasure, therefore, that he supported the
Resolution.

" MR. RATHBONE had resided for sixteen years in the Mauritius; he had considerable experience in the growth of sugar and
other tropical plants; and had full confidence in the capabilities
of Natal, as being not only equal, but in many respects far
superior, to that island.   Sugar, and a variety of other plants,
promise to grow more luxuriantly.   5,000℔s. of sugar *per* acre
is considered in the Mauritius a good average crop; but from
such superior canes as Mr. Morewood's he should anticipate
a yield of not less than 7,000℔.   Larger canes have been
realized in the Mauritius from a damp soil; but the cane
under such circumstances contains less saccharine matter, and is
not so profitable : but this plantation of Mr. Morewood's is on a
dry soil, and superior to any that he ever saw in the Mauritius
similarly situated.   One great advantage which Natal has over
that island is,—here the plough can be used to a great extent;
while in that country the land is generally so stony, that such a
thing is impracticable.   He only knew one estate where the
plough could be used in the whole of the Mauritius.   Pine-
apples thrive better here, and possess fine flavour : the queen
pine, which is the finest description of pine planted in the
Mauritius, grows here equal in size to the common Creole pine.
From observations as to what is being produced in Mr. Morewood's gardens, and other parts of the Colony, he is convinced
that ginger, pimento, arrowroot, turmeric, and many other plants,
usually grown within the Tropics, may be planted successfully.
Cattle are not so subject to complaints as formerly; and if ordinary care and attention were paid to them, less complaints would
be made.   Cattle are cheap: this is one cause of neglect; and
very little knowledge is possessed yet as to the nature of the
diseases affecting cattle, or the remedies.

" The Resolution was then submitted to the Meeting, and
carried unanimously.

" RESOLUTION II. (Moved by MR. THOMAS REYNOLDS, and

seconded by MR. MORILLIER.)—'That the want of good roads and bridges, as also of certain, available labour, are difficulties which materially interfere with and hinder the progress of the Colony; and the local government ought to adopt speedy measures to facilitate such arrangements as may secure to the settlers those advantages.'

"RESOLUTION III. (Moved by MR. LEWIS REYNOLDS, seconded by MR. RATHBONE.)—'That the schemes of emigration hitherto brought into operation have been seriously prejudicial to the best interests of the Colony; chiefly through the erroneous principles on which they have been established, and the bringing out of an unsuitable class of emigrants; and that any private scheme whatever, under present circumstances, would fail to secure public confidence, and on that account would be injurious in its results rather than otherwise.'

"RESOLUTION IV. (Moved by MR. MORELAND, seconded by the REV. MR. SHOOTER.)—'That the following plan of emigration is one especially deserving the consideration of the government, as being best calculated to insure to the Colony a useful body of emigrants, and to them the fullest information and protection :—

"'1st. The establishing a Local Emigration Board, to be composed of government officials or nominees, and landed proprietors, or others, equally interested in the welfare of the Colony; whose duties should be the collecting statistical information, and superintending generally the introduction of emigrants, guided by an efficient agency; and to furnish them from time to time with such instructions and information, as may guide and direct them in the performance of their respective duties.

"'2nd. An agent in England, to direct, advise, and assist intending emigrants in making their arrangements previous to embarkation, so as to avoid the wasteful expenditure of their means, by delays or other causes; to give all necessary information, with the view of preventing disappointment; and to select such a class of emigrants as will be most likely to prove useful colonists, and as far as possible deter those who are totally unsuited by previous habits or pursuits, or deficient of the necessary qualifications. The agency to be furnished with plans of the lands at disposal, public or private specimens or samples of the various mineral, vegetable, or other productions of the

Colony, and the publishing a monthly or quarterly report of such statistical information as may be supplied by the Board or other sources equally authentic.

"'3rd. The agent in the Colony, to superintend the landing of the emigrants, to provide for the shelter of themselves or goods for a limited period after arrival; to advise as to the character of the different districts in the Colony; be prepared to show them plans of lands in the market, public or private; refer them to the land-agents, or others, having such lands for disposal; assist in procuring servants for the colonists, and situations for the emigrants; to assist in obtaining waggon-hire; and, as far as possible, extend that advice and protection so desirable and so valuable to strangers, in order to prevent fraud and imposition.

"'The agents to be appointed and paid by the government, and to be restricted from participating in any scheme or any interest connected with emigration, so as to insure the faithful discharge of their duties.

"'The members of the Board, as well as the agents, should be men of experience in the Colony, and as far as possible possessing the public confidence.'

"RESOLUTION V. (Moved by MR. MOREWOOD, seconded by MR. THOMAS REYNOLDS.)—'That this Meeting, being of opinion that many mis-impressions are entertained in England with reference to this Colony and its great capabilities, feel every confidence in Mr. Moreland, that he will correctly represent them, and satisfy all inquiries, and have every reason to believe that the utmost reliance may be placed in this representative by persons about to emigrate.'

"The thanks of the Meeting were given to the Chairman, and the Meeting then dissolved; some of the company returning to the boiling-house to witness the operations there, and others to visit again the cane-fields and gardens of the enterprising proprietor, Mr. Morewood."

After the numerous, varied, clear, and full testimonies borne by the respective gentlemen whose names are appended to these documents, any additional remarks would be quite superfluous.

It has been said of Mr. Morewood that he will consult all parties, but still follow his own course. It has been fortunate for Natal that he has this characteristic; otherwise what is now

seen would not have been accomplished.   Three years ago, when
every thing was speculation, doubt, and uncertainty, and when some
were saying that Natal was worthless, (as stated in my letter on
emigration at the time,) this gentleman quietly persevered in the
labour and expense of preparing the ground, and planting the
canes, being content patiently to wait for the result; whilst
others stood by, commending the effort as praiseworthy, but
treating the whole as chimerical and ruinous.   Had Mr. Morewood listened to their discouraging notes, and acted upon their
depressing representations, he would have abandoned his important enterprise in despair, and added another to the number of
those who have so loudly exclaimed against the Colony.   But,
by pursuing his steady course, success has crowned his praiseworthy efforts, and both the country and the mercantile community will reap the benefit.   Hitherto he has realized very little
advantage himself; but it is hoped that he may not have all the
labour and expense, without considerable profit.

I should not thus lengthily have entered into these particulars,
but that, as this is the first successful effort in Natal, it deserves
to be recorded and transmitted to posterity, that those who follow
after may have some knowledge of the difficulties connected
with the developement of the resources of this country.   Should
Mr. Morewood visit England, he may be consulted with safety,
as being an honest practical man, and one also who can secure
Kafir labour, having no need to import Coolies.   He has about
twenty Kafirs employed on his estate, and seven Englishmen.
The population of Albert is increasing.

COFFEE.

THIS beautiful shrub has now become an article of great
interest at Natal.   It is proved, beyond the possibility of successful contradiction, that the plant will grow and bear well,
though attention and perseverance will be requisite in its production.   The subject is one of so much importance both to the
Natal resident and the English public, that I shall make no
apology for quoting the following able articles from the (late)
"Natal Observer" of September 19th and 26th, 1851.

I believe the author of these valuable papers is Mr. Wray,
who designed them for publication.   They would certainly, with

the succeeding ones, make a compendious and valuable companion for the agriculturist. Competent judges, who have resided in coffee-growing countries, pronounce the articles very excellent; and they will afford directions to all who wish to cultivate the plant.

"THE first great object with a settler, in a new Colony, is to provide the necessaries of life; and if engaged in agricultural pursuits, he naturally cultivates those articles which are required for the support of himself and family, and which will likewise find a ready market in his immediate neighbourhood. Hence we find that potatoes, Indian corn, wheat, barley, oats, and various garden produce, constitute the chief items in the agriculture of a new Colony. But as time goes on, and the supply exceeds the demand, it becomes a matter of vital importance, both to the agriculturist himself and to his fellow-colonists, that those particular products shall be cultivated which will form large and valuable exports. The chief of these are usually denominated 'staple productions,' and in course of time are ranked as such in every printed notice of the Colony.

"On the quantity and value of these staple productions the solvency or bankruptcy of the Colony must ultimately mainly depend; for exports alone can keep in it that amount of specie which is necessary to commercial vitality. It is consequently of great moment that the agriculturists of the country make a judicious selection in cultivating products for export; and it is in a great measure to assist them in making this selection, that I have undertaken the arduous task of writing this very comprehensive work.

"The varied information that I have gained during the many years of my life which have been devoted to agriculture, would, were I an idle man, perhaps descend with me to the grave; and my fellow-creatures would derive no advantage from the practical experience which I have gathered: but in the hope that my advice may benefit those who have had little or no experience in such agriculture as suits the soil, climate, and circumstances of this Colony, I will endeavour to place before them, in a plain and practical manner, all the information I myself possess.

"We are all more or less prone to error, and none of us are

infallible. I therefore must bespeak indulgence, wherever and whenever I err, in my information or my deductions; but my readers may be assured of my honest and zealous intentions.

"From the character of the country, and its varied climate, I think that the following are worthy of consideration, as likely to form permanent 'staple productions;' and I will endeavour to treat of their value and culture in as concise a manner as the several subjects will allow of.

" STAPLE PRODUCTIONS.

"Coffee, tea, sugar, dates, cotton, tobacco, rice, cocoa-nut, pindar-nut, olive, cacao, indigo, madder, safflower, mulberry, hops, grapes, arrowroot, sago, cassava, Indian corn, Guinea corn, ginger, nutmeg, pimento, clove, vanilla, cinnamon, cardamom, pepper, pine-apple, sunflower, aloe, flax, hemp, plantains, bananas, betel-nut, chestnut, walnut, filbert, almond, mango, fig, potatoes, oats, wheat, barley, beans, peas, &c.

"ON THE CULTIVATION AND CURING OF COFFEE.

"The coffee-plant is one which, at the present moment, claims the particular attention of Natal agriculturists, inasmuch as the soil and climate of the country are admirably suited to its growth, and to its bearing; and because its culture will speedily supply the great local demand, and likewise form a highly valuable export.

"The lands in the immediate neighbourhood of the town of D'Urban, and, indeed, all the coast-lands lying between the Umzimkulu and the Tugela, are peculiarly suited to its growth, as approaching more nearly to its natural *habitat* than any other in the Colony. But, because such is the case, it by no means follows that these are the only portions of the country in which it may be profitably cultivated. Coffee-plants are able to bear an amount of cold which is little known or thought of. The high and cold regions in Jamaica, near St. Catherine's Peak, and at the foot of the Great Blue-Mountain Peak, both situated at some six thousand feet above the level of the sea; and, again, the mountains of Arabia; furnish instances of the great degree of cold that the coffee-plant will endure.

"More than this: it is an established fact, that it bears a larger, plumper, and far more aromatic berry at these altitudes and in these cold climates, than in a lower situation and in a warmer temperature. I have lived for two or three years on a coffee-plantation near the foot of the Blue-Mountain Peak, in Jamaica; and I know that the coffee produced in those regions is the finest in the world. In Arabia, likewise, the cold at night is sometimes intense; yet who will dispute the goodness of Mocha coffee?

" Having had many years' evidence of the extreme hardihood of the coffee-plant, I am inclined to think that it will grow and bear fruit abundantly in all *sheltered* situations, even as high up the country as Pietermaritzburg; but at Pine Town, Field's Farm, and Botha's, I am convinced it would succeed admirably. This would give a large range of country for the culture of coffee; bearing in mind that a certain degree of cold is, in my opinion, essentially necessary to the production of really fine coffee-berries.

" In the culture of the tree there is a singular difference in the Western and Eastern Hemispheres, inasmuch as, in the former, shade is considered injurious; whilst, in the latter, it is held to be desirable, if not absolutely necessary. Contrary to the prac- tice and to my own experience in the West Indies, I have found that coffee-trees thrive much better under a well-regulated shade in the Eastern Hemisphere, and yield their fruit in much greater abundance, than they would otherwise.

" From the singular manner in which coffee was planted in the West Indies, on dry and bleak 'ridges,' in warm and fertile ' bosoms,' and moist ' bottoms,' the general average of a planta- tion was reduced to a very low rate *per* tree: even as low as a quarter of a pound *per* tree I have repeatedly known; whereas a full-bearing tree will yield from ten to thirty pounds of dried and marketable coffee. Fifteen to twenty pounds of thoroughly good cured coffee is the most that I ever knew one tree to yield in a year, in the high mountain-regions of Jamaica; but, in St. Ann's parish, Jamaica, and in the East, I have known thirty pounds of inferior coffee, well cured, to be produced by a single tree. What an extreme difference is there between thirty pounds *per* tree, and a quarter of a pound *per* tree!

" It seems to show that a course of grievous error was adopted, and persisted in, by coffee-planters, which it is difficult for strangers to understand: but the explanation is easy enough. A plantation of 150 acres in coffee would, perhaps, have 50 acres producing some 3 or 4 pounds a tree *per annum;* whilst 100 acres, being 'dry ridge,' would only yield a few berries *per* tree; which, of course, reduces the average produce of the whole plantation to something like a quarter of a pound *per* tree. But this should not be.

"A coffee-plantation, to pay well, should be made a most perfect garden-cultivation. If the plant can produce thirty pounds *per* tree, then make it yield that quantity, or as near to it as possible. Let us just look at the difference in three plantations :—

"NO. 1 PLANTATION.

"50 acres of coffee, say, 700 trees *per* acre, 10 pounds
　　of coffee, cured, *per* tree; in all, 350,000 pounds,
　　worth at least 6*d. per* pound £8,750

"NO. 2 PLANTATION.

"50 acres in coffee, say, 800 trees *per* acre, at 1 pound
　　per tree; in all, 40,000 pounds, at 6*d.* £1,000

"NO. 3 PLANTATION.

"437 acres in coffee, say, 800 trees *per* acre, at 1 pound
　　per tree; in all, 349,600 pounds, at 6*d.* £8,740

"These will show that, with proper care, 50 acres of land may easily be made to yield as much coffee as 437 acres now do under the ordinary mode of cultivation pursued in the West Indies. It is evident that a patch of 50 acres surrounding one's house, can be far more cheaply and far more effectually cultivated, than so large a tract as 437 acres. The plantation would be very compact, within a small circle, and consequently more easily manured, pruned, cleaned, picked, and fenced; whilst the carriage of the ripe berries from the field would be very short in distance, and inexpensive.

"If these few arguments are not sufficient to convince any one of the expediency of *garden culture* in a coffee-plantation, then I imagine that even volumes would not have that effect. My strenuous advice is, to keep a small and compact cultivation; to concentrate all the labour and energy of the plantation; to aim at quantity and quality of produce, and not at having a large and imposing extent of land under culture.

" Having expressed these general views, I now proceed to treat of the plant, and the mode of cultivation most likely to succeed in this country.

" The coffee-plant is described by botanists as *Coffea Arabica,* or *Jasminum Arabicum,* of the Pentandria order, &c.; but I should divide it into the Arabian, the Ethiopian, and the Indian varieties.

" Whatever its origin may have been, there can be no doubt that there are three kinds or species now grown, differing materially from each other.

" The *Arabian* or Mocha coffee is characterized by having a small and more brittle leaf, with branches shorter and more upright, than the Jamaica and Ceylon coffee; and by its berry being almost always, or at least very frequently, single-seeded, and the seed cylindrical and plump.

" The Jamaica coffee-tree has a larger and more pliable leaf, longer and more drooping branches, and berries almost always containing two seeds. (The *Ethiopian.)*

" The great difference now existing between the two kinds may possibly have originated in the change of soil, climate, and season, operating through a series of years; but this difference is so decided, and so strongly marked, that the veriest tyro can in a moment pronounce of either.

" The *East India* or Bengal coffee-tree differs exceedingly from all others, but is in every respect a veritable coffee. I found it growing in the garden of an indigo-planter at Monghyr, and took several plants to Calcutta with me, where they are now growing luxuriantly, and bearing fruit. The leaf is much smaller, and of a lighter green, than the foregoing variety; its berry is infinitely smaller, and, when ripening, turns black instead of blood-red. Coffee made from it is of excellent flavour, and much liked.

" The soil on which the coffee-plant will thrive is very various indeed; in fact, any fertile soil will suit it, provided that the climate be congenial, and the subsoil good and well drained. The tap-root generally runs down to a great depth; and it is essential to the perfect health of the plant, that it should meet with no *strata* that will exercise an injurious effect upon it. Cold, damp clay, marl, and stagnant water are extremely pernicious in the subsoil. Gently sloping hill-sides, properly sheltered from violent winds, and affording the benefit of an easterly aspect, are particularly desirable, as the natural drainage of such land is a grand consideration, and the morning sun is highly beneficial to the plant.

" Coffee is always propagated from the seed, and for this purpose the ripest and finest berries are chosen; which are planted about one inch below the surface of the ground. In about twenty days they will, in favourable weather, have made their appearance above ground; and, in a very few days more, the first leaves will have expanded.

" It is usual to form nurseries of well-prepared soil, in which the seeds are planted pretty close together; care being taken that the seedlings are well shaded, and that such shade can be removed at pleasure, to afford them a little of the morning sun, whenever they require it. They may be removed and planted out, almost at any period after they are two months old; always remembering that they must be carefully shaded still, and the soil kept thoroughly moist around them; otherwise they will be greatly checked and injured.

" At whatever age the young plants may be removed from the nursery, it will be found good policy to prepare a bed of one foot in diameter, to receive each plant; and in this bed some well rotted leaf-manure should be placed, and mixed up with pulverized soil. This will serve to give them a great impetus, which will in fact affect their growth for years, so that it is fully worth all the trouble and expense it may occasion.

" The space commonly allowed in planting out in the fields is 7 feet by 7, or 8 by 8; which latter, I think, is nearer the mark. In good soil I should myself allow 700 plants to the acre, which is very nearly 8 feet apart.

" The land should be carefully lined off, and the plants be placed in regular rows, each one equi-distant from the other; and in the space between the plants there might be plantains and bananas, to afford shade; or other trees, if these be not obtainable in sufficient abundance.

" As there would still remain ample space, Indian corn, arrowroot, beans, peas, &c., might be planted to fill up, and in order to get some crop to pay expenses until the coffee came into bearing. By a judicious selection of these auxiliaries, the expenses should not only be paid, but a considerable surplus ought to be realized.

"Cocoa-nuts likewise are very frequently planted on land destined to receive coffee; in which case the plantains, &c., are gradually removed, until at length there remain on the land cocoa-nut trees and coffee-bushes alone, the former shading the latter, in which manner they may grow together for very many years, yielding annually a double crop.

"Land planted and cropped in this way can be made very valuable indeed by maintaining a regular system of manuring; the coffee-bushes bearing for about 20 to 30 years, whilst the cocoa-nut trees will produce fruit during from 50 to 80 years.

"In eighteen months after being transplanted from the nursery into the field, the coffee-trees should begin to bear fruit; and will go on, gradually increasing in quantity, until the seventh or eighth year, when they may be considered to have arrived at their full bearing; although this is not always the case, many trees increasing until their twelfth year.

"When the young plants are about to be removed from the nursery to the field, it is by many planters considered beneficial to trim their roots, and cut off the tap-root; and I have myself frequently followed this practice, although I am now inclined to think that the benefits supposed to result are very much to be doubted.

"It is very certain that, under any circumstances, great caution should be exercised, and every attention paid to the time of year, quality of soil, and particular season prevailing.

"When the young trees have attained a certain height,—generally from four to five feet,—the West-Indian custom is to 'top' them, for the purpose of stopping their upward growth, and to cause the trees to expand, by throwing out lateral branches. This plan is admirably adapted to the peculiarities of certain elevated localities, such as the higher ranges of the Blue Mountains in Jamaica; but I am fully convinced that, under different circumstances, and in lower regions, the practice would be any thing but beneficial or proper. Careful observation and considerable judgment are required, even in practical and experienced men, to determine the extent to which this process may be carried; and I am sure that much injury and consequent loss are occasioned by an indiscriminate adherence to this custom.

"The variation in the practice may be appropriately evidenced in the two systems which I should recommend for adoption in Natal; namely, the Berea and coast-lands generally, and the higher lands, ranging from Field's Hill upwards. In the former, I should not think of topping, or cutting back, my coffee-trees, until they had attained a height of from six to eight feet, when they would speedily become large and spreading trees, capable, under judicious management, of bearing a very considerable quantity of really good coffee. In the latter, (namely, the higher lands,) I should almost invariably keep the trees at about five feet high, and no taller.

"The difference in produce I should calculate somewhat as follows: average of full bearing trees, in the Berea and coast-lands, say 20℔s. *per* tree, of good mixed quality coffee; and in the higher lands, say 10℔s. *per* tree, of superior quality coffee; —both cured and ready for market.

"I feel assured that time and carefully conducted experiments will serve to verify these opinions; but I am no less certain that, until local experience has proved me to be correct, there will be many persons who will totally disagree with my views on this point.

"Twenty acres of land, cultivated in the manner I suggest, would in a short time form a very valuable little property; and when the trees come into full bearing, a large income might be derived from it, as it should then yield 140,000℔s. of cured coffee, worth 6d. *per* lb.,—£3,500 *per annum*. This is a large sum; and the system is one so entirely different to that pursued in the West Indies, Ceylon, and other coffee-producing countries, that the most contemptuous incredulity will, I am sure, be exhibited by many experienced and highly esteemed planters, when they first read the principles I am now endeavouring to inculcate. Let any one, or every one, however, doubt my assertions to any extent he or they may please; but let the system be fairly tried, and I shall have no fear of the result.

"To obtain the large returns from each tree, as above estimated, the following rules should be carefully attended to in every particular :—

"1. Choose a good and fertile soil, containing a tolerable quantity of decayed vegetable matter, and having a generous subsoil, which is naturally well drained. Moreover, be careful that this patch of land enjoys the advantage of the morning's sun.

"2. Pick out strong and vigorous young coffee-plants, which take up (if possible) without breaking their roots, and with the earth around them: but if this cannot be done, then put the young plants into water immediately when they are taken up from the nursery, and keep their roots immersed until they are planted out in the field. Allow 700 plants to the acre.

"3. Let the ground be in a tolerably moist condition, and see that the weather is moderately rainy.

"4. Prepare holes (varying from 12 to 24 inches in diameter) with well rotted vegetable manure, and finely pulverized earth, into which place the young plants carefully, and fill up the holes, so as to leave no hollows wherein water may lodge.

"5. Be sure that these young plants are fully shaded, yet enjoy light and fresh air in abundance. As a shade, plantain, banana, or cocoa-nut trees answer admirably, and at the same time their produce is very profitable.

"6. During the early stages of their growth, the young trees should never be choked by weeds, but should be well attended to, and (whenever appearing) any dead wood must be removed by hand.

"7. All suckers and undesirable shoots ought to be destroyed, immediately they appear; and when the trees have arrived at a sufficient height, their tops should be pinched off, to stay their further growth upward.

"8. Each tree must, at all stages of its growth, be kept open, so as to insure plenty of air and light penetrating throughout every part of it; and consequently no matting of the branches can be permitted, nor the growth of moss on the trunk, or on any of the branches.

"9. The trees should be carefully pruned whenever they require it, so as to keep them open, and to preserve that portion of the wood only which will bear fruit abundantly, and of good quality.

"10. Dig-in manure around the roots of the tree, not close to the trunk, but in a circle as wide as the branches extend, that the roots, as they grow, may find a store of nutriment. The rule must be,—Manure well, but always dig that manure in about the roots of the plant.

" 11. The choice of manure must become a study, in order to give those kinds only which will exercise a particular effect on the tree. Highly stimulating manure is sure to occasion the growth of a quantity of useless young wood and numerous cross suckers, which are often denominated ' gormandizers;' and these are both very injurious to the tree. Only that kind of manure is desirable which will supply the requisite material for the formation of vigorous and healthy young wood, which will produce an abundant crop of sound berries. All portions of the plant itself and its fruit form a manure which cannot be equalled; but as these are rarely to be had in sufficient abundance, green grass, weeds, and other vegetable matter, dug in around the roots, act very beneficially on the plant. Cattle-pen and stable manure may be used with discretion; but bone manure (such as burnt and ground bones, either alone, or decomposed by the action of sulphuric acid) constitutes one of the choicest manures that can be applied to the coffee-tree.

" 12. Irrigate in the dry season, wherever it can be done; and the increased value of the crop will prove its great utility. It very frequently happens that a long spell of dry weather follows the general blossoming of the trees; and they are so parched from lack of moisture in the soil, that the young fruit is destroyed in setting, and the ground is found to be thickly strewed with the young sets, when no larger than very small peas. In this manner the hopes of a whole crop may be entirely dissipated in a few days. Irrigation, at periods such as these, will prevent this wholesale destruction, by supplying the plants with moisture, and consequent vigour, to perfect their fruit-bearing efforts."

These articles show the manner in which the plant is to be successfully cultivated; and are followed by others which describe the picking and preparation of the berry for use: but this information can readily be obtained elsewhere by those who desire it. Our object at present is rather to show the natural producing powers of Natal, than to describe the process of manufacture.

It is gratifying to find that many persons are beginning to obtain seeds and rear plants, by which means different localities will be tried, and their respective merits developed; and success will at once cut off one important item of family expenditure and of colonial import.

The quantity of coffee imported into South Africa is enormous. The Dutch, as well as the English, use it very extensively. Thousands of pounds of money annually go out of the country for this article alone; instead of which, if the plant is extensively cultivated, it will become a source of continued and increasing wealth. The writer has seen the shrub growing luxuriantly in different gardens, and it is as pleasant to the sight as it is profitable to the producer. The rich foliage, with its bright evergreen leaf, and the twigs covered with berries in all stages of growth,—some bright red, and others dark green,—all indicate the combination of beauty and utility, and call forth the admiration of the natural philosopher, and the gratitude of the devout Christian.

> " Part of THY name divinely stands
> On all thy creatures writ;
> They show the labour of thy hands,
> Or impress of thy feet."

CHAPTER XII.

THE KAFIR WAR.   ROADS.   SOCIETIES AND COMPANIES.   BANKS.
GOLD AND COAL.   MISCELLANEOUS.   CONCLUSION.

THE KAFIR WAR.—Great misapprehension has existed amongst
a large portion of the English public, on this subject.   This has
arisen from not sufficiently marking the particular locality in
which the war has been carried on.   Many have reasoned thus:
"The war has been in South Africa: But Natal is a part of
South Africa: Therefore the war has been at Natal."   This,
however, is not very sound logic, involving the fallacy of reasoning from the state of merely one part, to the condition of all the
other parts of a whole.   The war, it is true, has been in South
Africa; and Natal undoubtedly is a part of South Africa; but
yet the war has not been at Natal, *nor within five hundred miles
of it*.   For, though Natal is in South Africa, it is only a part of
it: and the war has not extended over the whole, but only over
one part of South Africa; and that part happily has not been
Natal, or any region near to it.   Therefore those who have felt
misgivings on this head may lay them all aside.   I am thankful
that this Colony has been preserved in peace during the whole
time of the war on the Frontier of the old Colony, and also whilst
commotion and war have been carried on in the Sovereignty,
which is at a distance of about two hundred miles.

I hope that peace will still be preserved, since a war in Natal
would be the worst thing that could befall it.   This is not the
opinion of some English people.   But, having personally witnessed
the dreadful effects of war in the other Colony in 1846, I have
no hesitation in saying that such an occurrence would be the
direst calamity that could happen.

ROADS.—A subject of great importance is good public roads.
Without these the transit of goods and produce is both a dangerous and expensive affair.   As to the roads of Natal in general,

they are very much better than those in the old Colony along the Eastern Frontier, except where new roads have been executed: but these are still sufficiently bad. Great improvements have been made on the line of road betwixt the Bay and Pietermaritzburg, by which many bad and dangerous places have been improved and made safe: but still much remains to be done, before it is at all what is desirable. An entirely new line of road is required, also, into the Sovereignty. This has been pointed out frequently, and called for loudly.

BRIDGES are also greatly needed. At most of the public drifts there are small boats by which individuals may pass; but, when the rivers are swollen, they cannot cross for weeks together.

These improvements cannot all be made at once, but they should command very serious attention, and as much money as can be spared should be judiciously expended upon them. Take New Zealand as an example, as shown in Mr. Hursthouse's work.

PROFESSIONAL LIFE ASSURANCE SOCIETY,

CONNECTING THE CLERICAL, LEGAL, MILITARY, NAVAL, AND MEDICAL PROFESSIONS, AND HOLDING OUT ADVANTAGES TO THE PUBLIC NOT HITHERTO OFFERED BY ANY SIMILAR INSTITUTION INCORPORATED.

Capital, £250,000.

THE directors of this Corporation, having had many applications from parties residing at the Cape of Good Hope for shares, have passed a resolution to allow 1000 original shares especially for the Cape of Good Hope, admitting the purchaser to all the great and numerous benefits held out to original shareholders.

In reference to shares the following particulars are worthy of notice:—

1. The entire capital of the Company is £250,000, arising out of 40,000 shares of £6. 5s. each; the greatest part of which has been actually sold and signed for.

2. The original deposit is 10s. per share, without the probability of a future call being made or required; the remaining £5. 15s. will be made up by the additions accruing from profits and bonuses.

3. By the deed of settlement no proprietor is liable beyond the amount of his shares.

4. The holder of from five shares up to fifty is entitled to one vote; and to an additional vote for every additional fifty shares held by him.

5. Interest is paid at the rate of five *per cent. per annum*, on all paid-up capital; such interest increasing year by year, as the shares increase in value, by the appropriation of profits; so that very considerable interest will be realized, until the amounts of profits shall be sufficient to pay off the shares in full; after which the Corporation shall be declared and constituted a Mutual Life Assurance Society.

6. Lastly. In addition to these advantages, there is one novel and most excellent feature, worthy of special attention; namely, that one-tenth of the entire profits of the Company will be reserved as an Annuity Fund:—

i. For aged and distressed parties, assured for life, who have paid five years' premium, their widows and orphans.

ii. For the relief of aged and distressed *original* proprietors, assured or not, their widows and orphans, together with five *per cent. per annum* on the capital originally invested by them; thereby securing advantages to the living, not to be found in any other existing Company, and constituting an absolute assurance against poverty, so that no one belonging to this Society can come to want,—a principle too excellent to require comment.

AGENTS.

MESSRS. WALTON AND BUSHELL, *St. George Street, Cape Town.*

J. LAING, ESQ., *Medical Referee for Cape of Good Hope.*

C. JOHNSTON, ESQ., *D'Urban, Medical Referee for Port Natal.*

AGENTS FOR THE COUNTRY DISTRICTS:—

MESSRS. AITCHISON, BROTHERS, *Port Natal.*

W. G. ATHERSTONE, ESQ., M.D., F.R.C.S.L., *Graham's Town.*

O. M. BERG, ESQ., *Stellenbosch.*

W. P. M. DIXON, ESQ., *Colesberg.*

MESSRS. KAY, HESS, AND CO., *Port Elizabeth.*

W. L. GLEASER, ESQ., M.D., *Worcester.*

NATAL FIRE ASSURANCE AND TRUST COMPANY.

Capital, £10,000.

Established April 11th, 1849.

BOARD OF DIRECTORS.

D. D. BUCHANAN, ESQ., *Chairman.*

J. HENDERSON, ESQ.	J. BRICKHILL, ESQ.
A. CLARENCE, ESQ.	P. FERREIRA, ESQ.
C. R. SINCLAIR, ESQ.	F. MAXWELL, ESQ.

J. Russom, Esq., and J. E. West, Esq., *Auditors ;* C. Behrens, *Secretary ;* J. Holmes, *Clerk.*

D. D. Buchanan, Esq., *Attorney.*

AGENTS AT D'URBAN.

G. C. Cato, Esq. | J. P. Kahts, Esq.

BLOEM FONTEIN.

MESSRS. BANMAN, BROTHERS.

NATAL AGRICULTURAL AND HORTICULTURAL SOCIETY, D'URBAN.

E. Morewood, Esq., *President.*

S. Beningfield, and J. P. Kahts, Esqs., *Vice-Presidents.*

J. R. Goodricke, Esq., *Secretary and Collector.*

G. C. Cato, Esq., *Treasurer.*

COMMITTEE.

Captain Smerdon; E. P. Lamport, Esq.; A. F. Dawson, Esq.; Mr. Jacques; Mr. W. Wood; W. Dacomb, Esq.; J. More-land, Esq; H. Jargal, Esq.; J. Sanderson, Esq.; J. L. Fielden, Esq.; E. B. Herbert, Esq.; W. Sanderson, Esq.; H. J. Barrett, Esq.; A. W. Evans, Esq.; L. Wray, Esq.; E. Dacomb, Esq.; J. Proudfoot, Esq.; H. Searle, Esq.

This Society has been in existence for a few years, but its operations were only on a limited scale. They have now, however, so far advanced as to have Agricultural and Horticultural Gardens established on the Berea, in a very suitable position. These are placed under the able management of Mr. M'Ken; and it is hoped that such an amount of encouragement will from year to year be given, that the Society may be in prosperous circumstances, as its success is nearly connected with the prosperity of the Colony.*

THE NATAL SOCIETY, PIETERMARITZBURG.

This Society embraces the Library, the Museum, and the Agricultural departments. The Library existed some time alone; but when it was found needful to have the other objects included, it was thought better to unite and combine the whole in one Society under the above general designation, than to have two

---

* An account of the Gardens and what is growing in them will be found in another place, pp. 275–277.

or three separate and distinct institutions, each of which might be feeble, and flag for want of sufficient support.

The Committee consists of—THE HON. H. CLOETE; THE HON. J. M. HOWELL; THE HON. J. ANDERSON; REV. MESSRS. GREEN, CAMPBELL, and PEARSE; J. ARCHBELL, G. MACLEROY, and J. MARQUARD, ESQS.; THE HON. J. BIRD, T. SHEPSTONE, and D. SCOTT, ESQS.

The officers of the Society are,—The HON. H. CLOETE, *President;* T. SHEPSTONE, ESQ., *Vice-President;* J. ARCHBELL, ESQ., *Treasurer;* — HENDERSON, ESQ., *Secretary;* and the REV. J. GREEN, *Committee-man.*

BANKS.—A Bank has not yet been established at Natal. This is a great *desideratum,* especially since trade has increased, and mercantile houses are now wishful of transacting business with England direct. Many bills of private parties have been returned dishonoured, which is a serious evil, occasioning great embarrassment and loss. It is a hard case, after cash has been paid upon them at Natal, to have the bills returned in six months, with all their attendant evil consequences. This seriously affects the credit of the Colony, as well as interferes with the success of mercantile houses.

It is to be hoped that the day is not far distant when this want will be supplied, and either a bank or a *banking agency* be established, which might become a profitable investment of capital, and, at the same time, confer an important benefit upon the Colony.

Since the above was written, I find that parties have been trying to do a little in the matter, and quote the following from the " Natal Times " of July 23rd, 1852, on the subject :—

" NATAL BANK.

" ANOTHER attempt is being made by parties at Pietermaritzburg to establish a Colonial Banking Company. A report of the Meeting held for the purpose appeared in the ' Independent ' of the 1st inst., and the Prospectus was advertised in the 'Witness' of the following day. The nominal capital of the proposed Company is to be £20,000, in £5 shares; of which, however, it would appear that only £8,000 is intended to be called up.

It is stated that 1,000 shares were subscribed for in two days. We recently urged the importance of a banking establishment to every class and interest of the community; but especially in connexion with the investment of British capital in undertakings for the developement of our manifold resources, and for the prosecution of the great industrial and commercial enterprises now germinating. We doubt exceedingly whether there as yet exists amongst ourselves a sufficient amount of spare capital, efficiently to conduct the operations of such an establishment as the one proposed; and we abide by the opinion, that the object would be best accomplished, *either* by an agency in connexion with some firm or company at the Cape or in England, *or* by means of capital imported for affiliated purposes, and worked in connexion with them. We do not perceive, in the Prospectus of the ' Natal Bank,' any intimation of a purpose to apply for a charter, with special provisions for limiting the liability of shareholders; nor do we think the government would sanction any restriction of liability in the case of a bank of issue, unless the paid-up capital, and all the other arrangements, were such as effectually to protect the interests of the public. This is a matter suggestive of useful hints for caution and guidance.

"It is very far from our wish to discourage, unnecessarily, an important movement of this kind, or to cast the slightest reflection on the parties who have, in so spirited a manner, embarked in it; but we must be permitted to say, that the numbers and, in some respects, the composition of the Meeting, as reported in the ' Independent,' were not of such a character as to command instant and absolute confidence in the project: and we do not recognise, either in the *historic* address of Mr. Russom, the chairman, commencing with the ' Athenian bankers,' and ending with Smith's ' Wealth of Nations,'—or in the style and phraseology of the Prospectus itself,—such indications of practical business knowledge and habits as would, of themselves, induce a cautious speculator to fill up the *blank* in the ' form of application ' for shares, appended to the document. ' Prosperity will dawn upon us, and we shall have enough and to spare,' is a very comfortable sentiment for an after-dinner speech, and would no doubt be received, on such an occasion, with ' thunders of applause;' but it strikes us as scarcely befitting a grave, matter-of-fact, business document, like the Prospectus of a Banking Company.

"We are greatly mistaken if these are not substantially the views entertained by the principal mercantile houses at this Port; and, without intending to imply any disparagement of the resources of Pietermaritzburg, or any doubt of the business capabilities of its many astute and public-spirited citizens, we think that obvious considerations point to this Port as the most eligible seat of banking operations.

"Since the announcement of the scheme in question, and apparently stimulated by it, a summary movement in the banking line has been made by private parties at Pietermaritzburg. A quantity of £1 notes, payable on demand, were issued, bearing the signatures of Messrs. Archbell, Lawton, and Puckering; and several parcels of them were transmitted to houses of business at this place. Being ignorant of the adjuncts of this undertaking, we cannot pronounce upon, nor do we think it at present expedient to discuss, its merits. The position and character of the senior member of this new firm may, we should conceive, be regarded by the public as a guarantee for cautious and prudent arrangements. And the same remark may doubtless apply to Captain Glendinning, whose chivalrous embarkation in an enterprise tending to the same *issue* was advertised in our columns last week. It would seem, the vulgar adage, ' It never rains but it pours,' is likely to be verified amongst us; and, if we are in no danger of being suffocated with the plethora of a ' glut of gold,' there is some risk of our being drowned by an inundation of £1 notes.

"Meanwhile, we see, as yet, no reason to modify the views embodied in the foregoing article.

"In the ' Government Gazette,' an advertisement appears of a Special Meeting of the ' Fire Assurance and Trust Company,' for the purpose of ' discussing and deciding on the expediency of investing a portion of the capital stock of the Company in shares of the proposed Natal Bank.' We presume this announcement indicates an intention to abandon the deposit and discounting business of the Company, in favour of the new establishment,—a procedure obviously tending to restore the former to its original scope and objects, as set forth in its designation. Whether the

proposed investment is a more *legitimate* application of its capital, it is for the shareholders, in the first instance, to determine;
though, we apprehend, the *insurers* of property will also claim
the right of exercising a judgment in the matter."

Upon the merits of this subject we do not attempt to enter,
but judge that the observations of the editor of the "Natal
Times" are just and well-founded, that gentleman having probably some practical knowledge of the subject, and being fully
competent to write upon it.

An emigration company is not required; but it is the opinion
of some practical men, that a COMPANY FOR MANUFACTURING
SUGAR might be advantageously formed, which should provide
all the works necessary for crushing, boiling, &c. These should
be on a small scale, and in as large a number as possible, being
established in suitable places and at convenient distances. By
this means the small farmers would be enabled to cultivate as
much as their circumstances would allow. Most of these cannot
grow sugar on a large scale, or purchase the expensive machinery
needful for the manufacture: therefore, unless something of the
kind above suggested is done, they must be excluded from the
benefit of producing that important article of consumption; which
would be a great loss, both to themselves and the Colony. If
there should only be one huge manufactory here, and another
there, conducted by large growers and wealthy producers, it would
be to the utter exclusion of *the many,* who might otherwise find
it to their interest and profit to cultivate; for a monopoly would
be established, which would operate very unfavourably upon the
community in general.

The object of Coolie labour, advocated by Mr. Byrne, is to
have them *to work in gangs;* but Natal does not want "this sort
of thing," and would be greatly injured by it. It wants *the
many,* who may employ just as much labour as their circumstances admit; in which case Kafir labour, with a portion of
English, would serve every purpose; the more so as Kafirs like
to work among the sugar, and will be content to do a hard day's
work for much smaller pay than any others would require. Mr.
Morewood has about twenty employed, and could get as many
more, if he required them.

It is not to be supposed that the cane will only flourish in one particular locality. The author has seen it growing seventy miles west of the Bay quite as luxuriantly as on Mr. Morewood's estate; and again, far beyond him, to the Umvoti river. There can be no reasonable doubt that the whole coast-line will be available for the same purpose, along which thousands of English and Kafirs might be labouring, and deriving a profitable subsistence, without importing the foreign, unnatural labour of Coolies from India or China, upon whom no moral influence for good could be brought to bear.

With this Company might also be combined others for the preparation of coffee, arrowroot, rice, &c., &c.

It has been currently reported that a MINING COMPANY was about to be formed in England, and a railway constructed to the mines; but most people in Natal would like to know where the mines are, and what they produce, whether gold or silver, copper or iron. There have certainly been strong indications of mineral wealth, especially copper; but nothing to induce parties to embark capital in the investigation; and it is generally thought that a gold mine would be a calamity rather than a benefit to the country, as it would take men from the true "diggings" to pursue that which would invert the order of nature, and prove an evil in the end. A friend of mine, the other day, when going to the plough, quaintly remarked, that he was going to the "diggings;" and some parties who left Natal for California are returning to the place from whence they went, thinking the "diggings" of the former country more pleasant, or profitable, than those of the latter. This is certainly a significant indication as to whereabout the real treasure lies.

The parts which give the strongest indications of mineral wealth are near the Umtwalumi river, near the coast, and not far from the Umzimkulu river. The primitive formations in these parts are very good; some fine specimens of quartz, felspar, syenite, mica, and other minerals, being found, as also a number of crystals. Iron ore is also very abundant, lying on the surface of the ground.

GOLD.—The following pieces are extracted from a Graham's Town newspaper, published in February, 1854 :—

"GOLD! GOLD!! GOLD!!!"

"MR. VOWE, late civil commissioner and resident magistrate of Smithfield, arrived in Graham's Town on Wednesday, and has brought with him some quartz, from which was obtained a small 'nugget' of pure gold, also in his possession. This gentleman states that the discovery is attributable to a jackal; that a party, while 'prospecting,' or looking for gold, came to a spot where he had taken to earth, some loose ground having been thrown out of the hole in which he had found shelter. Amongst this *débris* a piece of white quartz was picked up; and, being subsequently examined, was found to contain some particles of the precious metal. This led to further researches, and the specimen of quartz brought down by Mr. Vowe was dug out by himself, and the gold he produces extracted from it with his own hands. This quartz is of very curious formation. It is in size as large as the hand, and is a mass of quartz crystals cemented firmly together. It is of very irregular surface, many of its cavities being partially filled with a dull red ochre-looking clay, apparently tinged with oxide of iron. The specimen of gold obtained from this quartz is in weight about twenty grains, but many specimens have been obtained of much more considerable value, the gold being of extraordinary purity, and of great brilliancy of colour. As there can be no doubt of the rigid accuracy of the account given by Mr. Vowe, and as the existence of the precious metal in the locality in question is thus fully established, the question now to be ascertained is quantity; or, in other words, whether it is to be obtained in sufficient abundance to pay for working. Experienced men are very sanguine on this subject. It is thought that the true gold-field will be found in the great mountain-range that divides the Sovereignty from the Natal territory, but of which range very little comparatively is known. Speculation, however, need not be indulged. Many persons are moving to the 'diggings,' and doubtless before long we shall have such information as will dissipate those doubts which at present rest upon the subject. Should it warrant the expectations that have been raised, then neglected South Africa may look forward to a bright and glorious career.

"The following extract is from a letter, with the perusal of which we have just been favoured :—

" 'February 13th.—I am so far convinced that the veritable metal has been discovered, and that large quantities will be found, that I have purchased another waggon, and start from —— next Saturday. Alfred Coleman and some others were riding above Smithfield, when their attention was attracted by something shining at the mouth of an ant-bear hole. They alighted from their horses, and found there some small nuggets of the precious metal, one weighing sixty grains, the others smaller. This led to a search for more; and the whole population of Smithfield, even old ——, who was packed up to start, were violently excited by visions of future treasures. J—— and A—— have commenced a pit at Coetzer's Farm, and have arrived at the *stratum* which covers the gold quartz,—and that abounds in large quantities. But I must not write about one individual. After the discovery of the three nuggets in the ant-bear hole, the whole population hurried out, and all have found small nuggets *on the surface*. A pit has been commenced in the *vley*, in which, also, at the depth of fourteen feet, about twenty small nuggets have been found. The meeting to be held on the 15th, [with Sir G. Clerk,] at Bloem Fontein, has, however, called away the most active explorers; but, you may depend on it, old J—— would not dig unless he thought there was a great probability of its paying. The samples of gold are equal in purity to the Australian. Of the particulars I have given you I can vouch for the accuracy, and you must form from them your own opinion. Do not be biassed by mine, as I am one of the sanguine ones. But, depend upon it, that where gold is found in SMALL NUGGETS,—*nuggets*, mind, not *dust*,—it will be found in *large*, or there is no faith to be put in geology, or its principles either.' "

COAL.—This valuable mineral was found, some time ago, beyond Pietermaritzburg, but at a distance so great as to prevent it from being available at the metropolis, although fuel there is very high in price. The specimens which were brought have been mostly from the surface, and of inferior quality; but possibly, if labour and capital were expended upon working the mine, something better might be found.

The coast-range also presented promising indications of coal formation, which have now been realized by its being found on or near Compensation, (or Albert,) the estate of Mr. More-wood. This is distant about thirty-five miles from the Bay, and land-carriage would be expensive; but water-conveyance, if avail-able, would be much cheaper. The general impression is, that the mineral abounds to within a short distance of D'Urban: if so, it will be of the highest value to the Colony, as Natal lies so conveniently for the steamers which are just now beginning to ply between England, the Cape, India, and Australia.

I subjoin the official Report of Mr. Bird, Acting Surveyor-General, extracted from the "Natal Times" of July 30th, 1852.

"THE OFFICIAL REPORT ON THE COAST COAL.

"Surveyor-General's Office, *July* 21st, 1852.

"Sir,—I have the honour to state, that, in compliance with the directions of His Honour the Lieutenant-Governor, issued in consequence of a discovery, for the communication of which we are indebted to Robert Dickson, Esq., agent for Messrs. Chiap-pini and Co., of Cape Town, I have inspected the indication of coal, on the coast, near Compensation, the property of E. More-wood, Esq., about forty miles from D'Urban.

"In this inspection, I have availed myself of the valuable assistance of Messrs. Madigan and Turner.

"The vein of coal shows itself on the side of the cliffs over-hanging the sea; it is a distinct and very remarkable feature. The outer crust of the coal, exposed as it has been for centuries to the action of the air, is very difficult to kindle: at the depth of a few inches, this disadvantage sensibly diminishes. I have seen the coal used in a smithy, at Compensation, where every process of heating and welding iron is performed with the greatest facility.

"The *stratum* of coal on the cliff is not more than about two feet in breadth, and under several superincumbent *strata* of clay, sand, stone, &c. This at once forbids the hope of working it with advantage in the immediate neighbourhood of the coast.

"At the entrance of a small cave, however, the *stratum* of coal is seen to dip inland, and with a sensible increase in its breadth. It is therefore probable that, at some distance inland, the vein may be of sufficient breadth to be profitably worked; and it is still more probable that, below the first vein, a second,

XIX.—VIEW OF THE HOUSE AND LOCATION OF MESSRS. JAMES HALLETT AND HENRY DIXON, SITUATE ON THE
GREAT UMHLANGA RIVER, NEAR VERULAM.

more copious, and of superior quality, may be found. But this favourable conjecture requires corroboration by boring, before the discovery of coal near the coast can be pronounced important.

" I have made arrangements for the conveyance of six waggon-loads of coal to the Custom-house at D'Urban, in order that the officers of the steamer, now daily expected, may have it in their power to test its quality and value for steam-navigation.

" I have the honour to be, Sir,

" Your most obedient Servant,

" JOHN BIRD, *Acting Surveyor-General.*"

To bring down the information as to Natal to the latest date, an extract is subjoined from the " Watchman " of September 13th, 1854 :—

" The last accounts from Natal are those of the 21st of June, and present an exceedingly favourable picture of the progress of that Colony. An extraordinary degree of activity was exhibited in the trade with the interior. Trains of waggons, laden with wool, butter, ivory, and with other products, were daily making their appearance, each taking back merchandise and provisions from the warehouses and stores. Good roads, available through-out the year, and the opening of the nearer route to the New Free State, were alone wanting to secure to the Port of Natal the monopoly of a vast interior commerce.

" Beautiful samples of coffee have been grown near the Umhlanga. The berries are as large, clean, and full as any imported. The plants are from Bourbon seed, sown not quite three years ago. This is the first year of bearing ; and yet so heavy has been the crop, that several of the branches were borne downwards with the weight. The coffee-plant, it is now placed beyond doubt, grows vigorously and bears well in the district ; and its rapidly increasing cultivation will, before long, tell on the market.

" The field of mineral wealth opening up in Namaqualand appears to be immense, and seems likely to surpass any thing else in the world. In that portion of the Colony there are copper mines of almost unparalleled richness. The ores pro-duce, on the average, from forty to forty-five *per cent.* of copper ; and in some cases as high a *per-centage* as seventy-five *per cent.*

has been obtained. The ore appears to be obtained with the greatest ease, the mines, in most instances, having been hitherto worked as open quarries; and one miner and two assistants are able to extract and prepare for shipment about one ton *per* day. The proprietors of the principal mines have addressed the colonial government, with a view of obtaining such an extension of their leases as will make it worth their while to construct roads for the conveyance of the ore to the place of shipment. To this application the government does not appear disposed to listen, arguing that, as the ore can be delivered in England at £13 *per* ton under the present disadvantages, while its gross value may be computed at £30 to £40 *per* ton, the claim for better conditions than those existing is not sufficiently strong. The answer of the governor, however, hints that the colonial legislature may not feel indisposed to guarantee a fixed rate of interest upon the capital employed in making a railroad to serve the mineral districts; and it is very probable that the suggestion will be adopted."

The following extract is from the "Manchester Examiner," as cited in the "Watchman" of October 25th, 1854:—

"SILK FROM PORT NATAL.—A sample of silk from Port Natal has been shown to us, which, we believe, is the first that has reached this country from that Colony. The quality is considered good, though it is not quite perfectly reeled. We shall be glad to see that Colony continue its attention to the cultivation of silk. We are persuaded that it is an article which may be profitably cultivated in many parts of the world where it has been hitherto neglected; and, as we hope England will shortly afford a market for the cocoons, the difficulty and trouble which frequently attend the reeling at the places where it is produced, will then be dispensed with."

I HAVE now arrived at the close of my self-imposed task; and it must be for the reader to judge to what extent I have fulfilled my professions, and gratified the expectations raised.

There will doubtless be considerable variety of opinion as to both the plan and the execution of this work; and to expect to meet the views and wishes of all, were absurd. The plan and execution are my own, having had no prompter or director, but valuable and kind assistance, which I have recorded, and for which I again tender my grateful acknowledgments. It will now be for the public to judge whether I have been mistaken as to the nature of the wants in this case, and the value of the information imparted. The author has no literary fame, which, trumpet-tongued, might announce the production of his thought and pen to admiring multitudes; but he has to creep out of retirement into public notice, depending solely for success on the merit of his work.

The execution is far below what I should have wished; but in this I am entitled to every allowance which can possibly be made, having prepared it on the eve of departure from Natal, when numerous duties and engagements pressed upon me; and I have been obliged to snatch an hour, when I could, to write a little, and then again have been distracted by making further travelling arrangements.

If by this humble effort I am able at all to contribute to the interest, gratification, or profit of others, I shall be happy; and if I fail, I shall still have the award of our great poet, who declares, that he

"Who does the best his circumstance allows,
Does well, acts nobly : angels could no more."

I know it to be the opinion of some persons, that several of the topics which I have undertaken to discuss do not properly fall within the province of a minister of religion. But these censors ought to consider the intimate connexion that subsists between every man's dearest interests in this world, and those which are connected with eternity : and I have yet to learn, that my vocation precludes me from all attempts to communicate such knowledge as I think will benefit every one who comes within the range of its influence.

The information from this Colony has too often been partial and one-sided; tending to mislead the English reader, and to prevent him from drawing just inferences respecting many of the subjects brought under his consideration. Perhaps this may not in most instances have been done with a bad design, but has arisen in part from the constitution of our common nature. Every man of candour is aware of this personal predilection for his own views, and knows that time and opportunity are required before he can collect *data* for altering his preconceptions on various matters. When an object is placed prominently and continuously before the mind's eye, we are almost imperceptibly affected by the particular view which we obtain, and too frequently forget that others are intently looking at it in an opposite direction. A discreet man, standing in the centre between these extreme points, is in a condition to correct the conflicting and partially erroneous conclusions of both parties, and to show the relative importance of each point in its bearing on the whole. This friendly part I have endeavoured to enact on the present occasion; and have offered my reflections, without fear or favour, in plain language, but in a gentle spirit. In party-politics I have never been engaged; nor employed myself in delivering speeches at public meetings, or in writing leading articles for colonial journals. But, for many years, I have quietly moved through different parts of the country, and carefully noted all that transpired, without feeling my passions excited, or my interests assailed. Under these circumstances I think myself qualified, in some moderate degree, to perform the task which I have imposed on myself for the benefit of others; and my parting regret is, that I have not written in such an attractive style as accords with my wishes.

I subjoin, as an APPENDIX, a brief History of the Orange-River Sovereignty, and an exposition of the opinions and feelings of English settlers and others respecting the desirableness of that fine frontier remaining under the mild and fostering care of the British government, and their gloomy apprehensions of the disastrous consequences of its abandonment to the sway of incompetent and discordant rulers.

APPENDIX.

BRIEF HISTORY OF THE ORANGE-RIVER SOVEREIGNTY, SOUTH AFRICA.

OPINIONS OF THE COLONISTS RESPECTING ITS RETENTION OR ABANDONMENT.

THE SETTLEMENT OF THE DUTCH BOERS IN THE TRANS-VAAL TERRITORY.

A RECENT SPECIMEN OF THEIR COMMANDOES AGAINST THE NATIVES.

THE RENEWAL OF DOMESTIC SLAVERY.

JOURNAL OF A TOUR THROUGH THE KALAGHARE DESERT TO LAKE N'GAMI.

CONCLUDING OBSERVATIONS.

THIS APPENDIX was written, and ready for publication as a separate pamphlet, some months before the British legislature declined to interfere, when her majesty's ministers had determined no longer to retain the reins of government, which had been recently assumed, in the Orange-River Sovereignty. It contains much authentic intelligence on this "vexed question;" and the author has been advised to publish it for general information. A few paragraphs have been omitted; and others are presented in a form somewhat modified from that in which they were originally written. These changes were required, in consequence of the obvious difference between a result which was then only "under consideration," and one that has now become "an accomplished fact."

SKETCH
of the
British Colonies
SOUTH AFRICA.

BRIEF HISTORY

OF

"THE ORANGE-RIVER SOVEREIGNTY,"

SOUTH AFRICA.

OF "the Orange-River Sovereignty" but little is known by the British public; nor am I aware that sufficient interest is felt about it to induce people in general to make themselves acquainted with it. The gold-fields of Australia have become all-absorbing to many, who turn away from Africa with disdain. But if Africa does not abound in "golden nuggets," it is enriched with "golden fleeces," and well deserves, at any rate, the notice of the traveller or wayfaring man. But, in my modesty, (lest I should seem to be too obtrusive,) I propose to present the reader only with a very small work upon the "Sovereignty;" and thus shall avoid affrighting those who may condescend to notice this brief production.

Many persons, however, are desirous to have their knowledge enlarged about this important portion of Her Majesty's African dominions; and I have materials prepared for a large volume on the subject; but I am of opinion that I shall be able so to select and compress the requisite information, as to give, in a condensed form, a clear, connected, and satisfactory view of those parts which are most interesting.

Scraps of information in newspapers, in Government Proclamations, and in Blue Books, have from time to time appeared; but they have mostly been single and detached pieces, which could convey no adequate idea of the country, and have often a complicated or *ex-parte* character, presenting only one side of the topics under consideration.

Indeed, there must be great ignorance of "the Orange-River Sovereignty," and its relative importance and value to the Colonies of the Cape of Good Hope and Natal, as well as to Great Britain itself; otherwise the subject of abandonment, which has been entertained in many quarters, would never have found a place in the minds of thoughtful men.

In order to enable the reader to form a correct opinion con-

z

cerning this extensive portion of Her Majesty's dominions in South Africa, and also to accompany me in tracing the different points upon which I am about to treat, I have provided two maps on a small scale, which will convey with sufficient distinctness the relative positions occupied by the various tribes and nations whose interests are concerned in the decision of the paramount question of occupancy.

GEOGRAPHICAL POSITION OF THE SOVEREIGNTY.

TAKING the map of South Africa, and tracing the outlines of the locality in which "the Orange-River Sovereignty" is placed, the reader will find that the form of this large tract of inland country is not unlike that of a triangle, with the corners rounded off. It has three great distinctive boundary marks. On the south it is bounded by the Great Orange River, which is the northern boundary of the Cape Colony. On the east it is bounded by the gigantic range of the Quahlamba or Drakenberg Mountains, which separate it from Natal; and on the north and north-west, by the Great Vaal* River, which in Dutch signifies "Faded" or "Yellow River." This important river takes its rise high up in the Drakenberg to the north, flows along the whole north-western boundary, receives many large tributary streams and rivers, and then flows into the Great Orange River, which pours its mighty waters to the westward into the Atlantic Ocean. The Sovereignty lies in lat. 24° to 31° S., and long. 24° to 30° E.

This territory is divided into four districts:—THE CALEDON, the capital of which is *Smithfield;* BLOEM-FONTEIN, capital, *Bloem-Fontein;* WINBERG, capital, *Winberg;* and VAAL-RIVER, capital, *Harrismith.* Besides these, there is a large tract assigned to the Griquas or Bastards; and another, still larger, to the different tribes of natives. The relative positions which they hold to each other are these: The Caledon and Griqua-land extend to the south, along the Orange River: Bloem-Fontein and the Native Territory occupy the centre: and Winberg and Vaal-River occupy the northern part. The tract of country which is now distinguished as the "Vaal-River Republic," lies beyond the Vaal River to the north and west, but mostly to the north. Its

---

* *Faal*, in English pronunciation.

four chief towns are, Potchesstroom, Megaliesberg, Leydenberg, and Origstad. The two latter lie far north, probably in lat. 22° or 23° S., and the two former about lat. 26° to 28° S. Still further north is situated the Great Lake Ngami, in lat. 20° S., and long. 24° E. To the westward lies the country inhabited by the Nama-quas and the Damaras, reaching to the Atlantic or Southern Ocean.

Such is a general outline of the geography of the country lying north of the Great Orange River; a large portion of which has been thrown open to the exploring traveller only within the last few years, by the successful search for the long-reported Great Lake, by Messrs. Oswald and Livingstone.

It would, however, appear as though the all-wise Governor of the universe had, to some extent, placed at this point bounds to the course of civilized man. On the west lies a great waste, the Kalaghare Desert; a part of which was crossed by Mr. M'Cabe, whose journal will be given in the subsequent pages : and to the north the *tetse*, or " poisonous fly," becomes injurious and fatal, and fever prevails, often attended with fatal consequences :—all these declaring, " Hitherto shalt thou go, but no further."

NATURAL CHARACTERISTICS OF THE SOVEREIGNTY.

THE natural features of the Sovereignty are on a bold, broad scale. But little of the picturesque and beautiful presents itself to the eye of the traveller, bald monotony prevailing, except in some favoured spots. The plains, or " FLATS," as they are gene-rally called in South-African phraseology, appear interminable. The mountains rise high, until cloud-capped; the giant Quahlamba is lost in the heavens; whilst Moshesh's heights look blue, almost frowning black, in the distance. These apparently " everlasting hills" have on their summits long tracts of arable table-land, whilst, from their sloping or precipitous sides, " streams of water gush out." In some parts of the country purling brooks glide softly through, and in others large rivers force their impetuous currents into the Great Orange or Vaal River. But the country is not so well watered as Natal; yet I consider it to be better supplied with water than the old Colony. Drought, however, is some-times severely felt.

Whilst you keep to the mountain-range, this order of things prevails, until you approach the neighbourhood of the Great

Lake. In reference to it, let not the reader suppose it to be an insignificant affair, whilst he sneeringly turns to America, and reminds you of her inland seas, and points to the Great Mississippi, or talks of the magnificent St. Lawrence. No: we are writing concerning Central Africa; the reported " land of rivers without water," and pools, or " *fleys*," dried up; the land of solitudes and wastes, of sands and deserts.

The Lake Ngami is said to be one fine expanse of water, sixty miles long and twelve or fourteen broad, being probably one hundred and twenty in circumference. According to the report of the natives, another much larger lies far to the north-west.

The Zonga River is large; and the Zembese is said to be three quarters of a mile broad, deep to the very edge; when flooded, it overflows its banks seventeen miles on each side. These, with other mighty rivers, appear to invite busy man to appropriate their powers to his use, and probably empty their treasures into the Mozambique Channel towards Sofala.

The probability is that, in the higher altitudes of Central Africa, the different great mountain-ranges, powerfully attracting the clouds, cause immense quantities of rain and snow to descend; which severally feed the Nile to the north, the Niger to the west, and the Zonga to the east. From the remarkable facilities recently afforded to scientific and geographical exploration in every quarter of the globe, the time seems likely soon to arrive when the course taken by these vast streams, and the unknown regions which they contribute to fructify, will be accurately described and become familiar to us; and their resources be developed in a manner at present beyond our conceptions.

The intelligent reader must not suppose the Orange-River Sovereignty to be a waste desert, worthless and unproductive. On the contrary, in those parts where water can be commanded, vegetation is of the richest, rankest kind. Many of the mountains are of that peculiar formation, in which small fountains gush out about half-way down their slopes, and the water gradually spreads to the right and left in small and gentle rivulets, until, at the base, the whole of the surplus water is united, and moistens and enriches all the surrounding country. From the various points where the life-giving moisture descends, the natives or others commence cultivation; and sow the land with corn, or plant esculent herbs, as their wants may be. The sight of hundreds of acres waving with corn, girding the bases of the mountains, as was the case at Plaatberg, where I was long a resident, has a most cheering effect on the spectator.

As to the general fertility of the Vaal, Mr. Medhurst, who visited those parts, writes:—" Making every allowance for the latitude generally claimed by travellers, in the quotations which I have made, there can be no doubt that this is a vast producing country.   During my stay at Bloem-Fontein, few days passed without some waggons from Mooi River, Megaliesberg, or Mariqua, being on the public market, with meal, Boers' tobacco, brandy, Indian corn, dried fruits, &c., &c.; precisely the same as the waggons used to come from Oliphant's River and George to Graham's-Town market.   At Mooi-River Dorp, I saw the finest samples of wheat that can possibly be produced, and I was informed by Mr. Lombard, that it can be grown without limit."— NATAL MERCURY, December 29th, 1852.

But whilst the general producing powers of the country are thus great, its peculiar adaptation for growing wool is its most important feature.   It would appear from actual observation, that in rearing young lambs, whilst the old Colony gives 75 *per cent.*, the Sovereignty gives 95 *per cent.*, being 20 *per cent.* beyond the yield of the former.

This fine country abounds with all kinds of game; birds, beasts, and bucks; the lion, the tiger, and the elephant; the rhinoceros, the buffalo, and the gnu; the quagga, the eland, and the antelope.   These beasts of beauty or of prey are not found by odd ones, here and there, thinly scattered over the country; but most of them, being gregarious, in troops and droves of from ten to one hundred, and often one thousand, together.   Here they roam, and sport, and revel, as untamed lords of the land, and its only rightful proprietors.

BRIEF HISTORY OF THE VARIOUS RACES INHABITING THIS REGION.

HAVING now placed before the reader the geographical position of the country, and briefly sketched some of its leading natural characteristics, let us take a hasty view of the different races of human beings who have peopled it for the last half century.

I find this prepared to my hand by an able draughtsman, the Hon. W. Porter, Attorney-General at the Cape, who observes :—

"BETWEEN the Orange River and the Vaal River, and bounded by the Draaksberg range of mountains on the right, lies the new Sovereignty.

"About the year 1825, or perhaps earlier, colonial cattle-farmers, suffering from the droughts so common in the northern districts of the Colony, and tempted by the stronger springs and better herbage to be found beyond the Orange River, began to drive their flocks to the other side in search of temporary pasturage. Little or no opposition was made by any parties claiming to be the owners of the soil. The regions to which the Colonists first resorted for grass and water, could scarcely be said to have any actual possessors. The Bosjesmans, the true aborigines of the country, had either been exterminated, reduced to slavery, or hunted into holes and caverns in the mountains, by conquerors, partly Hottentot and partly Kafir. The whole territory was newly settled and thinly peopled. Things in that quarter had followed the common course of native conquest in South Africa; which has generally set-in from the north-east. If Chaka and his Zulus, moving southward, fell upon the Mantatees, the Mantatees, flying before these terrible enemies, fell down upon the Basutos, who, flying in their turn, fell upon such other Bechuanas as might be in their track, while those again fell upon the miserable Bushman.

"When all this was over, for the time, the remnants of the routed tribes found themselves each in a new country. Nor were portions of the Kafir family the only new arrivals in this vast region. There were also there the Bastaards, sprung originally from the intercourse of Dutch settlers with coloured women,—a mixed race who emigrated from this Colony early in the present century. It was some little time before they began to be regarded as a native tribe. Forty years ago, or thereabouts, a man of Negro blood, who had been a slave, but who had saved, by industry and thrift, money enough to buy his freedom, collected about him a number of the mixed race known as *Bastaards*, and of other people of colour, who looked up to him as their head. This was ADAM KOK, the great-grandfather of the present Adam Kok. Finding that his people had increased and were increasing, old Adam Kok quitted the Colony, and journeyed into the Bushman country, north of the Great River, where, after some wanderings, and (if report lie not) no small destruction of the aborigines, he settled in the territory, a large tract of which his descendant now rules, under Her Majesty the Queen. There he was joined by Hottentots and free Blacks from the Colony, and by refugees from various tribes, forming a community of a singularly mixed description; among whom were supposed to be the remnant of a Hottentot tribe, called by some name of which *Griqua* sounds like an abbreviation. At the instance of one of those missionaries whose labours amongst them can never be too much extolled, the degrading name of *Bastaard* was discarded, and Kok's people thenceforth assumed the name of *Griquas*. Under this name, political independence was claimed, or at least exercised; and Adam Kok, who exercised a rude sort of sovereignty amongst them, was declared to be supreme chief or captain. Disputes, however, soon arose, which split the population into two parts, and finally resulted in a Griqua government under Waterboer, at Griqua Town, and a Griqua government under old Adam Kok, at what is now Philippolis.

"Whether or not the Griquas were already in the country which they now occupy, when the Boers first began to cross the Orange River, is a point which I heard fiercely disputed in 1845, when I was in Griqua-land in attendance upon Sir Peregrine Maitland. That this point should ever have been mooted, showed the recent origin of Griqua right; and it is therefore no matter of surprise, that the Boer or his herdsman was so unresistingly allowed to lead his cattle to whatever spring or spot best suited him. At first, this sort of occupation was temporary, and ceased with the drought which led to it. But imperceptibly it became permanent, sometimes perhaps taken by strong hand, but more frequently made the subject of purchase from some Griqua, who, making little or no use of his land, was ready to sell it upon easy terms. But it was not until many years had elapsed, that the emigration became a matter of political importance. True, indeed, its beginnings were discountenanced by the colonial government. Our frontier authorities were enjoined as much as possible to prevent it. But, as in the case of every successive movement beyond the boundary for the time being, from the period when the Cape Colony was contained within the Cape-Town military lines, till now that it has reached the Orange River and the Keiskama, all the efforts of the colonial government proved unavailing. Down however to what may be called 'the great emigration' in 1836, the Boers beyond the boundary gave but little trouble, and excited, except in a few far-seeing men, little apprehension.

"But matters became truly serious when an emigration began which was in its character essentially political and anti-English, springing in no small degree out of old national feelings, embittered by what, conducted as it was, they considered and called *robbery*,—the slave-emancipation. The emigrants, through many dangers and much loss, reached Natal; and, after destroying Dingaan, the most powerful and ferocious chief who had tried to resist them, first by treachery, and next by force, they proclaimed a Batavian Republic. The assertion at Natal of British sovereignty by force of arms having become necessary, one effect of this measure was to send over the Draaksberg Mountains a number of emigrants, who carried with them, into what is now the Orange-River Sovereignty, a rooted antipathy to British rule: whilst another effect was, that the tide of emigration, instead of flowing into Natal, was thenceforth stayed at the Draaksberg, to spread and spend itself over the whole land between those mountains and the Great River. Then began a state of things too well known to need description. The Boers, with their guns in their hands, disputed native titles in all directions; and as their antagonists held in general only assagais, the Boers got the better in the argument.

"True it was, that there were native titles which covered every inch of the entire country; nay, that in many cases the same tract of land was loudly claimed by several chiefs at once. The disputes of Moroko and Moshesh, and of Sekonyella and Moshesh, (not to speak of others,) are well known to all who take an interest in such controversies. But the Boers regarded those native claims to immense possessions as the common foible of all rude tribes, and practically evinced their determination to judge for themselves what land was so occupied as to be really and legitimately the property of tribes who had come there, upon the same sort of errand as themselves, so recently before their own arrival. In this manner, and not without much mutual recrimination, it came to pass that emigrants from the Colony settled themselves down in many parts of what is now the new Sovereignty. They assumed absolute independence. They established something which they called a government, mimicked from the old Colony. They had their landdrosts, their field-cornets, their volksraads. All of them, even those living within the acknowledged territory of native chiefs, disclaimed being amenable to any native jurisdiction; but such Natives living amongst them, or near them, as they charged with having committed crimes against them, they themselves tried and punished. This state of things could not last: and it became apparent, that unless the British government interposed its authority, nothing but discord, violence, and crime, and an ultimate extinction of native rights, could arise from such a posture of affairs."—"Blue Book," pp. 7, 8.

This is a brief and general view of the parties that have recently taken possession of various parts of the Sovereignty, and the relative position which they occupy one to the other, and of their varied and conflicting claims to land, and their quarrels on this subject. But little is said about the different native tribes and clans; and it will be impossible, in the brevity of these notices, to make more than a passing allusion to them.

On the map will be seen the Griquas, or Bastards, under Adam Kok, along the Orange River, which extends towards the Vaal on the left; whilst another clan of the same people is occupying both sides of the Vaal, under Waterboer, who acts as independent captain over them. To the right will be found different tribes of Bechuanas and Basutos, upon two small locations in the Caledon district. Further to the north is Moshesh, with a large tract of country assigned him, along the left banks of the Orange River to its sources in the Drakenberg.

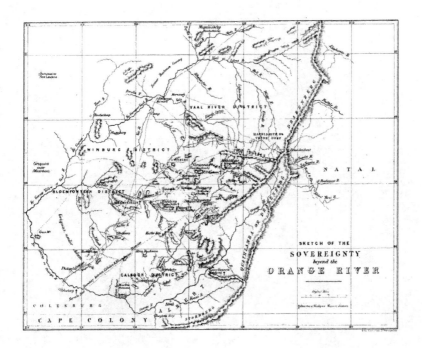

SKETCH OF THE
SOVEREIGNTY
beyond the
ORANGE RIVER

These are called Basutos. Further to the left, joining Moshesh on the right and Bloem-Fontein on the left, is the chief Moroko, with the Barolongs; near whom are the Bastards under Carolus Batge. Advancing toward the north, are the Batuing under Moletsani. Still further to the north, are the Koranas under Ged Taarbosch, betwixt whom and the upper part of Moshesh's country are the Mantatees under Sekonyella. Besides those who are here enumerated, many more natives are scattered over different parts of the Sovereignty. Nothing beyond the names and localities of these various tribes and peoples can now be ascertained.

In the preceding extract, the country is described as being thinly peopled; but when I passed through it, four years before that gentleman, it did not appear to be so; for, directly after passing the Orange River, there were the Bastards, extending right and left, with the Bushmans at Bethalie. As we advanced, we came to the Koranas at Betberg. Then, crossing the Modder River, we came to Thaba-Unchu, where the chief Moroko resided in the largest native town which I have yet seen. It was estimated to contain 10,000 people. Still further on, were the different tribes previously specified, who appeared to fill the land.

As to the precedency of the Griquas to the Boers in the occupancy of the country, the Attorney-General says,—" Whether or not the Griquas were already in the country which they now occupy when the Boers first began to cross the Orange River, is a point which I heard fiercely disputed in 1845, when I was in Griqua-land in attendance upon Sir Peregrine Maitland." But during the two years, 1840 and 1841, in which I resided in this neighbourhood, I never heard this question once mooted, it being universally allowed that the Griquas had a right to it by first occupancy; and the Boers invariably had, at that time, to take the farms from them on lease or by purchase. I mention this, not to invalidate the testimony of this gentleman, but simply to show on which side the preponderance of evidence concerning pre-occupancy prevails.

The native town at Thaba-Unchu was not only the largest I have seen, but the houses were of a much better description than the ordinary Kafir hut; and there was so much cleanliness and thriftiness about the people as was to me highly gratifying. They were the great tailors of the country, procuring the skins of various wild animals, and by a peculiar process rendering them soft and pliable. Out of these they made the various kinds of beautiful skin karosses, vast numbers of which have been sent to England. The Basutos about Moshesh and Plaatberg were then the great corn-growers of the land, and produced wheat in large quantities, which they exchanged with the Barolongs for their skin karosses. The Bastards were extensively employed in the merchandise of the country.

INTRODUCTION OF BRITISH CONTROL.

From these notices it will be evident, that the Orange-River Sovereignty was peopled with human beings, of all colours and nations, differing from each other in customs and languages, extending through every grade of society, from the civilized to the savage. It will be further evident, that in this Babel the state of society, if it may be so called, must be the most confused and disorganized imaginable. In this chaos, different interests must clash, and often the worst passions of our common nature be brought into hateful operation. The chief contending parties then were, 1. The Natives, who laid claim to the country as their undisputed right; 2. The Griquas, or Bastards, who claimed a large portion of it on the ground of occupancy; and, 3. The Dutch Farmers, who, fleeing from the face of the British government, resolved to seek, in the depths of the wilderness, freedom from its unwelcome and, what they believed to be, unjust restraints.

The Natives and the Bastards might have been left to manage their own affairs, and fight their own battles; but when the Boers entered, whom the English government claimed as its subjects, a third element of disorder was introduced, which at once demanded the interposition of British authority.

The great " trek " of these Dutch Farmers took place between 1836 and 1840. The chief causes of complaint with them were the loss of their slaves, and the unsatisfactory manner in which the Kafir war of 1835 was settled, with other matters of minor importance; which so chafed and irritated their prejudiced (and often ignorant) minds, that they left the old Colony in vast numbers, and have occupied extensive portions of the Orange-River

Sovereignty.   Many proceeded to Natal; of whom an account is given in the preceding part of this volume.

When so many different classes were in this manner thrown together, without any recognised authority or legitimate control, it is self-evident that disorder and crime must have extensively prevailed.   "Lynch-law was the order of the day, every one doing what was right in his own eyes."

In order to provide for this novel and disordered state of things, an Act was passed, (that of 6 and 7 Will. IV., cap. 57,) which was designed for the punishment of offences committed in the country north of the Orange River, as far as the 25th degree of latitude.   This was done with the design of extending to this distant point cognizance of offences and punishment of crimes, and, at the same time, of establishing an undefined control over those whom the government still claimed as its subjects, but who had expatriated themselves, in order to be beyond the reach and range of British authority.

This was good as far as it went; but the great defect of it was found to be, the assigning any particular limit; for these misguided men, with their unsettled habits and feverish dispositions, considered themselves to be at liberty to penetrate beyond this ideal line of demarcation.

MODE IN WHICH BRITISH RULE WAS ADMINISTERED.

From that time, the population of the country increased at a rapid rate, as there was then no war in the land.   Natives, Griquas, and Boers multiplied very fast; especially the Dutch, who were from time to time strengthened by the addition of fresh emigrants from the old Colony.   The natural result of this augmented population was, that disputes and complaints about fraudulent claims to land became rife and numerous; so that, in 1845, Sir Peregrine Maitland, governor of the Cape Colony, found it absolutely needful to interpose his authority; and promptly adopted arrangements for rectifying the evils which existed.   Under his orders, the native chiefs were instructed to distinguish and mark off the lands to be held by them and their people, from those to be held by the Boers; and to allow the Boers the privilege of obtaining leases of these lands from the native chiefs.   He likewise regulated the payment of quit-rents, out of which the expenses of maintaining certain magistrates and an efficient rural police were to be paid in the first instance. These regulations for the occupation of land and the application of the land-revenue,—with the establishment at the same time of a British resident, aided by a small body of British troops and a native contingent in case of need, and the official announcement to all parties, both Boers and Natives, that they were required to keep the peace,—at that time virtually constituted an extension of the authority of the crown of Great Britain over these remote regions.

" Not many months after Sir H. Smith had taken the charge of the government of the Colony of the Cape of Good Hope, his attention was called to the state of disorganization which continued in this territory, notwithstanding all that had been done; and he came to the conclusion, that peace could not be maintained without the existence of some more formal and regular government; and on the 3rd of February, 1848, he issued the Proclamation which is contained in the present papers, proclaiming the Sovereignty of Your Majesty over the territories north of the Great Orange River, including the territories of the native chiefs, Moshesh, Moroko, Moletsani, Sikonyella Adam Kok, Ged Taarbosch, and other minor chiefs so far north of the Vaal River, and east to the Drakenberg or Quahlamba Mountains." —" Blue Book," p. 87.

But the great evil still was, retaining the limit of 25 degrees south latitude, which allowed the restless and dissatisfied Boers to contemplate and attempt going beyond this boundary line; concerning which the Attorney-General makes the following just observations:—

" That an anxiety to get beyond the mysterious line (25°) extensively prevails, and that it stimulates some to retire further into the interior, cannot, I believe, be well questioned. To deprive parties of this temptation to penetrate beyond control, as well as to punish parties who might perhaps be made amenable for crimes committed even beyond the 25th degree of latitude; I respectfully recommend that the limitation of degree be wholly discarded. Even now, I do not feel it safe to *go to trial* without being prepared, by scientific observation, to determine the latitude of the seat of crime,—a costly kind of evidence. And I can, for my own part, see no evil likely to ensue from making British subjects triable in the Cape Colony for crimes committed any where in Africa. No English slave-traders from either the east coast or the west would, in all probability, be brought here;' and even were this otherwise, what harm could result?"—" Blue Book," p. 13.

Major Warden was the gentleman appointed by Sir P. Maitland as the British resident in the Sovereignty; who also urged upon His Excellency the extension of English jurisdiction, at any rate to the 20th degree of south latitude. But there appears to have been a most unaccountable dread of extending the British territory, as though it would be the greatest calamity which could be inflicted both upon Great Britain and South Africa; so that nothing could overcome the opposition on the part both of the Cape and Home government to this necessary measure, and accordingly the old boundary limit (25°) remained.

There would have been some reason for this determined resistance, if it had been intended to take-in the country of independent native tribes; but, instead of this, it was only to exercise wholesome control over her own subjects, whom England resolutely claimed as such;—or if this extension of territory had required an additional military force to guard a longer line of exposed frontier, which was not the case. On the contrary, it was to prevent a new and powerful foe from rising up; because to keep him in check might, in process of time, require the presence of a large military force.

Of the disposition or inclination of the Dutch Farmers to do this, there could be no doubt; for, immediately upon the issuing of Sir H. Smith's Proclamation, taking the Sovereignty as British territory, the Boers again tried their strength, as they had done before in Natal, and resisted Her Majesty's troops by force of arms, when they engaged Sir H. Smith at Boom Plaats, and were beaten and dispersed by that gallant officer; and a reward of £2,000 was placed upon the head of the Dutch commander, A. W. J. Pretorius, who then fell back to the north, and remained, may be, beyond this mysterious line of the 25th degree south latitude.

Had the recommendations of the intelligent residents—who, being on the spot, were well able to form a correct opinion upon the subject—been adopted, the probability is, that a vast amount of British blood and treasure might have been saved, and a settled and orderly state of things established, where anarchy only prevailed.

PERMISSION TO THE DUTCH BOERS TO ESTABLISH AN INDEPENDENT FORM OF REPUBLICAN GOVERNMENT NORTH OF THE VAAL RIVER.

THIS advocacy of a policy which would have excluded the Dutch Farmers from all hope of escaping British authority and establishing an independent form of republican government of their own, may by some be construed into unkind feeling. Such an impression, however, must be contradicted. There was no objection to their having that particular form of government which is most agreeable to their wishes. They have a perfect right to it, all other things being equal; and ought rather to be assisted in obtaining it than deprived of it. But the deep and abiding conviction of most persons was, that, in the present condition of this country, and especially in the very mixed state of the various classes and interests in the Sovereignty, it is a decided evil, and an evil as great to the Boers themselves as it is to all other parties, whether English or Native. South Africa, and the Sovereignty especially, require ONE *strong form of government; which could and would exercise full and efficient authority and control over all classes of the community: and any rival power in the present disorganized state of things must be a positive evil.*

The error here pointed out has, however, unfortunately been persevered in, and has produced its sad and painful results. "Confusion became worse confounded;" and the disorders of the Sovereignty increased, until, in 1851, Mr. Owen and Major Hogg were appointed a commission to hear and report upon all matters connected with the Sovereignty, when they decided to recommend to the home-government that the Dutch should be allowed to withdraw their allegiance from the British crown, and establish their own form of independent republican government, north of the Vaal River; which recommendation, I believe, has been adopted by the home-government, and the experiment is being tried. But it would appear that it has not been considered a benefit by all the Dutch; many of them being dissatisfied with it, and preferring the more orderly and better-organized form of English government. But here is one of its worst features,—it allows all the bad and fierce spirits to pursue the course which their evil passions dictate, without restraint or control. If there were not many Natives in the country, who are unable to cope with them or stand before them, the case would be different; but, as it is, the land has no rest, as the sequel will show.

ASSUMPTION OF THE GOVERNMENT OF THE ORANGE-RIVER SOVEREIGNTY BY THE BRITISH MINISTRY.

THE following is a "*Copy* of a DISPATCH from Earl Grey to Governor Sir H. G. Smith, Bart.," constituting the Sovereignty a British possession :—

"DOWNING-STREET, *March* 25*th*, 1851.

"SIR,—WITH reference to my Dispatch, No. 575, of the 11th ultimo, I now transmit to you Letters Patent which have been issued under the Great Seal of the United Kingdom for erecting the Orange-River territory into a separate and distinct government, and for empowering the governor of the Cape of Good Hope, or the lieutenant-governor of the said Orange-River territory, with the advice and consent of a Legislative Council, to make laws for the government of the said territory.

"I also transmit instructions under the Royal Sign-Manual and Signet, for regulating the power granted to you by these Letters Patent.—I have, &c., GREY."*

According to the instruction and permission thus given, a distinct and separate form of government was established for the Sovereignty, unlike any existing form either in the Cape Colony or Natal; some of the leading outlines of which I shall quote from the "Blue Book."

"REGULATIONS FOR THE FUTURE GOVERNMENT OF THE SOVEREIGNTY BEYOND THE ORANGE RIVER.

"NAME, EXTENT, AND MODE OF GOVERNMENT.—1. The territory between the Orange River, the Vaal River, and the Draakberg Mountains, over which Her Majesty's sovereignty is proclaimed, shall be designated 'THE ORANGE-RIVER SOVEREIGNTY.'"

"2. It is divided into four magistracies or districts, over which Major Warden, the British Resident, is the paramount authority, under His Excellency the High Commissioner :—

"(1.) The district of Griqua-land, of which Bloem-Fontein and the Queen's Fort is the seat of magistracy, and to which Charles Urquhart Stewart, Esq., is appointed magistrate.

"(2.) The district of Winberg, of which the town of Winberg is the seat of magistracy, and of which Mr. Biddulph is the magistrate.

"(3.) The district of Vaal River, of which the new town of

* "Blue Book," p. 98.

Vreededorp *(Peace Town)* is the seat of magistracy, and Mr. Paul Bester the magistrate.

" (4.) The district of Caledon River, of which Smithfield is the seat of magistracy, and Mr. Vowe the magistrate.

" 3. The Orange-River Sovereignty will be governed by Her Majesty's High Commissioner, aided by a local Council, to consist of the British Resident-in-chief, the four other magistrates, and eight counsellors, two for each district, to be nominated by His Excellency, from and out of the land-owners of such district holding their lands on quit-rent.

" 4. The mode of calling together, adjourning, or dissolving the council will be regulated by the High Commissioner, and hereafter announced.

" 5. Every unofficial counsellor shall serve for a term of three years, unless the council shall be sooner dissolved, or on his own resignation or incapacity.

" 6. The British Resident will be the President of the Council; which will meet with open doors, once a year, at Bloem-Fontein, and oftener, if summoned by order of the High Commissioner, for the consideration of such matters as may be suggested by His Excellency the High Commissioner, or proposed by the President, or any member, having for their object the benefit of all classes of people within the Sovereignty.

" 7. The authority of the Council as to the framing of laws shall extend over all persons within the Orange-River Sovereignty, not belonging to the tribe or people of any native chief or captain within the Sovereignty, in regard to acts done, or matters arising, within any of those parts of the said Sovereignty not belonging to any native chief or people. But in order that the reasonable and rightful authority of the native chiefs over their own people should be upheld, the Council will not be competent to entertain any project by which the exclusive jurisdiction of any chief over his own people, in regard to crimes or claims arising within such chief's land, and charged or made against any of his people, should be taken away or abridged; but, on the contrary, such exclusive jurisdiction, and the maintenance, in regard to the determination of such crimes or claims, of all native laws and usages not repugnant to decency, humanity, or natural religion, are hereby guaranteed.

" 8. Every unofficial member of Council who may desire it, will receive ten shillings a day during the sitting of Council, as well as ten shillings for every forty miles he shall have to travel to and from the place of meeting.

" 9. All measures resolved by a majority of votes in the Council, will be submitted through the President to His Excellency the High Commissioner, for his consideration and sanction; but no legislative measure shall have the force of law until the sanction of His Excellency the High Commissioner shall be signified by a notice in the ' Government Gazette ' of the Colony of the Cape of Good Hope. The High Commissioner may, in such notice, fix whatever time he thinks proper for the bringing into operation of any such measure; and if no other time be fixed, then the measure shall come into operation at the expiration of thirty-one clear days next after the day on which such notice shall be first published.

"10. The High Commissioner will cause a correct statement of the receipts and expenditure of all public moneys raised within the Sovereignty for the past year, to be laid before the Council at every annual meeting, as well as an estimate of the probable revenue and expenditure for the year next ensuing. It shall be competent for the Council to make to the High Commissioner any representations upon the subject, which the members shall think desirable, or likely to improve the administration of the district. The British Resident shall be the Treasurer-general of the Sovereignty.

"11. Considering the nature of the country, and the pursuits of the inhabitants, it is intended that the Council should combine with its other functions those of an Agricultural Society, and mature and propose to the High Commissioner plans for the advancement of agriculture, for promoting the planting of trees, for the construction of dams, many of which have been already completed in Griqua-Land, with great labour, and consequent advantage to the proprietors. In fine, it is meant that the people, acting through this Council, should devise measures calculated to advance their interests, civil, social, and religious; and minor obstacles shall not be suffered either to prevent or impede the accomplishment of any good object which they shall recommend."—" Blue Book," pp. 3, 4.

I think the justness of the plan on which the lands granted were to be regulated, must commend itself to every impartial person. The following are the terms:—

" TENURE OF LANDS.

"28. To avoid occasions of contention, prevent unjust encroachments in any quarter, and to preserve the just rights of all, the lands of which the continued and exclusive use shall be secured to the several native chiefs and people within the Orange-River Sovereignty, are to be carefully ascertained and defined.

"29. The lands within the Orange-River Sovereignty belonging to any native chief and people, are to be protected for the use of such chief and people; and shall be regulated by the laws and usages of such chief and people in regard to all rights of occupation or inheritance; and all questions touching the same shall, as heretofore, be determined by the tribunals of such chief and people.

"30. All lands within the Orange-River Sovereignty, not allotted to any native chief or people, shall be held from Her Majesty the Queen, by grant, on such moderate quit-rent as may be fixed; such grants to be in the name of the High Commissioner, acting on Her Majesty's behalf, and to be signed, under His Excellency's order, by the British Resident.

"31. The amount of such quit-rents, together with every sort and description of revenue raised within the Sovereignty, shall be applied exclusively for the benefit of the same."—" Blue Book," p. 6.

Such are some of the general laws for the government of this part of Her Majesty's dominions, which has no connexion whatever with the government of the Old Colony, and only with the Governor as High Commissioner. As no Lieutenant-Governor has been appointed in the Letters Patent, and for some time past the British Resident has been removed, the Magistrates, in their combined capacity, have recently tried a person for the gravest crime, and passed the extreme sentence of the law upon him. This is altogether a new and novel state of things in British jurisprudence, and probably will not long exist. The Government of the Sovereignty is self-supporting, of which the following extract will give some idea :—

"I still entertain no doubt that, but for circumstances at that time wholly unforeseen, the Orange-River Sovereignty would have been able to repay all sums lent by the Colony under this authority. But the rebellion in August, 1848, excited by certain evil-disposed persons, whose determined hostility to British rule was so inveterate as to blind them to the advantages of order and good government, retarded the means of payment of quit-rents, &c., so that a debt to the Colony has arisen, not from the expense incurred in the suppression of rebellion, but by the means of payment having been thus retarded. The position of affairs is now, however, satisfactory; and no infant settlement can more progressively improve. The Orange-River Sovereignty is now a self-supporting community, and, by its present position, fully bears out the remark with which the British Resident lately closed his address to the Sovereignty Council,—'that no new settlement, of equal standing, ever had brighter prospects.'"—"Blue Book," p. 66.

The revenue was chiefly raised by quit-rents and licences to traders; and would have been fully equal to the expenditure, had not the rebellion in 1848 seriously retarded the payment of the quit-rents for that year.

REASONS ADDUCED BY RESIDENTS WHY THE BRITISH SHOULD RETAIN THE GOVERNMENT OF THE SOVEREIGNTY.

AFTER all that has been said, written, and done in reference to the Sovereignty, it seemed strange, in this state of things, that the question of abandoning it should have been gravely raised, and that Sir G. R. Clerk should have been sent out for the purpose of ascertaining *whether it should be abandoned or not*. But since the objections against the abandonment are numerous and weighty, I shall take the liberty of giving some extracts from local journals, with the observations of their editors, and a few remarks of my own. I know of but one sentiment and feeling upon the subject among the English settlers in the Cape and Natal Colonies. The editor of the "Graham's-Town Journal," in a leading article, gives expression to that unanimous sentiment against its abandonment in the following language :—

"The affairs of the Sovereignty engross, as they ought to do, a large share of the public attention. Some there are amongst us who seem to think that British dominion will be withdrawn from that territory ; and they are estimating anxiously the consequences which must, they contend, inevitably result from so disastrous a step, should it be taken. We are not among the number of those who indulge in any such apprehension. We believe that, when the Government placed the matter in the hands of Sir G. R. Clerk, the Sovereignty was safe as a British possession, and that its interests will be promoted in a way they have never heretofore been. The great principle observed in the government of British India, the school in which this officer has been brought up, is non-retrocession ; and hence it is not to be supposed, that the contrary maxim will be observed in dealing with the natives of this country. And it should be observed, that this maxim of policy does not spring from a spirit of aggression, or a thirst for aggrandizement, but from the necessities of the case, and a clear perception of our inability to benefit the natives, or have them as safe neighbours, unless we keep the governmental power in our own hands, and are in a position to watch over the country, and to apply its resources to the maintenance of security, and the promotion of the common good.

"Abandonment of the Sovereignty would not be an act of mere shortsighted policy : it would be one of those suicidal deeds, the folly of which is only equalled by their atrocity. The Sovereignty is the great door or highway into interior Africa, as well as the link which unites the splendid territory of Natal to this Colony. Break this link, block up this highway, and incalculable mischief will be done, without any conceivable motive to justify the act. But, more than this, such abandonment could not take place without absolute dishonour to the British name and character. The Sovereignty is established as a separate and independent government under Royal Letters Patent ; and these cannot be rescinded without injustice towards those who have invested their property on the security of them, and consequent discredit to the Government by whose breach of faith their prospects would be blighted, and their property wrecked.

"Few persons, when they quietly speak of the abandonment of the Sovereignty, consider what is involved in such a measure. It is the break-up of the whole social structure, the abrogation of every law, the letting loose of every lawless passion, the introduction of the reign of anarchy and savage violence, and, in one word, the utter disorganization, as well as demoralization, of South-Eastern Africa.

"An immense deal of nonsense has been poured out in the House of Commons in reference to this country, leading the British public to believe that it is perfectly worthless, and retained merely because the Cape Colony has a peculiar *penchant* for adding desert to desert, for the mere pleasure of revelling in the enjoyment so graphically drawn by Pringle, when he wrote,—

' Afar in the desert I love to ride.'

"That this is not the case, may be proved by the fact, that the Sovereignty, so far from being a desert, is both a corn-growing and a wool-producing territory. By good management, it may be made at once a self-supporting settlement, a source of strength to the Cape Colony, and a large contributor to its revenue. The fact may not be generally known, but it is not the less undeniable, that to the Sovereignty the Colony is indebted largely for its supply of slaughter cattle; while, as respects the trade and commerce of South Africa, the most promising field for enterprise lies north of the Orange River, in which direction colonization must pursue its course, despite of difficulties, or all the hinderances which may be opposed by a short-sighted policy, by ignorance, or by any other conceivable cause.

"It has been well remarked, too, that the abandonment of the Sovereignty will involve heavy expenditure and flagrant wrong; while by its retention both will be avoided. Allegiance to the Crown, and protection of person and property, are reciprocal obligations; and, if so, the Government cannot withdraw the one without either sacrificing the other, or awarding to the aggrieved party full compensation for any loss which may be sustained by the act of one of the contracting parties. Viewing the subject under this aspect,—taking into account the absence of sufficient motive for abandonment, and the heavy loss and confusion such an act must involve,—we cannot but discard at once all apprehension on the subject. The Orange-River Sovereignty is, to all intents and purposes, part and parcel of the British empire, and cannot be dismembered from it but at the expense of great loss of property, embarrassment, and disgrace."—GRAHAM's-TOWN JOURNAL, *July 2nd*, 1853.

We supply a quotation which shows, in a different light, the strong claims for the retention of the Sovereignty as a British possession :—

"When we consider what was the condition of the Sovereignty five years ago, and what it has produced even during so short a period, we must acknowledge that the acquisition of this territory has not only proved a valuable addition to the Colony, but one of the soundest measures of policy that has emanated from the Government for many years. We have received from an intelligent correspondent at Bloem-Fontein some remarks on this question, so pertinent and sound, that it is with much pleasure we present them to our readers :—

"REASONS FOR RETAINING THE ORANGE-RIVER SOVEREIGNTY.

"ITS position and the nature of the country, open and flat, renders it easy of defence.

"Its superiority as a sheep *veld*, and the dry and cold climate, favourable for rearing the young lambs.   95 *per cent.* of their flock can be raised every year; in the Colony 75 *per cent.* is the average.

"It is required as an outlet not only for the surplus population of England, but also of the Cape; that Colony being now fully occupied, and the people pressing on here, and buying farms at enormous prices on the faith of Government.

"REASONS WHY THE SOVEREIGNTY CANNOT BE ABANDONED.

"TITLE-DEEDS have been issued in the name of the Queen of England, and, upon the faith of the Government, large amounts of money have been expended on improvements.

"There may be about one quarter million of money outstanding in the Sovereignty, and payable within fifteen years from this.   If it is given up, who is to guarantee the payment of this?

"What is to become of all the mortgage-bonds, and who is to enforce the conditions?

"But the greatest difficulty of all, because it is *really insurmountable*, is this:—What is to become of 'the Maitland Treaty,' *signed by Queen Victoria*, in favour of Adam Kok, *and the only treaty existing here that bears her signature?*   Dare this be broken?"—GRAAF-REINET HERALD, *June 15th.*

"VALUE OF FARMS.

"WE are glad to report that three farms—the property of Mr. Bingham—which have been advertised in our columns at various times, and which are close to the native boundary, have realized the gross sum of £1,800.   These farms are not large.   One brought £800, a second £550, and a third £450.   The farms are admitted to be good."—THE FRIEND OF THE SOVEREIGNTY, *June 16th.*

"We have been informed, on the best authority, that on the occasion of the last church held at the village of Sannah's Poort, (Fauresmith,) *erven* were sold at the rate of from £75 to £110.   This is the more extraordinary, considering that the village in question is situated within the Griqua line, and that the ground will, at the end of the current lease, (as the law now stands,) revert to the Griqua owner."—*Ibid.*

"THE SOVEREIGNTY AND NATAL:

"THEIR GEOGRAPHICAL AND POLITICAL RELATIONS.

"THE Orange-River Territory covers and protects Natal all along its west and north-west frontier, the east and south-east being protected by the ocean.   That settlement is thus rendered assailable only along a comparatively short line of frontier on its south-west, indicated by the river Umzimkulu, separating Natal from Kaffraria, but

which lies at a considerable distance from the occupied portion of
Natal. Then, as regards the eastern and north-eastern frontier of the
Old Colony, the Orange-River Territory acts as a bolster to it, beginning
with the Colesberg district, and ending at the Wittebergen, from
whence, and following the Quahlamba or Drakensberg range, it protects Natal as already described, until it touches the source of the
Ky Gariep, or Vaal River, which forms the boundary of the Orange-
River Territory north and north-west. Of course we do not pretend
to give our geographical account with infallible accuracy. Our intention is to state such bearings as will enable any intelligent person to
make a tolerably accurate chart for himself.

"To the north-west of the Orange-River Territory, the bulk of
the Bechuana tribes are to be found; and to obtain access to the
Colony and Kaffraria, they must either pass through the Orange-River
Territory, or cross the Orange River, traversing either of the Namaquas; or if they cross higher up the river, they must traverse a
country which may be literally termed a desert. If our readers will
endeavour to realize the idea that the Orange-River Territory, as a
British settlement, has been done away with, we shall endeavour to
convince them that certain inevitable evils would quickly ensue. In
the first place, the whole of the north and north-west frontier of Natal
would be exposed. From the Great Lake to D'Urban, not an interruption, in the shape of a British Government, could interpose. And from
the Damara and Namaqua countries, on the other hand, no obstacle
could intervene. A highway commencing at the Great Lake and
beyond, could be traversed to the mouth of the Great Kei River, or
that of the Bashee, without trespassing on the legitimate territories of
the Trans-Vaal Boers, far less on any British possession. In short,
from Delagoa Bay to the Great Lake, and from either point to Walwich Bay, and from all these to and from Kaffraria and the native
settlements of and around Natal, a trade in ammunition and arms
might be safely carried on to any extent. The Orange-River Territory
occupies the tract which all such routes would cross, and in which
they diverge and converge. Do away with the Orange-River Territory,
and Natal most undoubtedly will fall, and the whole Colony will gradually succumb, unless fifty thousand troops are constantly maintained. Fewer troops could not, in the event of this province being
suppressed, and having reference to the altered circumstances of the
Natives, maintain the frontier which would then present itself.

"The learned Recorder of Natal has, in the interesting lectures
delivered by him, and published, given a very accurate history of the
origin and progress of the occupation of the Orange-River Territory by
British subjects, long previously to the time of its annexation; therefore we need not enter upon this subject. A considerable time previous to the governorship of Sir George Napier, a formal treaty had
been entered into betwixt the British Government and the chief Waterboer, by which treaty this captain was recognised as the chief over
a certain extent of territory, defined in the treaty itself, and in the
possession of which the British Government obliged itself to maintain

him. Our readers are aware that Waterboer's territories lay partly north and partly south of the Vaal River. The fact of such a treaty having been entered into, would, in our opinion, be in itself sufficient to suggest to a contemplative mind, closely observing the progress of immigration from the Colony, the idea of the Orange-River Territory ultimately becoming of necessity a British province. It might be seen, that, to fulfil the terms of such a treaty, in the progress of occurring changes, the British Government must either occupy the country, or keep a force at hand to march into the country as often as required. In progress of time, the necessity for extending British supremacy over the country became very evident, and the Act (6 and 7 Will. IV.) was passed. In October, 1842, we find the late Judge Menzies, at Alleman's Drift, proclaiming the British sovereignty over the country. This measure was, no doubt, immediately repudiated by Sir George Napier. The idea was suggested to Mr. Menzies, in consequence of the difficulties which the neighbourhood of this country put in the way of the administration of justice. Previously to the manifesto of the learned judge, the Governor himself had seen the necessity of interposing in affairs on this side of the Orange River. On the 7th of September, 1842, he issued a very sharp Proclamation against the proceedings of certain emigrants in this country, in reference to the Griquas and Basutos. On January 12th, 1843, we find Colonel Hare, then Lieutenant-Governor of the eastern frontier, thundering forth a most resolutely worded Declaration against Her Majesty's subjects on this side the river. Now it was very evident that all those Proclamations and Declarations would have proved worse than useless, unless it was intended, on the one hand, and believed on the other, that their terms should be enforced. It would appear that, on one occasion, Colonel Hare did march troops towards the Orange-River Territory, which step had the effect, for the time, of putting a stop to, or at least ameliorating, the subjects of complaint against the emigrants.

" In 1845, matters had arrived at such a pass, as induced Sir P. Maitland to cross the river with a force, and fight a skirmish. He then entered into a formal treaty of good-will and mutual protection with the chief, Adam Kok, which was confirmed by Her Majesty. Sir P. Maitland, seeing, of course, that such a treaty would prove no better than waste paper, unless means were adopted to cause its being respected, appointed a British Resident, and placed at his disposal a small number of troops. If the treaty before existing with Waterboer might have suggested the ultimate necessity of proclaiming British sovereignty over the country, with what additional force would the treaty with Adam Kok inculcate the truth ! Under these circumstances, and the proceedings resulting in the battle of Boom Plaats, connected with the previous troubles in Natal, and the extension of the eastern frontier towards Tambookieland, we cannot see that Sir H. Smith could have acted otherwise than he did. The Act of William IV. itself would have proved inoperative, except in the cases of some very obnoxious English emigrants, unless some power were at hand to protect such as might attempt to enforce it. The evils which have led to the discussion as to the propriety of abandoning the Sovereignty, are not chargeable to the annexation, but to its subsequent administration, and handling of the country generally. These evils may be remedied, and the country restored to prosperity, if the proper means are only adopted."*

"Besides the revenues derivable from quit-rents, and a variety of other sources, and the admitted claim which the Sovereignty has to a share of the custom-dues collected at the colonial sea-ports,—which ought to be not less than five to six thousand pounds,—the transfer-dues alone would yield a very large amount, were the stability of the country once authoritatively declared. The rate of transfer-dues exacted in the Sovereignty is two *per cent.*, the half of the rate paid in the Colony. Were four *per cent.* to be made the rate here, a revenue of £5,000 or £6,000 would, in course of 1854, be derived from that source alone. The following sums received for four years prove, better than arguments, that this country has been progressing in spite of circumstances :—

				£.	s.	d.
" 1849 Transfer-duty received	....			356	5	2
1850	,,	,,	,,	783	2	0
1851	,,	,,	,,	1,141	19	9
1852	,,	,,	,,	1,849	10	1

" It is fairly calculated by persons acquainted with the wool trade of the country, that upwards of 4,000 bales of about 1,200,000℔s. of wool will, during this season, be sent out of the Sovereignty. This quantity will not, perhaps, appear large to persons who do not consider all the circumstances; but if it be kept in view, that only 1,220,000℔s. were exported from the Eastern Province in 1843, it will at once be acknowledged, that, for a province of only three or four years' existence, the progress in the growth of wool is most gratifying. If the new Home Government or Parliament would only say, ' Go a-head, and don't bother yourselves about the prospect of abandonment,' the country would go forward with a bound. Those who are here would carry on improvements of every description; whilst such as have been deterred by those reports of abandonment, would settle among us."—THE FRIEND OF THE SOVEREIGNTY, *March* 31*st.*

These four quotations give the voice of public opinion, in the Sovereignty, the Natal Colony, and on the frontier of the Cape Colony. That there will be diversity of sentiment upon some points, cannot be doubted; but nothing will be found at all affecting the validity of the quotations now produced.

---

* We have taken this quotation from the " Natal Mercury," which has copied it from the " Friend of the Sovereignty," and thus adopted it as its own.

OPINIONS OF THE BRITISH MINISTRY WHEN ASSUMING THE GOVERNMENT OF THE SOVEREIGNTY.

BEFORE dismissing authorities, having supplied the opinions of the general public in Africa, we shall also give the opinion of Her Majesty's Government, when met in Council with Her Majesty, upon this subject :—

" We are duly impressed with the importance of the opinion expressed in the dispatches of Your Majesty's Secretary of State, of the dangers attendant on the extension of the frontier of the Cape Colony, and of the policy of abstaining from any enlargement of the British dominions in Africa. But the question assumes a totally different aspect, when the consideration is, whether we should advise the abandonment of a Sovereignty already assumed, under the circumstances and in the manner which we have detailed.

" To disavow British sovereignty over this territory,—after the exercise of power by Sir P. Maitland in 1845, amounting to a virtual assumption of the sovereignty, after the actual assumption of the sovereignty in February, 1848, by the Proclamation of Sir H. Smith, recognised by Your Majesty's Government in the manner that has been stated ; and after administering the government of the territories up to this time,—would, in our opinion, be productive of evils far more serious than any that can follow upon giving legal validity to the assumption of sovereignty, and the form of government proposed for these territories.

" To adopt any other course than this, would, in our opinion, be productive of scenes of anarchy and bloodshed, probably ending in the extinction of the African race, over a wide extent of country. On the other hand, the exercise of British authority, merely through the people themselves, will probably preserve such a degree of order and security, as will suffice for the gradual diffusion of civilization, under the missionaries and teachers of religion, who are already making these districts the scene of their labours. It is neither necessary nor expedient, in the present state of society, to attempt more than a very rude and simple system of government.

" The native races it is proposed to govern through their own chiefs, and by their own laws and customs, so far as these are not repugnant to humanity.

" The authority of the British Resident will, it is hoped, suffice to mitigate the severity, so far as it is necessary to do so, of the exercise of their power by the chiefs ; and, as these people advance in civilization, there can be little doubt that new laws and institutions, suitable to the altered state of society, will, under the superintendence of the British authorities, gradually grow up amongst them.

" The Boers will be subject to a system almost equally simple, and one which, like the other, contains within itself the elements of future developement, as the wants of the society become greater.

"Thus it appears reasonable to anticipate, that, by asserting the sovereignty of the British Crown over these territories, Your Majesty may essentially promote the diffusion of civilization and of Christianity throughout Southern Africa. High and important as that object is, we are not prepared to say that it could be either wisely or justly prosecuted at the expense of the public revenue either of this kingdom or of the Colony of the Cape of Good Hope. That, however, is a question which has not actually arisen; because the expenditure incurred in subjugating these territories to Your Majesty's Crown has been already defrayed by the inhabitants of them. It is a question which is not likely to arise on the present occasion; because there is no reason, of which we are aware, to doubt either the power or the willingness of the inhabitants to sustain in future the charge, imposed upon them by Sir H. Smith, of maintaining the rude and cheap system of government under which he has provisionally placed them. Whenever that provisional system shall be superseded by any other scheme of colonial polity which Your Majesty may see fit to establish, the instruments to be issued for that purpose ought, as we apprehend, to declare that the exclusive liability of the colonists themselves to provide for the cost, civil and military, of their own government, is one of the essential conditions of any such grant."—"Blue Book," pp. 87, 88.

Thus thought, thus spoke, and thus advised Her Majesty's Ministers, "at the Court of Buckingham Palace, the 13th of July, 1850 : *Present,* the QUEEN'S MOST EXCELLENT MAJESTY in Council." And on the 25th of March, 1851, Letters Patent were dispatched by Her Majesty's Secretary of State, declaring the "Orange River Territory" to be "a separate and distinct government." If, then, the reasons why the Sovereignty should not be abandoned at that time were so cogent, are they not incomparably more so at the present time, three years later, when all the reasons then advanced have magnified a hundred-fold, many more having been created which, at that time, had no existence?

A CALM DISCUSSION CONCERNING THE RETENTION OR THE ABANDONMENT OF THE ORANGE-RIVER SOVEREIGNTY.

WITH these facts before it, the English Government should have acted with a promptness and decision equal to the emergency; and should have abandoned all right and claim to the Dutch Boers, as British subjects, when they crossed the colonial boundary. Had decisive steps been taken, this matter might have been set at rest for ever, and the possibility of their proceeding beyond the influence of British authority prevented. It is the want, in a great degree, of this firmness and vigour, which has been one of the most fruitful sources of the great disorder and mighty evils which have prevailed. In face of all these reasons, to talk of abandonment, appeared to be the very essence of weakness, folly, and injustice.

The British settlers reasoned in this way: It will not only be an act of flagrant injustice towards those parties who have invested capital in the Sovereignty, but it will cut off the high road to the interior, which is the connecting link of Natal, and cast away one of the most important and promising dependencies of the British Crown. Yet, great as all these evils must seem to those at a distance, who can but imperfectly understand all their bearings, they appear much greater to those who are on the spot, where they can be understood and appreciated. But all these considerations would be small and trifling, compared with the frightful consequences to property and life. This would be to spring a mine which must blow the population to atoms. A vast mass of combustible materials are there pent up; the trains are already set and heavily charged. It is only the strong hand of English power which holds in check these opposite and conflicting elements, interests, and principles. But let that sole controlling power be withdrawn, and, when the first accident lights the train, the whole will explode, and different parties, armed to the teeth, will rise up and destroy each other. It will then be white against black, and black against white, black against black, and each against the other. Confederacies will be formed and broken; then take a new shape, and again be annulled; until some power become predominant, and all the rest are crushed.

That the Dutch Farmers would be that power seemed to most men to be unquestionable, unless the English sent a very powerful military force to prevent it; in the absence of which, the Dutch Republic would be bounded by the Orange River, and probably strengthened and aided by several of our countrymen, who have been irritated and chafed, for many years, by what they regard as grievous wrong, or gross mismanagement. One army must then be kept up, to guard the Northern Frontier of the Old Colony along the Orange River against a Dutch

Republic; whilst a second will be required, to defend the Eastern Frontier against the inroads of the barbarous tribes of Kaffraria.

The Rev. F. Fleming thus expresses himself upon this point: "That the government of this territory is of a difficult nature, is not to be denied; but still nothing can justify the abandonment of it. If the Dutch in the Sovereignty, who are not, it is true, and never will be, well disposed to English rule, can only once gain sufficient unrestrained power to do there as they like, *the total extermination of the native tribes, by a war of colour waged to the knife, is certain to follow.* And, surely, it is the paramount duty of Britain to prevent this in a British possession."

The preceding reflections were considered by some persons to be dark and uncalled-for prognostications. But the battle of Congella at Natal, in which several of Captain Smith's brave little band were cut to pieces, and the remainder were so starved, as to be compelled to eat horse-flesh and forage-corn, whilst besieged by the Dutch, in their fortress of waggons;—and the battle of Boom Plaats in the Sovereignty, six years later, when the Dutch again mustered their forces under the same commandant, Pretorius, and gave battle to Sir H. Smith, and retreated only when they were opposed by superior force;—these two battles, with many other unmistakable proofs which they have shown of hostility to the English, created a general conviction that they would be quiet just so long as they found themselves unable to cope with a superior British force. But when they shall be able to meet us in the field, then the fine Colony of Natal will be added to the Republic, and a mighty power raised in the rear of the old Cape Colony, which might eventually threaten its existence.

Already were these restless and dissatisfied men seen penetrating into the unoccupied portion of Umpanda's territory, lying between the Tugela on the north-east boundary of Natal, and the actually populated parts of Zulu-land. Umpanda has long had this part ceded to him, for the purpose of affording greater facilities for detecting and seizing any Zulus who might be attempting to escape into the Colony; and we have yet to learn, that he has in any manner relinquished his right to this extensive tract of country. The following quotation from "the Natal Mercury," of June 9th, 1853, will convey some idea of the apprehensions entertained by many persons on this subject:—

"The great emigration of Boer families to the unoccupied portion of Zulu-land, on the northern border of Natal, has left one district of the Trans-Vaal almost without inhabitants, and greatly weakened that Frontier of the Boers. These families, we stated on a recent occasion, are founding a separate and second independent community, alike disowned by, and disclaiming fealty to, Pretorius. Let this emigration then progress at an equal ratio, and, within two years, the Boers will take possession of the whole of that beautiful and fertile tract of country lying between the Tugela and the Umhlatoos, with the coast on the east and the Quahlamba on the west. This being done, the entire line of boundary, from the Indian Ocean on the east, to the Atlantic Ocean on the west, will be occupied by them, taking the course of the Tugela to the Drakenberg, crossing that mountain range, and joining the Vaal River at the extreme north of the Orange-River Territory, following the course of that river, in a south-westerly direction, to its junction with the Orange River, and then along that majestic stream to its embouchure into the Southern or Atlantic Ocean. This is already the line of their boundary; and they require only the small part now on the borders of Zulu-land to fill it up. Let the English Government look steadily at this fact, and apply remedial measures before it is for ever *too late*."

1. "But," it may be asked, "why should it not be so? What evil will ensue?" The English intercourse with the interior is entirely cut off: a wall, stronger than that of China, will be run along the entire line, guarded by thousands of sturdy Boers, with their long guns pointed towards the Colony. "Nay," it is said, "but this is secured by treaty." Let the Boers acquire strength, and the treaty will become so much waste paper, and they will laugh in your face for your short-sightedness, weakness, and folly, having out-generalled you to perfection! "But I do not believe they would do it." Yet they have done it already: Messrs. M'Cabe and Bain were stopped,—the former tried, confined, and made to pay a fine,—for the unpardonable offence of trying to go to the Great Lake, and trade, &c.! Other officers and gentlemen have received similar treatment, which will soon become universal.

2. "But," it is further urged, "they will form a good body-guard along the Frontier, betwixt the natives and the English, securing the latter from the plundering incursions of the former."

On the contrary, they will first conquer the natives, and make them serfs and vassals; who will then be compelled to assist their lords in beating the English. This was being done at Natal when they summoned Umpanda for this service; but he found ways and means of excusing himself; for which he would probably have been afterwards severely punished, had not the Boers been repulsed by the English, and made to submit.

3. "But," it is added, "our commerce will be extended by it; our imports and exports will be increased; our revenue improved; and the Colony will flourish." Is it not more probable, if they get the branch of country down to the coast, that they will open a port, probably at St. Lucia, or at the mouth of one of the large rivers? They will then take the merchandise into their own hands, introduce their own shipping, and transact their own commercial affairs direct with Holland. Our present extensive and lucrative trade with the interior, both in Zulu-land and towards the Great Lake, will be cut off, and turned into this new channel, to the great detriment and injury of the Colonies of Natal and the Cape.

4. "These results, however, will not occur for many years to come; and by that time our Government will be strong, and our numbers greater; so that we shall be able to provide against all these contemplated disasters." This remark is misleading; for the Republic has already commenced active operations in promoting emigration direct from Holland. "The Raad have assigned 100 farms of 6,000 acres each to Mr. Stuart, for him to dispose of in Holland, at not less than 6,000 rix-dollars (£450) each. Mr. Stuart has already taken his departure. This gentleman is well known in Natal. He left for the Cape in the 'Annie,' on her last voyage."—NATAL MERCURY, *June 9th*, 1853. They design, by this movement, to procure a new infusion into their body of European blood, spirit, and enterprise, and to obtain the very means by which they may accomplish all that has been here stated as likely to take place, as well as to increase the amount of population.

5. It may finally be urged that this judgment of them is harsh; that they do not entertain these hostile views towards the English, and would not adopt such a course of opposition. In reply to this, it is sufficient to affirm, that this description of the Boers is

taken entirely from their principles and acts. Let any unprejudiced person glance at their past history, from the time when the emigration took place; and he will find that it commenced under strong anti-English feeling, which has not been softened or removed. Their exasperation under a sense of their wrongs has impelled them to resist the English by force of arms, both at Natal and in the Sovereignty; to stop our travellers, traders, and hunters, when penetrating into the interior, and compel them to return; and to adopt a course of continued and powerful resistance to British rule, which has led to the establishment of the Republic, and which, when carried out to its natural and legitimate results, will end in all that is here advanced, and probably in much more. Let not the reader, however, suppose that all the Boers are included in one sweeping charge. No: there are many very worthy and honourable exceptions to it. But it is the prevailing national feeling of the great majority of those who have passed the boundary of the Colony; and the more moderate men are often unable to curb the excesses of the more violent spirits.

SUGGESTIONS IN SUPPORT OF OUR RETAINING POSSESSION OF THE ORANGE-RIVER SOVEREIGNTY.

UNDER these circumstances, another important question arose: "What measures can now be adopted?" Much ground was considered to have been lost by weak and vacillating conduct on the part of the English Government. While it was still an open question, it was suggested:—

1. Instead of injuring all parties by abandoning the Sovereignty, at once take the most firm possession of it, and establish within it a thoroughly efficient English Government, adapted to the wants of the people, and conducted with such vigour and energy, that all parties may know and feel that the master is among them, and will be respected and obeyed; and that insubordination and rebellion are not weaknesses, but crimes, offences against the good order of the community, as well as against rightly-constituted authority.

2. Let the Government enter *instanter* into an alliance with Umpanda, offensive and defensive, to prevent the Dutch from seizing upon the unoccupied part of his country. In acting thus

promptly, no wrong would be done to the Boers; for it never entered into the arrangements of the Commissioners when the Vaal-River Republic was recommended to be established, that, ere the public documents were well signed, they should cross the Quahlamba, take possession of Zulu-land, and extend their border from the Vaal eastward to the sea. But much would depend upon the disposition of Umpanda himself; for, if he, as an independent chief, chose to give them permission to squat in his wide country, we have no right to interfere. From all that we have been able to learn, it would appear as though Umpanda looked upon this movement with considerable alarm; had already ordered some of his people to remove towards those parts of which the Boers were taking possession; and was anxiously waiting the result of present movements, intending, if the Boers advanced, to come nearer the English for security and protection. He, therefore, would be most desirous to enter into those political relationships by which he might forward the object here proposed. When the reader has perused the first part of my forthcoming work on the Natives, in which I have given the history of the Zulu nation, he will be able to understand, from what has transpired betwixt Umpanda and the Boers, the curious relation in which the parties stand to each other.

3. It would then be advisable to appoint a British Resident, or Diplomatic Agent, to reside with Umpanda; not only to watch the movements of the Boers, but also to look after deserters, and others, who might be doing much mischief at the residence of the black King, whilst they were actually runaway British subjects. A gentleman of suitable capacity and qualifications for such an appointment, might accomplish much good, and prevent much evil.

4. It has also been argued, that a large increase of English emigrants ought to be encouraged, by the English government, to settle in South Africa. The *three* great and powerful parties in the country are almost equally balanced;—the English, the Dutch, and the Natives. These three differ from each other in their views, feelings, prejudices, customs, and habits; and there is scarcely among them any common principle of cohesion. The whole forms a most heterogeneous mass, which it is most difficult to manage or govern. The law of the government here is pro-

fessedly English; but it is so mixed up with the Roman-Dutch law and with native customs, that confusion and embarrassment often prevail to a great extent, so as to render it irksome to carry on the functions of regular government. That which we most need is, a large importation of English spirit and English capital, and to establish one *paramount authority* throughout these dependencies, which, working out its legitimate results, may communicate an order, efficiency, and power, that will enable all the departments of the government and of the governed to proceed onward with energy and concord.

I question whether there is a finer country than this, to which people can emigrate. If they dislike too close a proximity to the Kafirs, they can choose locations at an immense distance from the half-civilized savages. Let peace continue, and good government be established, prosperity will then universally prevail. A few persons have emigrated from this Frontier to the inviting gold-fields of Australia; but some of them have requested money from their friends here, to enable them to return.

I would here again solemnly warn the English authorities against trifling with the Natives. Upon no consideration whatever exercise a weak and vacillating policy towards them. Let not one Governor adopt one line of conduct towards them, and then the next immediately pursue a contrary course of proceeding. Their ignorant minds, not having had the benefit of social experience, cannot comprehend this tortuous mode of procedure; and sometimes they attribute it to the most absurd and ridiculous causes, whilst confidence in these authorities, and respect for them, are greatly weakened, if not utterly destroyed. The present time is a most solemn and important juncture for the interests of tens of thousands of these people; and their future existence, as distinct tribes, depends upon a wise, firm, vigorous, and conciliatory system of management in their present state of transition.

In passing, I may also remark, that to abandon the Amatola Mountains again to the Gaika Kafirs, would, I fear, be a measure fraught with the worst evils to the interests of the natives themselves, as well as to the safety and prosperity of the Frontier of the Colony. The mistaken kindness of the English towards the Natives in general, has been attended with consequences almost as fatal as the reckless course pursued by some of the most fiery-spirited Boers. As they advance in useful knowledge, in civilization, and Christianity, let them gradually be introduced to the enjoyment of the same liberties and privileges as those of their more advanced white neighbours. But *at once* to place them in that position, is to destroy them, not to conserve them; is to inflict on them the severest evil, instead of conferring the greatest benefit.

I shall do myself the pleasure of inserting, in this place, the views of the Rev. F. Cumming, who has just published a small work on this part of South Africa, and who, being near the seat of operations, possessed excellent opportunities of forming an opinion concerning the subject about which he writes. Speaking of the Amatola, he says :—

"But, if its vast forests of timber were felled, and its waste acres of land apportioned out to able and industrious British emigrants, then a more lucrative result might be gained, while a home and livelihood might here be supplied for the swarming over-population of England.

"By this means, too, a strong border militia might be provided for the Cape Colony. For, by granting farms to these emigrants, only on condition of their serving as burghers, for the defence of their own farms and the Frontier, in case of future Kafir inroads; and by locating them, as such, in the Amatola Mountains, (the richest and most luxuriant district,) the double purpose would be answered,—of keeping back the Kafirs from the colonial line, and of helping to civilize and improve their social habits and condition, by nearer contact with European settlers.

"That nothing but an *increased English population*, stringent local British rule, and a large military force permanently retained there, will ever hold this Colony and dependency secure, few, who have ever visited it, investigated its condition and position, or know aught concerning the present state of its inhabitants, will for a moment doubt. Unhappily, these are not numerous amongst those who legislate for it.

"And when, in answer to such truths as these just stated, the reply is made, that 'such expense as their accomplishment entails, cannot be incurred by England, nor is the Cape Colony worth it,' it may very fairly be inquired, in return, 'Is England then prepared to relinquish this Colony, and, with it, her East Indian possessions ?'—for that the Cape is the maritime key to the East, few will be found to deny."

England, with her vast colonial possessions, does not seem to know how much the Cape Colony is worth. Now the man who would ascertain the relative value of the Cape to the British empire, must not make his calculation upon the sum expended in the maintenance of our military establishment; but he must view the Colony as the only available point for refreshing and victualling the vast navy of England. He must regard it not only as connected with India, but also with China, Australia, New Zealand, and the islands in the vast Southern Pacific, all of which are becoming yearly of still greater importance to us as a commercial nation. The loss of the Cape would throw the whole of our colonial possessions into a state of anarchy, would break the connecting link of our widely-extended empire, and produce disastrous consequences, beyond the power of man to estimate.

Besides, her value to England is unknown, in reference to the enormous quantity of wool, cotton, and, probably, silk, which she might export to the English market, in a raw state, and the incredible amount of manufactures which she would take in return. These are tangible facts, easily comprehended by the meanest capacity.

CONDUCT OF THE ENGLISH SETTLERS DEFENDED.

A FEW remarks on the conduct of the English border inhabitants, through the three most distressing Kafir wars which have desolated the fine Frontier of their Colony, are here subjoined. I can unhesitatingly declare, that, as far as my knowledge and convictions go, the Kafirs have been the sole aggressors in the whole of those disastrous proceedings. Seven years of my life were spent in this locality, extending from Colesberg on the northern Frontier, to the sea on the south-east; four of them at Fort Beaufort and near Fort Peddie. During these seven years, I not only mingled with the inhabitants on public occasions, but also visited very extensively their isolated dwellings, from the Winterberg to the sea, and as far westward as Cradock and Somerset. During that time, frequent inroads were made by the Kafirs in small parties; and the horses, cattle, sheep, and other property belonging to the English settlers, were carried off by these merciless people. But I never knew a single instance in which the white men entered their country, or took the value of a beast from them, though so strongly provoked and annoyed.

My belief also is, that these three wars have been forced upon the Colony by the frequent thefts and murders committed by the Kafirs; and that the chief cause of these wars was the too kind, but fitful and changing, conduct of the Government. It was *too kind*, not in itself abstractedly considered, but in reference to the relationship in which these people stood towards their white neighbours. As the avowed advocate of the Natives, I maintain that this kindness, though well intended, is the cause of their destruction. These Natives may be regarded as little children, not sufficiently advanced towards the manhood of Christianity and civilization to understand the nature of those privileges accorded to them; and these, like sharp knives in the hands of infants, have become the instruments of their own destruction. That which would have appeared severity and hardship if exercised on others, would have been the purest kindness when shown to them. Their liberties might have been enlarged, and favours extended to them, only in the ratio of their becoming gradually fitted to receive them, and able to appreciate their value, or to understand the influence they were intended to exercise in moulding their characters and ameliorating their manners. My own conviction has long been, that, had this cautious mode been adopted towards them, thousands of those who have fallen as victims of war, would have been alive at this day. Had due strictness and moderate encouragement been shown to the Natives, I have every reason to believe that, in their hopeful advances towards a qualification for enjoying the benefits of civilized society, the Fish River, and not the Kei, would at this day have been the boundary of the Colony.

But whilst thus exculpated from blame, I think them entitled, not merely to negative praise, but also to positive commendation. For on this very Frontier, when rebel Hottentots and ruthless Kafirs pillaged, burnt, murdered, and destroyed all within their reach, smarting under these intensely trying circumstances, the white population in connexion with the Wesleyan Society alone, contributed last year about £800 of their money to missionary objects,—for the very purpose of sending Christian missionaries amongst the barbarians and uncivilized of all lands. Nearly all these settlers had been grievous sufferers from the war; vast numbers lost their all, escaping only with their lives; and many of their immediate connexions lost their lives either in the field or on their homesteads. This is the Divine method of returning good for evil, and heaping coals of fire on the heads of the undeserving. Men imbued with such benevolent and fixed principles as these are entitled to the sympathy and commendation of their fellow-Christians. Many of them have felt warmly, spoken strongly, and acted manfully against these wholesale destroyers; but, in all this, they have never transgressed that moderation exercised by all well-informed Englishmen, when their painful duty has called them forth to hunt out those miscreants who, lying in dark lurking-places, watch for an opportunity to murder and destroy. The declaration of the law is, that all such bandits must be imprisoned, transported, or hanged, without reference to colour, name, or habitation; and I must confess, that I have frequently wondered at the almost universal absence of vindictive feelings in the whites towards the blacks, under provocations that seemed nearly beyond human endurance. In this well-merited eulogy on my own countrymen, must be included many worthy Dutchmen, whose character and conduct in all trying emergencies have been creditable to our common humanity and Christianity.

MISCONCEPTIONS ENTERTAINED IN ENGLAND CONCERNING THE NATIVE TRIBES.

On the 28th of February, 1853, "the leading journal of Europe" published in its columns a stringent article on the battle of Berea, in which Sir George Cathcart had attempted to inflict a severe castigation on Moshesh. This called forth the subjoined remarks from the editor of "The Graham's-Town Journal,"—

"The intelligence of the battle of Berea had reached England, and had occasioned, as it well might after the accounts transmitted immediately before, equal surprise and annoyance. The 'Times' of the 28th of February contains a bitter article on the subject, which we transfer to our columns of to-day. Looking at the antecedents to that battle, as well as to subsequent events, no one can doubt for a moment that the movement across the Orange River originated in some mistake, arising from imperfect information as to the cause of quarrel, and also as to the character and amount of the resistance which would be made to the advance of the British troops. That General Cathcart acted at the outset on a right principle, we are prepared to maintain; but that, in carrying out that principle, there was a manifest want of knowledge of the enemy with whom he had to deal, is equally undeniable. The

Basouta chief's own historian, the French missionary Arbousset, shows distinctly that Moshesh, when he first took possession of Thaba Bossigo, was merely a successful robber; that by his forays upon the neighbouring tribes he amassed large property in cattle,—the *summum bonum* of an aborigine of South Africa; and that, being successful, he, like David at the cave of Adullam, soon gathered around him those who were in want, or discontented, or in debt, or disposed to better their condition by a transference of the property of their neighbours to their own custody.

"The policy of Sir Harry Smith was to bring this chief within the circle of British jurisdiction, so as to place that degree of restraint on his aggressive movements which might afford some degree of security to that portion of the Colony which abuts on the territory that had been recognised as his lawful possession. But, besides this, there were the interests of 'the Sovereignty' to be secured; and this could only be done by checking the power of Moshesh on the one hand, and the spread of the Dutch Republic on the other. The recognition of the Sovereignty as a British possession, has been blamed as an act of mistaken policy, but, in our opinion, on very narrow and erroneous grounds. The fact is, the Imperial Government was powerless, in respect to staying the spread of colonization in this country,— every effort it had put forth with this view having only aggravated the evil. The motive for interference had always been ostensibly the protection of native rights; but this protection has been so given, as to create the most bitter feuds, and to raise insuperable difficulties,—in short, so to entangle affairs in this country, as that nothing but a display of the greatest determination, and an effort of the highest ability, will ever restore matters to a healthy and satisfactory state.

"In making these remarks, we are not hazarding a mere opinion; but are referring to facts which are patent to the whole public,—matters of historical record, and which, therefore, it is impossible to gainsay. Take, for instance, the state of the Sovereignty, when Mr. Justice Menzies in 1839 made an effort to stay and turn back the tide of insurrection which was then flowing from the interior towards the Colony, and had actually approached its very border. That eminent judge saw at a glance the threatened danger; and had there been at the time a man at the head of the Government of equal powers of perception, and of the same resolute will, a vast amount of evil, which has since befallen the Colony, might have been avoided. Unfortunately for this country, the Governor of that day, Sir George Napier, was one of the let-alone school; one who has gravely admitted that his principle of action was, *not to protect the colonists against plunder*, but to save the Home Government from any expense in the repulsion of aggression! Had a different course been pursued at that time, the battle of Boom Plaats would not have been rendered necessary, and the brave men who fell on that occasion might have been spared to their friends and country. The policy adopted by Sir Harry Smith, after that affair, was bold and statesmanlike; it went effectually to protect the Colony, and to place the native tribes in the best

possible position, from which to advance to social comfort and civilization. In stating this, we are not defending in any way mere matters
of detail. Many of these were, it may be, extremely faulty; but they
might, and, we doubt not, would, have been amended. A little time, with
the countenance and support of the Home Government, would have
consolidated Sir H. Smith's policy; and the native tribes from whom
danger was to be apprehended, would have been surrounded by so
strong a defensible cordon, as that the elements of mischief with which
we have now to contend, would have been effectually controlled.

"The 'Times,' by the use of random figurative terms, deprecates the
spread of colonization in this country, on the ground that it has
no conceivable limit. It seems to think that the Mountains of the
Moon will be no barrier, and that it will not cease until it meets the
stream of French colonization at its northern extremity. Were this
within the range of probability, humanity would be an immense
gainer; or the stories we have of the state of Interior Africa are mere
fables, got up to excite the imagination, and minister to a morbid
sentimentality, upon which not a few speculate from motives any thing
but akin to philanthropy. But all this is not merely improbable, it is
the wildest romance. The limit of European colonization is plainly
marked by the finger of Providence, and cannot be overstepped without tremendous risk of fearful punishment. Beyond a certain well-
known point the climate is fatal to the European constitution; and to
that point the tribes with which we have to deal are known, and may
be enumerated. Take, for instance, the whole of the tribes of Kafir-
land, which are at this moment surrounded by the white man; and
the whole do not number more than three hundred thousand souls;
and yet, instead of England placing these people under wholesome
restraint, and making them sensible of her superiority, she trifles
with them, supplies them with guns and ammunition, maintains them
in savage independence, and then occasionally stirs them up to an
assertion of it by an invasion of the Colony, which it takes years of
harassing work, and an immense expenditure of money, to repel,—
leaving matters much worse than at the commencement of the contest.

"We venture to think that the British Government cannot, on any
principle of justice, abandon the Colony to the tender mercy of the
savage hordes of this country, who have become formidable only
through the course of policy to which we have adverted, and over
which the colonists had no control. That policy alone has made the
Natives formidable; it has shown them their own strength, and the
most vulnerable parts of our border; and having done this, it may
be very convenient to leave the colonists to defend themselves as best
they may: but the question is, not whether it would be *convenient*,
but HONEST. We venture to think it would neither be politic nor
just, and that, moreover, such a procedure would tend to estrange,
not to say sever, this country from the British Empire. The germ
of a South African Republic has actually been sown, and that with
the connivance of the British authorities: a continuance of mal-
administration will force it into unnatural growth, and wither every

hope of the political regeneration of this fine, but mis-understood and mis-ruled, country."—GRAHAM'S-TOWN JOURNAL, *April 23rd.*

On this subject I would here make a few observations concerning some points which are not noticed in the "Journal."

In its very clever Article, the "Times" says :—

"This victory, independently of the profitless waste of life which it involves, is to be deplored, as showing how insensibly we are drawn on into the centre of this vast and savage continent, and how our quarrel with one savage tribe is sure to bring us, sooner or later, into contact with another. Once embarked on the fatal policy of establishing a frontier in South Africa, and defending that frontier by force, there seems to be neither rest nor peace for us, till we follow our flying enemies across the Congo, and plant the British standard on the walls of Timbuctoo. To subdue one tribe, is only to come in contact with another equally fierce, impracticable, and barbarous. We may conclude a peace with the conquered, but, even supposing their larcenous and murderous propensities to be thoroughly chastised, that peace only opens to us the certain preliminaries of a new war. Our quarrels with the Gaikas speedily involved the Tambookies. The Tambookies have led us, by an easy succession, to the Basutos. The Basutos are not the last of the human race, and will, doubtless, in their turn, introduce us to other tribes as barbarous, as thievish, and as pugnacious as themselves."

This passage would mislead a person unacquainted with the localities of the country : he might suppose that this was an onward and aggressive movement, beyond the bounds of the British possessions, and that the victory over Moshesh was only "the preliminary to a new war" with "other tribes" still more distant, but "as barbarous, as thievish, and as pugnacious," as those who were attacked. But, on examination of the part of the country which Moshesh occupies, it will be seen, that, instead of being beyond us, he is in the very centre of us. Instead of our being led into the "centre of these barbarians," they are in our centre, and we surround them on every hand for many miles. The Sovereignty surrounds Moshesh and his people, north, south, and west, and the Natal Colony encloses him on the east : so that to chastise him for his misdeeds, is not to destroy him, but to prevent him from destroying us.

But, besides this, it must not be forgotten, that the Sovereignty was, at that time, *bonâ fide*, to all intents and purposes, part and parcel of the British empire; and that our Government was not at liberty to neglect the interests of her own people and possessions, however distant. This battle was really fought on British ground, against those who were, in an important sense, (though not entirely,) her own subjects ; whose mischievous and plundering practices she was bound to restrain and chastise. Had Moshesh been so far corrected as to exhibit signs of amendment, it would have been a " blessing in disguise " conferred upon him and his people; whilst, in an equal degree, other tribes would have derived benefit from it, as well as all the colonists. But, in the absence of this, it will yet have the effect of teaching him that his conduct is watched, and that he must not commit crime with impunity.

With regard to the remarks on the Gaikas, the Tambookies, and the Basutos, I am not aware that there is the slightest connexion betwixt these three tribes. By a reference to the map of South Africa, it will be seen that several hundred miles intervene betwixt the Gaikas, the Tambookies, and the Basutos. The former are on the Frontier of the old Colony; whilst the Basutos are in the midst of the Sovereignty, and have no natural ties or land connexions. When we have had a war with Moshesh, it has always been as an independent enemy.

Let any one take the map of the Sovereignty, or that of South Africa, and he will perceive that Kafir-land Proper is surrounded by the English. On the south-west border is the old Colony; on the north-west is the Sovereignty; and on the north-east is Natal: so that a war with the Kafirs in any of those Colonies, instead of plunging the English deeper into the depths of barbarous Natives, only brings them nearer to the point of contact with each other. Abandon any one of these Colonies, and it brings barbarous tribes upon the rest with accelerated force, and magnifies a hundred-fold the horrors of the war, which, whenever it arises, must be waged upon the Frontier. It would be a libel both upon the Sovereignty and Natal, to say that we have waged any war with border tribes. We have had no war with Natives at all, in either of these dependencies of the British crown: the only battles that have been fought, have been with men who were then British subjects, (the Dutch Boers at Natal and in the Sovereignty,) and now with Moshesh at the Berea. In these two Colonies we have no armies, no line of frontier posts guarded by British troops. We have only a small number of soldiers at the capital of Natal, and at the capital of the Sovereignty.

It was the Kafirs who overran the Colony, plundering, burning, and murdering all before them; not the colonists who overran Kafir-land. For a long time the whole military force, and that of the Colony combined, were only able to stand on the defensive, and check the swelling deluge.

Governors of the Cape Colony do not appear to have been too anxious to have a large "military force at their disposal," and "fierce enemies against whom to direct it;" but, on the contrary, they have been desirous to have it as small as possible, and not to employ it until they were absolutely compelled so to do by the insufferable outrages of the Kafirs.

Let the reader try to realize the following description. Suppose he was travelling to a friend's house, a few miles from Fort Beaufort, or Graham's Town; and, before he could arrive there, darkness overtook him; so that, on his arrival, the barking of the dogs announced that a stranger was approaching, whom they had to meet with their guns in hand,—not knowing whether it was a party of marauding Kafirs. This was often my lot when travelling in those parts. At night the colonists would retire to rest, having seen their horses, cattle, and sheep, safely housed in the kraal; but they knew not that they would find them there in the morning. When they left their houses, and took a journey, however short, they bade adieu to their wives and children, but were afraid lest, on their return, they should find them the slain victims of the ruthless savage. This is not an imaginary picture. No : the writer has had to prosecute his labours for many miles all round Fort Beaufort, amidst this uncertainty of life and property. When he went into the country to preach on the Sunday, the probability was often realized of his congregation having gone to recover their stolen property. Sometimes, immediately on the close of the service, his audience have seized their guns, mounted their horses, and galloped off in pursuit of the culprits.

Such was the state of things before Sir P. Maitland issued a declaration of war, in 1846. It is probable that the very circumstance which hurried on the war of 1851, was the reduction of the "military force" on the Frontier by Sir H. Smith;

thus weakening the defences, and opening a chasm, to swallow up the treasure and the best blood of Britain. This reduction was made by orders from the Secretary of State, under the influence of such misleading articles as that on which I am now animadverting. At the same time the poor deluded savage has been led on to his own ruin, by seeing the defences weakened, and thinking it a favourable time to make his furious onslaught, regardless of consequences.

It is as the advocate of the Natives that I thus write. Is it not the consummation of all cruelty, to hold out, by weak and vacillating conduct towards them, a bait to hasten them onwards to their own ruin and the loss of their country? And would not real mercy dictate an opposite course? Would not the savages themselves be the parties that would derive the greatest benefit? Unless my whole mental nature deceive me, most assuredly they would be vastly the gainers. In confirmation of some of these remarks, I close this section with an extract from "The Graham's-Town Journal," of September 24th, 1853:—

"As bearing upon this subject, our attention has been arrested by a paper in 'Tait's Magazine' for June last, giving a very excellent and correct outline of affairs in South-Eastern Africa within the last few years. The writer confesses that he had consulted the pamphlet containing the three admirable lectures delivered at Natal by Mr. Recorder Cloete, as well as some communications which had been published in the local journals; and the deductions he makes from the facts before him, are such as will commend themselves to the understanding of every impartial inquirer into the affairs of this country.

"The writer then refers to the Sovereignty, and goes on to show the effect which the bare rumour of the abandonment of that territory had produced amongst the inhabitants; expressing a very confident opinion, that even should the Government have decided on such a measure, it cannot fail to be ultimately reversed. The passage is full of interest and importance, and we therefore extract it for the information of the reader:—

"'The announced intention of the British Government to abandon that Colony, has excited the utmost consternation among the settlers. The late mails from the Cape have brought to this country petitions from them, deprecating this abandonment in the most earnest terms. The petitioners pray that an elective government may be established in the territory, in accordance with the wishes expressed at the meeting of delegates in June, 1852; and they declare their readiness, when this is done, to undertake the entire defence of the Colony. It may be presumed, that this very reasonable request will be granted. We had intended to refer more particularly to some occurrences in that Colony, which are supposed to have led the Home Government to the conclusion that it must be abandoned. But as this conclusion, *formed in ignorance of the exact condition and wishes* of the inhabitants, has probably been already modified, and cannot fail to be finally reversed, there seems to be no necessity for dwelling upon this part of the subject. Should the Duke of Newcastle, or any other Minister actuated by the same enlightened views, remain at the head of the Colonial Department, there can be no doubt that, within a year or two, both the Orange Colony and Natal will have institutions as free as those which have just been granted to the Cape Colony. There will then be three British Colonies conterminous with one another,—similar in origin, in population, in laws, and in interests, and requiring to be united for some general purposes, such as postal communication, the levy of customs' duties, and the common defence. A Federal Government, similar to that which has recently been established in New Zealand, will obviously be the proper mode of effecting this combination......Such seems to be the natural solution of these South-African perplexities, which have heretofore caused so much endless embarrassment and expense.' "

A COMMANDO OF DUTCH BOERS AGAINST SECHELI, A KAFIR CHIEF.

I SHALL now bring before the notice of the reader another subject which has excited much attention in these parts. It is the case of Secheli, a native chief, who was residing in the direction of the Great Lake, and who has been attacked by the Boers, beaten, and, as it is affirmed, his children taken for slaves. I shall, however, first place the official Report of the Boers before the reader to speak for itself, and give their version of the affair.

THE TRANS-VAAL BOERS AND SECHELI.

(*From the Zuid-Oost Afrikaan.*)

" OFFICIAL REPORT OF THE ACTING COMMANDANT-GENERAL, P. E. SCHOLTZ, ESQ.

MARICO, *August 20th*, 1852.

" THIS day the Commando sent by A. W. Pretorius, Esq., assembled.

" I departed without delay, according to my instructions, to the rebellious Kafir tribes, who had constantly disturbed the country by thefts and threatenings. On the 23rd I sent from Maboiza an adjutant to the sub-captain of Cokkie, and the people left behind of Moselele, to offer and, if possible, to encourage them to peace; but received no answer from them. I proceeded on; and the following day they again had peace offered to them, but they were intrenched in caverns and jungle. I, however, ventured to send a couple of field-cornets with some men to within about one hundred yards of them, for the purpose of speaking to them; but they persisted in refusing. The patrol then endeavoured to take some of them prisoners, but they resisted; upon which I ordered a few shots to be fired at them. Towards evening the above-named sub-captain came out, and I made peace with him, and also restored to him all prisoners of war, on condition that he should forthwith return to his abode. On the 25th I went forward, and captured three of Secheli's scouts. During the march up to the 27th, I was informed that Secheli was making every preparation to fight, having assembled five captains of surrounding tribes about him. Upon these reports I determined to approach his residence as close as I could venture.

"I issued an order to the Commando, that no goods belonging to the missionaries should be touched, in accordance with the Lager Instructions; of which two men had made themselves guilty, who were tried by court-martial on the 27th and convicted, and sentenced to receive thirty lashes, or to be deprived of all burgher privileges of the Commando. They preferred the latter.

"The 28th, I pushed out to Secheli's town-water, about a quarter of an hour's walk from the town. To reach it, I had to march past the town, and to proceed through a narrow passage. I prepared every thing for self-defence, as every position was occupied by the enemy, who levelled their guns at and threatened us, but did not fire a shot, so that I gained my object without opposition; and as the day was far advanced, and it was also the last day of the week, I resolved, with the concurrence of the council of war, to abstain from every thing that could give rise to displeasure, not even to allow any one, except the commandants, to speak to Secheli's Kafirs, lest any misunderstanding should take place, and that we might observe the Lord's day.

"I at once sent to Secheli the following message :—

"'FRIEND SECHELI,—As an upright friend, I would advise you not to allow yourself to be misled by Moselele, who has fled to you because he has done wrong. Rather give him back to me, that he may answer for his offence. I am also prepared to enter into the best arrangements with you. Come over to me, and we shall arrange every thing for the best, even were it this evening. Your friend,

"'P. E. SCHOLTZ, *Act. Com.-Gen.*'

"Secheli replied :—

"'WAIT till Monday. I shall not deliver up Moselele : he is my child. If I am to deliver him up, I shall have to rip up my belly; but I challenge you on Monday to show which is the strongest man. I am, like yourself, provided with arms and ammunition, and have more fighting people than you. I should not have allowed you thus to come in, and would assuredly have fired upon you; but I have looked into the book, upon which I reserved my fire. I am myself provided with cannon. Keep yourself quiet to-morrow, and do not quarrel for water till Monday; then we shall see who is the strongest man. You are already in my pot; I shall only have to put the lid on it on Monday.

"(*Signed*) 'SECHELI.'

"SUNDAY, 29th.—We humbled ourselves before the Most High, who delivers both the weak and strong, and jointly beseeched Him to be merciful to us. After Divine service, Secheli sent two men to me to ask for some sugar, which I looked upon as a bravado. He also sent word to me to send two men to him on Monday, and that I should take care that the oxen did not depasture on the poisonous grass, for that he now looked upon them as his own. I briefly replied, that such a hero should rather use chillies instead of sugar.

"MONDAY, 30th.—I sent two men to Secheli to ascertain his meaning, and once more to offer peace to him. He replied, that he required no peace; that he now challenged me to fight; and, if I had not sufficient ammunition, he would lend me some. I again sent to tell him, that he should call to mind how he had ever to submit to the tyranny of Matselikatse, whom we had dispersed; that he, Secheli, was then poor and small, and, having now grown rich by the burghers, he should not become too arrogant by harbouring robbers and disturbers of the peace; that he should not harden his heart, as it might be productive of mournful results to him; that he would perhaps again become as little as he had been. His reply was, ' I want to fight.' I advanced with three hundred men close to his battery, and again sent messengers to prevail upon him to accept peace; and to inform him that, should he not wish to conclude peace, he was to set aside his women and children, or rather to come out with his warriors, that we then might fight man to man, as I would otherwise be compelled to fight with cannon, and this might endanger the women and children. All this I did to dispose him to peace. But he replied,— 'You have nothing to do with my women and children; they are mine; and I want to fight to-day, and experience which of us is the strongest.' Upon which, under a shower of balls, I advanced upon the battery, confiding my fate into the hands of the Lord. I stormed the intrenchments and caverns, under a severe fire which I encountered from three sides; took possession, set fire to, and stormed one side of the town, where one of my gallant burghers, named Jan de Clerk, was killed; and, in storming a rocky ridge, the gallant Mr. G. Wolmarans, Fs., and a Bastard were killed alongside of each other. After six hours' hard fighting, I had possession of two rocky ridges and all the enemy's intrenchments, with a large number of guns and prisoners. A good number of them had been killed. My loss was three killed and six wounded. I was compelled to retire, my men being knocked up, and night having closed upon us. The enemy had still possession of one rocky ridge. We again assembled to thank the Lord, and to offer Him our evening sacrifice.

"The following day I sent one hundred and fifty men out to reconnoitre, and to ascertain whether the enemy was disposed for peace;

upon which I found that they had evacuated their stronghold, and fled in various directions. I sent patrols after them, who found troops of them here and there, who fought in skirmishing order. But my party returned the following day with guns and cattle captured from the enemy, but without having sustained any casualty.

" On the 1st of September I dispatched Commandant P. Schutte with a patrol to Secheli's old town; but he found it evacuated, and the missionary residence broken open by the Kafirs. The commandant found, however, two percussion rifles; and the Kafir prisoners declared, that Livingstone's house, which was still locked, contained ammunition, and that shortly before he had exchanged thirteen guns with Secheli, which I had also learnt two weeks previously, the missionaries Inglis and Edwards having related it to the burghers A. Bytel and J. Synman; and that Livingstone's house had been broken open by Secheli to get powder and lead. I therefore resolved to open the house that was still locked, in which we found several half-finished guns, and a gunmaker's shop with abundance of tools. We here found more guns and tools than Bibles, so that the place had more the appearance of a gunmaker's shop than a mission-station, and more of a smuggling-shop than a school-place. This day young Smit, one of the wounded, died. We this day found two waggons hidden under a rock. On the 3rd I resolved to return, to refresh my cattle not far from the encampment. Having again encamped, I sent to all the tribes who had shown themselves our enemies, to offer peace to them, that those of them who accepted of it might return to their town or residence. I also sent to the disturber Monsua at Malopo, and appointed a place where I would meet him, because his subjects were continually plundering, and he was aware that they had committed serious depredations.

" The force returned with a booty of three thousand head of cattle, and a number of sheep, eleven horses, forty-eight guns, two waggons, and other articles, found in Secheli's retreat; likewise smiths' and gunmakers' tools found in the house of the missionary.

" Amongst the above cattle, many were recognised by their lawful owners as having been stolen from them by the Kafirs. I gave them back their property, which materially reduced the troop.

" The rest of the cattle, after defraying the expenses, I divided amongst the Commando in equal portions, except that I allowed something more to the wounded.

" The above expedition having, according to instructions, taken the field to ascertain what had become of the cattle that had been continually stolen, we found, on our advance, a part amongst the remaining herds of Moselele, who, along with the other vagabonds, was protected by Secheli. At Secheli's was the greatest smuggling-shop to be found in the whole settlement. He constantly deals in ammunition and guns, which he again exchanges with the other tribes; and an uncivilized nation, having fire-arms in hand, believe themselves to be invincible, and perpetrate the most heinous acts.

" This also was even Secheli's notion; who, though warned and exhorted to peace, deemed himself invincible, and not only desired to take our lives, but also all our waggons and cattle.

"*(Signed)*   P. E. SCHOLTZ, *Act. Com.-Gen.*
" Approved.
"*(Signed)*   A. W. J. PRETORIUS, *Com.-Gen.*
" The above report revised and approved.
" By order of the Volksraad,
"*(Signed)*   C. POTGIETER, *President.*"

Having thus allowed the Boers to give their own version of their doings, I shall quote a letter from the " Cape-Town Mail," which will throw some fresh light on some of the worst parts of the case, and which it is only fair to place by the side of the Report itself.

" SECHELI AND THE BOERS."
(*Cape-Town Mail, March* 12*th*, 1853.)

" AN article having appeared recently in the ' Zuid Afrikaan,' the purport of which seemed to be an attempt to excuse or justify the Trans-Vaal Boers in their late attack on Secheli, the chief of the Baquaines, permit me to make a few remarks concerning the fallacies thereof. The Boers, says the writer, feeling that Secheli was getting too formidable in arms, resolved to deprive him of them. He omits wholly to mention that the Boers, previous to their being acknowledged as no longer rebels, sent to Secheli several threatening letters, to the effect that he must always inform them of the arrival of English travellers in his country, otherwise they would inflict immediate punishment on him. Those threats were unheeded by him, as he was righteously unwilling to betray the trust reposed in him by the English. Pretorius, at the time that these letters were sent to Secheli, was himself an outlaw, with a price set upon his head ; of which circumstance Secheli was aware, and therefore he considered Pretorius to be usurping rights and forming laws for his own advantage, without the knowledge of the British Government. Feeling perfectly confident of his innocence as to any charge of a criminal or aggressive nature that Pretorius might feel disposed to prefer against him, Secheli nobly determined to brave the consequences that might ensue from his refusing to comply with his unjust demand. In the year 1850, a party of English gentlemen, while endeavouring to pass through the country occupied by the Boers, were intercepted by them, grossly insulted, and obliged to return to the Sovereignty. On this account, English travellers to the interior were under the necessity of proceeding through the country of the chief Secheli, where they felt perfectly secure from future interruptions.

" But let us now revert to the main point, namely, the recent attack upon the chief Secheli. A Commando, consisting of four hundred Boers and six hundred subjugated Kafirs, of the Bakonni tribe, occupying the country to the eastward of the Moriga, with nineteen waggons, arrived at the territory of Moselili, a chief occupying the country adjacent to the Boers. This chief, with the able-bodied men, had fled on hearing of the approach of the Boers; considerable numbers of old men and women remaining at the kraal, in the hope of obtaining peace from the Boers by peaceable remonstrance. This hope was delusive. Firing was immediately commenced on the part of the Boers, which killed and wounded a great number of men and women. The Boers then proceeded towards the residence of the chief Secheli, a distance of about fifty miles from the former chief, and arrived there on the 27th of August, 1852. Exorbitant demands were made by the Boers, requiring Secheli to deliver up guns, children, oxen, sheep, goats, and cows. The chief refused to comply, saying, 'I might as well be a dead man, and my tribe destroyed.' The Boers resolved to attack the kraal immediately, which they did on the 29th inst. They opened a heavy fire, and the people of Secheli, of course, returned it; and this murderous and unequal contest continued until night-fall, when those injured and unoffending people were compelled to retreat. The Boers possessed themselves of about twelve hundred head of cattle, about a thousand children, and two hundred women; also seizing all the property left by the English travellers in the charge of the chief, to the value of £1,200, which he had kept most carefully and honourably during the owners' absence. A party of these Boers then proceeded to the mission-house at Rolesberg,—where the Rev. Dr. Livingstone had long resided, but from which he was now absent, distant about twelve miles,—and, having rifled it of every thing that appeared useful in their estimation, destroyed his library and valuable medicine-chest, carrying away also doors, window-sashes, &c. We must not omit here to mention, that the Boers brought with them large quantities of brandy, to support their courage in the fight, and many were in a state of intoxication during the contest.

"Having thus collected as much booty as was within their reach, they then proceeded to the residence of Sentulie, a neighbouring chief; and, on their way, fell in with detached parties of Moselili's tribe, who were endeavouring to make their escape with their wives, children, and cattle. These wretched people they shot down in the most cold-blooded manner,—they offering no resistance whatever, but, on the contrary, wishing to surrender. Here the Boers also enriched themselves with numbers of cattle, women, and children. Sentulie, having sent as many of his women and children as he could to the mountains for safety, awaited the arrival of the Boers, who immediately opened a heavy fire. His men then also fled to the mountains; on gaining which, they returned the fire of the Boers, who then retreated. Here alone, it appears, they did not succeed in obtaining any cattle or captives; and they then returned to their Trans-Vaal, where a division of their ill-gotten booty took place.

"We have evidence from Boers themselves, as well as from Englishmen,—1. That many of these unfortunate captives were exposed for sale, and some have even been seen in the Sovereignty attending their masters, not knowing that upon British ground no one can be a slave. 2. That slavery to a great extent is carried on by the Trans-Vaal Boers, there is no doubt; and it only requires investigation to be clearly proved. 3. The main and real objects of these attacks appear to have been expressly for the purpose of obtaining native blacks for enslavement, and of enriching themselves with cattle. 4. Hence they show great unwillingness to permit the entrance of any English travellers, who could report on, and expose, their unrighteous conduct.

"It has been asserted or insinuated by the writer of the article in the 'Zuid Afrikaan,' that Secheli has been in the habit of selling slaves to the Portuguese of Delagoa Bay. This is an utter falsehood, and is in fact impossible; no Portuguese have ever visited Secheli's country. This unfounded assertion only exposes the ignorance of the writer in question, relative to the situations of the countries inhabited respectively by the Portuguese and the Baquaines, of whom Secheli is the chief. This letter has been written in the presence and with the sanction of two gentlemen, who have travelled for the past three years into the interior of Africa, who can vouch for its strict truth. I myself have also passed through Secheli's country several times, and once subsequent to the attack by the Boers, when I became acquainted with the facts I here relate.

"We know for certain, that Secheli is now on his way to Cape Town, preparatory to visiting England, and is prepared to confute any charges that interested parties may feel disposed to bring against him.

"I have, &c.,
"VERITAS."

According to the last paragraph in the preceding quotation, Secheli was expected at Cape Town, and he has since arrived there; yet, for some reasons not known to us, he proceeded no farther, but returned, and, on his way, passed through Graaf Reinet. Concerning his visit we find the following notice in the "Graaf-Reinet Herald." But I am not certain whether this was on his way to the Cape, or on his return.

"The chief Secheli, accompanied by Messrs. Edwards and Green, arrived here on Saturday afternoon last. We understand that £119 have been collected in Bloem-Fontein, and £10 in Colesberg, towards the expenses of the chief's journey to England.

"This object does not appear to find much favour in Graaf Reinet; and his account of the fight with the Boers, and assertions of their having made slaves of his people, are received with much coolness and suspicion. He states that thirty-five Boers were killed in the attack on his kraal, and fifteen wounded; while he had eighty-nine of his people killed, a thousand children and two hundred women taken prisoners by the Boers, and carried off into slavery. The Natives are described as very friendly to the English, but as having a wholesome horror of the Boers, who make plundering forays on them, for the sake of obtaining cattle and slaves.   The hostility of the Republic to English travellers is said to arise from a wish to conceal their treatment of the Natives from the eyes of the world, as well as from a desire to monopolize the trade with the interior.

"The sooner Mr. Pretorius gets his printing-press the better; as these stories, going about uncontradicted or unexplained, will excite a deep feeling of dislike against the Trans-Vaal Republic, and may possibly tend considerably to increase the difficulties of its position."

But that part on which we are desirous to have a little more information, is the assertion of the Boers that Dr. Livingstone had an establishment for making and selling fire-arms, &c.   I know not where this gentleman may now be, or whether he has had an opportunity of giving any explanations about it; but, in South Africa, no sensible man will, for a moment, receive such a calumny against one of the best men and most enterprising missionaries of the present age.   His character stands too high in this Colony to be injured by reports like these, apparently invented to cover dastardly acts of rapine, which are discountenanced in civilized warfare.   In Europe, too, his character is duly appreciated as a man of great intrepidity and of vast scientific attainments, and as a wonderful explorer and discoverer.   But his active piety, benevolence, and great moral worth have been highly esteemed in every part of the world, in consequence of the striking contrast which that modern Nimrod, R. Gordon Cumming, has unintentionally drawn between his own principles and conduct while in intercourse with the Natives, and those of his revered friend, Dr. Livingstone, whose religious and moral qualities he justly extols in his celebrated work, "The Lion-Hunter in South Africa."

It must also be borne in mind, that in those distant parts there are no carpenters, waggon-makers, or smiths : it becomes needful, therefore, for those who are permanent residents to have the means of repairing different articles for their own use and that of their friends and neighbours.   Nothing more than this seems to have been done by Dr. Livingstone; and as nothing was found to compromise his character, there could be no reasonable ground of complaint.   It is required of a missionary to be able occasionally to use a gun, to supply his family with a little animal food, which they might not otherwise obtain, the butcher's shop being far too distant. Besides, if the Boers had reason to suspect all was not right, they should have taken an honourable mode of finding it out, and not in his absence have broken open his house, and destroyed his property. The course which they adopted might have been expected from savages, but not from civilized human beings, professing Christianity.

RENEWAL OF THE SYSTEM OF SLAVERY BY THE BOERS.

In connexion with, and bearing upon, this subject, we quote from the " Natal Mercury," of June 9th, 1853 :—

" From the testimony of the gentleman referred to, as well as from that of other recent travellers, and numerous writers in the Cape and Sovereignty papers, we are compelled to believe, that, notwithstanding denials and evasions on the part of interested persons, a system of virtual slavery does extensively prevail amongst the Boers, under the plausible name of ' an apprenticeship ' or ' registration ' of prisoners taken in war ; and that one chief object of the frequent and bloody commandoes undertaken by the Boers is, in fact, to secure victims for this system of forced labour."

The following extract from a letter by " an emigrant of 1851 " we copy from " The Friend of the Sovereignty." It is dated from Megaliesberg : while it confirms the reported disunion that exists, it furnishes hopeful indications that justice and modera- tion may ultimately prevail over the rapacity of the war and slavery party.

" As to slavery, in spite of the treaty with the Assistant Commis- sioner, two Kafir boys have this very week been sold here,—the one for a hundred rix-dollars to a Boer, and the other for a hundred and fifty rix-dollars to a dealer living at Rustenburg. Last month, also, two were sold to Messrs. S. and G. Maritz, traders of Natal, and were immediately ' booked ' *(ingeboekt)* with the Landdrost of Potchesstroom for twenty-five years each ! Is this according to treaty ? If not, why does not Governor Cathcart interfere by force, if reasoning be unavailing ? for, without some force, I see little prospect of the Natives being saved from utter and universal slavery."

" The Graham's-Town Journal," of September 24th, in describ- ing the meeting of the Delegates at Bloem-Fontein, says :—

" We are credibly informed, that, in a private interview with Sir G. R. Clerk, one of the most respectable and loyal Boers, resident on a confiscated farm in the most disaffected district, ' *inter alias res,*' plainly told Sir George that he had some twenty or thirty Bushman children on his place; and that if Government withdrew, he must sell them in self-defence, as, if he did not do so, other persons would come and take them, and sell them. The reply, as stated to us, was to the effect, 'You have been too long a good subject, to lead me to think you would do such a thing now.' To this the answer was, 'I have been a good subject; but if Government will *make* me a rascal, I cannot help it."

These different kinds of evidence, coming from so many distant sources, and giving the particulars of direct and positive slavery, leave no reasonable doubt as to the real facts of the case; and, while they prove a direct and flagrant violation of the treaties on which the Republic was established, loudly call for decisive measures, to prevent the recurrence of such acts, and the perpetuation of the system of slavery.

But it is plausibly affirmed, that it only amounts to the apprenticing of *orphan children* until they are twenty-one years old, when they are grown up to manhood; and that this, therefore, is a boon conferred, rather than a wrong inflicted. This might be alleged as some excuse, had not the Kafir parents first been shot. When they have thus made them orphans, to take them as apprentices may be deemed an act of vast beneficence; but this view of the matter will be received only by those who derive benefit from the practice. How are these poor children to know when they are twenty-one years old, and the means by which they may seek and obtain their freedom? How can they know when they are entitled to their freedom? Their twenty-one may be thirty-one, or sixty-one, and will be completed when the grave closes over them.

I am aware that this is called " domestic slavery," and not like the slavery of sugar-growing countries, where the slaves are taken out and worked in gangs; but it still is slavery, by compulsory labour and compulsory detention. Yes; and the people know and feel it to be slavery, and do not prefer it to their former state. I had one of these apprentices (*aliàs*, slaves) in my employ at Natal; one whom the Boers had taken and bound in the same manner, before the English took Natal from the Dutch. This man assured me that he had been a slave, and that the Natives regarded this kind of apprenticeship as slavery. There are serious alarms among the late slaves residing in the Cape Colony, in reference to the new Constitution, as they find that

Dutchmen are to be admitted into the Parliament; and they dread the consequences, trembling lest they or their children should, under some plausible pretext, be taken from under the government of Her Majesty, and be again reduced to slavery. This fact has been pressed upon my notice by the serious apprehension of some of our own people, which could be removed only by the clearest explanations and most cogent arguments; and I have been informed, on the best authority, that this dread is not confined to a few, but is well-nigh universal. I could not have believed, unless I had witnessed it, that the remembrance of the bitterness of slavery could have been so fresh, and the feeling so strong, after twenty-four years of freedom.

But all that has hitherto been advanced relates to the *practices* of the Boers. I would now, for a moment, look at their *principles* and *convictions*. They are a religious people in their way, read the Bible, and profess to be regulated by its precepts; but, in reference to slavery, they look on the dark-skinned races as the " cursed sons of Cain," who are doomed by Heaven to perpetual servitude. Therefore they consider them-selves as performing the will of God, and doing Him service, when they inflict this cruel wrong on the Natives. You will, there-fore, find Commandant Pretorius conducting public worship in his camp, and devoutly praying for the protection and defence of Heaven, whilst engaged in these fierce forays. Those who fall in this warfare against the reputed enemies of the Lord, are considered as falling in a righteous cause, and to be sure of heaven. Now, the establishment of an independent Republic, in the midst of South-African tribes, by men who hold these principles, and act from such convictions, is a most serious affair. I gladly admit that there are some noble exceptions; yet I believe the preceding are the public national convictions of nearly all the Boers. Many of them have seriously quarrelled with their own ministers, for the unpardonable offence of teaching "these cursed people" the nature of religion; whilst the word *Zendeling*, properly signifying " missionary," is used by them as a term of reproach, and bearing the interpretation of a sort of artisan, pedlar, or hawker, who, whilst he tries to instruct the Natives, is engaged in secular transactions, and is a most dangerous man. It has been commonly reported that they will not allow a missionary to labour in the Republic; and my own impression is, that if it is possible to prevent it, they will do so. However some may attempt to deny or gainsay these statements, I believe them to be founded in truth, and confirmed by fact.

The consequence is, that if they see a tract of country which they like, having few inhabitants, they will go there and depasture their cattle; when the Natives, who think they have no business there, probably deceived by their fewness and their apparent weakness, will attempt to seize their cattle, and, perhaps, to murder some of the party. This quarrel is then taken up by the neighbouring tribes, and small reprisals are made, as in the case of Secheli and others; the result of which generally is, the loss of their independence, their property, and their lives. But is this just? Reverse this order of things, and suppose the Boers to be in the place of the Natives; would *they* be satisfied for others to come and say?—" The land is very thinly peopled,—only one family to six thousand acres of land. We can sit down here without doing harm to any one." Would the Boer be content to have it so? I think he would soon adopt effectual means for teaching this unwelcome intruder another lesson.

But let care be taken not to confound all equally in these censures. Very many Boers who have remained in the Colony do not maintain or defend these views. A gentleman, whose name is Gideon Joubert, in the Hauteur, near Colesberg, on this side of the Orange River, is a most honourable exception to the slavery and anti-English feeling. I mention his name here more especially, because he has received a requisition to become a member in the Council now forming under the arrangement of the new Constitution. The Council is the Upper House of Legislature. I believe that neither English nor native interests will suffer in his hands. Some of the plain and strong observations which I have made concerning these nefarious attempts to enslave the Natives, are not to be so construed as applying to them because they are men of another nation: my remarks refer simply to those principles and practices which characterize too many, and which are directly opposed to the rights of men, and to the good order of society.

DEATH OF COMMANDANT A. W. J. PRETORIUS.

MATTERS remained in the state described in the preceding sections, when, just at the close of the third Kafir war, and while Sir George R. Clerk, K.C.B., "Her Majesty's Special Commissioner for settling the affairs of the Orange-River Sovereignty," was about to enter on the functions of his important mission, a mournful event occurred, of which the following account is given in the "Graham's-Town Journal:"—

"The following, which we take over from the 'Zuid Afrikaan' of the 25th instant, confirms the report, given in our last, of the death of this remarkable man. Perhaps no one in this country has passed through more exciting scenes, or has been called to take upon himself higher responsibilities, than he; and it cannot but be a source of consolation to his friends, that he lived to overcome the difficulties of his position, and to establish, apparently on a firm foundation, the people who had chosen him as their leader and chief:—

"'By the last mail from the Trans-Vaal, we have received the mournful tidings of the death of that worthy man. Formerly an inhabitant of the district of Graaf-Reinet, where he enjoyed general respect, he emigrated from the Colony during the general expatriation of the Farmers; and—after having wandered several years in the desert, after innumerable collisions with the native tribes, after a host of adversities not necessary to be enumerated—he lived to see the object of all his endeavours, his sufferings, and privations, realized in the establishment of tranquillity amongst those by whom he was surrounded, and the independence of his people acknowledged by the British Government. We might say a great deal to justify the man's conduct during the latter part of his remarkable career; but the following few words embrace more than we can express:—*He was abused by several, but appreciated by many, and is universally regretted.*'

"The subjoined official account of his death will be read with interest. Heaven grant that amongst the Republicans a successor may be found who will worthily acquit himself of his duties, and who may be equally devoted to their real interests as the late Commandant-General! for in that case only will the Republic be prosperous, and will the Government and the inhabitants of the Cape Colony rejoice in their happiness:—

"'MOOI-RIVER, *August 4th*, 1853.

"'SIR,—Nothing is more painful to me than to inform you that, on Saturday, the 23rd of July last, our worthy guide, Andries Wilhelmius Jacobus Pretorius, Esquire, Commandant-General, departed this life, at the age of fifty-four years, eight months, and nineteen days. His illness was not of long duration. He suffered a short time from dropsy, which, owing to the want of proper medical treatment, increased, and eventually proved the cause of death. His last moments were tranquil. After having regulated all the papers relative to the government of the country, he earnestly admonished some of his sub-commandants and field-cornets to preserve unanimity and love, and they should do away with all party strife and ambition, in which case the blessing of God would be upon the Trans-Vaal Republic; that they should also take care of the Minister among them, the Rev. Dirk Van der Hoff, the faithful preacher of the Gospel and zealous labourer, so that morality and civilization might be disseminated among the old as well as the young. After having regulated all his worldly affairs, his thoughts were directed to the future: he committed his soul to our Saviour. Shortly before his death, he said, *I am reconciled with my Jesus, and about to be transferred to the regions above, where there shall be less troubles and sorrows than here;* and thereupon yielded up his spirit.

" 'Thus, then, has the hero of South Africa departed from us, whose name inspired all the native tribes with awe and terror. As regards his character, he was a man of great penetration. Humanity and humility were engrafted on his heart; and although frequently persecuted by his own countrymen, and an object of slander, he conducted himself calmly. His mode of life was moderate, tea being his most cherished drink. He never regarded himself, when necessity compelled him to be present on various occasions; and though frequently quite unwell, he only regarded the welfare of his countrymen. May his successor be imbued with the same abilities to direct a large number of people and the affairs of the Government, and to provide for the safety and tranquillity of the whites as well as the aborigines. Then may they, under God's blessing, be happy.

" 'I have, &c.,

" 'H. S. LOMBARD, SEN.'

" A private communication on the same subject states :—

" 'The death of Mr. Pretorius is most grievous to us: but we are consoled; for him to live was Christ, and to die was gain. We console ourselves with the paternal care of the Lord in this our bereavement. Death, which excuses no one, has often cut off members of society who could not be spared, and has also removed him whose memory will ever be dear to us. May the Lord sanctify his death to surviving friends and relatives! His indisposition, which lasted about a month, during which he kept his bed, was a constant preparation for eternity. Invariably did he engage in devotion and prayer; his prayers were heard for church and state. For his children and friends also did he pray fervently to the Lord; whilst all his subordinate officers were admonished to protect and maintain the church; and this he did until the vital spark at length fled. Great as we esteem our loss, dear as he was to us, yet we could minister nothing to preserve his life. It was most gratifying to us, when many of the chiefs of surrounding tribes, hearing of his indisposition, hastened to see their benefactor, and to bid him farewell. At his bidding they were admitted, and appeared at his bed-side loaded with grief, and kissed his hands. We are consoled by God's holy promise, *Blessed are the dead which die in the Lord from henceforth ; Yea, saith the Spirit, that they may rest from their labours.'*"—GRAHAM'S-TOWN JOURNAL, *Sept. 3rd,* 1853.

After some discussion of the question, true to their principles as Republicans, the Dutch Farmers repudiated the doctrine of hereditary succession, and chose in his place the member of another family, who had shown himself to be a brave and wise man, and well acquainted with the true interests of the rising Commonwealth.

ABANDONMENT OF THE SOVEREIGNTY.

IN the preceding sections of this Appendix, the reader will find a description of the state of the various parties whose interests seemed to be bound up in the determination of Her Majesty's Government on this important matter. On the arrival of Sir George R. Clerk, K.C.B., Her Majesty's Special Commissioner for settling the affairs of the Sovereignty, public excitement was raised to its highest pitch; while the colonial journals afforded ample expression to the feelings of all those whose welfare appeared likely to be imperilled by the abandonment of the Sovereignty. I quote part of a leading article from the " Graham's-Town Journal," which contains some just remarks on the abandonment or retention of the Orange-River Sovereignty :—

"Examine it, for instance, as a question of finance, and the arguments for retention will outweigh tenfold those in the opposite scale. We firmly believe, and are ready to maintain, that there is no British settlement that can be retained and governed so cheaply and so easily as the territory in question. It is true that a military force of some five hundred men have been maintained in that country; but let it be remembered, as a set-off to the expense, that they were in the healthiest climate in the world; that their duty was extremely light; and that their presence gave a degree of confidence to the infant settlement, which induced an outlay of capital, not merely in the improvement of the country, but for the extension of commerce, and increasing the production of raw material (such as wool) for the British market, which indirectly repaid fourfold the outlay incurred under this head. It would appear that the Governor has given an opinion that the retention of the Sovereignty will involve the maintenance of a military force of two thousand men in that country. There is not a single man of experience who concurs with His Excellency in this opinion.

"Another plea is, that the retention of the Sovereignty involves us in expensive and vexatious disputes with the native tribes. That this has been the case we may admit; while, at the same time, we contend that the objection is utterly futile and worthless. The fact is, we cannot, much as we may desire it, avoid interference with the Natives, unless we abandon the country altogether, and leave Africa to her fate. The British nation has a great mission in this country; an immense responsibility rests upon it, and this responsibility cannot be cast off or neglected, save at imminent hazard. It is absolute dishonour to shrink from it, nor can the attempt be made without entailing adequate punishment. The moral regeneration of the world *must* be accomplished, not by miracle, but by human agency; and we may be assured that those who put their hands to the plough and draw back, will become obnoxious to the penalty of unfaithful stewards.

" It would appear from the documents published in the ' Blue-Book,' an extract from which we give below, that the inconvenience of interference with the Natives is assigned as one strong reason for withdrawing from the country. But the question is, ' Will the withdrawal rid us of the difficulty ? ' The self-evident answer to this is, ' By no means.' Abandonment is only an equivalent term for anarchy : property would be wrecked, the evil influences of South Africa would be stirred up to their core, and the Colony, if it is to remain a British possession, would be obliged, in self-defence, to have such a force on its boundary as could maintain its integrity, and save it from the reflux of that tide of mischief which must inevitably overwhelm and destroy every thing within the range of its fatal influence.

" The following extract from the 'Blue-Book' is taken from Notes on the Sovereignty, addressed by Mr. Assistant-Commissary-General Green, the present Resident in the Sovereignty, to General Cathcart. These Notes go to show that Sir Harry Smith's Proclamation, promulgated while on a journey, to meet the exigency of the moment, required modification; which it would most unquestionably have received, had it not been for the breaking out of the Hottentot and Kafir rebellion. It is, however, a remarkable fact, that, in spite of the defects of the crude measure remarked upon, none deprecate more earnestly the withdrawal of British dominion from that country than the Natives themselves. That Proclamation, notwithstanding all its practical difficulties, bettered the condition of the Natives immensely, and was a rude charter, containing the germ of civilization; and which, had it been prudently cultivated, pruned, and dressed up by a skilful hand, would ultimately have produced golden fruit. Mr. Green remarks :—

" ' Had Sir Harry taken more time, and weighed well the wants of the country, instead of passing like a meteor through it, he would have ascertained that the greater part of the details of his Proclamation, written at the Great Tugela River, on the 3rd of February of that year, were diametrically opposed to the interests of nearly every class of its inhabitants.

" ' Had Sir Harry Smith confined himself to the establishment of equitable boundary lines between the white and native inhabitants of the country, and proclaiming the Queen's sovereignty over the former, leaving the latter to settle their own international disputes, the recent misfortunes of the country would have been averted. All the chiefs named in the Governor's Proclamation arrogated in consequence territorial rights, in which they looked to the Government to maintain them. Moroko and Moletsani held their land upon a very doubtful title; but the Proclamation was no sooner issued, than they set Moshesh and Gert Taarbosch at defiance.

" 'But, as if the Proclamation, as far as already noticed, were not sufficiently an apple of discord, thrown into the unhappy Sovereignty, there is a special clause in it to embroil the native and white inhabitants; for in the fourth paragraph we read, that 'one condition upon which Her Majesty's subjects hold their lands is, that every able-bodied man turns out with arms, or as a constable, for the defence of Her Majesty *and her Allies.*' Had the three last words *(and her Allies)* been omitted, no fault could have been found with the paragraph; but as, when two native chiefs are in hostility to each other, the one whose part is espoused by the Government is considered an ally, and the other an enemy, the effect was simply to bring the Boers into collision with other native tribes with whom they had no quarrel, and from whom they had always experienced kindness and respect.

" 'If the first consequences of interference in native international quarrels were bad, the ulterior ones were worse. It was soon discovered that a peaceable arbitration between contending tribes was out of the question; and that, generally speaking, it was necessary to coerce either one party or the other with a military force. Sir H. Smith would not hear of any of the extra expenses arising from such a cause being defrayed from imperial funds; and Major Warden, with his concurrence, hit upon the expedient of levying a fine upon the tribe he considered in fault for the purpose. An opportunity of applying this rule was produced on the following occasion :—

" 'In the month of September, 1849, in consequence of Sikonyella's tribe encroaching on the boundary line of the Winberg district, Major Warden moved a force into their country to punish them. Sikonyella acknowledged his fault, and agreed to pay a fine of two hundred and fifty head of cattle, which, however, have not since been exacted. While the troops were still in the Kafir country, a report was brought to the British Resident (who accompanied them) of an attack made by Moletsani on the missionary station of Umpukane, upon which he requested Sikonyella (our late enemy) to accompany him with a force to assist in punishing Moletsani, and called out Moroko for the same purpose. Moletsani was summoned to pay a fine of cattle for his late offence; he refused, upon the plea that he was not to blame in the affair; the combined force immediately attacked him, and succeeded in carrying off about three thousand head of his cattle, together with eleven waggons, the property of the Koranna chief, Gert Lynx, whose people were supposed to be partisans of Moletsani. All of this property was retained to pay the expenses of the expedition, and to divide among our native allies; part was sold at Bloem-Fontein for the former purpose, but the proceeds have not yet been paid into the commissariat chest.

"'The expedition had not reached Bloem-Fontein on its return, when accounts arrived that Moletsani, with the assistance of Moshesh, had compensated himself by an attack upon the outposts of our ally Moroko, and by sweeping off, according to the account of the latter, four thousand five hundred head of cattle, besides horses. Moroko having become a sufferer through his obedience to the call of Major Warden, it became incumbent on him to procure him restitution of his losses ; and an application to that effect was made to Moshesh, whose people had been principally concerned in the robbery. After the lapse of a considerable time, Moshesh restored two thousand head, and promised the remainder when he could collect them. This had not been done at the close of 1850, when Sir H. Smith determined, upon the representation of the British Resident, to compel him; and with this view had ordered the garrison of Bloem-Fontein to be reinforced with two companies of the 91st Regiment, whose march was, however, prevented by the breaking out of the Kafir war; and the cattle are still unrestored.'"—"Graham's-Town Journal," *September 3rd*, 1853.

Sir George R. Clerk proceeded with great courtesy and prudence in the execution of the unpalatable commission with which he had been intrusted. "The Graham's-Town Journal," of September 24th, says,—"We cast no censure on Sir G. R. Clerk, whose gentlemanly courtesy has won golden opinions from all men. He is simply acting upon instructions from those who have sent him hither to do an act of violence. Verily, if any thing could influence the British inhabitants of the Sovereignty to prefer a request to be absolved from their connexion with the British Government, it would be the series of mischievous blunders that have been made, of which this is the climax, in the administration of the affairs of that territory." "The Cape-Town Monitor" says,—"While much alarm and dissatisfaction prevail regarding this measure, we are happy to find that Sir G. R. Clerk is spoken of in all quarters in the highest terms. He is simply carrying the commands of the British Government into effect; and he will, no doubt, perform his mission, although an unpleasant one, in a manner worthy of his high reputation."

I close this section with an extract from "The Port-Elizabeth Telegraph," because it inculcates on the settlers the necessity of strenuous exertion and self-dependence, instead of uttering useless wailings: "On the withdrawal of British supremacy, and the abandonment of their territory by the British troops, the English residents should claim for themselves the same amount of protection and freedom from aggression which is guaranteed to native chiefs. We grant that the struggle at first would be an up-hill one; but the very sense of self-reliance would awaken new energies. The feeling that they had been abandoned, cast out, repudiated by the very country which, in word and deed, had pledged itself to protect and foster them, should fire them with a noble resolve to awaken, by a thousand acts of industry and self-denial, the mother-country to a sense of its errors. The course open to the Sovereignty is, to save Great Britain from the rashness of her own proceedings, and to exhibit to the world the example of subjects, wiser than their government, disdaining to turn their backs on danger and trial, although these may be multiplied by the faithlessness of their protectors."

Sir G. R. Clerk, having communicated in several meetings with all those who were personally concerned in the affairs of the Sovereignty, transmitted the result of his investigations and explanations to Her Majesty's Ministers. The following is an extract from his *ultimatum* :—

"The more I consider the position, relative both to the Cape Colony and to its own internal circumstances, the more I feel assured of its inutility as an acquisition, and am impressed with a sense of the vain conceit of continuing to supply it with civil and military establishments in a manner becoming the character of the British Government, and advantageous to our resources.

"It is a vast territory, possessing nothing that can sanction its being permanently added to a frontier already inconveniently extended. It secures no genuine interests; it is recommended by no prudent or justifiable motive; it answers no really beneficial purpose; it imparts no strength to the British Government, no credit to its character, no lustre to the crown. To remain here, therefore, to superintend or to countenance this extension of British dominion, or to take part in any administrative measure for the furtherance of so unessential an object, would, I conceive, be tantamount to my encouraging a serious evil, and participating in one of the most signal fallacies which has ever come under my notice in the course of nearly thirty years devoted to the public service."

The Home Government, as well as Sir George Cathcart, the Governor of the Colony and its dependencies, approved of the view taken of the matter by their Special Commissioner; and the fate of the Sovereignty was consequently sealed.

ATTEMPT TO REVERSE THE ORDERS FOR ABANDONMENT.

THE gentlemen most interested in this decision, which they had used all lawful means to avert, chose a respectable deputation to visit England, and to bring the entire case before Parliament. Having had several interviews with the Secretary and Under-Secretary of State for the Colonies, and with many influential Members of Parliament, they at length found an able advocate of their views and feelings in the Honourable Mr. Adderley, Member for North Staffordshire. Subjoined is a brief syllabus of the debate, which was brought on by Mr. Adderley, when he introduced his motion, May 9th, 1854.

MR. ADDERLEY moved an address to Her Majesty, praying that she will be pleased to re-consider the Order in Council for the pro-mulgation of a Proclamation, abandoning all sovereignty over the Orange-River Territory and its inhabitants in South Africa. His object, he said, was to vindicate the right of the people of this country to have a voice in the disposal of the dominions of the Crown. He reviewed the history of our connexion with this Territory, distributed into epochs, from its first occupation by British subjects, in 1836, to what he maintained was its unne-cessary abandonment; and put to the House the question, not whether the original occupation of the Territory was desirable, or whether its abandonment was expedient, but whether a territory annexed to the dominions of the Crown, and settled by British subjects, ought to be so abandoned. He discussed this question upon constitutional and legal grounds, contending that the Orange Territory was a colony, which the Crown could not alien-ate by its prerogative, and still less absolve subjects from their alle-giance, as had been done in this case. The manner in which the power of renouncing this possession had been exercised by Sir G. R. Clerk, he insisted, was informal and illegal, while the act itself was, he endeavoured to show, inexpedient, the Territory being the key and heart of the whole South African Colony, and affording, according to the testimony of Sir G. R. Clerk, a most favourable field for the introduction of Christianity.

MR. F. PEEL observed, that Mr. Adderley had discreetly laid his chief stress upon the alleged illegality of the course pursued by the Government, because, as respected its policy and expediency, he knew that they had only carried out the intention of their predecessors, who had resolved to abandon the Orange-River Territory; and it was considered that the Crown was perfectly competent to take this course without an Act of Parliament, the country being a peculiar one, not acquired by colonization, but by conquest. The measure had not been hastily adopted; and it was supported by great authorities, including Sir George R. Clerk, and Sir George Cathcart. The inhabitants of the Territory were either Natives who had never surrendered their independence, or Dutch Farmers who voluntarily expatriated themselves from the Cape Colony to escape British control. Enormous speculations in land had been made in the Orange-River Sovereignty, many of the owners being absentees at Cape Town. These lands were obtained at the cost of the native chiefs, who resented the encroachments of Europeans: a spirit of revenge was engendered, which led to war; and this was carried on at the expense of the British Government, the hostilities imparting an artificial value to the land thus acquired.

As the speech of Sir John Pakington embraces the views entertained by the most eminent British statesmen on this vexed question, it is given *in extenso* from the "Times" newspaper :—

"Sir J. Pakington said, that while he had filled the office of Secretary for the Colonies, his attention had been very much directed to South Africa, not only on account of the Kafir war, but also with regard to the question of the Constitution which was to be granted to the Cape Colony, and to this very difficult subject of the retention or non-retention of the Orange-River Territory; and he therefore felt bound to address a few observations to the House. He was sorry that he could not concur with his Honourable friend Mr. Adderley, who had brought the subject before the House, in all the opinions he had expressed. His speech was divided into two portions; the one relating to the policy of retaining the Territory, and the other to the legality of the means by which the Government had carried their object into effect. But the terms of his motion were so general, that, as he differed from him as to the policy of abandoning this portion of Her Majesty's dominions, it would be impossible for him to support it by his vote. He agreed in the wish which the Under-Secretary for the Colonies (Mr. F. Peel) had expressed, that we had never crossed the Orange River; and he regretted the policy which Lord J. Russell's Government had adopted, in acceding to the desire of Sir H. Smith that we should do so. When Sir H. Smith made that recommendation, Lord Grey expressed his strong disinclination to increase the territories of the crown in South Africa; and, although he nevertheless yielded to Sir H. Smith's representations, he desired in a short time to reverse the policy which he had adopted. When he (Sir J. Pakington) succeeded to the Colonial Office at the commencement of 1852, he found that Lord Grey had actually sent out directions to have steps taken for the abandonment of this Territory, and he had also sent out a commission of two gentlemen of great ability, Major Hogg and Mr. Owen,—one of whom, he regretted to say, had been prematurely lost to his country,—to inquire into the subject. He had postponed coming to any decision with regard to the Orange-River Sovereignty while he held the Colonial Office, in the hope of obtaining a Report from that Commission; but his individual opinion coincided with that of Lord Grey and of the Duke of Newcastle, and it was his intention to abandon the Sovereignty. Although he believed he had not consulted his colleagues on the subject, and therefore had no right to pledge their opinions, he had consulted the law-advisers of the Administration with regard to the proper mode of proceeding in order to effect that object. After the speech which had been made by the Under-Secretary for the Colonies, he would not detain the House by stating the grounds upon which he had come to the conclusion that we ought to reverse the policy which had been adopted, if we could do so consistently with our duty to the Crown and to those who had settled in the country in question. He need only refer to the map of Africa as one reason for doing so. He doubted whether the public were aware of the gigantic extent of our dominions in Africa; for he believed a large majority of them looked upon the Colony of the Cape of Good Hope as consisting merely of the well-known town and harbour, and of certain adjacent districts, although their eyes might have been opened by the Kafir war. Even exclusive of Natal and of the Orange-River Territory, the Cape Colony was not less than six hundred or seven hundred miles in length, and three hundred miles in breadth. The European population of that enormous district was most inadequate to its occupation, to its cultivation, or to its protection. On its eastern side there was a large space not yet added to the British dominions, and beyond it was the Colony of Natal. What were the circumstances of the Orange-River Territory which had been added to this territory, already too extensive? He believed that the territory between the Orange River and the Vaal River contained fifty thousand square miles of ground, and was occupied by one hundred thousand Kafirs, of whom sixty thousand acknowledged allegiance to the well-known chief Moshesh, and were among the most intelligent and powerful of the Kafir tribes with whom we had been engaged in a warlike struggle. General Cathcart, after having ended the Kafir war on the eastern frontier, had undertaken to settle the affairs of the opposite frontier; and the first step that he took had been followed by one of the most formidable of the struggles which had taken place between Europeans and the native tribes of South Africa. The European population of the Territory was said to be ten thousand; but a very small proportion of that number was British, the greater proportion consisting of Dutch Boers who had migrated to that very Territory, in order to escape from British dominion. He therefore thought his honourable friend must have been misled, when he stated that the general feeling of the inhabitants of the Sovereignty was in favour of retaining their allegiance to the British Crown; and all the dispatches of Sir G. R. Clerk confirmed him in the opinion, that it was merely a handful of British subjects who had speculated in land that desired to remain under the dominion of this country. Upon other occasions it had been argued, that we ought to retain this Sovereignty, on account of the danger and inconvenience of allowing an independent republic to be established upon our northern frontier. But could this be avoided? If the Dutch Boers crossed the Vaal, and established a trans-Vaal republic, ought a still greater extent of territory to be added to the British Crown, so as to include all these 'flying Dutchmen?' Was there any thing at all formidable in the establishment of such a power as it would be possible to establish on our northern frontier? His honourable friend had given an illustration of the helpless condition of that republic which had been established, when he alluded to the arrangements which were being made to get its wool to the sea through Natal, as it was four hundred miles distant from any port. Another point for consideration was the expense which this country would incur in maintaining its sovereignty over this vast territory, in which, as he had been advised, the authority of Her Majesty could not be supported, without keeping up an army of two thousand men, of whom five hundred at least ought to be cavalry. The Under-Secretary for the Colonies had not told them much with regard to the discovery of gold in this territory; and his honourable friend who had brought forward the subject, had not stated how much of the gold which had been discovered he had himself seen. He was far from saying that gold did not exist there; but he was now stating what were his impressions at the time he had held office, when the discovery had not been made; and when he had retired from office he had communicated to his successor what were his views with regard to the policy that ought to be adopted upon the question of the abandonment of the Sovereignty. The Duke of Newcastle, although he had adopted a course of policy, in a dispatch stated that he was still willing to consider any arguments which might be advanced against that policy; and if the honourable Member for North Staffordshire had advanced any well-founded argument opposed to the abandonment of the Territory, he should have been willing to pay it every attention. It appeared that Sir George R. Clerk was of opinion that the assertion of the British authority would be ridiculous, were it not also attended with the risk of perpetual struggles and reprisals. Sir George Cathcart spoke of the Territory as the 'Sovereignty incubus,' and strongly advised its abandonment. It appeared, then, that the opinions of the highest authorities were in accordance with the opinions which he had himself formed when he was connected with the Colonial Office, and upon those opinions he thought it only fair to the present Government to state that he was prepared to act. With regard to that part of the question, as to whether or not the Government were justified, in a point of constitutional law, he did not feel competent to give any opinion; but he had, when in office, consulted the law-officers of the Government with which he was connected, and, if his memory served him, his honourable and learned friend sitting near him (Sir F. Thesiger) had thought that it would be safer to abandon the Territory by Act of Parliament than by a declaration of the Crown. The present Government had thought it proper to pursue a different course, but he was not prepared to express any opinion as to the wisdom of the course which they had adopted."

After some remarks from Mr. V. Smith and the Attorney-General, Sir F. Thesiger said, he had never expressed an opinion that an Act of Parliament was essential in this case.

After a few words from Mr. J. Phillimore, and from Mr. Adderley in reply, the motion was withdrawn.

The leading article of the "Times" newspaper, on the issue of this debate, is one of those humorous and pungent productions which, at the time, irritate the parties to whom they more immediately relate; but which, on a re-perusal, long afterwards, are commended for much common sense, expressed in a witty manner:—

" One of the most frequent causes of private disaster is the difficulty of 'putting down' the smallest part of a costly establishment. It is declared 'impossible' to do without a town-house, or a carriage, or hunters, or a French cook, or a lady's maid, or any thing great or small that a man has once set up, even if he had never so little right to set it up. He finds it equally impossible to sell the property which he ought never to have purchased, and which lengthens his rent-roll and shortens his net income. He must go on or go back; and go back he will not: so he pushes onwards, till in a moment all his resources fail him, and he loses every thing because he would not make up his mind to sacrifice any thing. Now this folly is the bane of empires as much as of private estates. Wherever England has once planted its flag, wherever it has once proclaimed a conquest over a few naked savages or ill-tempered Boers, there, we are told, it must keep its hold. There is no help for it. It has put its foot into the slough of dominion, and there it must stick. It may hate its acquisition as much as it pleases; it may never make one step towards conciliating the good-will of the natives; it may find the new territory a constant item on the wrong side of the national ledger; it may incessantly abuse the generation or the Minister who saddled the state with so bad a property, yet it must not give it up. A certain class of patriots cry out, *Non progredi est regredi*, 'There must be no retreat; for the first step backwards is the presage of utter ruin;' and a certain class of jurists maintain, that the law forbids a state to renounce its dominion, or release its subjects from their allegiance. The fatal partnership, once contracted, with sterile acres or wild men, with pathless woods, untamed beasts, or unexplored wilderness, can never be broken. It must be transmitted in ruinous succession to reluctant heirs; and the unfortunate lords of savages, who never owned any allegiance, must persist against conscience, against interest, against the wish alike of the Sovereign and of the subject, to assert a barren claim, and secure, with fresh slaughter and cost, what it would most desire never to have possessed at all.

"Unless Mr. Adderley has done himself the grossest injustice, he is one of those patriots and one of those jurists. His patriotism has been aroused in defence of our sovereignty over the Orange-River Territory and its inhabitants. At all events, he is concerned to find that the Crown has the power, or supposes itself to have the power, of cutting the costly connexion without the fuss of an appeal to Parliament for a legislative divorce. The people of England, he insists, should have a voice in the matter; and his tone seems to imply, that the people of England would rush to the rescue of a territory of which they have no knowledge whatever, except that, to assert a nominal ownership, we have driven away the only civilized inhabitants, and are at constant war with some wandering savages. It is a mere conquest, declared to be such by the Crown in an evil hour. What is the precise nature of the tie which attaches the territory to the Crown, we leave to the lawyers, who appear to hold different opinions on that interesting point. We presume that, substantially, it is conquest, whatever the form and act of annexation; and, as the process took place without the intervention of Parliament, it seems almost necessary that the separation should be equally independent of that sanction. We have repeatedly seen territories declared by Proclamation to belong to the British Crown; and, by the rules of all logic, it seems a matter of course that the Crown, which can proclaim land to be its own, can proclaim it to be no longer its own. In the former case it deals with that which is originally not its own, and in the latter with what is confessedly its own; and if it has a right to take what is not its own, surely it has a still greater right to give away that which is its own, especially when the gift is to the original owners. If there is any doubt, by all means let it be given in favour of the Crown, as it was given last night, and had been given already by the law-officers of the Crown; for it is most desirable that the Crown should have the power of renouncing its own ill-advised, unfortunate, or questionable acquisitions. A certain degree of discredit attaches to all repudiations and changes of mind; and it is better the discredit should be confined as much as possible to the Crown than to the whole Legislature, which, in fact, had no direct voice in the matter from the beginning.

"The actual *finale* of our dominion over the Orange-River Territory appeared in our intelligence yesterday from the Cape; and the reader,

who has probably associated the name with intermittent wars, preda-
tory incursions, alternate cattle-driving, mutual mischief, and enormous
expense, would doubtless be edified at the very small sums that figure
in the negotiation. The new Government—of what sort, what origin,
what authority, we are only too thankful to be entirely ignorant—is
content to begin business with the moderate capital of £6,000. But
then there are certain other payments from the Special Commissioner.
Out of the magnificent sum of £500, damages are found for half-a-
dozen gentlemen illegally imprisoned, and as many widows of persons
unfortunately shot. The Rev. Dr. Tancred goes off a happy man with
£200; and, on the strength of it, is now the centre of hospitality, the
genius of improvement, and the soul of order, in the Clanwilliam district. The new government, besides taking powder and shot at a
valuation, have agreed to pay £95 for the barracks and other buildings
on the ordnance-ground in Bloem-Fontein. But, in the midst of this
rather sharp pecuniary settlement, it is pleasing to observe that the
British government, with its accustomed liberality, has presented the
new state of Orange River with the three large guns on the Queen's
fort, and sufficient shot, shell, and other ammunition to work them.
Possibly it occurred to the Special Commissioner that three cannons,
and as many pyramids of round shot and shells, would be an inconvenient addition to his luggage on his return from the discharge of his
office; and that, though gunpowder can be disposed of easily enough,
there is no such expeditious way of getting rid of thirty-two-pounders.
This remark, however, does not apply to another noble act of generosity, which, therefore, we trust will prove the foundation of an everlasting friendship between the United Kingdom of Great Britain and
Ireland on the one hand, and the Orange-River Territory on the other.
The new government of the latter has received all the government-
buildings and office-furniture in the different towns of the Sovereignty,
from the Special Commissioner, *gratis*. Tables, chairs, desks, shelves,
inkstands, green baize, safes, (like the similar articles that now constitute the sole relics of many a railway company in this country,) have
been freely sacrificed to the cause of peace; and the new State of
Orange River now sits on its own chairs, behind its own desk, with its
own inkstand before it, and, we dare say, a very tolerable stock of
stationery,—unless, indeed, the latter has been voted a perquisite by the
clerks of the retiring government. At all events, there is peace in the
Territory, and the last public act there done and transacted is of the
most pacific and edifying nature, besides being, what is more immediately to the purpose, exceedingly cheap."

SUPPOSED FAVOURABLE RESULTS OF THE ABANDONMENT.

No sooner had those who were most concerned in the determination of the Orange-River question received intelligence of its
final settlement, than they began, as became men of prudence and
energy, to accommodate themselves (in many instances with much

regret) to the novel position which they were compelled to occupy; and endeavoured to profit from such a great change, by developing and rendering available those resources which had till then been partially concealed, or carelessly neglected. In the brief space of eight months a marked improvement was visible in the general aspect of affairs; and if public prosperity proceed in the ratio in which it has begun, and if peace be preserved, which it is the highest wisdom of all parties to cultivate, this large territory will soon again become a flourishing colony, and constitute an integral portion of the British empire.

From the tenor of the debate in the House of Commons, it is very obvious that the leading men, of all political parties in the State, were unanimous in avowing their belief of the expediency and propriety of abandoning the Orange-River Sovereignty, and of allowing the Dutch Boers perfect liberty to improve their condition,—though their most approved methods of rising in life might not be in exact accordance with the views and practices of English settlers. Some of the Governors of the Cape Colony have been warm advocates for the adoption of a liberal policy towards the Dutch Farmers, whose ideas of social amelioration were not derived from the lights of history, but from their own experience, and that of their forefathers, in the rough patriarchal system, which, for two hundred years, had remained almost without change, and had made scarcely any perceptible advancement towards civilization. But no Governor exceeded Sir George T. Napier in the exposition and practical application of this benevolent policy; and a clever member of that brave and gifted family, Sir E. E. Napier, has lately published the following observations, under the date of April 9th, 1853 :—

" In another work of mine, called the ' Book of the Cape,' (edited by the author of ' Five Years in Kaffirland,' and published in 1849,) will be found, amongst other passages relating to the Boers, the following apposite remarks :—

" ' Let England consult at once justice, generosity, and self-interest, by declaring the independence of the Dutch Africanders, and then allowing them to establish whatever government they deem fit beyond the colonial limits. By following such a course, we should interpose a secure defensive belt between our possessions and native depredation ; establish pioneers of discovery, commerce, and civilization into the hitherto unknown regions of Central Africa ; and from bitter foes we should, no doubt, instantaneously convert the rebel Boers into our staunchest and most useful allies of South Africa.'—'Book of the Cape,' p. 260.

" Again, in the 'United Service Magazine,' for July, 1851, in an article bearing the title of 'Suggestive Remarks on the present Kaffir War,' and to which is appended my name, you will find the following passage with reference to the north-eastern frontier of the Cape:—

" ' Cease to persecute the emigrant Boers; conciliate them by friendly treatment; and, for their own sakes, they will be sure to keep aloof every savage tribe, and thus protect from molestation this extended portion of our frontier.' "—NAVAL AND MILITARY GAZETTE.

These sentiments, avowed by other persons of eminence, found favour among the upper and middle orders of society in England; and, as developing an experiment deserving of a fair trial, they have obtained, at least, a tacit acquiescence, if not a cheerful acceptance, on the part of the colonists. The horrors of such a fearful war as that which had then terminated, disposed the minds of all classes to encourage the attempt. Besides, England was then threatened with a great European war, which has since burst forth with terrific violence; and having, during the long continuance of peace, undertaken the defence of a large frontier, in the north-eastern regions of Asia, for the protection of her unwieldy Indian empire, she did not consider herself to be in a condition to engage in the occupation of another large boundary-line, to preserve her rising and thinly-peopled colonies in South Africa from the marauding aggressions of half-civilized barbarians.

In enumerating some of the motives which induced the mother-country to leave the colonists, in a great measure, to their own means of defence, it must not be forgotten that a strong opinion was entertained by Her Majesty's Ministers, as well as by others, that the colonists had not generally shown much promptitude in " turning out " on great emergencies, as a kind of *posse comitatûs*, when required by the Governor to act aggressively against the enemy. In the early part of the late war, the Kafirs were, in this respect, in circumstances far preferable to us; for all the men in the belligerent tribes were animated with one spirit, and were all under the control and direction of their own chieftains, whose word or nod was to them the supreme law of conduct. But whenever the parties who are actually engaged in offensive operations, or are called out as soldiers, assume the functions of a deliberative body, and choose to act or not to act for reasons which they can easily assign, they give a great advantage to the enemy. This is soon understood even by savages, who seem, in their late wars, to have universally adopted the maxim, "Union is strength," as the first principle of aggressive warfare. This unwillingness of the colonists to come forth as armed men, at the beck of any Governor that, on imperfect information or from personal pique, might hastily wish them to aid him in perpetrating what they considered to be acts of gross injustice against native tribes, whom both the English and Dutch settlers regarded as innocent, has more than once been made the subject of severe reprehension. Their reluctance to be made the facile instruments of the vindictive feelings of an irritated Governor, had been recently displayed in a remarkable manner towards Sir H. Pottinger and Sir H. Smith; and the unwilling portion of the colonists found encouragement in this course from the *vis inertiæ* presented by the inhabitants of the Cape Colony, when, as a deliberative and compact body, they successfully resisted the Home Government in the attempt to make that important part of South Africa a new penal settlement for the reception of convicts. It was well, for several reasons, that this ill-fated measure was frustrated. If it had been carried into effect, it would have operated as a vast encouragement to the Dutch Boers in trying to renew their former plan of domestic slavery; for they might then have pointed to the newly-imported species of servitude, and have triumphantly asked the philanthropic friends of the Natives, "Is your degrading system, or our mild one, the best method of treating men who are made in the image of God?"

But the three great parties in South Africa,—the English, the Dutch, and the Natives,—have lately been taught, by most painful experience, to entertain a better estimate of each other's good and bad qualities. This will tend to restrain all of them from those wanton aggressions and mischievous tricks, which, while deemed to be "fine sport" by those that practised them, have always rankled in the hearts of the injured, who usually made a fearful retaliation at the first convenient opportunity. Vast multitudes of the Natives are under instruction in Christian principles, and in the arts of civilization; and still greater numbers are desirous of obtaining the same means of elevating their characters and of improving their condition.   It is the paramount duty of the British Government, as well as of all true patriots and benevolent men, to encourage them in these laudable aspirations; for, if allowed to enjoy their undoubted rights without molestation, and if the different tribes live in amity with each other, in the course of a few years they will become the most numerous and powerful body in South Africa. How imperative, then, is it on us to give to the mental powers of this fine race a proper direction, which may issue in the greatest benefits to them, as well as to our own descendants and nearest connexions!

Many persons among us accustom themselves to complain of the measures introduced by the successive Governors of the Cape Colony and its adjoining provinces, and to attribute to them the chief disasters which have befallen the country and its inhabitants.   Others have been as loud in their blame of Her Majesty's Ministers at home, whose orders and instructions the Governors were expected to carry out; a liberal latitude being seldom granted to them for the exercise of a discretionary power.   Both these classes of critics are, to a certain extent, substantially correct.   But neither the different Governors of this extensive Colony, amounting, since the year 1814, to nearly a dozen, nor the combinations of men constituting the varying Ministries that have, during this period, been summoned by Her Majesty to assume the reins of government, will appear to be very blameworthy, if we compare them with others of their own rank and station in other quarters.   In England changes of administration are not uncommon in their occurrence; and, when not too frequent, they are usually reputed to be admirable safeguards of the British constitution, and the surest tests of its soundness.

In forming our estimate of human character, we must take into account the habits which the men have acquired, and the principal antecedents in their lives.   The Governors with whom the Cape colonists have been favoured, were generally officers in the army, who had long been used to obey as well as to command; and, when they came, required their orders to be promptly executed in true military fashion.   To the energy which they evinced no one can object.   It is rather to be viewed as a necessary qualification in the person that is invested with the attributes of government over such heterogeneous masses, a vast majority of the governed being half-enlightened savages. But when this promptitude is shown at the commencement of a new Governor's administration, it sometimes happens that a discovery is afterwards made of his energy in action having been misapplied, and perhaps an innocent chief and his tribe have been severely punished for crimes in the perpetration of which they never participated. It is in such emergencies as these that the different temperaments of mind are manifested. Some Governors, on making the unpleasant discovery, proceed at once to the redress of the grievance, and gain much deserved applause for their frankness in recalling the obnoxious orders, acknowledging that they had virtually been wrong-doers, and trying, by restitution and other means, to obliterate all traces of the injury which they had unwittingly inflicted. Others, under similar circumstances, display an inflexibility of character, which will not allow them to relax or modify any particle of their previous orders, though their injustice and precipitancy have become evident to all the community. These are the men who never own themselves to have been in error. They consider a softening of their sternness, and any approach to mildness or restitution, to be signs of personal weakness and indecision; and would not permit themselves to be compromised by the awkwardness implied in yielding to the moral force of equitable concession; which, when obviously a duty towards the party aggrieved, operates as an obligation only on minds of the highest order, who fulfil it with becoming grace and dignity.

Now, after all that has been premised, if we be inclined strictly to scrutinize the official instructions and the public actions of the various Lord-Lieutenants of Ireland, or Governors-General of India, who have been appointed since 1814, we shall perceive as strong grounds for vituperation in them, as we can find in the conduct of colonial affairs by the Governors placed over the British dependencies in Southern Africa. It scarcely ever forms a matter of dispute, whether these high functionaries, and those who promoted them to office, have not all had the best intentions in framing and carrying out those measures which they have devised for the benefit of the people whom they have been appointed to govern. In their general sincerity all are agreed, after making the ordinary abatement for human infirmity and errors in judgment. But the most common complaint preferred against these Viceroys in the dependencies now specified, is, that the principles on which they have severally acted often exhibit great anomalies and glaring contradictions. But in this they are not singular. The Romans, in the fairest days of their common-wealth, not unfrequently exhibited symptoms of the same inconsistency. The two consuls, and those eminent men who under them held proconsular office, often departed to the province which had been assigned to each, and there, *at the same time*, acted on principles decidedly antagonistic. But if we carefully study the effects of those remarkable discrepancies in the governing body, we shall find that they sometimes proved to be the means of eliciting a more equitable course of action, better suited to the altered condition of the people. Intelligent consuls who were subsequently elected, having suffered the first irritation of popular feeling to exhaust itself, wisely combined the conflicting theories of the two parties, and, by giving prominence at all convenient opportunities to sounder axioms of government, produced at length one harmonious plan, which worked well, and commended itself to all who enjoyed its benefits.

Such were the results perceptible among those ancient Heathens, who were not favoured with the pure light of Christianity as the true basis of all useful legislation and good government. In our days results very similar, yet still more remarkable, may be traced, by the Christian philosopher, in the management of affairs in our distant colonies; for in all of them the faults of the directing mind (to use a commercial phrase) " leave a large margin " for the interference of Divine Providence, and the display of its healing and ameliorating process :—

> " From seeming evil still educing good,
> And better thence again, and better still."

[For the sentiments contained in this article on " the Results of the Abandonment," and in that which precedes it, (pp. 399–411,) the author is not responsible. The editor thought it desirable to bring down the information to the latest date prior to publication; and, if he had waited to submit these two papers to the author for his approval, their transmission and return would have occupied more than six months.]

THE GREAT LAKE N'GAMI.

OUR geographical knowledge has been much extended by the discovery which Messrs. Oswell and Livingstone have recently made of the Great Lake N'gami, lying in about 20 degrees south latitude, and 24 degrees east longitude. The existence of this Lake had long been reported by the Natives; but the means of arriving at any certainty concerning it were unknown until these two adventurous gentlemen engaged in the undertaking. Dr. Livingstone had long resided at Kolobeng in lat. 25°; and from his accurate knowledge of every thing relating to the Natives, he was placed in favourable circumstances for entering on the enterprise. All being ready, he and his company left Kolobeng on June 1st, 1849. On the 4th of July they came to a large river about three hundred miles from Kolobeng; and, by following its banks three hundred miles further, they reached the long-expected Lake early in August. Thus, by great intrepidity and perseverance, they settled this doubtful point, and added a satisfactory portion of information concerning the Desert and Lake to our former treasure, which had till then been small and unsatisfactory. This has opened a new field of investigation, and already yielded a rich return to some of our enterprising traders.

I now introduce the deeply interesting journal of Mr. M'Cabe entire, as far as it has been published. His papers made their appearance first in "The Friend of the Sovereignty," and have been copied into "The Graham's-Town Journal;" from which I now take them for the instruction of the reader, as they give a very good idea of travelling according to African life.

THE KALAGHARE DESERT.

"WE transfer from 'The Friend of the Sovereignty' the following account by Mr. M'Cabe of a journey made by him across the Kalaghare Desert. The route, it will be seen, is one which can only be attempted by those willing to brave fatigue and privation of more than an ordinary character. Mr. M'Cabe relates his adventures with great plainness; and the public are indebted to him for his contribution to that stock of knowledge of this country, which has of late largely accumulated, exciting great interest both in this and in the parent country."

JOURNAL KEPT DURING A TOUR IN THE INTERIOR OF SOUTH
AFRICA TO THE LAKE N'GAMI, AND TO THE COUNTRY TWO
HUNDRED AND FIFTY MILES BEYOND, BY MR. JOSEPH
M'CABE.

" IN our late journey through the great Kalaghare Desert, to the
Lake N'Gami, and to the region two hundred and fifty miles beyond, we
took our usual course towards Kolobeng, having started from Bloem-
Fontein on the first of May, and reached the residence of the friendly
chief Secheli on the 29th of the same month. On our route to the
above chief, we passed the stations of two of the most hospitable of
Missionaries, Messrs. Ludorf and Edwards. Various considerations
induced me to try the route through the Kalaghare Desert; and, after
leaving a waggon, thirty oxen, some bags of coffee, sugar, meal, and
other articles, as a reserve, we pursued our course to the kraal of the
chief Sentuhe, forty miles south-west of Kolobeng, which we reached
on June 3rd. My reason for visiting him was, to obtain a guide,
knowing that his father, old Sebiege, chief of the Wanketse, had travelled that country, and dwelt for a long time on the border of the
Lake. From this tribe we obtained a good deal of information, and,
although by no means encouraging, we were determined to try and
overcome the difficulties which were said to form a barrier; and, having
obtained three natives as guides, we started on the enterprise on the
fifth of June, with good hopes of success. Our course then became
west by north. We travelled sixty miles, which took us three days,
through the sand, before we reached water; this at once proved to us
that we had entered the Desert. We halted at a Ballalla kraal, which
we reached on the 8th.

" These natives are very poor : they possess nothing, and subsist on
what game may fall into their pits or traps, on locusts and roots of the
Kalaghare. From them we ascertained, that a *vley* of rain-water was
to be found in the neighbourhood; and, after giving them some beads,
two men of the kraal, as guides, accompanied Mr. Maher and some of
my boys in search of it. After driving the oxen about fifteen miles,
they came to a *vley* of water, but so scanty that, in order to prevent
them from trampling the water into mud, only two oxen could be
allowed to drink at a time. While the oxen and horses went to the
water, I employed my time in gaining all the information I could possibly get from these poor creatures; and found that a well or pit, containing good water, lay in a northerly direction from where we
stood. Early on the 9th, I took my guide, and went in search of the
well; and, after proceeding some distance from the kraal, we fell in
with a foot-path which we followed for six miles, and which brought
us to a fine well. I examined it, and found it about fifteen feet deep,
and containing almost sufficient water for our stock. This well is
called by the natives Secuil. This little discovery was of great importance to us. I returned to the waggons, and found that Maher had
not returned with our cattle and horses from the water, which had
been sent the previous day. Late in the evening, however, all arrived

safe. The oxen and horses showed that they had been to water, for they looked full.

"On the morning of the 10th we made for the Secuil, which took us two hours with the waggon, Here we out-spanned, and took out our tin buckets; and, after forming a small dam by the side of the well, we posted three men to draw out the water: one went down to the surface of the water, another half-way down, while the other stood on the top. These pits are generally found with spars of wood fixed down the sides to support the drawers; and by this means we had all the water drained out, and thrown out into our temporary dam. Our guide informed us, that we should be four days without water: so, after filling our kegs and water-sacks, the oxen and horses were brought up to drink, and very little did they leave remaining. On the 11th, we resumed our *trek*, and, having the morning moon, we inspanned at four A.M. After four days' hard driving, from daylight till sunset, allowing only two hours for outspanning, we came to the Dowtley, a distance of eighty miles from the last well. On hard ground a waggon may travel a hundred miles in four days, but here we had heavy sand all the way. The Dowtley is a large pan with a good fountain, and several good pits with plenty of water. On our way to the Dowtley we shot several springbucks. These bucks are found where there is no water to be had, and so is the eiland, and the giraffe. Our oxen suffered severely, the sand covering the felloes of the wheel. The days were warm; and, being without water, we thought the oxen would kill themselves when they again reached a fountain. After drinking, they lay down close to the water, every now and then getting up and taking a fresh drink: thus the poor animals continued nearly the whole of the next day. We gave them a day's rest, and on the 16th we again entered on our journey.

"According to our guide's account, we had five days to travel without water: so, after carefully filling our water-utensils, we started at ten A.M. After three days' ride, we struck upon a kraal of natives possessing sheep and goats, also a field of Kafir melons which they had cultivated: this was quite unexpected. They received us in a friendly manner, and gave us a drink of goats' milk, and as many melons as we could carry away. The first inquiry we made was for water: they gave us to understand that there was no water within two days' *trek* from this. We then asked them where they obtained water for their sheep and goats: the chief pointed to the field of melons, and said, 'There is our water.' I found the natives of this kraal very reserved. I could get but little information from them respecting the route to the Lake, and they raised great obstacles to our success. As the waggon proceeded, I took my horse and made a huntsman-like search for water, and thus took a circuit of fifteen miles, but could not trace any path that appeared likely to lead to water. I now felt satisfied that their goats and sheep ate the melons as a substitute for water. We pushed on another day, this being again the fourth day without finding water; and, having travelled through heavy sand, several oxen dropped in the yoke. On the fifth day the oxen could pull the waggons no further, being quite overcome with thirst; and, according to information received from the Bushmen, the water was still a day's ride with the waggon.

"On Sunday, the 20th, while preparing to push forward with the oxen, horses, and boys to seek for water, two Bushmen made their appearance, but on our approach they fled. Maher and myself, being mounted, started after them; but, being mounted on thirsty steeds, we had some trouble before we could gain on these fleet-footed fellows. They often drive-in the eiland. We at length succeeded in bringing one to a stand. Having some beads and tobacco in my pocket, I presented him with a little of each, and coaxed him to my waggon, which he appeared to approach with great reluctance. He understood a little Sechuana; and, with the assistance of my interpreter, he gave us to understand that he would show us a field of melons not far off. I at once resolved to drive my oxen and horses to the spot, leaving two men in charge of the waggons. The remainder of us set off, accompanied by the Bushman, who took us about ten miles. The oxen then began to raise their heads to windward, and soon after to double their pace: shortly afterwards they increased their speed to a trot. At first they only came to an odd melon here and there; five or six oxen, joined by a horse or two, disputing a bite at the first they came to; and so they continued to do until the patch of melons became thicker. I soon had the satisfaction of seeing my oxen spread out and feeding the same as if they were on a field of sweet green grass. By sunset I felt satisfied that my oxen and horses were full, and their thirst quenched, so that we returned to the waggons that night.

"Early in the morning we inspanned, the oxen greatly refreshed. Leaving the boys to come on with the waggons, Maher and myself mounted to go in quest of game. We shot a giraffe, and drove-in an eiland. The waggons having travelled fifteen miles or five hours, we found them outspanned in the midst of a patch of melons. I was quite delighted to see our oxen and horses in the midst of a field of such an invaluable article in the Desert, and ourselves in possession of several slices off the ribs of a fat giraffe, while all hands were busy skinning a fine eiland, which we had driven in, and which was stretched out alongside of us. With a roaring fire, and ravenous appetites, being somewhat impatient for a mouthful, the kettle and gridiron were soon on the fire, and ere long the fat was dripping, and blazing away in the fire. We only grumbled because our gridiron, not being one of the improved kind, would not enable us to catch the fat; I must also add, that our kettle was but half full, for we had been on half allowance since the day before, on account of one of our *vatjes,* 'water-casks,' having lost the stopper, got upset, and the water, as a matter of course, ran out. Still we were as happy as kings after our feast. The eiland was cut up into *biltong,* salted, and stowed into the waggon. We then inspanned, and pushed on half the night; rode five hours, fifteen miles. Resumed our *trek* early next day, and at twelve noon reached the Kang, a large salt-pan with wells of water, very salt. This was now the seventh day without water, since we left the Dowtley.

"There is a nearer course from the Dowtley to Kang; but, for some reason best known to himself, our guide took us a long way round. The water being unfit for drinking purposes, except for the oxen, we dug a pit at the northern side of the pan, and found good fresh water, but so scanty that it took us a day and night to fill our water-casks. Our guide now pointed out two ways by which we could proceed. To the west, he said, we could get to the Lehutito, where we should find good water. By his account he made it four days' journey, which we calculated must be near ninety miles, and much out of our course. The other route being N.W., and in a more direct line, we adopted it: although without water, we trusted to the chance of finding melons. We had now to prepare for a journey of fourteen days without water. This appeared to us rather long; consequently our powder canisters were emptied, a number of water-sacks, and even ostrich egg-shells, were all brought into use, besides our half-aum, and two five-gallon kegs.

"Before we left the Kang, a number of Griquas arrived with several waggons, also endeavouring to make their way towards the Lake. They had barely outspanned before we were visited by them. Among the rest was a petty captain belonging to Sentuhe, who seemed to have the most to say, and conducted the party. After conversing some time as to the privations they had gone through before reaching the Kang, broad hints were thrown out by them that they wished to accompany us. He said he knew the direction well, and would be of great assistance to us. I would much rather have declined their company, but I knew not how to avoid them. I remained there on the 24th. At coffee time the whole gang came towards us, and, squatting all around our fire, intimated that their coffee and tea were used up, and that they did not know what they should do without. After finishing two kettles of tea, with a due proportion of sugar, and begging a couple of *treksels*—as they called it—of tea, and some sugar, they inquired when I intended to move forward: 'To-morrow,' was my reply. Accordingly, on the 25th, our fourteen days' supply of water completed, and all stowed away in the waggon, we inspanned and made a move, leaving the Griquas and their party behind.

"We travelled twelve miles, and then outspanned. We had not, however, long unyoked, when the cracking of whips announced the coming of the Griqua train; and before we had time to take some refreshment, up they came and outspanned, and said, 'We are glad to have caught up with you, and will now try and keep up with you.' Seeing our kettle on the fire, and our *karbonatjes* well peppered and salted, and producing rather a savoury perfume, they preferred the squatting system. The boys announced the breakfast ready, and, anxious to delay as little as possible, we ordered the breakfast to be served up. Our kettle being rather small,—the larger one being stowed away to prevent our being too free with the water,—these worthies did not forget to hint that they feared they should not get a cup out of that small kettle, while others remarked, 'That does not look like the kettle you had on the fire yesterday.' 'No,' answered one of my servants who understood the Griqua language: 'the kettle you refer to cannot be brought into use before we have the good luck to reach the Lake; and I expect, before we go very far, we shall have no water for the small kettle.' 'And what will your master do then? A white man cannot do without tea and coffee: he will have to turn back.' 'Not so long as melons are to be found,' said the boy. They then begged a *treksel* of coffee, and went to their waggons. We breakfasted, and ordered the boys to inspan the oxen, and rode till ten o'clock at night.

"Pursued our journey early next morning, and reached the Lat Lake, a large salt-pan. Here we found a Ballalla kraal, with a large flock of bucks. They had cultivated a large field of Kafir melons. From them I purchased some milk-goats. I found that goats travel much better through the Desert than cattle, feeding, as they do, upon the leaves of the different plants and shrubs. The people also supplied us with some melons, for which I was thankful. These melons are very good in a thirsty land. Here our oxen got a few wild melons; and we remained that day, it being Sunday.

"Monday, at eight A.M., continued our *trek*. On the 25th we reached another kraal of natives, who had a flock of goats, and a field of melons. From them I managed to purchase a patch for my cattle. The rest of the field was guarded by a number of women; the oxen and horses were then driven in, and much trouble had the women to keep them within bounds. Before long the patch was laid bare, and then the women had no chance of restraining them. A rush to the forbidden field was the result. My boys were obliged to run to the women's assistance. The oxen were brought up, inspanned, and at four P.M. we were again on the move, in company with the Griqua train. We travelled till late at night, and in the morning found ourselves outspanned at a small native village. They also possessed goats and a few sheep, and fields of melons which they had cultivated. From them I could get but little information; but, after some little difficulty, we learnt from them that a small distance out of our course we might find some melons. After presenting a few beads to the head man of the village, he gave us a guide; and, after driving the oxen and horses ten miles in a westerly direction, we came to where the melons lay thick on the ground. The cattle, after feeding for three hours, began to lie down full and quite satisfied, which clearly proves the invaluable qualities of the melon as a substitute for water. We returned to the waggons, but did not reach them before dark.

"I now found out, through one of the Griqua party, that Ghamma, a man of some note among the Wanketses, and conductor of the Griqua train, had put all the obstacles in my way, by warning the Ballallas and Bushmen in the country not to give the white man any information as to water, distance, or course to the Lake; he even sent men far in advance for that purpose. After hearing all this, I made up my mind to leave them, and take a different course, let the result be what it might. Early in the morning we were again on the move, and by midnight reached a Ballalla kraal. I was now told that this was the last kraal we should see, and that we should now enter upon a country inhabited only by wild Bushmen. The natives here appeared to know well the course to the Lake, but I found them very reserved. I did my utmost to obtain a guide, but in vain. The head man of this little village replied: 'If you were alone with only your own waggons, I would give you a guide; but you are aware that the Wanketse chief is close behind you. He has sent some of his men to warn me, that if I dare to give you a guide, or even give you the least information about the road, he will destroy us. But, never mind, I will give your own guide all the information I can.'

"Determined not to travel with Mr. Ghamma and his party, after making a few presents to the captain of the village, I inspanned early on the 1st of July, and continued our course, which now became N.N.W. We rode all that day, and at sunset we reached a patch of melons. Here we halted for the night. Next morning, as usual, we were early on the move, our guide leading us all this day and a part of the next a N.W. course. On the afternoon of the 2nd of July he disappeared. This brought us to a dead stand-still; so we outspanned: by sunset he made his appearance. On inquiring of him where he had been, he said, 'I saw a Bushman, and ran after him, and he took me so far that I lost the spot where I had left the waggons.' In the morning we resumed our course, still N.W., and continued the same all day.

"On the morning of July 3rd, our guide seemed to wander: every now and then he climbed up some of the highest trees he could find, and at last brought us to a halt. We were now obliged to outspan. This being the second day without melons, Maher and myself immediately went in one direction in search of them, while some of our boys started in another. Maher and myself succeeded; and in the morning we inspanned, and directed our waggons to the spot where we had found them, and which we had some difficulty in finding again. Here we shot an eiland. All this time our guide was missing. By the neglect of our herds, we lost a fine horse which had been separated from the rest, and not seen afterwards. I heard after, from Griquas who followed my *trek*, that the horse went back, and, trying to get a drink of water at the Kang, fell into the pit, and there died; so the horse must have gone back about two hundred miles.

"On the 5th, our guide returned, and informed us that the last two days he had been leading us wrong, and wished we would remain until the train of Griquas came up. This we at once declined, but inspanned and proceeded. He then turned us from N.W. to N.E. for about fifty miles. Our course then became north. On the 6th the herds lost seven oxen, but we did not miss them till the 7th. Mr.

Maher and Hendrik, mounted on horseback, took a little water with them, and went in search of the lost oxen. After going back about twenty miles they fell in with the spoor, which they followed another fifty miles before they found them. It was by mere good luck that they escaped the Bushmen; for, had they fallen in with them, there had been no chance of their recovery. There being no melons for our oxen and horses, when Maher left us, and our water fast diminishing, we could not wait for him; so we pushed on.

"On the afternoon of the 7th we *trekked* until sunset, and then halted for the night, but still without melons; our oxen, of course, thirsty. I could not help thinking of Maher and Hendrik, who had gone in search of the lost oxen: fearing that they would greatly suffer from thirst, I filled two bottles with some water, and tied them with some biscuit in a handkerchief, and hung it to a tree near the waggon-track, so that they could not help seeing it: and it was very fortunate for them I did so; for their horses knocked up, and they were obliged to foot it, distracted with thirst. The third day they came to where I had slung the handkerchief. Old Hendrik, a keen-eyed Hottentot, caught sight of it first, and soon hauled it down and examined its contents, each taking a hasty drink; but they wisely reserved a little in each bottle, not knowing when or where they might overtake the waggons. On the 8th of July I reached a large and rather deep valley, called by the natives Mugube Magoolo. This was the first appearance of a valley we had met with since we left Sentuhe's. Here the recent spoor of elephants and rhinoceroses was for the first time seen. This valley stretches from N.W. to N.E., and in many seasons holds water. On the south side it is lined with heavy sand-hills. It was at this place where a party of Griquas, three years ago, were disappointed in finding water, and were obliged to abandon their waggons and oxen, and nearly lost their lives from thirst; but, fortunately, a shower of rain saved them. Their waggons were burned, and most of their oxen fell into the hands of the Bushmen.

"On the 9th we found a small patch of melons, barely sufficient for our wants. Here I examined our supply of water, and found that we had only sufficient for one day; and as our guide could not tell us when we would reach the first water, I measured it out by pints, and, by reducing each man to one pint per day, I found I could make it do for five days. My men were accordingly put on this allowance. The Totties could not understand this at first; but, with the assistance of a melon now and then, they managed tolerably well. I must mention that, in measuring out the water, I did not forget Maher and Hendrik. On the morning of the 10th I again filled two bottles with water, and tied them with some biscuit to a bush near our waggon-spoor. The bush being rather low, a lion, following our track, came on the handkerchief, tore it down, and, after rolling the bottles about, and scattering the few biscuits, swallowed a piece of cheese, and walked off. Late in the day we arrived at another valley; and, after travelling up its course for four miles, we struck off to the north, following an elephant's path, and halted for the night without any melons. Oxen tremendously thirsty.

"On the 11th we pursued our journey; and, having travelled about three miles, the path divided into two; one struck to the N.N.E., and the other N.N.W. Our guide followed the one leading N.N.W. We travelled all the day through thick and heavy sand; shot an eiland; and halted at night without any melons. Early on the 12th, continued our route through thick sand. This day we were again without melons. Our oxen now began dropping in the yoke; as fast as they dropped, we replaced them with fresh ones. On the 13th our oxen could scarcely bring on the waggons. I left the boys to come on the best way they could with the thirsty oxen, while myself and Prince, a native servant whom I had obtained from the chief Secheli, started in search of water, both of us mounted on thirsty horses. After riding two hours, we fell in with a few melons, which we gathered and gave to our horses, not forgetting ourselves. Off-saddled for half an hour, and feasted upon the melons. Up-saddled, and proceeded on our search.

"After riding twelve miles further, we struck on a place where the trees and bushes had some years since been cut down with axes. Prince remarked, 'It must have been old Sebiego's people that had done this, and we cannot be far from water now.' We pushed on through this place where the trees had been cut down, when all at once we fell in with a fresh rhinoceros spoor; and knowing that this animal never goes far from water, unless he is much hunted, which I knew was not the case here, we followed the spoor; though it gave us a great deal of trouble to do so, still we kept it, and found, as we proceeded, that the track was joined by another, until it led us to a foot-path where many fresh spoors were visible; and ere long we came upon several pits, but so scarce was the water, that we barely got enough for ourselves and horses. However, we went round to all, and found that by opening them we should be likely to succeed; and, to crown this success, we found that at a short distance to the west lay a fine field of wild melons. I immediately started Prince back to the waggons, to inform the people that relief was at hand; that we had found water. When he reached the waggons, a short halt was made. All the water was brought out of the waggons, and divided amongst them, and not a drop did they leave. While Prince went back to hurry on the waggons, I amused myself by opening one of the pits, which had been stopped up by Bushmen. While very busily throwing out sticks and stones, I perceived a rhinoceros coming towards the water, within fifty yards of me. My rifle being close at hand, I treated him to a bullet behind the shoulder; blowing and snorting he ran for about a hundred yards, with the blood streaming from his nostrils, when he tumbled over to rise no more.

"After working some time, I had the pit cleared to the depth of three feet. It was nearly sunset before the waggons arrived, and by that time I had obtained sufficient water for our immediate wants.

My people were so impatient, that, before unyoking the oxen, they ran to the pit and drank heartily; the oxen were then outspanned, and both they and the horses were driven to the melons, where the herds remained with them the whole of that night. 'Coffee!' was now the cry, and two kettles were accordingly brought out and filled; and ere long the fire was blazing away under both; and not many minutes elapsed before we were enjoying that refreshing beverage, in addition to our biscuit. The Bakuains and Wanketses, of whom I had eight in my service, stood the nineteen days without water, and not even a murmur escaped them. They did not ask for so much as one pint of water, but satisfied themselves with the melons. Early on the 14th of July I dispatched Alexander and Prince, two native servants, each with a led horse, some water, and provisions, in search of Maher and Hendrik, with directions to keep the waggon-spoor. They rode for about twenty miles, and found Maher and Hendrik sitting under a tree, taking rest. Of course the water met with a hearty reception; it was immediately taken from the horses, and the two thirsty men relieved. They had found the oxen; but their horses had both knocked up, and they were consequently obliged to foot it, greatly fatigued.

"After they had taken some refreshment, Hendrik and Alexander mounted the fresh horses, taking with them what water they had left, and went back to try and relieve the two knocked-up and thirsty horses; but they found one dead, and the other too far gone to leave any hope of its recovery: so both animals perished for want of water. Leaving Prince to come on slowly with the oxen, Maher mounted the horse I had sent to him, and at five P.M. he reached the waggons in safety. We felt rejoiced at having met again; he could not help remarking that the little water I had occasionally left on the waggon-track had saved them from perishing of thirst. They fully expected to find the waggons deserted; and were surprised that the oxen had pulled them such a distance, through the deep sand, without water, and with so few melons. On the 14th we were all busy clearing out the several pits; and by evening we had got a good supply of water. After having been nineteen days without drinking any thing, our oxen and horses were brought up, and driven to the water; but, having been in a good field of melons all day, they did not drink so much as we expected. The oxen were now nearly worn out, consequently we resolved to give them two days' rest. The Griquas and Mr. Ghamma again caught up with us; and we heard from some of them that they had found water two days ago, though we had found none. Mr. Ghamma was astonished to find us here, and said, 'You have travelled well, and beaten me.'

"We had now crossed a Desert of five hundred miles in breadth; which the scarcity of water, heavy sand, and a bad guide rendered no easy task. In many parts—

'Not a bird was to be seen,
And the stillness of death reigned over the scene.'

A deep and unceasing sand, covered with a kind of thin grass, and a low sort of hooked thorn, which often checked the oxen, continually lay before us, and greatly impeded our progress. Hundreds of Bushmen villages were scattered through the latter part of this Desert, but were all at this time deserted, some very recently: the smoke from their fires appeared in all directions. The country to the west and north-west of our route was inhabited by them. While the Griquas were at the pits, they managed to catch two of these Bushmen; they were fine strapping fellows, much superior to their southern brethren.

" The country to the W. and N.W., up to the Atlantic Ocean, is occupied by the Damaras, a powerful tribe, rich in cattle; they wear but very little clothing or covering of any kind. The country to the S.E. of them is inhabited by a horde of Corannas, under one Jonker Africander. This tribe often goes out on a foray against the Damaras, and succeeds in taking droves of cattle. A party of Baralongs and Batlaries from over the Vaal River, lately made a trading expedition to their country, and actually brought back two hundred head of cattle.

" On the 18th we left the pits, accompanied by the Griquas. Our course now became nearly east. Maher and myself mounted, and went in quest of game, and drove-in a fine fat eiland. We reached the Ganse late on the 19th. Here we found good and sufficient water for all our wants. Mr. Ghamma and his party shot two rhinoceroses: the horns they bartered to me in exchange for tea and coffee. On the 21st we continued our journey, leaving the Griqua train behind. We travelled twenty miles, and halted for the night in a field of melons. Early next morning we were again on the move, and fell in with a *borielle*, or black rhinoceros, and shot it. Here we unyoked the oxen for two hours, and took breakfast. Again we inspanned, and continued till four P.M., when we found a small pit with a little water, and halted for the night.

" Early on the 23rd we again pushed on; but had not gone far, when we came upon another well, containing sufficient water to fill our *vatjes*, (water-casks,) and enough for our horses; but the oxen got none; a few hours' work at the well would have procured us abundance, but we were anxious to push forward, and therefore started again immediately. Our guide wandered from the proper course as usual, consequently we were another day without water. We now regretted that we did not remain at the last well till we had opened it, and given the oxen water. Our oxen would not have suffered so much, had our guide directed us properly; for we should not then have been without water.

" On the 24th the forests through which we passed were so thick, that we were obliged to bring our axes into play, to clear a road for our waggons. After travelling eighteen miles, daylight was fast disappearing, and yet no signs of water; and we had again made up our minds to halt, and spend another night without finding any, when Alexander accidently noticed that one of our dogs appeared rather playful, and, after calling him, found him quite wet. This caused a general turn-out; and in a few minutes every one at the waggons, including Kafirs, stood round the dog, and found that he had, without doubt, been to water. A general search was made, and before long we found a *vley* of good water, about three hundred yards to the north of where we had stopped. The waggons were drawn up to the *vley*, and as each ox was unyoked he ran to the water. They were very thirsty. At supper-time the poor dog who had found the water was not forgotten; every one treated him to a piece of meat. On the 25th, having good water, and plenty of sweet grass, we remained at the *vley*. Maher, myself, and after-rider, saddled-up and went in pursuit of game. We had not gone far from the waggons, when we came upon another large *vley*, supplied by a good spring; many geese, ducks, and other wild fowl on its surface, and so deep that a horse might swim in it. This *vley* must contain water in the driest seasons.

"We had not long left the *vley*, when we observed a troop of giraffes quietly feeding, standing at a short distance from us. We rode up towards them; but, when within three hundred yards, they got scent of us, and made off. Our trusty steeds soon brought us up to their heels; for some few minutes we were hidden by the dust; ere long we were riding by their sides. We turned out two of the herd, and tried to drive them towards the waggons; but we soon perceived that their race was run; they got obstinate, and would go no farther: a bullet from each of our rifles laid them low. We then returned to the waggons. When our Bakuains and Wanketses heard of our success, they followed our horses' spoor to where the giraffes had been shot, and at midnight returned loaded with flesh. On the 26th we continued our course. The country hereabouts must have been visited with heavy and late rains, for all the *vleys* were full of water. Far in the horizon we now observed a blue speck; but as the sun passed the meridian, it gradually disappeared, and at last we lost sight of it altogether. We travelled on until ten o'clock at night, and then halted at a pool of rain-water. Maher and myself, expecting game, lay in wait at the edge of the water; we had not waited long, when we saw two objects approaching, which turned out to be rhinoceroses coming to drink. We waited until they gave us the chance of giving them a broadside, when both of us fired at one; wheeling round, they both set off, the one severely wounded.

"On the 27th, at an early hour, we were again on the move; and as the sun showed its rays above the horizon, a chain of hills distinctly appeared in the distance. At two A.M. we unyoked the oxen for two hours, breakfasted, again inspanned, pushed on, and at five P.M. reached the foot of the hills, where we found a *vley* of rain-water. We unyoked for two hours. I took my spy-glass, and climbed to the top of one of the hills to look out for the Lake; but, the day being far gone, my glass was not powerful enough for the distance, which was, by our guide's account, thirty-five miles. At seven o'clock in the evening we again moved on, and continued until ten o'clock at night. We inspanned early on the following day, with the hope of reaching the Lake about sunset. We had not proceeded far, before we fell in with the spoor of three bull elephants. Leaving the waggons to push on, with instructions to the drivers to reach the Lake if possible, Maher and myself, with two after-riders, and three of our Bakuains, followed on the spoor of the elephants, which took us about twenty miles to the westward, where we found that a number of Bushmen had also fallen in with the spoor, far ahead of us, and had dispersed them; so the result of our day's work proved fruitless.

"We then gave up the chase, and off-saddled for an hour. After saddling-up we went in search of the Lake; shot a rhinoceros; the sun went down, and yet no sign of the Lake. We again pushed on; and, long after dark, we for the first time heard the sound of the mighty waters. The sound at first put me in mind of the distant sea. By ten o'clock at night we reached its banks, which are rather boggy, and being thickly covered with reeds, and very dark at the time, we had some trouble to get to the water. However, we succeeded at last; and, after we, as well as our horses, had taken a hearty drink, we went in search of our waggons. Seeing a light at a distance, we made for it, and found it to be a kraal containing sheep, goats, and a few cattle; to our surprise, we found our herdsman and horses here. On inquiring of the herdsman where the waggons were, he replied, 'I cannot say; the horses took fright about the middle of the day, ran off, and I followed them.' The horses were well secured on account of the lions being rather troublesome. We off-saddled and remained at this place for the night; got a drink of milk, made a good fire, and lay down for the night; having nothing to cover ourselves, we found it very cold. Long before day-light we were up sitting round the fire, impatient for the appearance of the sun.

"At dawn of day, we were in the saddle in search of our waggons. We rode along the shore of the Lake for about six miles to the S.E., where we found them outspanned. They had reached the Lake about ten o'clock at night, at its most southern point. One of the waggons stuck fast in a kind of quicksand, and we had some trouble in extricating it. We remained here the whole of the 29th and 30th, to give our now jaded oxen a little rest. Maher and myself, with an after-rider, mounted our horses and took a ride round the Lake, from W. to N., until we struck the river Teougha. This took us four hours and a half, (about twenty-seven miles,) from the point where the waggons stood. We touched at a Makowa village, on the Teougha River. The Natives received us in a very friendly manner, and gave us corn for our horses. We made inquiries as to whether there was a passage round the Lake to the Batuane village, or Sebitoane's country. 'No,' was the reply, 'you cannot cross the Teougha; there is no drift. The Teougha is about thirty to forty yards wide, and eight feet deep, with a rapid current, and large reedy swamps stretching out far and wide in every direction, which entirely obscure the river; consequently you can only approach it at a very few points.'

"Not feeling satisfied as to there being no drift, so soon as our horses had eaten their corn, we saddled-up, and went in search of one, being determined to find our way down the river as far as its junction with the Lake. The many reedy swamps greatly impeded our progress; and, as night overtook us, we were obliged to off-saddle, and halt for the night. Surrounded by swamps, we felt the night rather chilly. Early next morning we continued our course. By nine A.M. we succeeded in making our way through the reeds and marshes, and found that the Teougha here extended to more than two miles in width, and that at a mile further down it supplied the Lake with an immense sheet of water. The noble river before us here proved a magnificent sight; and many of the Lake bucks, of which I shot two fine specimens, capering about, enlivened the scene. We now determined on wading through the river; and several Makowas came up, and did their best to prevent us from attempting to cross, saying, ' The water is deep, and full of crocodiles.' However, we would not be stopped. We waded through the river, and found it in the deepest part only three feet in depth, with a sandy bottom, hard enough for waggons to cross. We were delighted at our success, and I immediately sent Alexander, our after-rider, back, to bring up the waggons.

" The Teougha enters the Lake almost due north; but as it ascends, its course inclines to the west. Bakowas dwell on the banks of the river. They build their villages among the reeds; and possess canoes, huts, lines, and harpoons. Although they grow corn, still they live principally on fish, and often harpoon the sea-cow. Their robust and healthy appearance proves that they live well. Hordes of Bushmen also inhabit the Teougha and its vicinity. Our waggons arrived on the 2nd of August, without our Wanketse guide. He told Alexander that the chief of the Lake would certainly kill him, if he dared to take us round to the north of the Lake. He accordingly left the waggons, and proceeded by a different route to Lethulitebe, chief of the Batawana town, to inform him that he had brought the white man to the Lake, and would still have guided him to them; but, like most men, he would sometimes follow his own course, and the waggons had gone round by the Teougha. This startled the chief, and accordingly he dispatched a party to turn us back, and bring us the way our guide wished us to go.

"Early on the 3rd of August we inspanned, and commenced fording the river. Our first waggon got over well, but the other stuck fast in the sand. This was the fault of the driver, who held still too long, and gave the waggon-wheels time to sink into the bed of the river. We unyoked the span of oxen in the first waggon, and put both spans to the waggon that was stuck fast; and by the united exertions of twenty-four oxen, we got the second waggon extricated; and by ten o'clock A.M. we were across all safe. We now pushed on for the Batawana town; and on the 5th of August, at six P.M., reached it. The party the chief had sent after us, finding we had already crossed the Teougha, relinquished their pursuit. The N. and N.W. shores of the Lake are lined with a chain of sand-hills of some height. The shore on this side is open and free from reeds, and can be approached to the edge of the water; for it is not boggy as in many other parts. From the top of one of the sand-hills we had a beautiful view of the broad water. Below and around us stood many magnificent trees, including the mimosa, which adorn the scene. With the assistance of a telescope, I may venture to say, I almost feel satisfied that I could see the trees all round the Lake, from the point where my waggons first touched the shore. I travelled round north to the Batawana town; and, reckoning by my watch, I made the distance, as near as possible, sixty-five miles. The remainder of the distance has been travelled by other parties, who calculate it to be fifty miles. This would make the Lake one hundred and fifteen miles in circumference, and fifty-seven and a half miles in length, and about twelve miles in breadth.

" As we approached the village of the chief Lethulitebe, he sent three men to conduct us to a spot for our encampment. We had scarcely unyoked our oxen, when I received a message from the chief, to the effect that he was anxious to see me. I accordingly paid him a visit, accompanied by Andries, my interpreter. The chief's messenger guided us to the village, which we entered by a long and narrow path, very winding, and wattled on both sides. This brought us to the *gotla*, or ' council-chamber,' an open spot or square in the centre of the town, where all public business is generally transacted. In all villages where a chief of any note resides, you will find the *gotla*. Here I found the chief seated with his councillors. After greeting his highness, I presented him with a cloak decorated with about four gross of glittering brass buttons; for which he thanked me and seemed pleased. He then asked me from whence I came, and many other questions, which I answered. He seemed astonished that we had succeeded in reaching him through the Great Kalaghare Desert. He said, ' I was not aware that white people could cross the Desert in waggons. When I heard of your being in that direction, I sent a party to meet you, to see who you were; but they did not fall in with you. I am not pleased at your coming round N'gami ' (the Lake) ' to my residence, a route which I have forbidden. There is only one way by which I am accustomed to see travellers, and by that way only I expect them. I find you have every appearance of being friendly visitors, and therefore I will not say much on the subject.'

" The interview now being over, I bid him good day and returned to my waggons. Dinner—which consisted of very good rhinoster and giraffe steaks—being prepared, the chief not having offered me anything to eat, I felt rather hungry, and accordingly ordered it to be dished up immediately. While we were sitting at our meal, the chief made his appearance with a number of followers. I offered him a stool, and he sat down, his followers squatting around him. He did not give us time to invite him to dinner, but exclaimed, ' *Nama u enkile eona e la monate,*'—' That meat you have there must be very good;' at the same time, stretching out his long arms, he laid hold of the dish, and, placing it on his knees or lap, after looking round, and dealing out some to his men behind him, he very summarily finished the remainder. I then poured out a basin of coffee for him, which I sweetened agreeably to my taste: he took a mouthful, put the basin down, and asked for the sugar-basin, which was of course handed to him, when he immediately emptied its contents into his coffee, stirring it well, until it became nothing but a basin of treacle, which he swallowed with a due proportion of soaked biscuit. After finishing it, he said, 'I like the white man's honey better than ours.' He now appeared anxious to know what we had in our waggons, and said he would like to trade with us. On showing him our beads, brass wire, and other articles, he seemed pleased at seeing so many varieties. He said, 'It is now *perimela*,'—'the sun is down,'—'put your goods away: I will come over to-morrow.'

"Early next morning he arrived, accompanied by many followers, with some tusks of ivory; and a greater Jew I never had to deal with. The day was nearly gone before the bargain was closed, and the ivory secured. All this time our waggons were surrounded by at least a hundred spectators; and when the market was over, and the crowd dispersed, we found that we had lost a bundle of clothes containing two pairs of trousers, three shirts, a jacket, and waistcoat, besides another good waistcoat of mine, in the pocket of which was my compass, the only one I had. A search and every inquiry was made, but of no avail. I then sent to the chief to acquaint him with my loss, and requested his assistance in recovering it. He replied, that we ought to have taken better care of our goods. I offered him a reward if he would but find the compass, and return it to me, but it was not to be found. I felt the loss of it very greatly on my way to Sebitoane's country.

"One morning the chief Lethulitebe came down to our waggons, with some followers, leading a horse which he had purchased from some traveller. He said, 'I have brought down this horse to show you; and I wish to purchase one from you: it must be a horse that can run well.' My horses were soon brought up, and I pointed him out a good quiet pony: he asked me the price, and I told him. He then said, 'If it can beat mine, I will give you your price.' Jockeys were selected, and the course pointed out was about a mile long. The horses started: pony took the lead, and won easily. He sent for the ivory, and the bargain was concluded. He next required a bridle and saddle, which I also sold him. He was very much pleased, and wanted to ride his new horse; the horse was accordingly saddled; the chief mounted; his feet were placed in the stirrups, and the reins put into his hands; all this time he had two men holding the horse by the bridle. It was full ten minutes before he was ready; the horse was at length led a little way, and then let go. Pony began to trot towards his companions, who were feeding a short distance from the waggons: the chief let go the reins, and clung with both hands to the saddle, lying flat on the horse's back. The loose horses, being astonished, no doubt, to see such an awkward rider, lifted up their heads, and began capering and prancing at almost full speed; pony, as a matter of course, followed, and, seeing his companions rather playful, followed their example, and took a part in the performance. The first BUCK he made laid his rider prostrate: the ground, however, being sandy, he was not much hurt. The horse was caught, and brought up to the waggons: when a consultation was held, and it was decided that 'the horse must be taken to the village, fed with Kafir corn, and kept there for three days; then he will become tame and more accustomed to us; but now he only knows the white man!' The horse was accordingly taken up to the village; and, on the third day, he was brought down by the chief already saddled, with the pommel hindmost. The bridle the chief carried in his hands, and requested one of my boys to put it on for him; the boy then bridled the horse, and altered the saddle. He then sent for his old horse, and asked me to allow one of my men to ride with him, at the same time requesting me to tie up all my horses, lest he should meet with the same disaster as before. I then called Hendrik, who mounted with him, first warning him not to go faster than a walk. After an hour they returned; and the chief, quite delighted, said he should soon learn to ride.

"Finding him in such a good humour, I thought it a good opportunity to intimate to him my intention of proceeding to Sebitoane's country, and to obtain a guide from him. In reply to my request, he said, 'You cannot go to Sebitoane's; the *tsetse* will kill all your oxen, and you and your people will catch the sickness. Besides, Sebitoane has no ivory, and there are very few elephants in his country.' I told him I believed all he had said; but that I would risk it, if he would furnish me with a guide. After a great deal of talk, he at last promised me a guide, provided I would remain with him a few days longer: this I agreed to do. He asked me where Mr. Oswell and Dr. Livingstone were, and when Mr. Oswell was coming to see him again. I told him that I thought Mr. Oswell had gone over the 'great water' to England. He said, 'Should you see him, tell him he must come one day and see me again.'

"I found fish very plentiful at the Lake; we were well supplied while there. The Bakowas brought us an abundant supply every day for a few beads. On the 11th of August I went to the chief, and told him that I was anxious to start for Sebitoane's, and that I should like to move in two days' time; at the same time reminding him of his promise to give me a guide. He replied, 'You are determined then to go. I know I have given you my word to furnish you with a guide; but we must first agree about the payment. You must give me gunpowder and lead; for you know that you are on my side of the river, and that you cannot reach Sebitoane's country without crossing the Tamalukan; and *that* you cannot do without my canoes.' All this I was well aware of, but refused to pay him in powder and lead, on the grounds that I had but a scanty supply, but would pay him in other articles. However, nothing would do but the powder and lead; so I was at last reluctantly compelled to give him ten pounds of powder and two bars of lead. Even then he did not seem satisfied, so five pounds of beads were added, and all was settled, and we got every thing ready

for a start the following day. On the 13th of August I started with a
waggon and twelve oxen, accompanied by a driver, leader, interpreter,
two Backmanes, and the guide; leaving Mr. Maher in charge of a
waggon, thirty-six oxen, my horses, and the remainder of my people.

"At eleven P.M. we inspanned, and rode twelve miles; and outspanned on the banks of a small stream of clear water, the surface of
which was covered with hundreds of wild fowl of various kinds, of which
I bagged thirteen ducks. There were beautiful trees of great height,
which added greatly to the beauty of the scene. We again inspanned
and pushed on, continuing up the stream for six miles, and then halted
for the night. Our waggon was drawn up under a large and magnificent tree. This stream is called by the natives the Gonier. Early on
the 14th we were again on the move. We now crossed the stream,
and in the course of the day had to cross several other streams.
In passing through one of them, my waggon stuck fast; great
exertions were made to extricate it, but without effect. In this
predicament we remained all night. A Bushman village being near
at hand, I went over and got fourteen of them to come to our
assistance. My boys took the axe, and chopped down several spars,
with which we succeeded in lifting the wheels, and, with the
assistance of the Bushmen and oxen, all united, we managed to
extricate it by eleven P.M.

"After rewarding the Bushmen for their assistance, we proceeded,
and crossed two more streams, the last being nearly a hundred yards
in width, and four feet deep. All these streams were called by the
name of Gonier. The last one we crossed is the principal stream;
the others are caused by the annual rise and overflow of the rivers.
We continued our course up this stream all day, and did not halt till
the evening. About midnight I awoke, and, after lying some time
listening, I heard a noise rather familiar to my ears; I got up and
awoke the boys, went a few yards from the waggons and listened attentively; I then distinctly heard that the noise was made by elephants.
The night being dark, we could not exactly tell on which side of the
river they were. But at daylight in the morning, leaving the leader in
charge of the waggon, myself and the driver, with a number of Bushmen who had followed our waggon, went towards the spot from
whence the noise had proceeded in the night. We found the spoor of
a small troop of cow elephants, and followed it for about three miles
up the river. The spoor then crossed the river, which we waded
through. The water was about four feet deep. We followed the
spoor for five miles further without seeing any thing of them, when
all at once we came in sight of eleven cow elephants within a stone's
throw of a large patch of reeds, growing in deep water, and the
ground around very boggy. We approached them as quietly as possible, but a slight puff of wind blew from us towards them; consequently
they got our scent: lifting up their trunks, and making a shrill noise,
they dashed into the reeds. This I anticipated, and, running as fast as
I could, just arrived in time to send the contents of both barrels of

my eight-to-the-pound smooth-bore gun into the stern of the hind-most cow.

"They were now completely obscured in the reeds. I sent the Bushmen round to make a noise, and told them to try and drive them to our side, while myself and the driver entered some short distance into the reeds; but soon found that we could get no farther, the water becoming deep and even muddy. We stood here for some time, wait-ing to see whether the Bushmen would succeed in driving them towards us, when two dogs unperceived by us got to the elephants, and presently we heard a bark from a dog, then a shrill trumpeting from the elephants, and down they bore upon us. We were obliged to clear the way in haste; but being deep in reeds and mud, we had some difficulty in doing so, and keeping in front of them, for the dogs were pushing on behind. They came close up to the edge of the reeds, one cow coming almost out; we had two good shots at her, putting both bullets into her ribs. With a loud trumpet-like noise she dashed back, and became separated from the rest. The dogs, finding she was wounded, kept to her. We tried hard to get another shot at her, but the reeds were so thick that we could not for some time get sight of her, till at last the enraged elephant made a charge at one of the dogs. The dog clearing his way out, she followed him till she was clear of the reeds, and stood with outspread ears. Her shoulders and head were now exposed; I levelled my gun, and took aim at her fore-head, fired, and laid her prostrate.

"While we were standing round the cow, making remarks on her death, a Bushman came running up, beckoned to us, and then ran off. We followed as fast as we possibly could; he took us about a mile, when another Bushman came up nearly out of breath, took me by the hand, and, leading me to a *vley* of rushes and reeds, pointed into it. On looking into the reeds I saw the backs of two bull elephants, standing motionless as statues, with the exception of the moving of their ears; but I could not get a glimpse of either of their shoulders, nor of any vital part at which to take aim. For some time we stood watching them; but, the day fast declining, we had no time left for further consideration; so levelling the gun at the back of one of them, and drawing down the muzzle, as I thought, low enough for his shoulder, I fired, and the ball told loudly; they both wheeled round and rushed deeper into the reeds. Numbers of Bushmen now kept coming up and closing round the reeds; they brought some dogs with them, and three of these daring Bushmen went in and encouraged the dogs until they came in contact with the elephants. The trumpeting of the elephants at once told us that the dogs were at them; dashing at the dogs, and making their shrill trumpet-like noise all the time, and cracking and trampling down the reeds, so they continued for more than an hour. The sun was now nearly setting, and we were afraid we should have to leave them; but fortunately a Bushman arrived with some fresh and plucky dogs. They dashed into the reeds, and tormented the wounded bull so much, that they several times brought him within gun-shot of us. Not an opportunity did we allow to escape, and soon put two bullets into him: at length the sun was all but down, when he made a charge at a dog, and thus gave me an opportunity of putting a ball into him which broke his shoulder, and brought him down with his head resting on his tusks.

" A Bushman, who was close to me at the time, gave a loud halloo, and in less than ten minutes many of his companions crowded around the elephant. Some of them ran up and stuck their assagais into him; the enraged animal, endeavouring to plunge upon his assailants, through his shoulder being broken, fell forward, under the weight of his body, and there lay prostrate. Three more shots finished his career. The sun being set, we bivouacked there for the night. We cut down a quantity of grass for our bedding, and made our supper off some elephant flesh. I was greatly amused at the Bushmen, who continued the whole night cutting away at the elephant; every now and then a dispute arose amongst them as to who should have the best piece of meat. Many roaring fires were blazing all around, and large quantities of elephant's flesh roasting at each; so the Bushmen continued feasting all night. In the morning I found they had got the upper tusk of the elephant extracted; but the lower one lay deep in the mud and water, and was not got out until near eight o'clock in the morning. The tusks being now extracted, four Bushmen accompanied us back to the waggon, two of them carrying the ivory. We found the cow elephant, which we had previously shot, entirely cut up, and more than half of it carried away: the trees around were red with the flesh which they had hung up to dry. The ivory had been already extracted and sent to the waggon: so we proceeded on our way, and reached the waggon about two P.M. The leader had prepared us a good dinner and plenty of coffee, so we sat down and made a hearty meal. The day being now far gone, and the driver and myself rather fatigued, we lay down and had a good sleep.

" Early on the 17th we continued our journey for four miles farther up this river (the Gonier); we then left it, and passed through a dense forest, which occasionally obliged us to use the axe. Travelled eight miles, and struck upon another river about twenty-five yards wide, and four feet deep, called by the natives the Ingotego. Here we outspanned for an hour, pushed on again, and halted for the night without water. Early next day we were again on the move, rode for about six miles, and came to another fine little river; it flowed rapidly, and was about sixty yards in width, and in some parts very deep. It is called by the natives *Mazeppa Petsie*, or, in plain English, ' Horse-dung.' It derives this name from the quantity of quagga-dung brought down by it when flooded. We crossed it about three hundred yards above its junction with the Tamalukan. The drift was deep, and the stream rapid.

" After crossing the river, we passed through a small but thick forest; and, striking the bank of the Tamalukan, continued up its course for ten miles. Here we were met by three Bakowas, who stated that their canoes were waiting for us; and, after proceeding a mile farther, we accordingly found three canoes ready to paddle us over.   We unyoked the oxen, took the waggon to pieces, and by sunset our waggon and goods were safely landed on the opposite side; the oxen swam through the river.   The country between the Tougha and Tamalukan has every appearance of being a complete swamp.   As far as the eye could reach, nothing but water and reeds appeared in view, except some little islands, formed by dark forest-trees.   The whole of this country is more or less infested with the poisonous fly *tsetse*, and travelling through it with an ox-waggon is undoubtedly impracticable.

" We continued our course up the Tamalukan for fifty miles; then, leaving that river, entered a sandy country thickly covered with a grey and weather-beaten looking forest from sixty to seventy miles long. In this forest there are several *vleys* or pools of muddy water; it is consequently frequented by buffaloes, rhinoceroses, and other wild animals that drink at the *vleys*.   One night, as we were outspanned at one of these *vleys*, I lay watching till about midnight, when a buffalo came to drink within fifteen yards of me.   I fired at him, but without knowing the result till the next morning, when the natives followed his blood spoor, and found him dead.   It was a fine old bull.

" On the 25th of August we reached the Mobabe, a large swamp about ten or twelve miles in width.   Many small villages, inhabited by Bakowas, Bushmen, and others, are situated on its banks.   The country around the Mobabe is in many parts infested with the *tsetse*, or ' poisonous fly.'   The guide I obtained from the chief of the Lake, here refused to proceed farther, and turned back; so Majando, head man of one of the Mobabe villages, now became our guide to Sebitoane's country.   He took us round the swamp; and, after travelling for eighteen miles, we halted near a native village.   After unyoking the oxen, I went up to the village, and found a number of natives sitting round their fires, roasting mice; this they accomplished by fixing them on sticks, which they stuck in the ground in a slanting position over a slow fire.   They feasted upon these mice all night.   Next morning we resumed our journey, and entered on a large, level, and boundless plain, on which there was little or no grass, with the exception of here and there an odd patch very rank and coarse, more like reeds than grass; yet hundreds of the blue gnoo, the sasabe, and quagga were to be seen passing in long files before our waggon.   Of these we bagged three gnoos, two sasabes, and a quagga, of which our native followers made good use: little was left for the vultures.   It took us six hours to travel across this plain, after which we reached another village; but finding the inhabitants had to bring water from a distance of about five miles, I declined stopping for the night, but unyoked the oxen for an hour.   When the moon rose, we inspanned, and pushed on until twelve o'clock at night.

" Early next day we started again; and, after travelling nearly the whole day, found that the water was still a considerable distance off, and the oxen worn out by the deep sand through which they had pulled the waggon, besides being greatly weakened by the bite of the *tsetse*. I outspanned, and taking Prince, my Bakuain boy, and several other natives, and leaving the driver and leader in charge of the waggon, set off with the oxen to the water. After driving them about ten miles they suddenly came to a stand, lifted up their heads, and began sniffing the air. One of the natives went forward, and immediately returned, exclaiming, ' *Shugoro!*' I ran forward, and the moon shining brightly enabled me to see a rhinoster standing directly in our path. On my approach he trotted a few yards, and then stood. I levelled my gun, fired, and made a lucky shot, considering it was night : the ball, entering behind the shoulder, passed through the head. He ran a short distance, and then, grunting like a pig, rolled over to rise no more. A fire was immediately kindled, and the natives who accompanied us soon began cutting away at the carcase with the full intention of remaining there for the night, and requested me to do so also. My oxen having been already two days without water, it was not very likely I should accede to their request ; so, after a great deal of remonstrating, I got two of them to guide us to the water, and after travelling five miles farther we reached the Tarrara, a *vley* of good water. Here I remained all the next day, shot a roan antelope, and at sunset started back again to where we had left the waggon.

" On the 29th, my oxen being in rather better condition, we inspanned them, and brought the waggon to the water, where we remained two days, during which time I sent two messengers to acquaint Sekeleto, now chief of the Makalolo, Sebitoane's tribe, that I was on my way to visit him. My oxen were now rapidly falling off, and were so weak that they could barely pull the waggon. On the 30th the messengers returned with instructions from Mataljana, a petty captain under Sekeleto, who has charge of the southern part of that great country, under the sway of the Makalolo, that I was to come on as speedily as possible. He also sent three men to meet me. The distance was reported to be a hard day's *trek*, and to be also greatly infested with the *tsetse*.

" On the 31st we started at five o'clock P.M., in order, if possible, to get through this dangerous country by night, and so to avoid the further destruction of my cattle by the poisonous fly. We pushed on, and passed the Zonda by night. Here my first ox died. In the morning we still found ourselves amongst the fly, and it was not until twelve o'clock at noon, that we reached the river Chobe. I was met in the most friendly manner by Mataljana, who immediately made preparations to get his canoes ready to convey my oxen across to the north side of the river Chobe, where they would be safe from the *tsetse* fly. It is singular that this river alone divides the country infested by these destructive flies, the north side of the river being entirely free from them. The Makalolo are rich in cattle, which are all kept in the country north of the Chobe and other neighbouring rivers. My oxen were taken over the river safely, and kept there so long as I remained on the Chobe. I found two of Sekeleto's head men had arrived from the residence of that chief, to await my arrival, with instructions from their chief to inquire what I had got in my waggon, and whether I was a trader; if so, he would trade with me. As his messengers had to return, I availed myself of the opportunity for sending Prince and my Bakuain head man with a message and a present to his highness. They proceeded in a canoe, which was soon got ready and pushed off. The residence of the chief being about thirty miles distant down the river, it took them the whole day before they reached it.

"The third day Prince returned with several of Sekeleto's principal or confidential men; amongst whom was the father-in-law of the chief, who presented me with twelve buckets of Kafir corn, carefully put up in bark, worked together in the shape of a calabash. Each of these bark calabashes contained about a bucket of corn. He also presented me one of the same sort of calabashes filled with a kind of sweet earth-nut, a pot of good honey, and two slaughter oxen. These articles were all presented by the father-in-law of the chief: who at the same time stated that 'Sekeleto sent you this as a token of friendship; and being aware of the difficulty you must have had in penetrating into his country, he fears you must be hungry, and has therefore sent you food to eat;' and further that Sekeleto himself would be with me to-morrow. The whole of Sekeleto's men appeared pleased at meeting us. The chief did not arrive till late in the afternoon of the 5th. One canoe arrived first, bringing the intelligence that the chief would soon be here. Very shortly afterwards I perceived twelve canoes paddling up the river, all in a line, and in less than fifteen minutes the great chief landed with a considerable number of followers, and came up to my waggon. He was introduced to me by his father-in-law. After greeting him, I offered him a stool, and invited him to sit down. He is a young man of about twenty years of age. He was dressed in a pair of blue moleskin trousers, drab moleskin jacket, and broad-brim hat. He is far from good-looking, and has by no means a prepossessing appearance. He had but lately taken over the chieftainship from his sister, who ruled the tribe for some time after the death of her father, Sebi-toane. It appears that she, having taken a husband, thought it advisable to give up the government of the nation to her brother, who is now the chief. British manufactures find their way up to this country, both from the east and west coasts. I saw several of the natives dressed in print garments, also in blue-striped shirts. According to their account, they are frequently visited by the Mambari, a tribe living far to the west, and who bring down these manufactures, as well as guns and gunpowder; and, pointing to my waggon-chain, they stated that the Mambari also possessed chains like that. These articles they bring down for the purpose of bartering for slaves, in which traffic they are often successful. While I was staying on the Chobe I was visited by several natives differing in language from Sekeleto's people, such as the Nohukolumba, Batoka, and Borotse people. These tribes have already been ably described by Dr. Livingstone."—FRIEND OF THE SOVEREIGNTY.

This interesting and valuable Journal has not been published beyond this point. Taking into consideration the unsettled state of that district, and the absurd claims of the Trans-Vaal Boers to their own exclusive "right of road" in all the approaches to the Desert, Mr. M'Cabe evinced much prudence in withholding from the public the rest of his narrative. He did not proceed further north; but, after accomplishing his purpose, returned safely to the Colony with his waggon-loads of produce in ivory, skins, curiosities, &c. The value of these articles, and of this trade, may be conceived from the fact, that these loads realized some £1,300 in the market, if my memory serves me correctly.

The reader must carefully observe that this journey was through the Kalaghare Desert, or rather on the eastern extremity of it, as from this point it stretches far west, and is very thinly peopled in many parts by native tribes: consequently European colonization cannot extend farther in that direction. The other route to these distant regions is probably nearer, and the parties travelling are not exposed to similar hardships. But it would be highly dangerous for parties to attempt it, who had not a good general knowledge of the country, and who did not understand how to manage in reference to oxen and people, and the best mode of arranging so as to provide against all the casualties which might arise. Without this practical knowledge they would be in danger of dying in the Desert from want of water, or of their cattle dropping, unable any longer to bear drought and fatigue. How great must have been the powers of enduring thirst, hunger, and labour, possessed by Mr. M'Cabe's oxen, in this unexplored wilderness! How merciful and wise are the arrangements of that Gracious Being, who, in the order of His providence, provides the cooling watery melon in the midst of the drought and the burning sand of the Desert, by which the most pressing wants of man and beast are supplied, and life is sustained! These melons must consist chiefly of vapour, or watery particles supplied by the atmosphere; which, when once imparted, are retained, and serve the most valuable purposes.

It must also be noted, that, at the point attained, the *tsetse*, or "poisonous fly," and the prevalence of deadly fever, have determined the bounds of colonization in that direction; and we find this natural demarcation existing across the whole space of the continent, in that latitude, from the Mozambique Channel on the east, to the Atlantic or Southern Ocean on the west.

AN ACCOUNT OF THE DAMARA COUNTRY.

THE following interesting account of the country lying betwixt the Lake and the western coast, with the different tribes of inhabitants, their manners, &c., I copy from the "Blue Book," as given by Mr. Kolbe :—

"THAT country on the western coast of Africa, which commences from the 25th degree of south latitude, and which is generally called Damara-land, is inhabited by a nation divided into two principal tribes, the Ovaherero and Ovampantera. This country is bounded on the west by the Atlantic Ocean ; its northern and eastern boundaries, however, are not yet ascertained. The bordering nations to the south are the Great Namaquas and the Hill Damaras ; which latter is a Negro race that speaks the Namaqua language. To the east is a nation called the Ovatjaona. It is this nation that lives on the coast of the newly discovered Lake. There are also tribes residing near this Lake which speak a dialect of the Damara language, as we learn from the discoverers of the Lake. To the north of the Damara country resides a nation called the Ovampo, a Negro race, living in a fertile country in large villages, and governed by a King. They work in trades, and have agricultural habits. Slaves are exported from amongst them. They have no clicks in their language ; and it so much resembles the Damara, that the two nations are able to converse with each other.

" To the south, Damara-land is hilly. The northern part consists of wide plains, covered with thorn-bushes, low shrubs, and grass. All the rivers are periodical : on their banks grow high and thick trees, chiefly of the acacia kind. Compared with Namaqua-land, the country is well watered. Besides mineral springs, wells are frequently found, which are dug by the natives ; so that the want of water is not felt in travelling.

" The rainy season commences about October, and lasts till March or April. The climate, during the remaining months, is very agreeable, being clear and bracing, though sometimes piercingly cold in the night.

" The country abounds in wild beasts. Lions, leopards, rhinoceroses, hyænas, buffaloes, giraffes, zebras, gnus, roe-does, and other kinds of antelopes, are found in great numbers.

" The Damaras are a numerous people, being, as we suppose, forty thousand in number. They belong to the Kafir race. Their appearance, habits, manners, religious ideas, and particularly the similarity of the construction of the two languages, place this fact beyond doubt. They are nomades, and have no agricultural habits ; but are very rich in cattle and sheep, on which they almost entirely live.

Some of the chiefs possess from six thousand to eight thousand head of horned cattle. On account of their few wants, (cattle supplying both food and clothes,) very little trade is carried on with other nations. Utensils, assagais, and other things made of iron, (which is much valued by them,) they procure from the Ovampo, and from the Colony, by means of the Namaquas.

" The Damaras are divided into tribes, each tribe being governed by a chief; who, again, has other inferior chiefs under him, that rule over villages containing from one hundred to four hundred people. They have no fixed laws ; but the chiefs, although they have the power of governing arbitrarily, yet venerate the traditions and customs of their ancestors ; so that tyranny is seldom heard of amongst themselves. The names of the richest and most powerful chiefs are, Katjokura, Omunaunda, Katjemaha, and Kahitzene. The latter is the most influential man among them ; he unites with good sense energy and bravery. He is respected and feared both by the Damaras and Namaquas. The tribes are constantly in a state of enmity with each other, and frequent wars take place between them. In battles between the Namaquas and the Damaras, the latter generally are beaten ; for they are not so well provided with fire-arms as their enemies, and betray much ignorance in conducting a war, and seem unacquainted with the disunion of the tribes. Their religion resembles that of the Kafirs and Bechuanas. They have no clear idea of a Supreme Being. Pointing to the north, they speak of Omukuru as the highest being they know of ; but whether he is considered a god, or only as their great ancestor, is uncertain. They practise circumcision, offer sacrifices of beasts, and pray to the shades of the dead. There are many sorcerers and rain-makers amongst them.

"About six years ago, the mission among the Damaras was commenced by the Rev. H. Hahn and the Rev. H. Kleinschmidt, of the Rhenish Society; and this Society has now two stations in that country, New Barmen and Otjimbinque, both situated on the right bank of the Swakop River. The first is presided over by the Rev. H. Hahn, and the other by the Rev. J. Rath. The time has been too short, and the preparatory works (such as acquiring the language, printing books, building, &c.) too many, for us to see much success ; but the work is encouraging : some hundreds of people attend the places of public worship, and send their children to the schools. Some of the Damaras are, at least outwardly, much improved ; so that we may cherish the hope that the work will become prosperous.

" The country lying between the limits of the Colony and Damaraland is inhabited by Namaquas and Hill Damaras. The names of the chiefs are : Araham, of Nisbet Bath ; Willem Fränjman, John Binkes, and Umap, of Fish River ; David Christian and Paulus Goliat, of Bethany ; Narup, chief of the Velds Choendragers ; Willem Zwarthoi, of Rehoboth ; Oasip, chief of the Red Nation ; Omral, of Elephant Fountain ; Frederik Willem, of Stehmen's Dorf at Walwich Bay ; and Jonker Africander, of Concordiaville. The highest estimate of the number of people governed by these chiefs is ten thousand; the country which they inhabit is so waste and barren, and the supply of water so small, that very little intercourse can be held with Damaraland and the Colony. The shortest and easiest communication is by way of Walwich Bay.

" (*Signed*)   F. N. KOLBE,
" *In the service of the Rhenish Missionary Society.*"*

DR. LIVINGSTONE'S FURTHER DISCOVERIES IN THESE REGIONS.

THE vast importance, moral and commercial, of the discovery of Lake N'gami and its tributaries, is now beginning to be developed. The subjoined brief account of Dr. Livingstone's latest movements, and of those which he has in contemplation, is full of interest. It is the substance of a communication read before the "Royal Geographical Society," March 26th, and is copied from the "Athenæum" of March 31st, 1855 :—

"'DISPATCH from Loanda, respecting Dr. Livingstone's Exploration of Central Africa,' communicated by Consul Brand through the Foreign Office.—Dr. Livingstone left the Cape of Good Hope in May, 1852, for the purpose of exploring the interior of the continent, and establishing Mission-stations beyond Lake N'gami, which, in company with Captain Oswell, he had discovered on a previous journey. After travelling for eight months, he reached the River Leeambye, or Zambeze, where it bends from a southerly to an easterly course, between 17° and 18° S. latitude, and about 24° E. longitude. He was received by Sekeletu, the chief of this country, in a most friendly manner. He acquired a knowledge of its geography, its inhabitants, and their language; and remained there, instructing the people in Christianity and civilization, for eight months. With the assistance of Sekeletu, he continued his travels up the Zambeze River and its affluent as far as 11° 30' S. latitude, into the Balonda country, the chief of which (named Matiamvo) is reputed to be the most powerful in this part of Africa. The subjects of this chief treated him with kindness, but his desire to push on for the west coast prevented him from visiting their master.

" In passing through the countries adjacent to the frontier of the Portuguese territory of Angola, he experienced great difficulties from the rapacity of the tribes, who now intercept the traffic passing between the coast and the interior, and are permitted to levy extortionate imposts on every thing which comes within their grasp. But having reached the limits of Angola, the Portuguese protected him from all annoyance, and assisted him to reach Loanda, where he was treated with marked attention and friendship by the Governor, the

* " Blue Book," pp. 36, 37.

Bishop, and the whole population,—having thus accomplished a journey of two thousand five hundred miles through unknown countries.

"In an address to the Portuguese settlers at Loanda, Dr. Livingstone maintains the opinion that two or three years of honest commercial intercourse would result in establishing a profitable trade with the interior. Bees'-wax, and other articles of commerce, with which the country abounds, are now thrown aside as useless. Ivory is abundant, and a ready sale would increase the supply. Cattle thrive marvellously in the Borotse Valley, on the river Zambeze. At present the obstacles to commerce are, the absence of roads, and the rapacity of the border tribes. About ninety men are now required to carry a load in Angola, which a Cape merchant would convey in two large bullock-carts, with cattle and five Hottentots. Dr. Livingstone urges on the Portuguese merchants the construction of a road from Loanda to Matiamvo's country, with the concurrence of that powerful chief, as the best means of overcoming the difficulties of transit, as well as the extortion of the intervening tribes, and yielding a profitable revenue from moderate tolls. Dr. Livingstone adverts to the remarkable fertility of the province of Angola. Its coffee stands high in the London markets; it grows throughout the whole of the interior, and trees once planted continue to bear fruit even when entirely neglected. The country is particularly suitable for cotton, and the introduction of a better quality of seed is desirable.

"Dr. Livingstone left Loanda with his faithful African attendants, on his return into the interior, on the 20th of September last. He had perfectly recovered from the effects of his extraordinary journey; and he is the bearer of a friendly communication and a present of a quantity of trade goods from the merchants of Loanda to his friend the chief Sekeletu. After his return to Sekeletu he intends to trace the river Zambeze to its mouth, with the expectation of reaching Quillimane, in the Portuguese territory, on the east coast, in November next. The Governor of Angola has given him letters to all the Portuguese authorities; and Lord Clarendon has been requested to cause one of Her Majesty's ships on that station to make occasional inquiries for him at Quillimane, and enable him to proceed to the nearest port to England."

COPPER MINING OPERATIONS IN NAMAQUA-LAND.

In the twelfth Chapter of this volume, mention has been made of the recent discovery of rich mines of copper in Namaqua-land. To afford the latest intelligence on this subject, the editor has ventured, in the absence of the author, to introduce, from "the Leading Journal of Europe," under date of February 8th, 1855, the subjoined important extract:—

"THE advices by the Natal steamer from the Cape of Good Hope are of unusual importance, from the facts they contain regarding the spread of the Namaqua-land copper mining mania, which has plunged the Colony into a state of excitement such as prevailed with regard to gold three years ago at Melbourne. The following letter, from an experienced merchant, gives full information of the precise position of affairs at the latest date, accompanied by some practical views of the mining movement likely to have a salutary effect in checking those speculative attempts in connexion with it which are certain to be made on this side :—

" ' THE rage for speculating in mining shares can only be conceived by those who recollect the railway-share mania in England a few years ago. Perhaps, in proportion to population, it exists to a greater extent at the Cape; for if one-third of the nominal capitals of the various companies were called up, the shareholders could not meet it. I do not say there is not sufficient capital in the Colony to meet all the calls that might be made, but I assert the present holders would, in the main, be found defaulters; and there can be no question that a reaction will ensue next year that will entail more misery upon the community than the unthinking calculate upon.

" ' From all the accounts I have been able to collect, there can be no doubt that the district of Namaqua-land abounds in copper ore; some of which is exceedingly rich, producing sixty, seventy, and even eighty-five *per cent.* of pure metal, and, being found on the surface, is easily worked. It is difficult, however, to say if it extends to any depth; and probably, as long as the surface ore lasts, few shafts will be sunk. Much of the ore, however, yields from twenty to twenty-five *per cent.* only, but a large portion thirty-seven *per cent.*

" ' The great difficulties are, the distance from the coast, the means of transport, and the heavy and destructive state of the roads—or country, for I understand there are no roads. The climate also, although represented as healthy, is during the summer months so hot that it is naturally extremely debilitating to European constitutions. The want of harbours is another considerable drawback; for although there is tolerable anchorage on several parts of the coast, occasionally the rollers set in fearfully. One of Her Majesty's ships of war is at present surveying that part of the coast in which the mines, or rather fields, of copper ore are situated.

" ' The manner in which individuals or companies acquire the right to work the Namaqua-land copper fields is as follows :—A spot is selected, and application is made to the Government for a lease. An imaginary circle of one mile from the spot is drawn, and the applicant is authorized to select as much as forty or eighty *morgen* (a *morgen* is about two acres) in an unbroken lot. It is then surveyed at his expense, and a lease granted to him for a period of fifteen years, at the rate of £1 per morgen *per annum.*

" ' These spots are in local phrase termed *centres;* and, as no limit is placed by the Government to quantity, individuals or companies are proprietors of the leases of many centres. This, in fact, is the cause of the present most unhealthy speculation in mining shares.   An expectation is very prevalent that large capitalists from England will, on being assured of the abundance of copper ore in the Colony, (and of course the speculators think they will be as easily assured as themselves,) purchase these centres at any price.   This is the base of many of the companies.   One company possesses, I am told, about sixty or seventy centres, and is still seeking for others.   Now, if these companies are so satisfied that such vast quantities of ore exist, and that it is of easy acquisition, why not work their centres, instead of investing their paid-up capital in the leasing of more ground?

"'In 1849 or 1850 the first copper mining company was formed, and £1 *per* share was paid up.   From some cause or another the mines or fields were not worked, and the shares fell to 5*s*.   When it became known that so much copper ore existed in the district, these shares rose rapidly.   The Directors secured more centres; £3 *per* share has been paid up, and the shares have, I believe, been as high as £30; they are now £23 each.   But I am not aware that this company has shipped a single ton of ore to England!

"'Another company is formed thus:—The proprietor of the lease of three or four centres disposes of them on the following conditions:—five thousand shares are to be created of £5 each, of which he is to receive one thousand shares, without paying a sixpence, and out of the first profits (!) the sum of £15,000.   Would you credit that the company was formed in less than an hour, that the following day 5*s. per* share was paid, and that in the course of a fortnight they were selling at £5 *per* share?   Do the annals of railway speculation archive such monstrous advances as this?   Now, supposing the whole capital to be paid up, namely, £20,000, and that the centres are as rich in ore as some of the shareholders believe, how long will it be before any profits are realized?

"'Messrs. Phillips and King, who are proprietors of copper fields in Namaqua-land, have, under almost incredible difficulties, been able to ship about eleven hundred tons of ore, averaging, it is said, thirty-four *per cent*. of copper; and, to procure this quantity, it is generally believed their outlay could not have been much below £30,000.   It is true that a considerable portion of this outlay was for implements, stock, &c., which remain in their possession, and the future expense will be considerably lessened.   But when I inform you that, for the transport of ore from the mines to the coast, the enormous sum of from £8 to £9 *per* ton is paid, and from £2 to £3 thence to Table Bay, you may form some conception of the expense, and all the world knows that individuals can work cheaper than companies.

"'Railways and tramways are talked of, and I am not prepared to say they would not pay a handsome dividend, if economically constructed; but before the people of England subscribe to any thing of the kind here, they should be well assured the quantity of ore is inexhaustible, as is asserted.   One thing is certain,—until the means of transport are much cheaper, none but rich ores can be shipped.

"'I am sorry to say that speculation is not confined to mining shares. In every little village dignified by the name of a town, where there are two or three shops, a joint-stock bank is started, and the newspapers of the day are full of prospectuses. Hitherto the community of the Cape has been tolerably free from the panics, crises, &c., which have been not unfrequent in the sister Colonies in the northern hemisphere, and even in older communities; but I fear we shall not in future escape those disasters.'"

ANOTHER COMMANDO OF THE DUTCH BOERS AGAINST THE KAFIRS.

"THE Times" newspaper of March 15th, 1855, contains large quotations from the Report of young Pretorius, who joined Commandant-General Potgieter in an attack on some Kafir tribes, one of which is alleged to have been guilty of several acts of atrocity against the Dutch settlers. But, assuredly, these belonged neither to the Griquas, nor to any of those Kafir tribes who fought against the British troops under Sir George Cathcart; otherwise the result would have been very different from that which is here recorded, and no necessity would have existed for challenging the Kafir chief, a second time, "to come out of the caverns, with all his men," to answer for his gross misdeeds. They must have been a tamer and more pusillanimous people, who had never encountered the Trans-Vaal Republicans in battle. Pretorius junior is the chronicler of his own exploits; and in a thinly-peopled country, where public opinion is unknown and exercises no influence, the art of mystifying is sure to receive no check from the remarks of dispassionate spectators. The hero of a dozen skirmishes with unwarlike savages, in such circumstances, may safely give his own version of the tragedy in which he enacted the principal part, and "return" the number of the unhappy sufferers either smaller or greater than it actually was, according to the preponderance within him of the two rival principles,—"vanity" and "prudence." In this instance "vanity" seems to have been in the ascendant; and we may, therefore, reasonably compute the "upwards of nine hundred men who had fallen *outside* the caverns," and "the *much greater* number who had fallen *within*," to have been really fewer than the young general, flushed with an inglorious victory, has been induced to reckon them.

I give only two extracts from the official dispatches of General Pretorius. Having been unsuccessful in his attempts "to blast the rocks above the caverns" in which the frightened natives had concealed themselves, he says,—

"This having failed, I gave orders to besiege the caverns day and night, and to cut off, as far as possible, all supplies. With this view I had some fences constructed on the rocks, behind which I posted one hundred men day and night. During this work the Kafirs fired incessantly out of the caverns, but without injury to us, while our patrols daily shot down some of the enemy. On the 6th of November I proceeded to the caverns, accompanied by Commandant-General Potgieter: we had ordered the bushes, which obstructed us at night, to be cut down. My colleague, while urging on a party of friendly Kafirs who were working for us, having gone too far in advance, was struck by a bullet fired by the enemy at the very mouth of one of the caverns; it entered the right shoulder, and came out between the left shoulder and the neck, so that he was knocked down the *krantz* upon which he had been standing, a height of about twenty-five feet, and fell right in front of the enemy's fence. I at once ordered the fence to be stormed, and thus secured the body, which I had forthwith escorted to the camp, to be buried there. On the same day his brother, the Commandant H. Potgieter, was provisionally appointed to succeed his brother as Commandant-General. The chief command of the whole force there engaged was, however, confided to me, as the executive Commandant-General: and this task I readily accepted. Deeply, indeed, was I grieved at the loss of my colleague, whom I had learnt to love as a brother. In every thing we consulted each other. To his praise it may be said that he was a warrior in the fullest sense of the term; undaunted, and educated in the war with the Kafir tribes, he despised them, and knew no danger; wherever duty called him he was present, and was enabled at all times to point his men to his own example. The loss of my gallant colleague strengthened, if possible, my determination fully to avenge the blood which had already been shed."

This is in every respect a most lamentable affair. On the death of the first Commandant-General, A. W. J. Pretorius, recorded in pp. 392–394 of this Appendix, the eldest of the brothers Potgieter was chosen as his successor. This gentleman had brought a large detachment of Boers, to form a junction with those under the command of young Pretorius, for the purpose of avenging the murder of his brother, Field-Cornet Potgieter, and some of his companions; but was suddenly killed, while indiscreetly exposing himself, "at the mouth of one of the enemy's caverns." As the highest post of honour has thus, once more, become vacant, it will probably soon be occupied by the warrior who figures so conspicuously, like a second Cæsar, in this *bellum crudele et infandum*. His constituents are the best judges of his qualifications for the elevated station to which he aspires. But, from the imperfect *data* which he affords as to his own doings, a stranger to his merits will find some difficulty in ascertaining the particular line in which his personal energy is usually displayed. The only glimpse of it which I have been able to obtain, is in that passage of his dispatches in which he intimates his wish to personate "the undertaker :"—"I at once ordered the fence to be stormed; and thus secured the body, which I had forthwith escorted to the camp, to be buried there." This was certainly a very safe and discreet course for a model Commandant to adopt in those uncultivated regions, and among a barbarous people, who had not appreciated the hardihood of his deceased colleague in the unnecessary exposure of his person.

Our next extract is of a still more truculent and unmanly character :—

"The siege was a work that proceeded much too tardily. Fruitlessly had the Kafir chief been challenged to come out of the caverns with all his men, to answer for the butchery which he had committed. On the 8th of November I determined to block up the openings of the caverns, which are from forty to fifty feet wide, and twenty-five to thirty-five feet deep. Fifty span of oxen, with an adequate number of labourers, were employed upon that work on the first day. During the next five days this work was vigorously prosecuted, during which time fifteen hundred drags of trees, and as many loads of stone, were brought on, and thrown down the caverns, by three hundred friendly Kafirs in our employ. Meanwhile the Kafirs commenced at night to sally forth to procure water ; a large number of women and children, suffering from want of water, also sallied forth, but died after they had drunk a little. Among these was a male Kafir, who surrendered, undertaking to point out where the ivory of the murdered man was secreted. Lieutenant Paul Krieger was dispatched for this purpose on the 11th instant, with a small guard, and returned in the afternoon with twenty-three large, and fifteen small, elephants' tusks. The first, 1,010℔s. in weight, belong to Mr. Uckermann, trader, of Pietermaritzburg ; the latter belong to the murdered man here. This afternoon two horses of the late H. Potgieter also fell into our hands. On the 16th of November a large number of women and children again rushed out of the caverns, while, on our part, we continued to approach the same, so as to be enabled to look into them for some distance. The following day part of my men entered the caverns almost without opposition ; they took twenty-four guns, fourteen shot-belts, mostly filled with powder and balls, a bag of slugs, some pieces of lead, two chests of clothing, (some unfinished,) forty pounds of coffee, and numerous other small wares. Among the booty captured there was much belonging to the families of the murdered, which was returned to them. The rest, after consulting the council of war, I caused to be sold, besides half the ivory belonging to Mr. Uckermann, to defray expenses. I moreover caused all the sheep and goats to be sold. The whole realized three thousand eight hundred rix-dollars; part of which was given to the men of the late General Potgieter, while the rest I have reserved to cover the expenses of ammunition, &c."

This is truly a horrid description of merciless internecine warfare; the most harrowing part of which relates to "a large number of women and children, suffering from want of water, who sallied forth" from the caverns at night, "but died after they had drunk a little." The attempt to obtain water occurred more than once, but is narrated in very obscure and unsatisfactory language. Under a marvellous semblance of innocence on the part of himself and followers, the new *"executive* Commandant-General*"* gives these distressing details; but leaves his readers to draw their own inferences respecting the *modus operandi;* and, with commendable discretion, avoids all mention of the pitiable females and children who were cruelly shot down, on those dreadful nights, when trying, at the risk of life, to escape. But the nature of the facts disclosed cannot be mistaken by the most careless reader. The besiegers were divided into relief-parties; who, "posted behind fences constructed on the rocks," undertook, in turns, by day and by night, the easy duty of quietly and safely watching behind them for stragglers. On hearing the first tread of a foot or the rustling of a few leaves, they were ready to discharge their rifles in the direction from which the sound came, without stopping, during the darkness of night, nicely to ascertain the size or the sex of the hapless fugitives; few of whom would have an opportunity of reaching the streams to slake their own thirst, or stealthily to convey some of the precious water to those in the caves who were dearest to their hearts.

It would be a profitable employment for such a redoubtable Commandant and his dashing adherents, before they venture on another campaign of extermination, to study attentively the clever treatise of their celebrated countryman, Grotius, *De Jure*

Belli ac Pacis. Since its first publication in 1625, it has been the hand-book of every great European general who was distinguished for strategic talent and bravery, and for splendid victories; as well as for uniform humanity towards women and children,—inviting them to come out from besieged cities, and assuring them of a safe-conduct to a place of security. I recollect the exquisite delight which I felt, when a youth, on reading Du Bosc's and other accounts of the campaigns of the Duke of Marlborough and Prince Eugene, and of the accomplished commanders who were their opponents in honourable warfare; and the supreme disgust which I conceived when perusing the ruthless butcheries of the Duke of Alva and his infamous imitators. With the former class of heroes, I found myself transported far back into the most illustrious ages of ancient chivalry, and all its accompanying amenities intended to assuage the horrors of that which was regarded as "a necessary evil;" while in the latter class I was reminded of the reckless enormities of the most ferocious and brutal savages that are recorded in history, the rapacious blood-hounds of murder and desolation. In palliation of the cruelties of the Duke of Alva it may be urged, that the ameliorating treatise of Grotius had not been published in those days of darkness and tribulation: but this cannot be pleaded in extenuation of the misdeeds of young Pretorius, who seems to glory in these chronicles of his own infamy and degradation.

STRICTURES ON COMMANDOES OF THIS DESCRIPTION.

After having presented to the public copious extracts from the Report of General Pretorius, the "Times" newspaper of the following day (March 16th) contained the subjoined strong and pungent remarks on the *salutary* effects of these cruel expeditions:—

"The dispatches just received from the Cape of Good Hope contain an incident of a nature so striking in itself, so terrible in its details, and so instructive in the lessons it conveys, that we bring it prominently into notice for the consideration of the public.

"We are not the only Europeans settled in South Africa. The Dutch were there before us; and there, in no inconsiderable numbers, they remain still. Not being very well satisfied with our Government,—though discontented probably rather with the policy of our proceedings than with our supremacy itself,—some of the representatives of these older colonists have penetrated more and more deeply into the interior of the country ; and have acquired a species of independence, by escaping from the immediate vicinity of the British provinces.   One of their settlements is ' the Trans-Vaal Republic,'—a title which will explain both the political and geographical position of the community.   Here, like ourselves, they border upon the Kafirs, and are exposed accordingly to the self-same liabilities in the shape of frontier alarms, attacks, and depredations.   That they do not, however, content themselves with our mild system of reprisals, or deal in our fashion with their savage enemies, will be only too evident from the story which we are about to relate.

" The Kafirs had given the Trans-Vaal Boers most dreadful offence. They had murdered seven or eight men of the settlement, including a field-cornet, or officer of colonial levies, and had put to death several women, with circumstances, as we are told, of the most frightful barbarity.   In the month of October last, therefore, (for so long are accounts in reaching us from these remote regions,) General Pretorius, accompanied by Commandant-General Potgieter,—a relative, apparently, of the murdered officer,—proceeded on an expedition to avenge the blood which had been shed by the Kafirs. The force altogether was about five hundred strong, the greater part being mounted ; and they had a hundred and sixteen waggons, and two field-pieces.   Towards the end of the month they reached certain subterranean caverns of vast extent, in which the offending Kafirs, under their chief Makapan, were known to have intrenched themselves.   These extraordinary caves are described as being upwards of two thousand feet in length, and from three hundred to five hundred in width, intersected by several ' walls,' —we presume, of natural construction,—and so dark that no eye could penetrate the gloom.   Arrived at this retreat, General Pretorius appears to have debated, without scruple or hesitation, how he could exterminate his enemies with the greatest facility ; and at ' a council of war' it was resolved, we are told, to blast the rocks above the caverns, and thus crush and bury the savages alive under the ruins. This scheme was attempted forthwith, but failed, in consequence of the stone proving unfavourable to the operation.   The caves were then surrounded, and rigorously watched day and night, to prevent the entrance of any supplies ; so that the wretches within, who seem, by the accounts, to have represented the whole population of a Kafir village, wives and children included, might be reduced to the extremities of famine.   At first fences or barriers were constructed round the rocks, behind which the Boers maintained incessant watch ; but, as the work proceeded, enormous loads of timber and stone were brought up, and thrown into the openings of the caverns.   The pangs of thirst, however, soon forced through these obstacles some of the miserable creatures within, and a ' large number of women and children,' we are told, ' suffering from want of water, sallied forth, but died after they had drunk a little.'   Meantime the patrols kept ward night and day, and with their rifles laid every Kafir dead who showed himself, in his exhaustion or misery, at the cavern's mouth. As this barbarous siege was actually protracted through the greater part of three weeks, it is plain that the savages must have had some small amount of provisions with them : but the work at last came to an end. On the 17th of November the besiegers, as they advanced towards the rocks, encountered little opposition; and the silence of the caves, together with the horrible smell of the dead, told them how effectually their object had been accomplished. The miserable savages had perished in their holes, and the estimate of their losses gives a frightful idea of the tragedy. Women and children in considerable numbers appear to have escaped; but upwards of nine hundred Kafirs had been shot down at the opening of the caverns; and the number of those who had died by inches within was, we are assured, 'much greater.' Such is an incident of Kafir warfare, as conducted by colonists !

" Every one will rejoice that so horrible a massacre was not perpetrated by British soldiers, or under cover of the British flag; and the example may, perhaps, be reasonably appealed to by those who protest against committing the conduct of such wars to any but regular troops. It is impossible, however, to overlook the disadvantages in which such a policy places us. Judging from experience, we could not have done so much towards curbing the Kafirs in a long campaign, or after an expenditure of millions, as General Pretorius did in two short months with a handful of volunteers, at probably little or no cost to his countrymen, and with a loss of only two killed and five wounded. The whole expedition was contrived with a rude simplicity, which, though barbarous enough in its results, was successfully adapted to the purpose in view. The settlers of the Trans-Vaal Republic turned out to hunt savages after a savage fashion. The Kafirs had not only butchered their countrymen, but had added cannibalism to murder; for pots were found containing the roasted limbs of the victims. To such offenders no more mercy was shown than to so many wolves; and, when they had been tracked to their dens, they were starved and shot without respect to the usages of more civilized war. After the expedition was over, the booty collected was sold for the public good; a portion of the proceeds was assigned to the widows and families of the murdered men; the rest was reserved to pay for the ammunition, &c., expended; and with this primitive settlement the Kafir war of the Boers was closed.

" We, it is plain, do not fight with such enemies on fair terms. The Kafirs, in passing from peace to war with us, forego little, sacrifice little, and hazard to a very small extent even their own savage lives. We export soldiers thousands of miles; every man of whom has cost us the worth of a Kafir province in training, and who are expected to encounter treacherous and sanguinary barbarians, in their own deserts, according to the punctilios of regular war. The result is, that the losses are almost exclusively our own. The Treasury is drained of million after million; our best officers and men perish in the thicket; and, after the lapse of a year or two, the ' Kafir war ' is concluded, to be followed in a few months by another. We doubt very much if as many Kafirs have fallen by the bullets or bayonets of our troops in the last three wars, as were destroyed in this single expedition of Pretorius. It would be hard, indeed, to argue that such an example should be followed; but of this we are convinced,—that, if the colonization of South Africa is to be continued, the savage tribes of our frontier can only be successfully encountered, like the savages of all other regions, by acts resembling their own. The backwoodsmen of Kentucky pursued the Red Indians as the Red Indians pursued them, and victory in the end fell to the superior race. It would probably be the same at the Cape; but to expect that the contest should be conducted without offence to civilized feelings, is altogether vain. We simply put the case, by aid of this illustration, before the eyes of the reader. Handled as those on the spot could handle them, the Kafirs—those bugbears of our statesmen and economists—could be kept down with little outlay or trouble; but the system would be only too sure to involve shocks and scandals to the humanity of the nation. This, however, we must needs add, that if such an alternative be rejected, the border provinces ought to be relinquished altogether; for the country can no longer afford or tolerate those periodical wars of which the cost is found so great and the fruit so little."

The writer in "the Times" has, on this occasion, as well as on others, arrived at the conclusion, that this Trans-Vaal exterminating warfare is the only eligible mode to be pursued towards the marauding Kafirs. But while much truth is apparent in his observations, he has not thought fit to exhibit to his readers the still darker side of this foul picture,—the deteriorating effects which such wholesale butchery produces on the morals and characters of the successful executioners. To support his view of the matter, he adduces very appositely the case of the men of Kentucky. This, however, is an instance which makes more against his argument than in its favour : for it must be borne in mind, that the earliest of that class were the descendants of the first English settlers ; young men of good families, possessed of great courage and enterprise, who could not be confined within the limits of the large estates of their fathers. Accustomed from boyhood to the use of the rifle, indulging in a roving disposition, and smitten with the love of more perilous adventures than home afforded, they found appropriate employment for their newly-directed energies in attacking the bears of the dense forests, and the dwindled and retreating race of Red Men in the prairies. The vagabond life which they had chosen did not, in the course of years, tend to soften their manners, or to ameliorate their dispositions; the destruction of the Indian, by any and by every means, was regarded in the light of a gallant act, quite as useful and meritorious as that of "bagging" the wild game of the forest, or of entrapping "Bruin" in a pitfall, and impaling him alive. As the tide of emigration began to flow on with a ten-fold force, these young men of enterprise were soon joined by some of the more restless new-comers, whose antecedents were not of that order which would bear strict inquiry, and who too often had been the scum of European society. The downward course would have continued, though perhaps not quite so rapidly, without the aid of these fresh importations; for, under such malign influences, the debasement of men's natures is a gradual process, in the ratio of their advancing years. Cruelty to the inferior animals, or to men "formed in the image of God," hardens the hearts of those who delight in the vile practice, and renders them, in the end, brutal and cowardly. Novelists have smoothed down the disgusting asperities of the common life of the early backwoodsmen, and have succeeded in exhibiting them as little heroes; but the stern realities of their downward career can never be obliterated from the records of their country. These men may, in courtesy, be called "the pioneers of civilization," and "the superior race." But, with all their warlike appliances,—their powder and shot, and long-range rifles,—it is very doubtful whether they would ultimately have gained the mastery over the Red Indians, had they not been thrust forward and pushed onward by the yearly-increasing masses of European auxiliaries, who trod on their heels, and supplemented the *lacunæ* which their skilful and wary foes had made in their ranks. The contest between the two races was long and sanguinary. Yet, in all that desultory and indiscriminate carnage, the Red Indians, like the Arabs and some of the South-African races, (the structure of whose languages usually gives undeniable tokens of ancient refinement and patriarchal origin,) retained much of their native sense of rude chivalry and honour, and of the inviolable duties entailed on them by the rites of hospitality; while the Kentucky backwoodsmen, within a few years, lost all traces of their recent descent from a Christian ancestry, and sank far lower than the Indians in all that was mean and discreditable.   Long practice in the low tactics of circumventing Indians and destroying buffaloes had reduced some of the most courageous of mortals into arrant poltroons and barbarians.   The monitory results are soon told and easily understood :—The cool and deliberate murder of any one who had offered an affront, Lynch law, the brutal art of " gouging " the eyes of a prostrate foe, and other dastardly *et ceteras*, at length rendered the name of *a man of Kentucky* " a proverb of reproach and shame " to his own countrymen.

Such is the fate of all those who, brasen-faced and iron-hearted, have " gloried in their shame," while indulging in acts of meanness and cruelty towards abject inferiors.   It is capable of as varied and satisfactory proof from the pages of ancient history, as from the modern records of Kentucky.   It is the fate which awaits the Trans-Vaal Boers, if they restlessly persist in the perpetration of such dastardly crimes as those which Commandant Pretorius has proclaimed to the world with vast satisfaction.   It is a rapid descent towards barbarism, which cannot be checked, except by a complete abstinence from the unmanly practices which I have deemed it a duty here to expose and condemn.   Those respectable Boers who constituted a portion of the grand emigration from the Cape Colony in 1836–1843, but who, many years ago, chose to locate themselves in Natal, have recently shown their Trans-Vaal friends " a more excellent way " of suppressing incipient Kafir outbreaks, and preventing a repetition of their marauding and cattle-stealing habits.   It is contained in the next section of this Appendix.

But it would be derogatory to the grace of God, and an indelible stigma on the pious descendants of the North American backwoodsmen, were I not to allude to the means by which many of these " sheep that had gone so far astray " were brought back " unto the Shepherd and Bishop of their souls."   The authentic chronicles of their speedy and remarkable recovery to Christianity and civilized life, are to be found in the churches of every evangelical denomination in the United States, but more especially in those of the Baptists.   These intrepid messengers of Divine Mercy considered their peculiar vocation to consist in the baptism of adults, after they had been instructed in the first elements of Christian doctrine.   In the spirit of self-denying

piety, their most zealous efforts were directed to overtake the
brutalized and untamed wanderers, and proclaim to them in all
directions the Gospel of salvation; which produced exactly the
same effects as it has always done on those who feel themselves
to be the "chief of sinners." To some of the self-righteous
among His hearers our Saviour once said, "The publicans and the
harlots go into the kingdom of heaven before you." In the con-
version of the worst of men, this "true" saying of Christ has
always had its fulfilment. But, in every age of the church, this
startling proposition has sorely perplexed and mortified both
philosophers and malignants. Yet the great truth which it
involves is the same as that which is found in another of His
first principles : "They that be whole need not a physician, but
they that are sick. I am not come to call the righteous, but
sinners to repentance." The meaning of these words is obvious
to all; yet they seldom mortify human pride, because it is the
culpable infirmity of all men, who, in their natural state, "have
their understanding darkened," to place other people in the
category of "sick" and flagrant "sinners," but themselves in
that of "the sound" and "the righteous." "Christ crucified,"
implying the necessity of His atonement, always was and ever
will be "unto the Jews a stumbling-block, and unto the Greeks
foolishness; but unto them who are called" by Divine Grace,
and feel their urgent need of this blessed remedy, "Christ is the
power of God, and the wisdom of God." So it was in the
case of the adventurous backwoodsmen : there was no attempt at
gainsaying. "They were convinced of all, they were judged of
all, and thus were the secrets of their hearts made manifest."
"A very great number believed, and turned unto the Lord," at
the first unfurling of the banners of the cross. It was, indeed, a
memorable and almost universal transition, which gladdened the
hearts of all who witnessed the blessed event. For mutual
defence and security, most of the families, like those of the
Dutch Boers, consisted of descendants from the patriarchal
stock down to the third or fourth generation. The Baptist
evangelists found in numerous households a great-grandsire,
with descending gradations of grandfathers, fathers, and
children ; and, after suitable instruction and probation, received
all these adults into the fold of Christ Jesus. The genuine

Kentucky men are now represented to be as exemplary in spirit and orderly in conduct, as any of their countrymen. If, in the streets of some of the large cities of the Union, brutal encounters, emulating in ferocity those which have been described in these pages, occasionally take place, it will seldom be found that either of the culpable parties belongs to the race of Kentucky. They are usually from some other State, in which the ancient atrocities of backwoodsmen form the choice code of chivalry for all irreclaimable blackguards; or they are combustible materials, recently imported from Europe, where all those who attempt openly to indulge in lawless and destructive passions are sure to meet with speedy and condign punishment.

A LESS REPREHENSIBLE AND MORE EFFECTUAL COMMANDO.

To many persons it will appear a strange co-incidence, when they are told that the same number of the "Times" newspaper, which gives the extracts from the "Graham's-Town Journal," March 15th, contains in its columns another from a Natal paper, which inculcates a doctrine and practice very different indeed from those of Commandant Pretorius. Short though it be, it teaches by example a more innocent and sensible method of repressing or punishing Kafir depredations than that on which I have briefly animadverted. It proceeds on the sound principle of apprising the chief culprit of his misdeeds, and of its consequences in the prompt retribution with which he would be visited, if the stolen property were not restored on demand. The oldest and the best of books expounds this wise political axiom in very energetic language :—"Because sentence against an evil work is not executed speedily, therefore the heart of the sons of men is fully set in them to do evil." Encouragement to crime is undoubtedly afforded by the appearance of too much lenity, and by deferring to inflict the threatened punishment. When the party aggrieved has fixed on a reasonable amount of compensation for the injury inflicted, which he knows the offender is well qualified to pay, it is an act of real charity to the culprit himself to be prompt in the exaction of payment, after having given due warning. The natural logic, in which the Kafirs are great adepts, is exceedingly curt and conclusive :

"Since the exaction of the penalty is deferred, it is virtually abandoned; and I shall now have ample opportunity stealthily to convey my best cattle to a place of safety." But when "sentence against an evil work is executed speedily," the criminal finds little scope for the exercise of such deceptive and injurious chicanery. The following extract from "the Times" supplies a good exemplification of these remarks :—

NATAL.

"AN expedition against the chief Dushani had been successful, without having been obliged to resort to bloodshed. The 'Natal Mercury,' of the 27th of December, states that Dushani was terrified at the demonstration against him :—

" 'He confessed the most abject submission to the Lieutenant-Governor, called himself *a dog*, &c., and, as usual, attempted to shift the blame from himself, by pretending that the thefts of cattle had been committed by new comers among his people, or without his knowledge or power of prevention, and other plausible excuses of a like kind. The result, however, was, that he paid the fine and compensation insisted on, namely, one thousand and thirty-eight head of cattle; and some minor chiefs in the same neighbourhood were fined in smaller quantities for other offences, making the entire quantity, we believe, about one thousand four hundred head. Some of the cattle brought in were identified as having been stolen several years ago.

" 'On the whole, this demonstration of a determination, on the part of Government, to visit promptly and severely such conduct as Dushani and his tribe have been guilty of, has produced the most salutary effect on the minds of the Natives, and will have a powerful tendency, together with the new ordinance, in checking the offence of cattle-stealing.

" 'Besides the good effect produced on the Natives by the mere strength of this demonstration, the thorough union exhibited between the Dutch and the English greatly surprised them, and appeared at once to produce the conviction that resistance or evasion was hopeless. This cordial union has also produced the best results as regards the two European classes themselves. It is the first exhibition of combined action to any thing like the same extent, that has occurred in this district; and such co-operation, extended to the peaceful and ordinary pursuits of life, will do more than any thing else to improve our social condition, and to secure permanent tranquillity.' "

This opportune display of promptitude and decision, by the Lieutenant-Governor of Natal, towards as noted a pilferer of other men's cattle as any lawless Rob Roy ever was, is a fine specimen of prudence, skill, and humanity. Dingaan and his warriors were not of that puny race of Natives described in the dispatch of Pretorius, but were stout and sinewy men, capable of vast exertions and great resistance. Yet, at the sight of this firm and orderly demonstration on the part of the European settlers, the half-civilized savages became discreetly submissive and obsequious. After reluctantly acknowledging themselves to have been wrong-doers, they instantly made the required restitution; and thus the affair ended, without injury to either of the parties. We can scarcely imagine a greater contrast than that which is presented between this well-planned and successful expedition, and the one undertaken by Pretorius. Most assuredly, the Trans-Vaal Boers, and the defenders of their cruel and exterminating system, may find, in this brief narrative, much to admire and imitate. It contains some valuable lessons in clever strategy, good policy, and in a due regard for human life, which is a distinguishing trait of a true Christian. This is indeed, in every respect, a preferable and " more excellent way " of treating savages, than that which has been the recent subject of animadversion.

As the remarks in this Appendix, from p. 443 to the end of the volume, proceed from the editor, he is happy, at the close of this section, to adduce, in confirmation of most of them, from the author himself, the following paragraphs in his eighth Chapter :—

" But let not those who are invested with a little brief authority use it in playing all sorts of fantastic tricks, or something worse. A Kafir has a sharp sense of justice ; and whilst he will respect and reverence the officer who will give him just punishment for his misdeeds, he will abhor the man who does him wanton wrong, and may be tempted to settle accounts in his own way.

"The Kafirs must be treated like children. If a man has a large family, and leaves them without restraint or control, his children become a plague to himself and a scourge to the community. The Kafirs are children of a larger growth, and must be treated accordingly,—*children* in knowledge, ignorant of the relationships of civilized society, and strangers to many of the motives which influence the conduct of the white man. But they are *men* in physical and mental powers,—*men* in the arts and usages of their nation, and the laws of their country ; and the great difficulty in governing them is, to treat them as men-children, teaching them that to submit and to obey are essential to their own welfare, as well as to that of others.

" Besides, it should not be forgotten that what appears to be severe to us, is not so to them, since many of them have lived under the iron rule of cruel, capricious despots, with no security for life or property, and are consequently unable to appreciate or understand our excess of civilized kindness, being strangers to those refined feelings which operate in the breasts of the Christian. The result of too mild a policy is, that in a few years they are changed from crouching, terror-stricken vassals, to bold, lawless, independent barbarians."

All his reasoning in that Chapter, especially in pp. 210–238, is highly worthy of perusal, and demands deep consideration from every philanthropist.

CONCLUDING OBSERVATIONS.

THE causes of the long delay in the completion of this volume are detailed, by the editor, in the Preface, and will be received as the only apology that can be offered for some of its defects; though, as a first attempt under great difficulties to delineate a variegated and very extensive tract of country, and the social and moral condition of the several races by whom it is peopled, it will be regarded by every candid reader with much indulgence, if not with complacency.

How many momentous events have transpired, (which are now proceeding yet more fully to develope themselves,) since the first sheets of this work were put to press! The termination of a desolating and most expensive Kafir war;—the partial exploration of Lake N'gami and its principal tributaries;—the sudden abandonment by Great Britain of the Orange-River Sovereignty; —the grant of a liberal constitution to the Cape Colony;—the appointment of a new governor;—the discovery of vast mineral wealth in Namaqua-land;—the facilities, in the countries north of Natal, for water-communication with the interior;—the elasticity of commerce and agriculture, and their gradual recovery from recent depression;—and the hopeful progress of sound principles and good conduct among several of the half-civilized natives:— These and other important occurrences have taken place in little more than two years; and the arrival of every mail brings us current information concerning matters of stirring interest, which will be hailed, by every lover of his species, as flattering presages for the future. Some gifted historian of Natal and the Orange-River Sovereignty may hereafter arise, on whom will devolve the duty of faithfully narrating the benign triumphs of religion and civilization, which have displayed themselves as the blessed consequences of a long and profound peace, and of the close union subsisting between the various races who occupy these vast regions. A man of philosophical mind will then have a fine opportunity of tracing to their proximate causes the fruits of good government in every department, and of suggesting many improvements, which might in due season be advantageously tried. Such an opportunity was not afforded to Mr. Holden when he wrote this "History;" for the administrative acts of the successive governors were not always based on the same principles, and often ended in a manner very different from that which the projectors had expected. The restlessness of the half-enlightened mind of the natives rendered the government of the Cape Colony one of continual experiment; and few of those who administered it were allowed sufficient time, before they were superseded, to test the correctness of their own measures. Yet they were all intended for the general benefit of the community: and even when they were proved to be palpable failures, they bore the impress of the real benevolence of their promoters.

In connexion with these matters it is well to invite the reader's attention to the great solicitude evinced by the British government for the permanent welfare of the surplus portion of its teeming population, and the vast expenditure incurred in encouraging colonization. Very different were the circumstances in which the first English Protestant settlers found themselves, when they landed on the shores of North America. Beyond their own strenuous exertions, they had no arm on which to depend for aid, except that of the Almighty. Let all British colonists in every quarter of the globe peruse the exceedingly interesting History of the Peopling of New England, written by the celebrated Nonconformist historian, the Rev. Daniel Neal; and they will be induced gratefully to acknowledge that, on the whole,—however the acts of particular governors may in certain instances seem to have militated against individual interests,—"the lines are fallen to them in pleasant places, and that they have a goodly heritage." For more than a century past, Great Britain may be regarded as a state truly parental, in granting opportune and substantial encouragement to her rising colonies, often at a serious outlay of capital, for which she has seldom received any of the ordinary tokens of thankfulness, but abundance of that grumbling in which it is averred John Bull and some of the most prosperous of his descendants delight to indulge. To these general remarks the case of the North-American colonies, at the time of their rude severance from the mother-country, forms no exception: that unfortunate outbreak was hastened by an error in judgment on the part of the English ministers, which would soon have been rectified by their successors, had both the dissentients been sincere in their desire for an amicable settlement of their differences.

It has long been a favourite maxim with our best ministers of state, that every British colony should remain in a state of pupilage, or leading-strings, no longer than till she had become self-supporting, and proved herself to be qualified, by obvious social progress, to undertake the task of self-government. The natives of a considerable part of South Africa are in a state of transition from barbarism to civilization; and by careful moral culture they may gradually rise to an equality with their whiter and now more refined neighbours, who fringe the immense coast-line from the Cape of Good Hope to Zulu-land. The latter are able and willing to raise a revenue by equitable taxation, and to superintend the disbursements from their own exchequer, to general advantage; and they have lately been put into possession of this valuable initiatory privilege. Under the judicious management of a clever and skilful governor, such as Sir Charles Grey has shown himself to be in New Zealand, both these classes will make satisfactory advances in all that is fair and praiseworthy, that tends to elevate and ennoble human nature, and to enhance that well-poised combination of mental and physical enjoyment which constitutes the most important portion of earthly felicity.

But in all the British dependencies, as well as in those of other nations, great hindrances are opposed to this progressive improvement in the scale of civilization, which the united wisdom of a vigilant and prudent governor, and of a legislative council, cannot directly prevent or neutralize. For instance, one of the earlier settlers becomes an eager land-jobber, holding in his hands all the good plots which he can procure, and doling them out, at highly-advanced prices, to those who may require smaller portions. Another is a dashing speculator in mines; by dabbling in which, he assures his fellow-colonists, they may soon become very rich capitalists. Some are large holders of prime cattle, suitable for the improvement of the indigenous breeds, on which they hope to obtain vast profits; while others are general traders or wandering merchants, who ask exorbitant prices for the multifarious articles in which they deal. The principle on which all these acute men proceed, does not seem, up to a certain point, to be unreasonable. Each of them adopts this mode of arguing: " I have fruitful fields, profitable minerals, the finest of cattle, or such excellent articles of merchandise as are in universal demand. Now, this new country is very thinly peopled, and I cannot obtain for my property or produce the prices which I might have in a richer and more populous locality, and which I ought to have in these regions, considering the numerous risks to which I am liable. Therefore, instead of *a large and quick sale with moderate profits,* which, together, are not attainable here, I must fall back on the old principle of *large profits and a slow sale,* and thus ultimately secure an adequate remuneration for my outlay and labour." This is a description of one of the partial evils with which every colony is visited at some period or other of its infancy, and from which those of South Africa cannot boast of having escaped. All such schemes, supported by this very natural mode of reasoning, may be frowned on and privately discouraged by the authorities; but any attempt beyond this to put them down would be viewed as an impolitic tampering with the freedom of trade, which is most sensitive in its nature, and cannot bear undue interference. All excessive trading-speculations soon meet with a check; and a sudden reaction is the usual remedy. Competition is not long in making its appearance; and every vendible commodity then commands a price in the market nearly approaching to its equitable value. The sales of land, effected by government in all new colonies, have a wonderful tendency to keep down prices, except for prime lots, in the choicest situations. New comers with a small capital have only to push forward to some of the recent settlements at a distance from the coast, where the number of uncultivated acres seems interminable, and the population on the surface is thin and scattered; and they will buy, at a reasonable rate, land enough for their money. When a settler has thus realized his wishes in the purchase of a good location, he has only to exercise ordinary prudence in abstaining from undue expenditure in needless articles of dress and furniture, and from all hazardous undertakings, how specious and attractive soever may be the shapes which they severally assume. For all these occasional excesses in the social system, and for others that will arise in every new colony, Providence, it will be seen, usually has an adequate cure in reserve. But in all projects relating to the construction of roads, wharves, and bridges, with other emergent necessities, which cannot be achieved by individual efforts, but require the concentration of local talent and capital, every sensible man will unite with his neighbours in contributing his quota for improvements affecting the future value of his own property, as well as that of others. The sober and industrious farmer, who has not indulged in any of the modish risks of the day, is the only one who carries within him the materials for mental tranquillity, while others are enduring the horrors inseparable from depressed quotations and ruinous reactions. Seeking the blessing of Heaven on his honest labours, he will be favoured with present success, and is in the high road to ultimate enjoyment. His healthy descendants, following in his steps, may exultingly chant the juvenile pastoral of one of our sweetest poets :—

> " Happy the man, whose wish and care
>   A few *paternal acres* bound;
> Content to breathe his native air
>   *In his own ground :*
>
> " Whose herds with milk, whose fields with bread,
>   Whose flocks supply him with attire;
> Whose trees in Summer yield him *shade,*
>   In Winter, *fire :*
>
> " Bless'd, who can unconcern'dly find
>   Hours, days, and years slide soft away,
> In health of body, peace of mind,
>   Quiet by day :
>
> " Sound sleep by night; study and ease,
>   Together mix'd; sweet recreation;
> And innocence, which most does please,
>   With meditation."

The axiom is universally received by the soundest writers on political economy, that it is the true interest of every new country to devote its chief attention, for the first century of its existence, to the cultivation of the soil, and the accumulation of agricultural wealth. They adduce, in proof of this position, the error of the United States of America, in too soon becoming a manufacturing nation; and aver that the inhabitants of those vast and fertile regions would have been more numerous, wealthy, and prosperous, had they never embarked in those projects, when they could have been furnished with all textile fabrics, both for common and luxurious dress, at less than half of the price which they now pay for their home-productions. For the encouragement of this unnatural branch of industry, they are compelled to resort to the imposition of enormously high duties, which are levied with much strictness, by comparatively few officers of customs, on an extent of coast which cannot be adequately watched. The arguments against this species of industry become, every year, less plausible; since improved machinery, for which the Americans have long been famed, continues to supersede the demand for manual labour, and consequently diminishes the cost of production, and enables the maker to sell his articles at lower prices. But the strictures of these gentlemen were never intended to apply to those who, on account of their distance from the few great marts of trade, are compelled, for many successive years, in every new country, to prepare and spin their own wool and flax, to dress the hides of the animals slain for food, and to weave or knit all their garments; and who are, in fact, the earliest manufacturers of all articles of prime necessity. But the great political economists declare, that the same objections do not lie against the immense commercial transactions in which the rich American merchants, in the cities at the mouths of the large rivers and along the coasts, are profitably engaged. In this respect they have been highly favoured by Providence, and have promptly and skilfully availed themselves of these advantages, by establishing a commercial intercourse with almost every nation on the face of the earth, from which they draw ample and well-earned riches in the shape of mercantile profits.

No fear is entertained concerning the colonists in Natal, and in the adjoining provinces, that they will prematurely erect factories, and fill them with machinery, while they have all the choicest elements of agricultural wealth already within their reach, and while many of its most profitable sources are in their possession in farms and large locations, the latent capabilities of which are as yet only partially developed.   The adventurous settlers, also, on the coast, and those who have found a home for themselves still further along, near Delagoa Bay, will, in due time, be in a condition to compete, in commercial pursuits, with the most favoured of their brethren in other climates. When a complete survey shall have been made of that long line of coast; and when every one will have been put into a con- dition to perceive the facilities afforded to him, in safe harbours for his ships, and in the scientific means of avoiding dangerous shoals, sunken rocks, or deceptive currents; he may then with confidence embark in lucrative traffic with foreign nations.   But not only is this preliminary application of science required along shore and at sea, but the entire inland territory also demands a full exploration.   It has lately been said by an accomplished geographer, A. Petermann, Esq.,—"There is scarcely a region of Africa which offers so extensive and interesting a field to travel- lers, as the eastern half of that continent between Natal and the Equator, containing, as it does, the key to the Limpopo, the Zam- bezi and Leambey, the Nyassa, the sources of the Nile; while it comprises the celebrated country of Sofala, the Snowy Mountains near Mombas, and other highly interesting and important points." This quotation assuredly opens out a grand prospect, sufficiently discursive and varied to gratify the aspirations of the most daring and sanguine spirits, whether they be philanthropists, traders, or mere lovers of adventures.   The beneficial results anticipated from these discoveries and improvements, will be ultimately enjoyed by the clever and persevering colonists, who have for years been in a course of preparation to hail the first approach of the wonderful changes in society which will soon ensue.

But no such results will be witnessed by the present genera- tion, unless the grand ameliorating influences of religion, morality, and benevolence compose the main elements of this epiphany, this glorious outbeaming of providential lustre. Every man of mature age and of ordinary understanding, who has beheld the last three Kafir outbreaks, quickly succeeding each other, is convinced of the benign and powerful effects of religious instruction on the native mind. While these barbarians are made familiar with the paramount duties which they owe to their Maker, Redeemer, and bountiful Benefactor, "the grace of God teaches them that, denying ungodliness and worldly lusts, they should live soberly, righteously, and godly in this present world; looking for that blessed hope, and the glorious appearing of the great God and our Saviour Jesus Christ." As to the transcendent importance of such teaching, no one in South Africa is any longer sceptical; for every man has seen Christian natives who were placed in circumstances of great peril and temptation, remain true to their principles, and come out of these fiery trials without a stain on their characters, or the slightest impeachment of their integrity. In this volume Mr. Holden has shown the necessity of a steady perseverance in the same course of religious and moral culture, as the best means of realizing those happy consequences which are predicted in the beautiful and figurative language of the prophet:—"The wolf also shall dwell with the lamb, and the leopard shall lie down with the kid; and the calf and the young lion and the fatling together; and a little child shall lead them. And the cow and the bear shall feed; their young ones shall lie down together: and the lion shall eat straw like the ox. And the sucking child shall play on the hole of the asp, and the weaned child shall put his hand on the cockatrice' den. They shall not hurt nor destroy in all my holy mountain: for the earth shall be full of the knowledge of the Lord, as the waters cover the sea." (Isaiah xi. 6–9.)

THE END.

LONDON : PRINTED BY WILLIAM NICHOLS, 32, LONDON WALL.

PREPARING FOR PUBLICATION.

In One Volume, 8vo., with numerous Illustrative Engravings,

THE NATIVE KAFIRS

OF

NATAL AND AMAZULU.

IN THREE PARTS.

BY THE REV. WILLIAM C. HOLDEN,

AUTHOR OF THE "HISTORY OF THE COLONY OF NATAL."

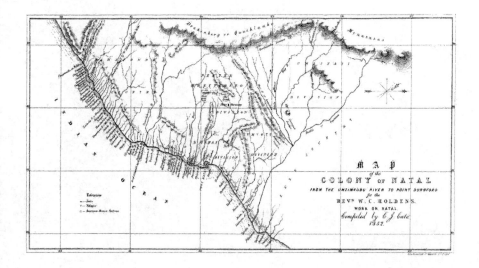

MAP
of the
COLONY of NATAL
FROM THE UMZIMVUBU RIVER TO POINT DURNFORD
for the
REV.ᴰ W. C. HOLDENS.
WORK ON NATAL
Compiled by C. J. Cato
1852

CPSIA information can be obtained
at www.ICGtesting.com
Printed in the USA
BVHW030444211022
649951BV00005B/144